SAN DIEGO PUBLIC LIBRARY

http://www.sandiego.gov/public-library/

Presented by

CITY OF SAN DIEGO
ENVIRONMENTAL SERVICES
DEPARTMENT

http://www.sandiego.gov/environmental-services/index.shtml

Forests in Landscapes

Ecosystem approaches to sustainability

The Earthscan Forestry Library

Forests in Landscapes:
Ecosystem Approaches to Sustainability
Jeffrey A. Sayer and Stewart Maginnis (eds)

The Politics of Decentralization:
Forest, Power and People
Carol J. Pierce Colfer and Doris Capristrano (eds)

Plantations, Privatization, Poverty and Power:
Changing Ownership and Management of State Forests
Mike Garforth and James Mayers (eds)

The Sustainable Forestry Handbook 2nd edition
Sophie Higman, James Mayers, Stephen Bass, Neil Judd and Ruth Nussbaum

The Forest Certification Handbook 2nd edition
Ruth Nussbaum and Markku Simula

Forests in Landscapes

Ecosystem approaches to sustainability

Jeffrey Sayer and Stewart Maginnis
assisted by Michelle Laurie

IUCN
The World Conservation Union

EARTHSCAN
London • Sterling, VA

First published by Earthscan in the UK and USA in 2005

Copyright © IUCN – The World Conservation Union, 2005
All rights reserved

ISBN: 1-84407-195-2

Typesetting by IUCN Publications Services Unit, Cambridge, UK
Printed and bound in the UK by Cromwell Press, Trowbridge
Cover design by Susanne Harris
Cover photo: A log landing at Malinau in East Kalimantan, Indonesia, Intu Boedhihartono
Illustrations by Intu Boedhihartono

For a full list of publications please contact

Earthscan
8–12 Camden High Streeet
London NW1 0JH, UK
Tel: +44 (0)20 7387 8558
Fax: +44 (0)20 7387 8998
Email: earthinfo@earthscan.co.uk
Web: **www.earthscan.co.uk**

22883 Quicksilver Drive, Sterling, VA 20166-2012, USA

Earthscan is an imprint of James and James (Science Publishers) Ltd and publishes in association with the International Institute for Environment and Development

A catalogue record for this book is available from the British Library

Library of Congress Cataloging-in-Publication Data has been applied for

Printed on elemental chlorine-free paper

Contents

Foreword
  Achim Steiner and Ian Johnson   vii

Preface   ix
  Jeffrey A. Sayer and Stewart Maginnis

Acknowledgements   xi

Acronyms and Abbreviations   xiii

Chapter 1   **New Challenges for Forest Management**   1
  Jeffrey A. Sayer and Stewart Maginnis

Chapter 2   **Economics Issues in Ecosystem Approaches to Forest Management**   17
  Roger Sedjo, Josh Bishop and Jeffrey A. Sayer

Chapter 3   **Information Needs for Ecosystem Forestry**   31
  Robert C. Szaro, Per Angelstam and Douglas Sheil

Chapter 4   **Global Standards and Locally Adapted Forestry: The Problems of Biodiversity Indicators**   47
  Bryan Finegan

Chapter 5   **Changing Forest Values in Europe**   59
  Per Angelstam, Elena Kapylova, Horst Korn , Marius Lazdinis, Jeffrey A. Sayer, Victor Teplyakov and Johan Törnblom

Chapter 6   **Empowering the Forest-Dependent Poor in India**   75
  Sushil Saigal, Kinsuk Mitra and Pankaj Lal

Chapter 7   **Balancing Conflicting Values: Ecosystem Solutions in the Pacific Northwest of the United States and Canada**   101
  Richard W. Haynes, Robert C. Szaro and Dennis P. Dykstra

Chapter 8   **Wildlife, Loggers and Livelihoods in the Congo Basin**   115
  Jeffrey A. Sayer, Cléto Ndikumagenge, Bruce Campbell and Leonard Usongo

Chapter 9   **Poor Farmers and Fragmented Forests in Central America**   129
  José Joaquín Campos Arce, Róger Villalobos and Bastiaan Louman

Chapter 10   **Australian Forestry: "Beyond One Tenure-One Use"**   147
  Ian Ferguson

Chapter 11   **The Political Ecology of the Ecosystem Approach for Forests**   165
  Tim Forsyth

Chapter 12   **Forests in Landscapes: Expanding Horizons for Ecosystem Forestry**   177
  Jeffrey A. Sayer and Stewart Maginnis

References   193

Annexes: 227

Annex 1   **CBD Principles of the Ecosystem Approach**   229

Annex 1a   **FSC Principles and Criteria**   232

Annex 2   **Improved Pan-European Indicators for Sustainable Forest Management as adopted by the MCPFE Expert Level Meeting 7–8 October 2002, Vienna, Austria**   243

Annex 3   **List of Contributors**   248

Index   251

Foreword

To many people the apparent lack of progress with conserving and managing the world's forests embodies all that has gone wrong with respect to the modern world's stewardship of its natural resources. There are still too many places where deforestation and degradation continue unabated, forest-dependent people slip further into poverty, governments and other forest owners lose large sums of potential revenue to illegal logging, and climate change now threatens the remaining forests. World leaders make commitments but appear to be unable to find workable solutions. This catalogue of woes makes for depressing reading. However, the reality on the ground is that when the right incentives exist and when forest governance is fair and predictable, progress can be achieved. When these conditions are right, solutions will emerge, tailored to local circumstances and taking into account both short-term development needs and long-term sustainability.

Sayer and Maginnis have drawn together in this volume a series of case studies that show that local reality is often well ahead of international rhetoric with respect to the conservation and sustainable use of forests. In many parts of the world people are organizing to manage forests better. Faced with scarcity of the goods and services that they need from forests, people are cooperating to produce locally workable solutions to forest problems.

In order to allow this trend to continue, we need to resist the temptation of shoe-horning the science and the art of sustainable forest management into a one-size-fits-all straitjacket of standards and norms. The international processes dealing with forests have often been referred to disparagingly as international talk-shops. They may have focused too much on top-down definitions of "principles" or "criteria and indicators" or other approaches to sustainable forest management. But they have also provided inspiration for many of the positive things that are happening. Local success has not just suddenly emerged from a vacuum; it has been nourished and shaped by the debates that have been occurring at the meetings of the Convention on Biological Diversity and the United Nations Forum on Forests. Recent thinking emerging from these two bodies is leading to a new and exciting understanding of how forests can be managed as "ecosystems" and to new concepts and tools for Sustainable Forest Management.

The idea for this book came from the ongoing discussion at both the Convention on Biological Diversity (CBD) and the United Nations Forum on Forests (UNFF) on the relationship between the Ecosystem Approach and Sustainable Forest Management. This book demonstrates that these are neither alternative methods of forest management nor are they simply complicated ways of saying the same thing. They are both emerging concepts for more integrated and holistic ways of managing forests within larger landscapes in ways that optimize benefits to all stakeholders. The best bet for the sustainable and equitable management of the world's forests will be locally adapted solutions that are inspired by the latest thinking on both the Ecosystem Approach and Sustainable Forest Management. Ultimately, every forest situation is different and we need a plurality of solutions, each grounded in local realities. International processes do seem to be contributing to a more enabling environment in which successful local solutions can emerge.

So the conclusion is that not all the news on forests is bad. Over the past couple of decades, a quiet revolution in forest management has been gathering momentum. This revolution has been initiated not in boardrooms or national assemblies but through the practice of communities, individuals, foresters and conservationists, often setting aside their differences and starting to act together.

Achim Steiner
Director General
IUCN

Ian Johnson
Vice President, Sustainable Development
The World Bank

Preface

This book was stimulated by discussions held at the third meeting of the United Nations Forum on Forests (UNFF) on the relationship, as applied to forests, between sustainable forest management (SFM) and the Ecosystem Approach Principles developed under the Convention on Biological Diversity (CBD). It also responds to a decision at the 6th Conference of the Parties of the CBD seeking clarification of the relations between the two concepts.

The book grew out of a workshop held in May 2004 in Begnins, Switzerland. This meeting brought together a group of 20 people representing forest managers, academics, specialists in integrated approaches to natural resources management and forest conservation practitioners from about 15 countries. The group shared experiences on recent trends in sustainable forest management concepts and in the use of various forms of ecosystem approaches to forest conservation and management problems.

The case studies in this book were, with the exception of the Australia chapter, written by persons attending the Begnins workshop. But the workshop also triggered an intense set of interactions amongst both the participants and people from the wider IUCN network on issues related to ecosystem approaches and sustainable forest management. We have drawn heavily on this network of experts and on the rich recent literature on SFM and ecosystem approaches in editing this volume.

It was apparent from the beginning that there had been numerous attempts to manage forests at the scale of "ecosystems" during recent decades. The terms "Ecosystem Management" and the concept of managing and conserving "forest ecosystems" had been around for a long time before the CBD Principles were developed. Much of this practical experience anticipated, and undoubtedly con- tributed to, the Ecosystem Approach concepts articulated by the CBD. Almost all of the case material in this book relates to practical experiences that were already initiated long before the publication of the CBD Principles. We were not able to identify and so have not drawn upon any examples of forest management initiatives that had been undertaken as a direct response to the CBD Principles. The use of the term "ecosystem approaches" in this book therefore refers to forest management experiences that are consistent with, but were not a response to, the CBD Principles. We have used the lower case, ecosystem approach, when we are referring to general approaches to managing forests at a large spatial scale for multiple environmental and social objectives in ways that are consistent with the CBD Principles. We have used the upper case and definite article – The Ecosystem Approach – when we are referring specifically to the CBD Principles.

This book is written largely from the perspective of the forester. Foresters have been widely criticised for taking a narrow commodity focus to forest resource management. They have been primarily interested in timber and are perceived as treating everything else as secondary to timber production. We believe that this book shows that this stereotype is no longer valid and has not been for at least a couple of decades. Foresters and forest departments have in many cases been at the cutting edge of the development of more integrative approaches to resource management. In many cases this has been because they were subject to strong pressure from civil society to give more prominence to the broad social and environmental values of forests – but the fact remains that the past two decades have seen a remarkable evolution of the profession of forestry. We would argue that foresters may have moved further and quicker in the direction of ecosystem approaches to management than other resource managers – and certainly further than they have widely been credited.

A major conclusion of our work is that ecosystem approaches manifest themselves in very different ways in different situations. The term "ecosystem approach" is understood in different ways by people depending on the situations in which they have worked. In Western Europe the issues that have driven the need for ecosystem approaches have been biodiversity conservation and amenity. In India and Central America it has been poverty alleviation and local people's rights to forest resources. In North America and Australia it has been an environmental lobby for the preservation of old-growth forests. In Russia it has been the protection of employment and rural economies in the face of destructive and illegal logging. When asked to write about experiences with ecosystem approaches people from these different geographic origins focussed on the issues that had been the drivers of change in their own forests.

This leads us to the overall conclusion that it is unhelpful to focus too much on any one formula for forest management. The future of forestry should lie in pluralism. Every forest system is different in its biophysical, economic, social and political attributes. Every situation needs a response tailored to its present needs and these needs will inevitably change over time. The skill of the forest manager is to be able to draw upon the rich literature on the ecology, economics and social values of forests and work with all stakeholders to develop the best management regime for the location at that point in time. The forester then has to stay engaged and be alert to the need to change management when the time comes to do so. We do not believe in management by formula or by any single "cookie-cutter" approach, guideline or criteria and indicator set. However we do conclude that the CBD Ecosystem Approach Principles and their supporting documentation are an excellent resource for forest managers and should be widely consulted and the Principles should be respected. We also conclude that the recent literature on sustainable forest management and the numerous sets of criteria and indicators that have been developed to monitor and evaluate its performance also represent valuable sources of guidance and accumulated knowledge and make valuable contributions to addressing the challenge of better management of forests worldwide.

Jeffrey A. Sayer and Stewart Maginnis
Gland, Switzerland
June 2005

Acknowledgements

IUCN and PROFOR/The World Bank would like to acknowledge the large number of people who have been involved in the project that led to this book:

At the World Bank, Jill Blockhus, David Cassells and Kathy MacKinnon attended the original meeting in Switzerland and they and Laura Ivers remained supporters of the project throughout. Jim Douglas contributed to the ideas expressed in the chapter on Economics.

Mette Bovenschulte, Mette Loyche Wilkie, Rodolphe Schlaepfer, Rosalind Fredericks, Sandeep Sengupta, Tomme Young and Russel Diabo, all helped organize or took part in the Swiss meeting.

Jack Hurd, Bo Larsen, Dave Rolf, Sven Wunder, Robert Nasi, Charles Doumenge, Neil Byron, Sergio Rosendo, Dennis Dykstra, Richard Haynes and Reidar Persson, reviewed various chapters.

A number of persons in the IUCN secretariat or involved in the work of the IUCN Commission on Ecosystem Management contributed ideas and comments as the work progressed, in particular we would like to thank William Jackson, Gert Bergkamp, Simon Rietbergen, Gill Shepherd and Don Gilmour.

A number of people helped in the preparation of the manuscript and we would like especially to thank Intu Boedhihartono, Elaine Shaughnessy and Jennifer Rietbergen-McCracken. Rob West of EARTHSCAN was supportive throughout.

This publication was made possible through funding from PROFOR donors: the Finnish Department for International Development Cooperation, the Japanese International Cooperation Agency (JICA), Swiss Development Cooperation (SDC), and Department for International Development (DFID) of the United Kingdom.

Acronyms and Abbreviations

ACICAFOC	Asociación Coordinadora Indígena y Campesina de Agroforestería Comunitaria Centroamericana (Central American Coordinating Association for small-scale Agroforestry)
ACOFOP	Asociación de Comunidades Forestales de El Petén (Peten Association of Forest Communities)
AFLEG	African Forest Law Enforcement and Governance
AMAs	Adaptive Management Areas
AMI	Areas de Manejo Integral (Integrated Management Areas)
APEC	Asia-Pacific Economic Community
AREAS	Asian Rhino and Elephant Action Strategy
BOSCOSA	Cooperación en los Sectores Forestal y Maderero (Forest and Wood Sector Cooperation)
CACH	Centro Agrícola Cantonal de Hojancha (Hojancha Cantonal Agricultural Centre)
CALM	Department of Conservation and Land Management-Western Australia
CAR	Central African Republic
CATIE	Tropical Agricultural Research and Higher Education Center
CBD	Convention on Biological Diversity
CBFP	Congo Basin Forest Partnership
CCAD	Comisión Centroamericana de Ambiente y Desarrollo (Central American Commission for Environment and Development)
CEFDHAC	Conference on Central African Moist Forest Ecosystems
CFM	Community Forest Management
CGIAR	Consultative Group on International Agricultural Research
CIB	Société Congolaise Industrielle des Bois (Congolese Forest Industry)
CIFOR	Center for International Forestry Research
CIRAD	The International Centre for Agronomic Research for Development
CITES	Convention on International Trade in Endangered Species
COMIFAC	Comité des Ministres des Forêts d'Afrique Centrale (Committee of Forest Ministers of Central Africa)
CONAP	Consejo Nacional de Áreas Protegidas (National Council for Protected Areas)
CRZ	Coastal Regulation Zone
CT	Commercial Thinning
CTFT	Le Centre Technique Forestier Tropical (Technical Centre for Tropical Forestry – France)
C&I	Criteria and Indicators
DRC	Democratic Republic of the Congo
ECOFAC	Ecosystèmes Forestiers en Afrique Centrale – An EU sponsored programme

EDC	Ecodevelopment Committee
EIA	Environmental Impact Assessment
EsA	Ecosystem Approach
ESA	Endangered Species Act
EU	European Union
FAO	Food and Agriculture Organization of the United Nations
FD	Forest Department
FEMAT	Forest Ecosystem Management Assessment Team
FMU	Forest Management Unit
FONAFIFO	The Fondo Nacional de Financiamiento Forestal (National Fund for Forest Finance)
FREEP	Forestry Research Education and Extension Project
FSC	Forest Stewardship Council
FSI	Forest Survey of India
FUNDECOR	Fundación para el Desarrollo de la Cordillera Volcánica Central (Foundation for the Development of the Central Volcanic Range)
GEF	Global Environment Facility
GIS	Geographic Information System
GMO	Genetically Modified Organism
GNP	Gross National Product
GoI	Government of India
HCVs	High Conservation Values
ICBEMP	Interior Columbia Basin Ecosystem Management Project
ICDP	Integrated conservation and development project
IEDP	India Ecodevelopment Project
IFF	Intergovernmental Forum on Forests
IIFM	Indian Institute of Forest Management
INBio	Instituto Nacional de Biodiversidad de Costa Rica (National Biodiversity Institute, Costa Rica)
IPF	Intergovernmental Panel on Forests
ITTO	International Tropical Timber Organization
IUCN	The World Conservation Union
JFM	Joint Forest Management
MAB	Man and Biosphere Programme
MASS	Montane Alternative Silvicultural Systems
MCPFE	Ministerial Conference for the Protection of Forests in Europe
MoEF	Ministry of Environment and Forests
MoU	Memorandum of Understanding
MUSY	Multiple Use–Sustained Yield
NBSAP	National Biodiversity Strategy and Action Plan
NEPA	National Environmental Policy Act

NESDB	National Economic and Social Development Board
NFMA	National Forest Management Act
NFP	National Forest Programme
NGO	Non-governmental organization
NIMBY	Not In My Back Yard
NIPF	Non-industrial Private Forest
NRSA	National Remote Sensing Agency
NTFP	Non-Timber Forest Product
NWFP	Northwest Forest Plan
PA	Protected Area
PDBL	Desarrollo del Bosque Latifoliado (Development of Broad-Leaved Forests)
PES	Payment for Environmental Services
PNW	Pacific Northwest
PNWW	Pacific Northwest-Westside
PCT	Pre-commercial Thinning
PYME	Pequeñas y Medianas Empresas (Small and Medium Enterprises)
PPA	People's Protected Area
RCA	République Centrafricaine
RDC	République Démocratique du Congo
RFD	Royal Forestry Department – Thailand
RPA	Renewable Resources Planning Act
SBSTTA	Subsidiary Body on Scientific, Technical and Technological Advice
SFM	Sustainable Forest Management
SMEs	Small- and Medium-Scale Enterprises
TFAP	Tropical Forestry Action Plan
TNS	Tri-National de la Sangha
TOF	Trees outside Forests
UNCED	United Nations Conference on Environment and Development
UNFF	United Nations Forum on Forests
UNDP	United Nations Development Programme
UNESCO	United Nations Educational Scientific and Cultural Organization
UPA	United Progressive Alliance
USAID	United States Agency for International Development
USDA	United States Department of Agriculture
USFS	United States Forest Service
WCS	Wildlife Conservation Society
WSCG	Women's Savings and Credit Group
WTI	Wildlife Trust of India
WWF	WorldWide Fund for Nature (World Wildlife Fund in North America)

1 New Challenges for Forest Management

Jeffrey A. Sayer and Stewart Maginnis

The concluding decades of the 20th Century saw unprecedented changes in forestry. New realities emerged in both industrialized and developing countries. In the industrialized world there were strong movements towards the privatization of production forestry. Internationally the sustainability of the tropical timber industry became a major issue. A small number of multi-national corporations came to dominate the pulp and paper industry worldwide. In the developing world considerable attention has been given to expansion of local ownership of forests and agroforestry has assumed greater importance as a major platform for improved livelihoods. Throughout the world there has been a re-examination of who makes decisions about forests and how these decisions are made. Attempts have been made to establish a global regulatory framework for forests through existing and proposed intergovernmental agreements, principles and broadly-accepted criteria and indicators for sustainable forest management. In parallel there has been a strong tendency towards more participatory, localized decision-making. These changes were seldom initiated by forestry agencies. Political pressures, the media and activism by civil society groups have been the main drivers of change. In a number of countries forest stakeholders have clashed in the courts and the judiciary has had to take key decisions on how to manage forests.

Almost all countries are moving away from a tradition of centralized, technically-driven forestry. Forest departments are no longer primarily concerned with maintaining the status quo. They are abandoning top-down, 'command and control' traditions and evolving a more adaptive, pluralistic vision of their own role. Instead of establishing and enforcing regulations, forestry departments are now facilitating negotiations and providing an 'enabling environment' for broader-based and more inclusive management of forests. Instead of dealing exclusively with the forests placed under their control they are now addressing the needs for forests and trees in broader multi-functional landscapes. Many of the long-standing laws and institutions for dealing with forests were created when forest boundaries were well-established and stable over time – now we are witnessing expansions of forest areas in many industrialized countries and the continuing conversion of forests to other land uses in many developing countries. The range of forest products and services and the arrangements for providing them from our emerging multi-functional landscapes are constantly changing. Trees both inside and outside forests are assuming increasing importance, or at least greater recognition, for their role in the provision of fuel, fibre, habitat for biodiversity, carbon storage and amenity.

The Ecosystem Principles adopted by the Convention on Biological Diversity and the various sets of Criteria and Indicators for sustainable forest management all mirror these changes in the expectations that our societies have for their forests. To a greater or lesser extent they capture the public's growing recognition of the global values of forests and the emerging demands for locally-adapted forests with control firmly in the hands of civil society. The chapters in this book attempt to capture the richness of some of these changes and to draw general conclusions about the elements that should make up our approach to forestry for the 21st Century.

Background

Sustained yield forestry, sustainable forestry, and sustainable forest management (SFM) represent a progression of basic forest management concepts that have a long history. The different terms refer to attempts to 'sustain' the flows of different sets of forest goods and services. In general there has been a recent trend to greatly increase the range of goods and services for which 'sustainability' is sought and to look at forests as integral parts of dynamic landscapes. The term SFM is increasingly used to describe approaches to forest management that take account of very broad social and environmental goals. A range of forestry institutions now practice various forms of SFM and a wide variety of methods and tools are available that have been tested over time. Forestry institutions have adapted their skill mix and structures to address these new broader definitions of SFM and forestry-training institutions have also been evolving rapidly. University Forest Departments have often broadened their mandates or merged with other departments to form departments of 'Natural Resource Management' or 'Environmental Sciences'. These general trends in forestry institutions are occurring almost every-where, though the speed with which they are occurring is variable. In a number of countries the transformation of forestry in recent decades has been revolutionary. In other countries changes are less apparent and in many developing countries laws and policies may have changed but the capacity to translate these intentions into realities on the ground has been lacking.

The Forest Principles adopted at The United Nations Conference on Environment and Development (UNCED) in Rio de Janeiro in 1992 captured the general international understanding of SFM at that time. Since then a number of sets of criteria and indicators (C&I) have been developed to evaluate the achievements of SFM at both the country and management unit level. These were all attempts to codify and provide for independent assessment of the degree to which the broader objectives of SFM are being achieved in practice. Many of these initiatives to refine sets of C&I have been conducted at a regional level by groups of countries sharing similar problems. These processes have themselves provided valuable opportunities for learning lessons and sharing experiences between countries. The development of C&I has often been a participatory process. C&I were originally developed to measure progress but the processes that produced them have been major drivers of change. The C&I phenomenon is an example of the swing from "hard" formal government-determined legal frameworks towards "softer" rules developed and imposed by civil society.

A good definition of the present day understanding of the term SFM was developed by the Ministerial Conference on the Protection of Forests in Europe and this definition has now been adopted by FAO. It defines SFM as:

> *The stewardship and use of forests and forest lands in a way, and at a rate, that maintains their biodiversity, productivity, regeneration capacity, vitality and their potential to fulfil, now and in the future, relevant ecological, economic and social functions, at local, national, and global levels, and that does not cause damage to other ecosystems.*

Throughout the world, trained professional foresters and forest technicians practice SFM to varying degrees. A vast literature exists and there is a very large body of accumulated knowledge and experience of how the diversity of management goals for forests can be met. Professional practice, science and the literature have made enormous progress in recent decades in addressing the requirement of the diverse stakeholders who wish to see the objectives of SFM broadened. [1]

---

1 Ferguson (1996), Schlaepfer (1997) and Angelstam *et al.* (2004) give interesting overviews of current thinking on SFM from different perspectives.

Ecosystem Management as Applied to Forests

Ecosystem management is a concept of managing entire ecological units in an integrated and holistic way. The term has been used in a number of different contexts. The term was first widely used in the 1980s within discussions on the need for more integrated management of coastal and marine resources, especially fisheries. In the late 1980s, a major public challenge to conventional forest management approaches in the USA Pacific Northwest was addressed by the adoption by the US Forest Service (USFS) of ecosystem management. A conflict resolution NGO, the Keystone Center, conducted a major series of public hearings to clarify and build consensus on precisely what ecosystem management entailed. A large body of literature was produced in the USA at this time on ecosystem management and ecological stewardship. Accounts of the North American experience of Ecosystem Management and of the science that underlay it are given in two important publications – *Ecological Stewardship – A common reference for Ecosystem Management* (Johnson et al., 1999) and *Creating a Forestry for the 21st Century* (Kohm and Franklin, 1997). These remain excellent compilations of North American experience of the application of ecosystem management to forests.

Originally, and especially in the USA, the term ecosystem management was used to describe an approach that was heavily based upon understanding and managing ecological processes. More recently, and especially in Europe and in developing countries, the term has been used to describe social-ecological systems – so people and their institutions have come to be considered components of the ecosystems under management.

The Ecosystem Approach

Discussions of the Ecosystem Approach have been prominent on the agenda of the CBD since the first SBSTTA and the second meeting of the conference of the parties in Jakarta in 1995. The CBD definition of the Ecosystem Approach and a set of principles for its application were developed at an expert meeting in Malawi in 1995 – the so-called Malawi Principles. The definition, 12 principles and five points of 'operational guidance' were adopted by the Conference of the Parties at its 5th meeting in 2000. The CBD definition is as follows:

> *The ecosystem approach is a strategy for the integrated management of land, water and living resources that promotes conservation and sustainable use in an equitable way. Application of the ecosystem approach will help to reach a balance of the three objectives of the Convention. An ecosystem approach is based on the application of appropriate scientific methodologies focused on levels of biological organization, which encompasses the essential structures, processes, functions and interactions among organisms and their environment. It recognises that humans, with their cultural diversity, are an integral component of many ecosystems.*

In many respects the USFS use of the term ecosystem management is a logical progression from SFM. It is simply SFM defined more broadly and providing for more participation and management for a wider range of goods and services. It remains a managerial approach and is firmly anchored in a set of tools and methodologies to enable it to be made operational. The CBD use of the term Ecosystem Approach is – as is stated – a set of general principles that can be applied in a wide range of circumstances. It is not linked to any particular operational approach nor does it contain a vision of clear targets. Sedjo's (1996) criticism of ecosystem management could also apply to the Ecosystem Approach: "Ecosystem management has no clear goals and cannot therefore be operationalized". In reality the CBD Ecosystem Principles were never intended to be a management prescription. They provided an internationally-negotiated set of principles that described what are considered to be desirable attributes of management systems for the implementation of commitments under the convention. Nevertheless Smith and Maltby (2003) have made a first attempt at examining how the CBD understanding of the Ecosystem Approach might be translated into operational terms. Shepherd (2004), working with the IUCN Commission on Ecosystem Management, has proposed operational guidelines for implementing the Ecosystem Approach.

In this book we have deliberately drawn a distinction between the CBD statement of Principles for the Ecosystem Approach and the practical, on-the-ground, reality of forest departments, land managers and communities attempting to locate their operational work in a broader landscape or ecosystem context. We refer to the latter, collectively, as "ecosystem approaches". The reason that we do this is to draw a clear distinction between the overarching philosophy of broader and more holistic management of forest systems and earlier commodity-oriented approaches to management. This book is largely about the actual experiences of forest managers in attempting to work at the scale of social-ecological systems. We consider that attempts to categorize these as ecosystem management, ecosystem approaches, landscape approaches etc. are largely questions of semantics. Our case studies therefore cover a very broad range of practical experience of approaches that are consistent with the spirit of the CBD Principles. None of them is about attempts to implement those Principles and we are not aware of any formal attempts to do so in relation to forests.

The Broader Context

The emergence of the concept of the Ecosystem Approach and the rapid broadening of the concepts of SFM must be seen within the context of a general trend towards greater integration of societal concerns in all natural resources management in recent decades. Debates similar to those that have occurred in relation to forests have also taken place in relation to almost all terrestrial and marine systems – both natural areas and heavily man-modified systems such as farms. A plethora of terms has been used to describe these more integrated approaches. Integrated conservation and development projects (ICDP) were attempted around many protected areas in the 1980s and 1990s and in several respects can be seen as a precursor of the Ecosystem Approach of the CBD. Integrated range, integrated river basin and integrated watershed management also have much in common with the Ecosystem Approach (SFM). The basic need to manage large complex natural systems in an integrated way was already rather well articulated in the UNESCO-sponsored Man and Biosphere Programme (MAB) that was initiated over 30 years ago. MAB now has the endorsement of 186 UNESCO member states and is operationalized to a greater or lesser degree in 440 biosphere reserves in 95 countries. A rich literature has emerged on the theoretical underpinnings of integrated approaches to natural resources (Berkes *et al.*, 2003; Gunderson *et al.*,1995; Lee, 1993).

Parallel to these trends towards integrating different forms of management of a single area of land, there has been a strong wave of interest in the problems of dealing with issues at larger spatial scales. There is an emerging recognition that the different components of landscape mosaics combine to form a dynamic whole that is 'greater than the sum of the parts'. Interest groups ranging from agricultural researchers to conservationists are attempting to use the 'ecoregion' as a unit of analysis. Many different groups are attempting to manage large areas of land in an integrated way to optimize the multiple-functions of different components of landscapes.

Many scientists and resource managers are grappling with the difficult issues of the 'scale-dependency' of sustainability. Management that is sustainable within the management unit may have negative impacts on adjoining areas – it is therefore unsustainable when judged at a larger spatial scale. Management that can supply today's needs sustainably may not allow for adaptation to meet future needs. Our understanding of the word "sustainable" is evolving. We no longer see sustainability as a permanent continuation of the present situation. Sustainability now embraces the concept of the ability to adapt to changing needs. There has been much debate in forestry about the relative merits of single or 'dominant use' and 'multiple-use' as competing paradigms. However it is clear that these are not necessarily competing or mutually-exclusive at the larger landscape level. In some situations, sustainability may be best achieved by fine-scale integration of use across the entire landscape. In other situations, segregation of uses at fine or larger scales may provide the best outcomes. SFM has traditionally focused on the 'fine-scale integration' model; Ecosystem approaches can accommodate both integrated and segregated models.

The concepts of eco-regions, landscape functionality, integration of conservation and development etc. are better reflected in the CBD Ecosystem Principles than in the definitions and C&I related to SFM. The SFM debate has been led by foresters, who often have mandatory responsibilities to produce goods and services profitably from land under their control. The Ecosystem debate has been led by people more concerned with limiting the damage that resource extraction can do to natural resource systems.

There is a large element of the 'Precautionary Principle' in the Ecosystem Approach discourse. Some advocates of the Ecosystem Approach appear to seek to eliminate all risks before taking decisions. This was never how the precautionary principle was intended to be applied. The Precautionary Principle should be interpreted as a rational and transparent approach to taking decisions where risk currently cannot be quantified. Risk can never be eliminated or even fully quantified in managing natural resource systems and perceptions of risk change over time. However, in spite of this, risks must be managed and the task of professional natural resource managers is to make good judgements on the basis of their assessment of the risks involved.

The concepts underlying SFM and ecosystem approaches have evolved dramatically in the past decade. A similar evolution of conceptual frameworks has been taking place amongst managers of other categories of natural resources. There are guidelines and manuals on integrating conservation and development (Wells and McShane, 2004). Rich bodies of literature exist on the integrated management of a number of different natural resource systems. Spatial planning and decision support tools have been widely applied in a variety of contexts where complex landscape mosaics had to be managed. This literature is reviewed and many of these definitions and approaches explored in Sayer and Campbell (2004), their definition of integrated approaches to natural resource management could be applied to current concepts of SFM and ecosystem approaches:

> Integrated Natural Resource Management is a conscious process of incorporating multiple aspects of natural resources use into a system of sustainable management to meet explicit production goals of farmers and other users (e.g. profitability, risk reduction) as well as the goals of the wider community.

This definition as applied to SFM and/or ecosystem approaches has the attraction of referring to 'explicit production goals' and the 'goals of the wider community'.

The Drivers of Change in Forest Management Systems

People have been managing forests since the dawn of time. Formal forest laws and institutions first emerged in 18th Century Europe and were a reflection of those less egalitarian times. They were mainly driven by the need to protect timber and hunting 'rights' of royalty and other national elites against the local subsistence needs of the peasants. The need to ensure the availability of large timber for building ships in Western Europe in the 17th and 18th Centuries set a pattern for forestry that has had an impact on the development of forestry institutions throughout the modern world. However many things have changed and today's forestry institutions have to meet very different needs in a world that has become more connected and is putting more pressures on its environment.

The global discourses on SFM and ecosystem approaches must be considered in the context of a myriad of local innovations in resource management systems. Many successful initiatives have included ideas that are reflected in the definitions and principles of SFM and the Ecosystem Principles. They range in scale from community-managed forests to the application of integrated management to large industrial timber concessions or trans-frontier protected areas. There has been considerable interest in multiple- use protected areas where productive activities are integrated into attempts to conserve biodiversity (IUCN's categories V and VI – Protected Landscapes, Resource Management and Multiple-use Reserves). These have many similarities to the biosphere reserves under the UNESCO Man and Biosphere programme and respond to many of the concepts that figure in the SFM and ecosystem approach discourse.

Some of the more important underlying trends that are creating the need for more integrated and holistic management systems for forests and that are providing the context in which SFM and ecosystem approaches have to operate include:

1. **Broadening forest management objectives:** At all scales, from the community to the global enterprise, forest owners and managers are being urged to deal with a much broader range of social and environmental issues than in the past. Forests have values within the landscape for hydrology and amenity. Forests can also have 'global values' for biodiversity and carbon storage and these often do not correspond to the values perceived by local people. Society is making more explicit demands for longer temporal scales and larger spatial scales to be addressed in forest management.

2. **Codifying good practice:** Regulators, certifiers and civil society are developing C&I and other performance standards against which they can assess the 'quality' of forest management or the 'health' of forests. Governments want to apply norms and capture rents for publicly owned forests, the private sector wants to reduce costs and maximize profits, local people want to defend rights and assets, and environmental groups want to ensure long-term sustainability and promote best practice by all forest users.

3. **Recognition of pluralism in forest management:** The reality that all forests are different is increasingly recognised and is accompanied by growing awareness that promoting a 'single best' management system may be counter-productive. The predominant concept of a single best way to manage 'state forests' is giving way to the recognition that there are many different systems of ownership and use of forests that are likely to be sustainable.

4. **Decentralization – devolution:** While the locus of decision-making on some forest issues is moving from the national to the global level, many governments are decentralizing control of forests and divesting themselves of forest assets. Responsibility for forests is being placed in

the hands of regional, municipal and local governments and communities. When this is done too quickly or in response to crisis situations it may result in a free-for-all and a degradation of forest resources. Sometimes it takes time to develop local capacity to manage forests but decentralized systems can be good at achieving local integration of different forest functions. They may be less good at making sure that features of global value are conserved.

5. **Globalization:** In parallel with the moves to decentralize forest management, the forces of globalization are having major influences on forests. Multi-national corporations, banks, trade regulations etc. all have strong impacts on how forests are managed and are usually out of local control. A small number of multi-national corporations now dominate the pulp and paper sector and control over vast areas of forest plantations is concentrated in their hands. Trans-national payments for environmental services may become increasingly influential. Macro-economic forces and poverty reduction measures all have a major impact on forests. The number of international meetings at which forest conservation is discussed is proliferating and some forest issues are the subjects of inter-governmental processes.

6. **Climate change:** The uncertainties created by the potential impacts of different climate change scenarios have major implications for forest conservation and management laws and institutions. Eco-climatic zones are shifting by hundreds of kilometres, new pest and disease problems are emerging, and invasive weed species are posing increasing threats. Climate change adaptation will be the major challenge for all forest managers in the future. Climate change mitigation – through carbon sequestration – may provide some opportunities to offset the costs of sustainable forestry but may also create a whole new set of problems. The problems posed by managing forests in periods of rapidly changing climates are better addressed through ecosystem approaches than through conventional SFM.

7. **Governance:** Running through all of these issues are different aspects of the issues of forest governance. In developing countries and in some countries with economies in transition institutions are weak and have difficulty taking on the new challenges of conserving and regulating forests. "Tragedies of the commons" are played out at all scales from local to national and regional. Illegal exploitation, land conversion and corruption are all major issues for forests. Forests are only well managed when formal institutions are effective and civil society is mobilized to defend the interests of diverse stakeholders. Forests are never well managed in countries that lack an effective judiciary system.

Changing Paradigms for Forest Management

The 'drivers of change' listed above will require us to re-think conventional forest conservation and management paradigms. Institutional arrangements, organizational cultures, training and research must all be adapted to address these new challenges. The concepts underlying ecosystem approaches are enriching the debate and are challenging forest conservation and management professionals to reflect upon some changes to which, in many countries, they have traditionally been resistant.

The regional and national case studies that make up the bulk of this book have been deliberately selected to illustrate the diversity of the changes that have occurred in forestry in recent decades. We have concentrated on places where significant changes have taken place but in each location the driving forces that led to change were different. Not surprisingly, the responses to these changes were also different. The changes are often consistent with the CBD Principles for the Ecosystem Approach and they are all manifestations of sustainable forest management. But the actual outcomes on the ground are predominantly driven by local context. We see this emergence of local, national or regional approaches positively. It shows that internationally-negotiated principles, criteria, indicators and other normative guidelines can enrich the local debate but must not constrain it. The case study authors were instructed to write about the extent to which the changes that had occurred in their regions reflected emerging concepts of ecosystem approaches and SFM. It was interesting to see the diversity of interpretations of the concepts of ecosystem approaches that exist. It became clear that the CBD principles were sufficiently general that they could be subject to very different interpretations in differing situations.

It will always be frustrating to attempt to capture and codify the richness and diversity of the changes occurring in forestry in sets of simple definitions and principles. Much energy can be wasted in discussions of semantics. It is important to focus international debates on those issues that need to be addressed internationally. Too much time should not be spent trying to fine-tune international sets of principles of ecosystem approaches or definitions of SFM to encompass the diversity of change that is occurring in the world's forests. The principle of subsidiarity must be applied more consistently, and issues that can be achieved through local or regional processes should not be attempted at an international level.

Box 1   **CBD's Twelve Principles of the Ecosystem Approach**

1. The objectives of management of land, water and living resources are a matter of societal choice.

2. Management should be decentralized to the lowest appropriate level.

3. Ecosystem managers should consider the effects (actual or potential) of their activities on adjacent and other ecosystems.

4. Recognizing potential gains from management, there is usually a need to understand and manage the ecosystem in an economic context. Any such ecosystem-management programme should:
   (a) reduce those market distortions that adversely affect biological diversity;
   (b) align incentives to promote biodiversity conservation and sustainable use;
   (c) internalize costs and benefits in the given ecosystem to the extent feasible.

5. Conservation of ecosystem structure and functioning, in order to maintain ecosystem services, should be a priority target of the ecosystem approach.

6. Ecosystems must be managed within the limits of their functioning.

7. The ecosystem approach should be undertaken at the appropriate spatial and temporal scales.

8. Recognizing the varying temporal scales and lag-effects that characterize ecosystem processes, objectives for ecosystem management should be set for the long term.

9. Management must recognise that change is inevitable.

10. The ecosystem approach should seek the appropriate balance between, and integration of, conservation and use of biological diversity.

11. The ecosystem approach should consider all forms of relevant information, including scientific and indigenous and local knowledge, innovations and practices.

12. The ecosystem approach should involve all relevant sectors of society and scientific disciplines.

So far, this paper has attempted to show that SFM and ecosystem approaches are emerging or evolving in response to a set of underlying driving forces. The paper prepared by FAO on 'Sustainable Forest Management and the Ecosystem Approach' (Wilkie *et al.*, 2003) carries the subtitle 'Two Concepts, One Goal'. Wilkie *et al.* conclude that the CBD Ecosystem Approach and SFM are basically different ways of expressing the same ideas and they only differ because they evolved from different origins. Our study suggests that they are not simply different ways of saying the same thing and that there are differences in both the scope of their application and their underlying philosophies. However we do not see this as necessarily negative. Indeed the SFM and Ecosystem Approach discourses have been complementary and mutually enriching.

A recent paper by Ellenberg (2003) provides additional useful ideas on the relationship between the CBD Ecosystem Principles and SFM. He expresses the concern that the application of the Ecosystem Principles to forests would result in further layers of restrictive regulations. He portrays a scenario where foresters would be more subject to the concerns of 'environmentalists' and would be forced to 'jump through even more hoops' in order to exercise their profession. It is possible that a narrow interpretation of the Ecosystem Principles could manifest itself in this way. However, this is not inevitable and would depend upon how countries choose to apply them. It would be preferable if the Ecosystem Approach were to be regarded as a different process of decision-making rather than an additional layer of regulation.

So, what really are the differences between these two concepts and what are the practical implications of these differences? Table 1 is an attempt to characterize the differences between SFM and the CBD Principles. It deliberately does not attempt a direct comparison between the CBD Principles and any particular SFM definitions, principles or criteria. It is based on a review of the more general literature on SFM and ecosystem approaches, and tries to distil out some underlying conceptual differences. Some of the characterizations may seem arbitrary and will be contested. The two terms are used so broadly that some people may feel that the simple characterization exaggerates the distinctions. This comparison is simply a starting point for discussion.

Criteria and Indicators for Assessing Forest Management

Criteria and Indicators have emerged as a tool for third party certification that forests are managed sustainably. However they can also be seen as part of a more pluralistic, negotiated approach to decision making about forests. Instead of "hard law" imposed by the state they can be seen as an emergent "Soft law" developed and applied by civil society. Certification may be emerging as a form of alternative forest governance. It can be seen as a soft regulatory framework for making modern concepts of ecosystem approaches and sustainable forest management operational.

Certification is a product of ...*a new paradigm of policy planning...(which)...focuses on governance processes which take place in policy networks or bargaining systems. Networks are informal groups of interacting political actors of the policy making process. State and society are not hierarchically separated but interacting* (Gluck 1997 cited in Elliot 2000). Certification can be seen as part of the tendency towards broader-based and more participatory models of forest management which are grouped under the general heading of 'ecosystem approaches'. However some industry interests might still see certification as the imposition of a radical environmental agenda on legitimate commercial operations.

Certification was initially motivated by the desire to ensure continued access to markets where there were threats of boycotts from environmental groups concerned about forest destruction and adverse impacts on local communities. There were also hopes that certified forest products would command premium prices and that this would offset the higher costs of sustainable management. However certification has evolved into a movement to improve forest management in a number of different ways and these are generally consistent with, and driven by the same pressures as, those promoting ecosystem approaches and modern concepts of sustainable forest management.

Table 1. Characterizing the differences between SFM and the CBD Principles

Criteria for Comparison	Sustained Yield Forestry	Sustainable Forest Management	Ecosystem Approaches
Tangibility of goals...	...is high – commodities.	...is high – products and services	...is low – equity and sustainability
Resource management objectives...	...are based on long-standing technocratic traditions and legal mandates, focused on production	...incorporate broader range of environmental and social objectives	...are a matter of societal choices
Control of resource management decisions...	...is generally centralized under responsible forest management agency	..is still usually centralized though other management options are emerging	...is decentralized to the lowest appropriate level
Hierarchical approach...	...is one of command and control – "we manage"	...is slightly more open – "we manage, you participate"	...is replaced by the concept of social learning – "we are learning together"
Spatial scale is considered...	...at site level only (i.e. management unit)	...primarily at site level, though with some consideration of externalities	...to incorporate the wider landscape-scale linkages
Knowledge is based on...	...scientific and technological knowledge	...expert knowledge, supplemented with broader stakeholder inputs	..a more balanced use of scientific and indigenous and local knowledge, innovations and practices
Sectoral approach is...	...narrowly focused	...broadly focused	...cross-sectoral
Assumes...	...predictability and stability	...adaptive management – but within defined limits	...need for resilience, anticipation of change
Associated tools...	...are those of classic silviculture	...include codes of forestry practices, criteria and indicators etc	...are not yet available. EsA have no case law and need practical testing
Primary concern...	...is on sustainable commodity production	...is on balancing conservation, production and use of forest goods and services	...is on balancing – and integrating – conservation and use of biological diversity

Successful certification systems have been associated with more pluralistic, participatory approaches to decision-making on forests. They have given civil society a more significant role in forest management and are seen by some as a form of 'democratization of forestry'. Others see them as an intrusion on private property rights. Most certification schemes have gone beyond simply improving harvesting techniques and now address broad social and environmental issues. Certification has also helped to raise public awareness and understanding of the issues of sustainable forest management. Criteria and Indicators have helped structure the public debate on forests and have provided a simple message on sustainable forestry that is accessible to the media and through them to the public. This has resulted in much broader acceptance of the desirability of using forest management as a route to forest conservation and has convinced many environmental activists to support sustainable forest management. This is exactly what ecosystem approaches are all about.

Certification has itself been associated with a number of changes in the 'policy narrative' concerning forests. Originally it was widely believed that a single, globally applicable set of principles, criteria and indicators would be a basis for assessing SFM. Now it is widely accepted that there are multiple ways in which forests can be managed, all of which qualify for certification. While certification began as a product of environmental special interest groups, it is now often determined through broad-based multi-stakeholder negotiations. And, while assessments have tended to pass or fail forests for certification, there are recent moves towards progressive, stepwise approaches consistent with the use of certification to exert pressure for the gradual incremental improvement of forest management.

Although certification was initially driven by the potential for price premiums or the avoidance of boycotts, today it is motivated more by a desire to demonstrate corporate social and environmental responsibility. For some producers it is essential to maintaining market share and retaining access to the most lucrative markets. Some governments and forest agencies initially saw certification as a challenge to their authority, many now often welcome it as one of the tools that can help achieve the objectives of SFM and maintain their legitimacy. Certification initially focussed on large industrial concessions but now there is much more interest in certification of small private and community forests. Certification has evolved from the concept of a single uniform system and now recognises that multiple and competing systems are legitimate.

Certification has thus emerged in just a single decade from the tool of special interest activist groups to part of mainstream approaches to improving forest management. Over 200 million hectares of forest are now certified by one or other of the major certification schemes. Certification is highly consistent with, and a powerful tool for achieving, ecosystem approaches to forest management. Certification is another reflection of the same underlying trends that led to the emergence of ecosystem approaches and current concepts of sustainable forest management.

Multiple Forest Stakeholders with Diverse Objectives

It may seem self-evident that all forests should be managed in accordance with local conditions and societal needs. These are fundamental principles in the ecosystem approach. But this is quite an innovation for forestry – the general tendency in the past has been to establish management approaches or models and apply them widely. The acceptance of diverse management approaches is very evident in the regional and national case studies in this volume. All of the authors were given the same instructions and all describe the progress in applying ecosystem approaches in the forests of their countries. But the approaches that they describe differ considerably. The changes in management described were all consistent with both ecosystem approaches and present-day concepts of sustainable forest management but the way in which these were translated into on-the-ground reality were determined by the specificities of the local context. This is an emerging trend. When C&I were first being developed it was generally assumed that one could eventually negotiate a single set that could be applied globally. The recent history of C&I has seen the emergence of a rich range of sets responding to local, national and regional needs. The change in focus of the work in this area of the Center for International Forestry Research is indicative of the way perceptions have changed. CIFOR began by researching a uniform approach to C&I but has now shifted its focus to research on Adaptive Collaborative Management. The latter implies that every single situation needs its own independently-negotiated indicators as a basis for local adaptive management. In a similar move, the Canadian Model Forest Programme has gone from an attempt to form a global network of forests managed according to Canadian best practice to one where a greater diversity of models qualify for membership.

This acceptance of multiple possible approaches to forest conservation is reflected in the agendas of the main international environmental conservation bodies. Many of them have moved from an almost exclusive focus on protected areas to a pluralistic approach that recognises the need for landscapes to contain forests that are protected, sustainably managed and where conservation investments can target restoration of critical forest functions.

Subsidiarity: Local Forest Rights and Assets

The solutions to many of the problems of forest loss and degradation are often portrayed as lying in more secure and more decentralized ownership and control of forests. If people or corporations know that they will reap the benefits of future flows of goods and services from forests, then they will practice better forest husbandry. Recent studies have shown that an increasing proportion of the world's forests are coming under local ownership (White and Martin, 2002). However, forests often exist as common property or common pool resources precisely because the benefits of any patch of forest often accrue at different scales and to different interest groups. Control of forests is often vested in the State on the grounds that the State will protect the public goods values of the forest. But in many cases the state has focussed excessively on a small subset of forest values – notably timber.

The same forest may in reality be valued in very different ways by different stakeholders. A forest fragment in the highlands of East Africa may be valued globally for its rare plant and animal species but locally as a source of fuel, fibre and clean water. Furthermore different local groups may depend on the forest for a differing mix of local benefits. Attributing ownership of this forest to any one group will be a difficult process to negotiate. Much good forestry practice in the past has aimed to balance the conflicting and overlapping needs and expectations of multiple beneficiaries. Many modern forest agencies see this as their prime function. Ecosystem approaches to management attempt to seek equitable trade-offs between different actors but the goals of ecosystem approaches could be threatened by the present trend towards local ownership?

In an economically efficient, globalized society, private ownership for specialized uses would appear to be a logical development. Indeed in many countries this is precisely what one observes. Everyone from industrial corporations to nature conservation organizations and from private individuals to pension funds is seeking to obtain ownership of forests. But in parallel to this drive towards private ownership there is a parallel and conflicting tendency towards the imposition of limits by civil society on what private owners can and cannot do with their forests.

This tension is manifest in countries such as the United Kingdom and Australia where urban majorities value forests for amenity and environment whilst rural minorities are more interested in employment and local economic benefits. The majority seeks to impose severe restrictions upon what the minority of forest owners can do with their forests. One could interpret this in two ways: Either in the search for improved productivity and efficiency, we have moved too far along the privatization spectrum or, that the majority are prepared to use their position to impose their value sets on the minority without offering any form of compensation. Perhaps the future needs of more integrated societies, many of whose members are engaged in service industries, lie in greater public influence over forests matched with fair and adequate compensation for forest-owning individuals and communities. In some European countries the restrictions upon what a private owner can do with forests are so great that ownership comes to resemble a 'transferable use right'. Even under devolved management arrangements, recognised property rights tend only to confer a limited number of entitlements to use.

Economic Integration and Trade Liberalization

Foresters have always struggled to achieve multiple uses of their forests. This was the essence of professional forestry – at least in the days before economic pressures drove the need for more specialized and efficient production systems. Globalization may now be changing that. Economic integration is a powerful force for increased efficiency and this translates into more intensive production systems, greater dependence on external inputs, and perhaps on GMOs etc. There is a prospect that we may move inexorably towards a world of homogeneous super-productive plantations and the diverse, multi-functional forest systems that so enrich our lives may disappear – or be relegated to a few protected areas. Forestry institutions have to confront the challenge of managing forests to optimize the full range of forest benefits. There will be a need for strong incentives or rules if we wish to preserve some of the rich and diverse traditional forest management systems that create the landscapes in which we live. All the indications are that civil societies throughout the world want to retain diverse multiple-functional forests.

An alternative interpretation of the impacts of more integrated economies on forests is that it will create a framework under which payments for environmental services can readily be transferred between countries. The numerous attempts to introduce such payment systems are struggling with the practical difficulties of how to measure environmental services. The current World Trade Organization negotiations are forcing the European Union and others to abandon some of their agricultural subsidies and to focus more attention on ways in which traditional rural livelihoods can be supported through environmental service payments. This is a precedent that could have significant long-term impacts on achieving multi-functional forest management.

The current interest in landscape-scale forestry is one manifestation of this resistance to excessive specialization and segregation of production and conservation functions. The global initiative for 'Forest Landscape Restoration' also reflects a desire for forestry to integrate environmental and social concerns with those of fibre production. These tendencies recognise that optimizing forest functions at a larger scale cannot be achieved by simply maximizing forest productivity at the scale of the management unit. There are complex issues of connectivity, downstream and offsite impacts, aesthetics etc. that must be taken into account. The European Union is ambitiously experimenting with 'multi-functional landscapes' and 'multi-functional forests' to counter the negative impacts of intensification.

The International Tropical Timber Agreement is an interesting example of how a commodity agreement has successfully integrated its primary objective of promoting the sustainability of the trade in tropical timber into a broader context. It has realized that the promotion of the trade in tropical timber species from a sustainably managed resource does not stop at ensuring good performance within the forest management unit but must also address the issues of networks of protected areas, restoration of degraded forests, non-timber forest products and the recognition of local and indigenous people's rights. The subsequent International Tropical Timber Organization (ITTO) is an unusual example of the mainstreaming of some ecosystem principles into a trade-related dialogue.

Achieving multi-functional landscapes and forests appears to be possible but it requires that the environmental and social roles of forests be given a value and that the sectors of society that benefit from these values are made to pay for them. It seems likely that the concepts of multi-functional landscapes and environmental forestry in general will only be possible in practice if such payments are introduced on a large scale. Tentative efforts to introduce such payment schemes suggest that they probably can only work in situations with strong institutions and clear, defensible land-rights. The full application of current concepts of ecosystem approaches and sustainable forest management requires that forest uses are integrated at the management unit and landscape scale and in general this will only be possible where environmental payments are made.

The inter-connectedness of the world's economies and of global environmental measures is illustrated by the complexity of the potential impacts of some measures that were initially conceived to improve the environment. The Clean Development Mechanism – in the unlikely event that it ever becomes a major factor in forestry – could result in pressure to establish forest plantations on a large scale. If this were to happen it could create pressures on some natural habitats and increase the opportunity costs associated with restoring multi-functional natural forests in degraded landscapes. If avoided deforestation were finally to qualify for credit under the clean development mechanism then this in turn would lead to a new set of challenges and trade-offs. For instance there would be a conflict between the need to maximize the amount of carbon stored with the requirement to allow fires to occur as a habitat management measure. The spectre of large-scale biomass fuel plantations covering vast tracts of the humid tropics with sugar cane or palm oil plantations poses similar threats for those seeking to conserve tropical rain forests. Even such large-scale land developments could be subject to the ecosystem principles but this is only likely to happen within the context of transparent and consistently applied regulatory frameworks and environmental service payments.

Conclusions

The changes in arrangements for forest management will undoubtedly continue. Opportunities will be needed for countries to share their ideas, experience and learning on the options that exist for more integrated and holistic management. However, there will be only limited returns from attempts to further fine-tune definitions and principles to describe ecosystem approaches and SFM. It is more important to have more in-depth debates on some of the underlying issues and to ensure that forestry professionals have the skills and incentives to produce management approaches that achieve the desired outcomes on the ground. Countries will have to determine the institutional landscape that best meets their forest needs. This will inevitably differ from country to country. Furthermore any set of management arrangements for any particular country will have to evolve over time. Both foresters and conservationists will have to get used to living with dynamism rather than pursuing stability. For instance the laws and institutions that best serve the needs of a country with low forest cover will not necessarily be the same as those appropriate for a forest-rich country. The real challenge is to make forest management operational in a way that increases the net benefits to society and protects the rights and livelihoods of individuals and communities heavily dependent on forest resources.

Forest conservation and management is entering a period of new challenges and greater uncertainty. The traditional skills and knowledge of professional foresters are going to be of ever-greater value. However, new skills and processes are going to be needed. Ultimately there is still a need for pragmatism. The marginal benefit of adding new competencies or further broadening the remit of forest agencies must exceed the marginal cost of doing so. The ecosystem principles advocate the use of the Precautionary Principle. But, this must be used only as a tool to navigate through uncertainty; if not properly applied, the Precautionary Principle can simply be an obstacle to progress, generating excessive opportunity costs and risking counterproductive outcomes. For example a private sector company with a well established social and environmental track record may abandon a difficult project area leaving the way open for less scrupulous operators. There are many recent examples of very high costs being incurred to resolve uncertainties or negotiate trade-offs in forest use. There have always been risks, uncertainties and trade-offs in forestry and these will certainly increase in the future. Ultimately the ecosystem vision tends more towards process and negotiation for resolving such difficult issues whereas the SFM tends more towards the application of professional judgment. Ecosystem approaches will have to be revisited and negotiations re-opened over the course of time. Sedjo *et al.* (1996) argue persuasively for economic sustainability to be given more weight in discussions of SFM. The 'transactions costs' of negotiating and implementing the broad ambitions of both SFM and ecosystem approaches can be high and will have to figure in economic analyses.

A number of forest issues that are currently high on the international agenda could benefit from being examined through the different lenses of SFM and ecosystem approaches. Initiatives dealing with the problems of illegality and crime, adapting to climate change, determining how best to utilize forest resources for poverty reduction, and safeguarding global forest values in decentralized forest management systems might all look different from an ecosystem and an SFM perspective, and the best solution might be a pragmatic mix of responses drawn from both.

Realizing that both ecosystem approaches and SFM are evolving concepts, it will be useful to continue to maintain an international dialogue on new and innovative ways of organizing sustainable forest conservation and management. Many countries have already embarked on reorganizing their institutions. Indeed, many developing countries have been encouraged by aid donors to engage in continuous processes of legal and institutional reform. The underlying differences in philosophy and vision found in the CBD Ecosystem Principles and SFM are significant for countries that plan to change their way of organizing forest conservation and management in biophysically, economically and socially-dynamic landscapes. Thorough and open debates on the underlying issues are important; 'one size will not fit all' and no single paradigm has a monopoly on the truth.

Institutional reform should not be attempted solely or even largely in the abstract conceptual sphere. Rather, the emphasis should be on experimentation and lesson-learning. The best solutions for forests and other key natural habitats will vary in different landscapes. This suggests the need for mixing and matching elements of ecosystem approaches and SFM. This approach should logically involve:

- Developing culturally and politically-appropriate mechanisms for defining both the production goals of immediate concern to local resource user groups and the environment and development goals of the wider society. In essence this will involve developing a process of participatory social choice to decide what should be sustained, for whom, where, when and how. Inevitably it will also mean that trade-offs will have to be made and that some arrangements will have to make do with simply keeping options open in order to retain the choice of delivering certain values at a later date.

- Developing programmes to negotiate the institutional arrangements for integrated landscape management and define processes that will maximize positive synergies and minimize negative synergies between forest and other land uses.

- Clarifying fair and workable institutional, policy and legal arrangements with respect to the rights and responsibilities of forest ownership and use.

- Aligning and reforming resource access prices, payments for environmental services and fiscal constraints and incentives to encourage resource sustainability and the internalization of all externalities associated with particular resource use patterns.

- Developing participatory monitoring, evaluation and review mechanisms that will allow iterative improvement in land use allocation and management processes in response to new scientific information, changing environmental, social and economic conditions and the experience gained from landscape management.

The thematic case studies that follow examine aspects of some of these important cross-cutting issues in more detail. We begin with additional perspectives on the culturally-based assumptions that underlie much of the policy narrative on forests. Examples of the impacts of macro-economic forces are then presented to show that these constrain the options for different approaches to forest management. The practical issues surrounding the use of generalized sets of criteria and indicators are then discussed. We follow this with case studies from a diversity of countries and regions where forestry has undergone rapid change in recent years. These studies further emphasise the diversity of conditions that exist and the need that this creates for a diversity of solutions. Following these studies, we look at what this all implies for our needs for information on forests. Lastly we offer some conclusions on how forest institutions need to respond and some thoughts on emerging forest management issues. Ultimately this entire review could be subsumed under the single rubric of "Natural Resource Governance". We have not singled this out as an issue but have attempted to weave the governance issue through the entire text.

intu

Economic Issues in Ecosystem Approaches to Forest Management

Roger Sedjo, Josh Bishop and Jeffrey A. Sayer

Introduction

Ecosystem approaches seek to conserve the cultural and environmental benefits of forests whilst ensuring that these forests continue to provide economic benefits, both to local communities and as a contribution to national growth. A balance therefore has to be found between management for timber and non-timber products and management for recreation, landscape, watershed protection, soil fertility, biological diversity and carbon storage values. The latter benefits can be provided by creating protected areas, but this is not the only, or necessarily the most effective way. Today, forests devoted to commodity production are also expected to provide environmental and cultural benefits. Ecosystem approaches require that forests are managed together with agricultural, urban and other lands as part of the broader landscape. This ecosystem has to be managed to secure social, economic and environmental benefits.

To many people it may appear self-evident that forests should be managed using integrated, ecosystem approaches. However economic forces will have a profound impact on both the long-term and short-term behavior of forest stakeholders and will ultimately determine the balance that occurs between the different competing objectives of management. This impact will be apparent both at the level of local markets – it will impact on demand and prices for forest goods and services – and at the macro-economic level where the general conditions for investment, trade and profitability are determined.

Increasing awareness of the many benefits that forests provide has stimulated development of new methods for realizing forest values. Recent years have seen widespread innovation in the use of market-based approaches to ensure that forest managers as well as consumers take account of environmental and social values in land use and product purchasing decisions. Experience suggests that market-based mechanisms can help secure new sources of funding for forest conservation, ensure that forest benefits are provided in a cost-effective manner, and also contribute to rural development.

At the same time governments often use fiscal reform, exchange rate control, monetary policy, export promotion, tax increases, privatization and land reform as tools for addressing perceived economic imbalances and or to encourage improved economic performance. These macro-economic measures will often have major impacts on natural resource systems and on those who depend upon them and these are often not adequately taken into account by economists. Critics have argued that a singular focus on economic growth, trade liberalization and increased primary product exports increases pressure on natural resources. Others argue that getting macro-economic conditions right is a precursor to being able to implement good environmental policy. Forest sustainability has often been part of that concern. However the issue of forest sustainability has almost always been equated with increased or decreased intensity of either forest use or pressures for forest conversion. Little is known about how such economic measures might impact on approaches to forest management.

This chapter gives an overview of some recent work on how macro-economic measures may impact on the conditions under which forests are managed. It then describes how local market mechanisms may be used to help retain a full range of forest products and services.

Macro-economic Impacts on Forest Ecosystems

In recent years, there has been widespread concern that macroeconomic policies oriented toward currency stabilization and structural adjustment in the developing world may have a negative impact on incomes, poverty and the environment – notably on forests. The World Bank and, particularly, the International Monetary Fund (IMF), have been criticized for their stabilization and structural adjustment programmes. These often require stringent macroeconomic policies in return for the external financing necessary for servicing the debt associated with large external borrowing that has grown out of the control of the particular country. The question of the impact of these types of macroeconomic adjustment policies has begun to be addressed in the literature. For example, their impact on poverty within a country is discussed by Easterly (2001) and on the environment of the country by White (1992). Some studies (e.g., Reed, 1996; Repetto and Cruz, 1992; Kaimowitz et al., 1998; Sunderlin et al., 2000) have concluded that structural adjustment can result in negative outcomes, particularly in the developing world, by creating pressures on the environment and on forests. However, other studies (e.g., Munasinghe, 2001; Munasinghe and Cruz, 1995; Reed, 1992; Warford, 1994) report ambiguous and sometimes positive results, with income and environmental benefits often accruing as the structural adjustments removed price distortions and market impediments and allow market incentives to work more effectively. The success or failure of a structural adjustment policy may have less to do with the economic prescriptions and conditionality and more to do with the political climate and degree of local ownership within which the adjustment package is implemented (Mallaby, 2004). Recently, an attempt has been made to statistically assess the impact of structural adjustment programmes on forests across a large number of countries (Pandey and Wheeler, 2001).

Structural adjustment programmes are designed to improve macroeconomic performance of countries experiencing serious trade, balance of payments and fiscal deficit problems. Typical policies involve cuts in the government's budget, fiscal reform, trade and market liberalization, emergency loans from foreign sources (e.g., the IMF), budget support, etc.

Pandey and Wheeler (2001) undertook an empirical study of 112 countries to determine the relationship between structural adjustment and its impact on the forest, as measured by its impact on roundwood production. However, they found no significant statistical relationship between an adjustment and roundwood production. A possible explanation of these results may be that many of the countries included had no comparative advantage in forestry, and the features of the structural adjustment did not change that situation. Another explanation, not necessarily incompatible with this, is that "other factors" are not adequately included in the analysis. Finally, the assumptions about links between deforestation and industrial roundwood production may not have been correct. One problem with these sorts of analyses is that they do not consider economic activities in the informal sector. For instance illegal logging might increase under certain adjustment scenarios but this would not show up in government statistics on roundwood production.

The point here is that the empirical evidence indicates that structural adjustment alone does not appear to be sufficient to generate increased forest products production for all countries, or even a significant number of countries. The empirical evidence suggests that the outcomes of the same set of macro-economic policy prescriptions on forests could vary by country and perhaps be related to the nature of their forest resource. A country with a comparative advantage in forestry (usually a forest-rich country), which is already exporting forest products, might increase its forest products exports in response to a structural adjustment package. However, this outcome would not occur for a country without a comparative advantage in timber production. Such a country may have limited forest resources and a comparative disadvantage that is not overcome by the effects of a structural adjustment, even should it include exchange rate depreciation.[1] Fuel subsidies often are major determinants of the profitability of extractive natural resource industries. When such subsidies are reduced as part of adjustment strategies the pressure of logging in remote areas may be reduced. More expensive fuel can also create pressure to harvest and transport timber more efficiently. Increased fuel prices might also drive a switch from kerosene back to wood for domestic fuel needs.

Trade Liberalization and Forest Ecosystems

A number of studies have been undertaken to address the question of the effects of various trade policies on global wood flows and on forests. Bourke and Leitch (1998) examine the effects of trade restrictions generally. Barbier (1999) estimates the effects of trade liberalization resulting from the Uruguay Round of tariff reduction on selected forest products exports, while Brown (1997) estimates the effects of trade liberalization on Asia-Pacific forest products trade. Sedjo and Simpson (1999) examine the question of the expected effects of tariff liberalization on forest products trade and global forests in the context of the proposed accelerated tariff liberalization proposed by the Asia-Pacific Economic Community (APEC) (*Federal Register*, 1999). All of these studies look at the general effect on forest products of the liberalization of trade. The general approach in these studies is to assume that the exchange rate would not change, since the macroeconomic impacts for individual countries were expected to be small. However, the studies did provide information on the anticipated changes in forest products trade and the subsequent impact on the forest environment, including forest land use. These studies generally found that forest exports would be expected to increase in forest-rich countries (e.g., countries with a comparative advantage in forest products), both developed and developing, while forest exports would decrease in countries lacking a forest products comparative advantage; these are mostly forest-poor countries. Overall, wood production and trade should increase, but only very modestly. For example, Barbier (1999) estimated the effect of the Uruguay Round tariff reduction would increase selected forest products exports by an overall average of 1.6–2.0%.

The forest and biodiversity implications of this finding for developing forested countries is that they would experience some increased pressure from commercial logging on their forests, while developing countries that are marginal forest producers might expect a very modest reduction in pressures for commercial logging. A negative consideration for the countries that are marginal forest producers is that forest land that becomes nonviable for logging might become a target for conversion to other uses.[2] Scherr *et al.* (2004) have raised the issue of market liberalization increasing pressure on small-holder multi-functional forest managers in Central America who are unable to compete with cheap imports of plantation timber from Chile.

---

1 For countries without a comparative advantage, a structural adjustment even with an exchange rate depreciation might simply result in a decrease in their imports of wood, while not producing a significant increase in wood exports.

2 Amelung (1991), among many others, argues that most deforestation is due to land use conversion, usually conversion to agriculture, and not due specifically to commercial logging.

Resource Rich Developing Countries – the Dutch Disease

Dutch Disease refers to the distortions in economies caused by the foreign exchange earnings and appreciation of exchange rates that result from exploitation of natural resources. In Holland the appreciated exchange rates provoked by oil and gas exports made imports less expensive, and created new competition for domestic producers. Thus, various sectors of the Dutch economy found their competitive position compromised. This was further exacerbated by the attraction of domestic resources, e.g., labour, to the natural gas sector, thereby increasing labour costs in the domestic economy.

The same phenomenon has been observed in developing countries. Demand for forest and agricultural products declines as the high exchange rate reduces the competitiveness of these products. The empirical information available on the effects of a dominant resource-export industry on forests in the developing world is substantial, including a number of detailed case studies provided by Wunder (2003).[3] Wunder confirmed that the appreciated exchange rates dampened foreign demand for both agricultural and forest exports, while encouraging their import. Also, expanding non-traded sectors (services, construction, etc.) drew domestic resources, including labour, away from forestry and agriculture. All of these factors discouraged productive forest activities. In addition, since they also discouraged agricultural activities, there was little incentive to convert forest lands to agriculture. There are situations, for instance in Southern Europe, where biologically and culturally valuable forest landscapes (e.g. the Dehesa in Spain) maintained by traditional agricultural activities are abandoned as a result of competition from more intensively produced crops. The overall diversity of the landscape therefore tends to decline and some wildlife species and amenity values are lost.

While the results vary a bit by country, reflecting the wide diversity of individual conditions and circumstances, these findings suggest that the general outcomes are very similar. The overall effect tended to reduce pressures for harvesting from the forest resource, and was assumed to reduce forest damages and losses. However the hypothesis that the reduced level of activity in the forest sector might lead to reduced investments in forestry institutions and forest management was not explored.

Forest Values in the Market Place

The value of forests for timber production depends on their location and accessibility, vegetation type and management, as well as changing human demands. The same factors determine the value of forest environmental benefits. Demand for forest recreation, for example, is strongly influenced by average income and distance from population centers (Bateman *et al.*, 1999). Attempts to manage forests for a balance of goods and services must be sensitive to these differences.

Most forest owners are aware of the ecosystem services that their lands provide. Public forest agencies in many countries make special efforts to provide environmental benefits, for example, restricting logging in areas of exceptional natural beauty for the sake of recreational uses or, on steep slopes, to protect water quality and reduce the risks of flooding downstream. Similarly, some private companies, particularly in developed countries provide access to their land to hikers, hunters and fishermen on a voluntary or fee-paying basis.

---

3   The countries examined by Wunder were Gabon, Venezuela, Cameroon, Ecuador, Papua New Guinea, Mexico, Nigeria and Indonesia.

While such efforts are welcome they are generally insufficient. The reason is that forest owners and managers in most countries receive little or no financial reward for adopting ecosystem approaches. In both the private and the public sectors, land owners and managers focus on the direct costs and tangible benefits of their activities. Foresters produce timber they can sell. Farmers convert forest land to grow agricultural crops for profit or subsistence. Environmental benefits, on the other hand, typically generate little or no revenue for forest owners, even though they may be important to neighbouring land owners or to the general public.

Where forest benefits cannot be marketed, private land owners will have little motivation to produce them, unless compelled to do so through incentives or other means. By the same token, public forest agencies may under-estimate the importance of such benefits, which are often less visible than the revenue, taxes and jobs generated by commodity production.

Even where forest benefits are traded, they may escape notice. In many developing countries, rural populations exploit non-timber forest products such as bamboos, rattans and edible fruit for subsistence and sale, but this activity is rarely recorded and easily ignored by public authorities. Similarly, in the developed world, entry fees to recreational forests often grossly undervalue the true willingness-to-pay of visitors and thus the full value of recreational benefits.

The fact that forest environmental benefits are neither traded nor have any observable market price is not a problem in itself. However, using forests to produce tradable goods such as timber or non-wood products can reduce their value for recreation or biodiversity conservation. Conversion of forest land to agriculture or other non-forest uses is even more destructive of non-market values. Environmental regulations can reduce such negative effects, but compliance is often grudging and resources for enforcement are limited. As a result, in many countries, large areas of land are cleared illegally, hunting for "bush-meat" is excessive or excessively destructive logging practices are used. Potential environmental benefits are foregone, sometimes irreversibly. While a few people may benefit in the short-term, ecosystem values are lost.

Who Benefits from Ecosystem Approaches?

Conflicts over forest values reflect the differing interests of stakeholder groups. For example, the designation of forests as protected areas can be seen as a means by which certain interest groups (typically not the poor) secure recreational, amenity or non-use values. This may result in a loss to other groups, such as subsistence farmers who rely on forest land for extraction of non-timber forest products, or for shifting agriculture. Similarly, logging or converting a forest represents a victory for certain economic interests at the expense of others. Where the values of domestic and foreign stakeholders differ widely, the resulting conflict may be international in scale, as shown by heated debates about forestry and the timber trade.

Efficiency and ecosystem approaches do not often coincide. Markets respond to the preferences and purchasing power of people with money, rather than the needs of the poor. Similarly, market-based approaches to conservation may favour forest values and land uses that are inaccessible to poorer groups, due to their limited access to land, capital and information. These groups must therefore confine themselves to "inferior" uses. For example, a study of a new national park in Madagascar determined that the value of recreational benefits to international tourists was 2–3 times greater than the loss incurred by local villagers, in terms of foregone agricultural output (Kramer *et al.*, 1995). While such a change in land use may be economically efficient, since the potential for compensation exists, it will aggravate poverty if compensation is inadequate. This highlights an important issue with respect to macro and micro- economic incentives and policies for both SFM and ecosystem approaches. While critically important these policies are not sufficient by themselves to underpin good forest management. They need to be implemented in tandem with non-economic policies that clarify governance arrangements and secure use-rights of individual groups of stakeholders.

Estimating the Benefits of Forest Conservation

Forest environmental benefits are gifts of nature but not free of charge. Protecting or enhancing environmental benefits often implies a sacrifice of competing values, for example by increasing the costs of extracting timber or preventing the conversion of forest-land to high-value agriculture. Whether such sacrifices can be justified in economic terms depends on the value of environmental benefits compared to alternative forest uses and values, and on the extent to which multiple benefits can be obtained from a single site or management system.

Because forest environmental benefits often have no market price, economists have developed many indirect methods for estimating non-market values.[4] Most valuation methods measure the demand for a good or service in monetary terms, that is, consumers' willingness to pay for a particular benefit, or their willingness to accept compensation for loss of the same. Monetary measures of value are generally considered an accurate reflection of the relative preferences of consumers for different goods and services.[5]

Applications of valuation methods can be found for virtually all forest benefits.[6] In industrialized countries, valuation studies have focused on recreational and non-use benefits. In the developing world, valuation studies focused initially on non-timber forest products (NTFPs), reflecting greater concern for production and subsistence benefits (Hearne, 1996). The under-lying premise of the latter studies was that NTFPs were sufficiently valuable to justify the conservation of forest land.

More recently, there has been increasing attention to the indirect benefits of forests, notably the environmental services of carbon sequestration, watershed protection and biodiversity conservation (Daily, 1997). In the case of carbon, valuation has been made possible by improved data on the impacts of climate change and better understanding of carbon flux in forests. Estimates of the value of carbon storage by forests are comparable to the value of forest management for timber production (Pearce *et al.*, 2002; Willis *et al*, 2000). Moreover, when carbon and timber values are combined, they can compete with agricultural uses in some cases (de Koning *et al.*, 2002).

Watershed protection is another indirect forest benefit that economists have tried to value. One obstacle they face is the lack of reliable information on the impact of vegetation cover and forest disturbance on the quality and quantity of water supply downstream (Calder, 1999; Chomitz and Kumari, 1998; Willis, 2002). This may be one reason why the conclusions of existing case studies are mixed. Another is that watershed protection benefits tend to be site-specific, depending on water uses downstream. While in some cases forest conversion or selective logging can have devastating effects downstream, in other cases the negative effects may be minimal, short-lived and/or offset by

---

4   Among many texts published in recent years see for example: Abelson, 1996; Boardman *et al.*, 2001; Dixon *et al.*, 1994; Freeman, 1993; Hanley and Spash, 1994; Kopp and Smith, 1993; Munasinghe and Lutz, 1993; OECD, 2002; Pearce and Turner, 1990; Vincent *et al.*,1991.
5   Some people reject the notion of comparing market costs and benefits with non-market social and environmental values while others take issue with the assumptions and methods used to estimate non-market values (Bennett and Byron, 1997). Although monetary valuation methods are far from perfect, and not the only way to assess forest benefits, they can be useful for illuminating trade-offs.
6   The methods used to assess non-market forest values include travel cost, choice models and contingent valuation, hedonic pricing and substitute goods approaches, as well as methods that express environmental values in terms of their impacts on the costs of producing marketed goods, or the costs of replacing them (IIED, 2003).

positive impacts related to increased water yield (Aylward *et al.*, 1998). Nevertheless some water users, notably in Central America are less concerned with the lack of hard evidence and prefer to make payments to local farmers for maintenance of forest cover as a relatively cheap form of insurance. This provides an interesting application of the precautionary approach to ecosystem functions by the private sector.

Valuation of forest biodiversity has focused on recreational and non-use ("existence") benefits (Hanley *et al.*, 2002). Some studies have estimated the value of biological material as an input to the biochemical industry (Adger *et al.*, 1995; Kumari, 1995; Laird and ten Kate, 2002) or the value of pollination services provided by forest-based insects (Ricketts *et al.*, 2004). Initial estimates of the value of tropical forests as a source of new drugs and biochemical products were extremely optimistic. Subsequent analysis suggests that biological information contained in wild forest species has significant economic value, but usually not enough by itself to justify forest conservation on a wide scale (Simpson *et al.*, 1996; Barbier and Aylward, 1996; Rausser and Small, 2000).

Despite considerable effort by researchers in many countries, aggregate estimates of the non-market value of forests are not readily available. There is an urgent need for better estimates of the total economic value of forests, to guide public and private decision-making. At the same time, the lack of such information need not prevent efforts to "internalize" non-market values in forest management. There is growing experience of bringing non-market values into the market-place, so that forest managers may adopt the more environmentally-friendly practices that Ecosystem Approaches require. Doing so requires a clear understanding of why the market tends to neglect environmental values in the first place.

Why Markets Neglect Forest Environmental Values

In theory, markets will allocate resources efficiently if prices reflect both the full marginal costs of production and the full marginal benefits of consumption. However, where prices do not reflect all costs and benefits the so-called "invisible hand" of the market does not work and resources may be used inefficiently, resulting in a loss of welfare (Baumol and Oates, 1988).

There are several reasons why market prices may fail to reflect environmental costs and benefits. In the case of forests, two of the most important reasons for market failure are what economists call "public goods" and "externalities". Both Ecosystem Approaches and the more recent visions of Sustainable Forest Management are basically concerned with ensuring that the "public goods" and "externalities" associated with forests are addressed in management.

Public goods have two key features: (i) no one can be effectively prevented from consuming them and (ii) increased consumption by one person does not reduce the availability of a public good to others. For example, no one traveling on a public highway can be charged for enjoying a beautiful view, even if the land in question is privately owned. Nor does one person's enjoyment of the view detract from that of another (provided there is no crowding). Such aesthetic value is one of many public goods provided by forests, together with carbon storage and biodiversity conservation. However, because no one can be prevented (or charged) for enjoying public goods, the market will tend to under-provide them. In response, governments may provide public goods directly or secure such goods through contracts and/or regulation of private enterprise.

Externalities are uncompensated costs or benefits arising from economic activity. An example in forestry is the decline in availability of game or other NTFPs due to logging. Unless the logging company (or land owner) pays compensation to hunters and gatherers for their loss of livelihood, the full economic cost of extracting timber will not have been paid. Whether hunters and gatherers have a legitimate claim in such cases will depend on the distribution and formal recognition of property and use rights, including customary rights as well as formal title.

In addition to public goods and externalities, markets may fail to reflect forest environmental benefits due to lack of information about their contribution to economic welfare, distortions in prices arising from public policy and regulations, lack of clear or secure property rights over forest lands and other factors. The role of economic policy in driving deforestation has been widely discussed for many years.[7] Reducing or removing subsidies that encourage forest destruction, including under-pricing of harvesting rights as well as government support for extensive agriculture or road building in environmentally sensitive areas, remains a priority in many countries. Similarly, much improvement can be achieved by strengthening forest tenure and legal regimes governing environmental damages, or by introducing more comprehensive social and environmental reporting requirements for private companies.

Bringing Forest Environmental Values into the Market Place

Forest regulation, tenure reform and reporting can create powerful incentives for sustainable management. In addition, there has been considerable interest lately in using market-based approaches to encourage forest conservation (Daily and Ellison, 2002; Gutman, 2003; Powell et al., 2001; Scherr et al., 2004). Such mechanisms can complement conventional approaches such as land set-aside and regulation of extractive uses (Table 1).

An early innovation was to extract more value from recreational uses of publicly-owned forests. Economists had demonstrated that public forest and wildlife agencies, in particular, were failing to recover the full willingness-to-pay of hunters, campers and other visitors, or were handing out valuable concessions to commercial operators for minimal return (Loomis and Walsh, 1997). Such research led to widespread reform of license, entry and concession fees, initially in North America and subsequently in other parts of the world (Mantua, 2001). In many cases the revenue generated was reinvested to improve recreational facilities and services, attracting yet more visitors and increased income.

Another example builds on the observation that residential property values are often higher in the immediate proximity of natural forests and other environmental amenities (Garrod and Willis, 1992; Powe et al., 1995). In other words, home buyers and renters will pay more to live near forests. This has led some far-sighted property developers to devote significant portions of their projects to maintain or restore forests, rather than adding more residential units, which add less value to the project as a whole. This can create another suite of problems, particularly in fire prone areas. The management regime of the forests may have to be drastically altered in order to address the security concerns of home owners thus diminishing other forest values.

Yet another approach that has gained wide support is the notion of payments for ecosystem services. The idea is to create positive incentives for forest managers to behave in ways that increase, or at least maintain, certain environmental functions. Recent applications of market-based incentives have focused on a sub-set of ecological services provided by forests, notably carbon sequestration,

---

7   Much of this research focuses on the causes of deforestation in the Amazon. Key references include: Amelung and Diehl, 1992; Andersen et al., 2002; Angelsen and Kaimowitz, 2001; Barbier et al., 1994; Chomitz and Gray, 1996; Brown and Pearce, 1994; Browder, 1985; Margulis, 2004; Ozório de Almeida and Campari, 1995; Repetto and Gillis, 1988; Vincent and Gillis, 1998; Wunder, 2003.

watershed protection, the provision of habitat for endangered species, and the protection and maintenance of landscapes that the public finds attractive (Johnson *et al.*, 2001; Pagiola *et al.*, 2002; Swingland, 2002).

Table 1. Instruments to Promote Forest Environmental Benefits

Lead Actors	Instrument	Examples	Who Pays?
Government	Public direct management of forest resources	National forests and forest protected areas	Government (taxpayers)
Government	Regulation of private forest resource management	Harvest permits, rules on logging methods	Private forest owners and managers
Government	Support services for forest owners/users' own initiatives	Technical assistance program for forest owners to improve management	Government or NGOs
Government	Public pricing policies to reflect ecosystem costs and benefits	Lower tax rate on forested land	Mixed; indirect incentive (outcome not measured)
Gov't/Market	Open trading deals under a regulatory cap or floor	Carbon trading under the Kyoto Protocols	Consumers or producers subject to cap (least cost)
Gov't/Market	Public payments to private land and forest owners to maintain or enhance ecosystem services	Agro-environmental payments for forest conservation easements on farms	Government
Market	Self-organizing private deals	Payments by a water bottling company to upstream watershed managers	Private company, NGO, community (user)
Market	Eco-labeling of forest or farm products	Forest certification	Consumer, intermediary

The forms of, and participants in, systems of incentives for ecosystem services are very diverse. Some governments and non-governmental organizations make *direct payments* to farmers and other land owners, in an attempt to encourage conservation-oriented land uses including forestry. Examples include the FONAFIFO system in Costa Rica (Box 1) and the BushTender Programme in Australia, among many others.[8] Often these payment schemes are administered by agricultural ministries as an alternative to food price supports or input subsidies. The vast majority of successful examples of such market based mechanisms for securing the delivery of a particular ecosystem value come from countries that have good and transparent governance systems, equitable and secure property rights and an absence of corruption and cronyism that undermines respect for the law.

---

8   BushTender is a pilot scheme covering 3,000 hectares in the State of Victoria, Australia, under which private land owner's are paid to provide habitat conservation services to state agencies (Stoneham *et al.*, 2003).

Box 1   **Payments for forest environmental services in Costa Rica**

The Fondo Nacional de Financiamiento Forestal (FONAFIFO) pays forest owners and the protected area authority in Costa Rica for reforestation, forest management and forest conservation under 10–15 year contracts (Pagiola *et al.*, 2002). FONAFIFO acts as an intermediary between forest owners and buyers of various ecosystem services, including carbon sequestration, watershed protection, scenic beauty and biodiversity conservation. As of the end of 2001, almost 4,500 contracts had been written covering over 250,000 hectares, at a cost of US$50 million, with pending applications for another 800,000 hectares (Snider *et al.*, 2003).

A variation on direct payments is the elimination or reduction of public subsidies that encourage the wasteful use of natural resources and result in the loss of ecosystem functions. These include subsidies for "land development" or highway construction in environmentally sensitive areas. Direct payments and subsidy reform can be extremely cost-effective mechanisms for achieving conservation goals (Ferraro and Simpson, 2002).

Another incentive for the provision of ecosystem services is the *purchase or leasing* of land or of resources on the land, from either public or private owners, for the purpose of conservation or sustainable use. For example, some NGO buyers actively engage in rural land markets to acquire threatened habitat, purchasing development rights from private land owners, or competing with timber companies to secure long-term concessions on publicly-owned forest land (Hardner and Rice, 2002; Ferraro and Kiss, 2002).

There has also been a proliferation of voluntary *eco-labeling and certification* schemes, which seek to encourage sustainable forest management practices through consumer preferences (Upton and Bass, 1995; Bass *et al.*, 2001; Eba'a and Simula, 2002). The premise of such schemes (rarely borne out in practice) is that consumers will pay more for certifiably "sustainable" forest products. This is combined with a hope that enough money will be left over, after deducting the costs of certification itself – including elaborate chain-of-custody arrangements for commodities that are hard to distinguish – to allow certified suppliers to cover their production costs, which are often higher than the costs of conventional, uncertified practices.

A third category of incentives for ecosystem services involves the creation, by government, of *new rights and responsibilities* affecting the use of natural resources. One recent example is the commitment by many governments to reduce or mitigate emissions of greenhouse gases. This has led to new national legislation assigning emission reduction targets to industry, as well as the purchase by polluters of carbon credits from forestry operators *et al.* (Lecocq, 2004).

Other examples of this approach include the emergence of wetland and endangered species "banking" in the USA (Box 2), trade in forest conservation obligations in Brazil (Chomitz *et al.*, 2003), and emerging markets for groundwater salinity credits in Australia (van Bueren, 2001). What these initiatives have in common is the possibility of trading environmental obligations to meet government mandates. Without a trading mechanism (or another financial incentive such as a tax credit), there is only the legal obligation to comply with the mandate. While the latter may be sufficient to achieve environmental goals, assuming an effective enforcement system, it does not constitute a positive incentive to provide environmental benefits and is likely to result in higher costs of compliance (Stavins, 2003; Tietenberg, 2002).

Box 2   **Habitat banking in the USA**

In the USA, public agencies and private firms are required to avoid, minimize or mitigate adverse impacts on certain types of habitat. This requirement is imposed as a pre-condition for the issuance of permits authorizing land development. The obligation to protect habitat is mandated at a Federal level by the 1972 Clean Water Act, which includes provisions to protect wetlands and aquatic resources, and the 1973 Endangered Species Act, as well as by relevant state and local laws. This legal framework has stimulated the emergence of environmental entrepreneurs ("mitigation bankers"), who sell habitat offsets to land developers (Clark and Downes, 1995; National Research Council, 2001). Purchases of wetland offsets alone cover more than 50,000 hectares (Wilkinson and Kennedy, 2002).

Market-based Forest Conservation and Rural Development

Market-based incentives for forest ecosystem services appear to have the potential to reduce poverty and inequality while also conserving the environment. One reason is that most of the demand for ecosystem services arises in or near urban areas. Millions of urban residents need water, energy, food and fiber, recreation and other goods and services. Increasingly, they want, or must buy, environmentally-friendly products. Meanwhile, the supply of forest ecosystem goods and services comes mainly from rural areas. In general, urban populations are better off than rural residents. So at an aggregate level, there is reason to believe that markets for forest ecosystem services would involve transfers from richer to poorer. The argument is even more persuasive where financial transfers are from North to South, as in the case of the Clean Development Mechanism and, to a lesser extent, some other types of payments for ecosystem services such as forest conservation concessions or certified timber. These approaches to treating environmental services as commodities do carry risks – the benefits may still be captured by elites and denied to the poor. Richer and more influential landowners are said to have benefited disproportionately from payments to restore forests in the creation of the meso-american biological corridor.

At the local level, the picture is more confused. Market-based incentives for ecosystem services may not always be good for both the environment and the very poorest of the poor (Landell-Mills and Porras, 2002; Orlando *et al.*, 2002; Scherr *et al.*, 2001; Smith and Scherr, 2002). The evidence is thin on the ground, as markets for forest ecosystem services are still relatively new, but some observations can be made.

Firstly, very poor people may find it difficult to sell ecosystem services.[9] Where payments are made to land owners, the poor may be excluded because they don't own any land, or because they lack clear legal title. Where markets for ecosystem services require prior certification of production processes, the poor are hampered by their small-scale operations, which may be too small to support the costs of getting certified. In other cases, poor producers may simply lack access to the capital, information and expertise needed to engage in markets for ecosystem services. In this regard, markets for forest ecosystem services may have the same "anti-poor" characteristics as markets for timber, which are capital, technology and skill intensive, involve large economies of scale, aim at specialized consumer markets, and require large, long-term investment (Sunderlin *et al.*, 2003).

---

9   The poor are also consumers of ecosystem services and could be made worse off by new market-based incentives, for example when payments for watershed protection are added to water tariffs. In most cases, however, the impact of payment schemes on the costs of life's basic necessities is likely to be modest.

There are also *indirect linkages* between markets for ecosystem services and poverty. On the supply side, one must ask whether the activities that produce ecosystem services, such as pure protection or environmentally-friendly production practices, are more or less labour intensive than alternative uses of natural resources. The concern here is that a shift to conservation-oriented forestry may reduce demand for unskilled or low-skilled labour, depressing rural wages and exacerbating rural unemployment.

Note also that markets for ecosystem services may not result in the construction of roads in rural areas, unlike logging, mining and other uses of forest resources which require road access. While this implies less risk of subsequent agricultural encroachment or hunting, it also means that local populations will not enjoy the benefits that roads can bring, notably improved access to markets and social services.

A further concern is that environmentally-oriented land uses and production practices may limit access by the poor to forest resources on which they traditionally rely, including wood and non-wood products. Moreover, where there are economies of scale in the production of ecosystem services (as appears to be the case for carbon), new markets may lead to concentration of land ownership or the exclusion of existing small-scale land users.

Developing Markets for Forest Environmental Benefits

Capturing the economic benefits of forest conservation is not easy. In effect, some of the value enjoyed (often for free) by environmental beneficiaries must be extracted from them, in the form of cash payments or other transfers, and channeled to land users in order to create incentives for conservation or sustainable management. For this to occur, participants in such transactions need information on the value and volume of environmental benefits being exchanged. They must also have opportunities to negotiate payments. Most importantly, property rights over environmental benefits must be well defined and enforceable.

In most countries, rights over forest land and timber are well established in law or custom (although law and custom may not always coincide). This is not the case for forest environmental benefits. Disputes may arise and investment will be discouraged so long as it remains unclear who owns the carbon sequestered in forest biomass, the genetic or other useful information contained in forest biodiversity, or the quantity and quality of water flowing downstream from a forested hillside. A prerequisite of market-based approaches to forest conservation is to determine the ownership of forest environmental benefits so they can be subject to commercial contracts.

In many countries, the state claims ownership of most forest land (White and Martin, 2002). In practice, however, weak government authority in remote areas often means that forest lands are effectively managed (or mismanaged) by private land users. In such circumstances the state may rely on local communities to monitor and enforce incentives for forest conservation, with only limited government support.

Where government agencies act as buyers or sellers of forest environmental services, changes in their mandates may be necessary. For example, water companies in Costa Rica needed regulatory approval in order to charge additional fees to water consumers for watershed protection (Pagiola, 2002). Costa Rica had to pass a special law establishing the principle of payments for environmental services, creating FONAFIFO and allocating funds.

Conclusions

It has long been recognized that large external shocks can have major impacts and repercussions on an economy, affecting many sectors, including the agricultural and forestry. The literature shows that in many cases forests can be affected, both positively and negatively, depending on the nature of the shock and other conditions. However, in the literature it has been difficult to demonstrate a connection between macroeconomic policies and incentives and structural adjustment programmes and the deterioration of the ability of forests to provide ecosystem functions.

While in many cases structural adjustment programmes can be expected to affect the forest sector, in some cases they will not. Furthermore, even when there is an impact on the forest, it need not be detrimental to environmental and ecosystem values.

Increased harvests and exports would tend to occur when the country experiencing the structural adjustment has a comparative advantage or near-comparative advantage in forest resource production. Then, the structural adjustment would need to include an exchange rate depreciation sufficient to increase the country's existing comparative advantage or to push its near-comparative advantage into the actual-comparative advantage category. Even then the resulting increased activity in the forest would not necessarily generate negative environmental or socioeconomic impacts on the forest.

In general, for a developing country with a large portion of the population in the rural sector, an emergency devaluation such as often accompanies structural adjustment will likely result in increased pressure on land. This may result in negative effects on the forest. To the extent that the agricultural sector is small or disassociated from the forest sector, we would expect the extent of damage to forest ecosystems to be reduced. Also, should the exchange rate depreciation be sufficient to trigger a new resource-based or industrial sector, these damages may be avoided.

Increased timber harvest from working forests, within the context of sustainable management, will not be environmentally destructive. However, the impact may be sufficiently large to cause harvest in excess of sustainable management or provoke uncontrolled or illegal logging by the informal sector. It might also encourage human incursions into protected forest areas threatening critical habitat or generating undesired land conversion. In these situations structural adjustment programmes would clearly generate negative environmental externalities.

Similarly trade liberalization will tend to increase the intensity of forest exploitation in forest rich countries and reduce the intensity in countries that do not have a comparative advantage in forestry. How this will translate into impacts on the integrated management of ecosystems will depend upon the broader economic and social context. In the United Kingdom the decreased profitability of timber production resulting from competition from imports led to forestry shifting towards a focus on environmental and amenity values (Grundy, 2005). In less developed economies a decline in profitability of forestry might open the way for agricultural expansion or smallholder encroachment into forested areas. It might also encourage smallholders to convert multi-functional agroforestry systems to other, more intensive land uses.

At a local level the economic benefits of forest conservation are significant but they remain poorly documented and they have insufficient impact on decision making. Information on forest environmental benefits can and should be incorporated in private property rights, forestry regulations and pricing policy. This potential has not been realised, largely due to market imperfections and policy failures. As a result, in many parts of the world, valuable forest benefits are lost due to inappropriate or ineffective policies. In these circumstances ecosystem approaches to forest management will be unlikely to succeed.

Market-based incentives for ecosystem services may be the best hope of generating significant new investment in forest conservation and sustainable use. For this to be realized, however, it is important to:

- Match payments for ecosystem services with people's real willingness to pay;

- Pay for changes in resource management to deliver the full range of forest benefits that people demand;

- Link incentives for ecosystem services to better support the current network of protected forests; and

- Ensure that poor countries and poor resource users benefit from new market-based incentives for forest conservation.

- Ensure that economic policies and incentives are accompanied by concomitant non-economic policies that address land-use related governance and property rights arrangements.

We can take some comfort from an overall increase in transfers from richer segments of the economy to less affluent segments. Increasing funding is being made available both nationally and internationally to pay for the broader ecosystem values of forests. On the other hand, there is reason to worry that the truly poor may find themselves unable to participate as suppliers of ecosystem services. Both externally imposed forest industries and conservation programmes often displace them from their jobs and deprive them of access to natural resources they previously exploited. Market-based approaches to forest conservation should not be rejected on social equity grounds, but extra care must be taken to ensure that poverty is not exacerbated by such approaches and to assist the poor to participate actively as suppliers of forest ecosystem benefits.

3 Information Needs for Ecosystem Forestry

Robert C. Szaro, Per Angelstam and Douglas Sheil

Introduction

The Forest Principles adopted at UNCED (Rio de Janeiro, 1992) constituted a commitment to sustainably manage all types of forests: "Forest resources and forest lands should be sustainably managed to meet the social, economic, ecological, cultural and spiritual needs of present and future generations." The concept of ecological approaches to forest management arose as a reaction to the predominantly top-down, command-and-control approaches to natural resource management that were directed at what could be removed from the forest (Grumbine, 1994; Christensen *et al.*, 1996). In contrast, an ecological approach to management can be thought of as an operational framework under which forests can be sustainably managed with a focus also on what remains in the forest (Sexton and Szaro, 1999).

Obviously, issues differ, problems differ and consequently solutions and information needs differ between boreal, temperate and tropical forests and even within forest types within these biomes. Our focus here is on the broad categories of information that might be considered in making decisions for sustainable forest management. Specific information needs will be assessed and determined by local conditions and issues keeping in mind the potential impact of forest management within a broader regional context. How much information is collected in the process will also be influenced by the amount of existing information as well as the resources available to fill information gaps.

The roots of the developing ecologically based approach to management have evolved from increased understandings and articulated values provided over time by the scientific community, natural resource managers, international treaties, state legislative actions, judicial reviews, and widespread public comment (Szaro and Boyce, 2004; Angelstam *et al.*, 2004b). Yet, much of the controversy surrounding resource management questions is not from the lack of science/information, or disagreements about the state of nature, but instead involves basic disputes about human values. Science can aid in the development of informed choices and sustainable solutions by incorporating human needs and values with our best understanding of the environment. Any decision invariably requires the integration of multiple components that can only be accomplished by value-based weighing of tradeoffs among those components (Szaro and Boyce, 2004). Science is concerned with identifying and clarifying uncertainties and with weighing competing hypotheses (Sheil *et al.*, 2004). As Stage (2003) notes, "A decision is 'science-based' to the extent that all relevant and acceptable hypotheses of effect have been used to display the consequences of the management actions. Verifying that the relevant hypotheses of effect have not been ignored is a crucial role for scientists in the decision process. That is very different from having scientists make the decision!"

Table 1. Keys to Sustainable Forest Management (adapted from Szaro et al., 2000)

Information

* **Information development** is required to address the underlying causes of forest degradation and ways to assess progress towards sustainable forest management.

* **Information dissemination** is crucial, for information not distributed is wasted and oftentimes leads to duplication.

* **Information translation and transfer** to allow technical research results and analyses to be accessible and utilized in practical ways by users.

Innovation

* **Innovative mechanisms** are necessary to strengthen both individual forestry research units and the linkages between them to enable the concept of a "world-wide web of forest researchers" to function effectively and be closely linked with real-world forest management problems.

* **Innovative research programs** are needed to address the integrative and multi-disciplinary science needed to address the complexities of sustainable forest management.

* **Innovative human resource development** requires new concepts and approaches in addressing training needs, incentive mechanisms to encourage staff retention, and developing appropriate centers of excellence.

Implementation

* **Implementation of practices and solutions** for sustainable forest management, e.g. this role of various management practices in both allowing for extractive uses and maintaining ecological processes and functions.

* **Implementation of funding mechanisms** that aid in the strengthening of research capacity and in development of research priorities that address the needs of stakeholders.

* **Implementation of institutional restructuring** that ensures the basic framework is in place for development of the information and knowledge needed for sustainable development, and to create a nurturing environment for innovation.

Perhaps one of the most significant elements of an ecological approach to forest management is that it deals with information and analyses at multiple spatial and temporal scales (Sexton *et al.*, 1998). Historically, characterization and analyses tended to focus intensely on individual projects and programs based on the area and scale they directly affected. Ecosystem approaches require that resources and landscapes be considered at several scales simultaneously during assessment and analysis (Angelstam *et al.*, 2004a). Collecting and analyzing information at several scales provides a relational context at multiple levels and supports an improved understanding of linkages and re-lationships within and between scales. This supports a better understanding of connections between features, patterns and processes and helps characterize potential effects and outcomes. Because of constraints surrounding the selection of appropriate scales and the need to scale up as well as down for management, it is useful to consider assessment along gradients of land use intensity and with the natural environment as a reference (Angelstam *et al.*, 1997).

Managing large landscapes is a multidimensional challenge in balancing conflicting and overlapping uses and values. Managers are confronted with stakeholders demanding a broader range of goods and services, as well as a voice in setting priorities on the use of forests (Szaro *et al.*, 2000; Angelstam *et al.*, 2004b). As a result, management needs to become more sophisticated and adaptive, as it strives to achieve balance among multiple products and services. To do this, managers need the best possible information on which to base their decisions. Good science has a vital role in generating new information that can provide input to the international dialogue on sustainable management of forests through the provision of synthesis of existing information and knowledge; the generation of new policy-relevant information in identified priority areas; and the input of expert technical advice as requested by international bodies (ICRIS, 1998).

But what can be done to ensure the generation and flow of the required information and knowledge? The scale, scope, and complexity of natural resource and environmental issues have dramatically increased, yet the urgency to solve these issues often requires immediate information that spans disciplinary boundaries, synthesizes material from a variety of sources, draws inferences, and identifies levels of confidence (Szaro and Peterson, 2004). Although science information and knowledge are only one consideration in making natural resource decisions, credible science information is increasingly necessary to gain public support and acceptance. In order to provide this information, scientists need to adopt a multidisciplinary, or even transdisciplinary, approach (Jakobsen et al., 2004). This is not easy to do given that scientific activities in the forest sector have traditionally been oriented by discipline.

To fully understand and appreciate these challenges to forest science, it is useful to establish an appropriate background against which they should be viewed and suggest how to improve our capability to deliver knowledge for a sustainable future. There are three keys to making this a reality: information, innovation, and implementation (Table 1). Consequently, we wish to focus on what are the information needs, what are the tools/innovations needed to assess social-ecological systems, and how science can be integrated into the decision-making process to implement sustainable forest management.

Information Needs for Sustainable Forest Management

Lee (1993) points out that the crucial constraint on what he calls civic science is that in learning to manage large ecosystems there must be a partnership between the science of ecosystems and the political tasks of governing. From the perspective of the science community, the lack of clarity in the socioecological problems creates a barrier to distinguishing issues reflecting different personal values among the governing partnership from those attributable to the lack of information (Haynes and Perez 2001). Furthermore, this lack of clarity around the questions leads to confusion about the appropriate spatial and temporal scales of our responses to various problems. Many of the issues reflect a transformation (underway in the past several decades) in the way that knowledge is produced and used in society (see Gibbons et al., 1994). For example, the emphasis on producing new knowledge in the context of its relatively immediate application is one of these trends, as is greater emphasis on "transdisciplinary" research (Jakobsen et al., 2004). Finally, given an engagement in civic science, there is greater social accountability expected of the science and resulting knowledge. Part of this accountability is recognition that science not only needs to be judged by disciplinary peers, but also on its social acceptability.

Full consideration of the relevant and available scientific information can help improve the decision-making process by providing an understanding of the natural and human systems and their interactions (Table 2). A science foundation helps people understand a system in which they are all interested and improves their ability to estimate consequences and risks of decision alternatives (Mills et al., 2002). Science insights may occasionally lead to a wider range of management alternatives that increase the potential compatibility among people holding differing values for how the land should be managed and used (Mills et al., 2002).

Table 2. Information and Science Needs for Ecological Approaches to Sustainable Forest Management

	Information/Science Need	Description of Need	References
1	Assessment of current resource conditions	As management objectives broaden and more stakeholders needs have to be addressed the need for management information changes. We need multiple-resource assessments and more participation in designing and carrying out assessments and inventories.	Lessard et al. (1999) Basset et al. (2000) Karr et al. (2000) TBFRA (2001) Wong et al. (2001) Shiel et al. (2002, 2003) Wear et al. (2002) Corona et al. (2004)
2	Assessment of current science base	Oftentimes there is a considerable body of science concerning an issue or particular ecosystem but it is scattered throughout an amazing assortment of both peer reviewed and grey literature sources. Bringing this information in a synthesis form is an essential resource for making management decisions.	Hawksworth et al. (1997) Graham et al. (1999) Sheil and van Heist (2000) Kates et al. (2001)
3	Ecology on multiple scales	There is a well-known discrepancy between the typically very small scale of species or habitat specific ecological research projects and the larger geographic scales upon which ecosystems are managed. Yet environmental management in general focuses on geographic units such as whole watersheds, coastal zones, or national forests or parks. Highly localized studies are part of the basis for understanding some of the functions of larger ecosystems, but there are ecosystem processes on landscape or greater scales that are incompletely understood.	Noss (1996) Scott et al. (1996) Allen and Hoekstra (1993) Haufler et al. (1999) Sexton and Szaro (1999) Poiani et al. (2000) Turner et al. (2000) Bailey (2002)
4	Multiple species science	There is a great deal known about the biology of single species, but very little about the interactions between species, groups of species, and the habitat that supports them. Managing for a single species, such as for maximum harvest for food or fiber, has often resulted in harmful effects on other species and other ecosystem functions. Better understanding of the natural and human factors that determine habitat quality for different species groups is needed to improve our ability to model the effects of possible management decisions on populations.	Purvis and Hector (2000) Roberge and Angelstam (2004)

Table 2. Information and Science Needs for Ecological Approaches to Sustainable Forest Management

			References
5	Monitoring and Evaluation	Ecological monitoring is an indispensable part of sustainable forest management because it can provide periodic feedback on how management policies and techniques are working, whether regulatory compliance is occurring, and when adaptive management changes should occur. The limited investment in baseline monitoring restricts our ability to observe the direction of trends in degradation or recovery, and our ability to predict future ecosystem condition and responses to management actions.	Dallmeier (1992) Heyer et al. (1994) Boyle and Boontawee (1995) Goebel et al. (1998) Sheil (2001; 2002) Williams et al. (2002) Wright et al. (2002) Busch and Trexler (2003) Corona et al. (2004)
6	Benchmarks of ecosystem condition	Understanding the composition, structure and function of the benchmark conditions as defined in policies. There is a shortage of information and methods for comparing degraded ecosystems with fully functional ecosystems. These "benchmarks" include fully functional reference sites, measurable indicators of ecosystem condition, and measures of progress by which management actions can be tracked and modified if necessary. Indicators and measures of progress are priority areas for research and development. In the selection and development of benchmarks it is essential to get a measure of the variability of the benchmark.	Peterken (1996xx) Angelstam et al. (1997) Noon et al. (1999)
7	Socioeconomic sciences and valuation	Ecological approaches to management are complicated by the need to integrate information on myriad biological, physical and socioeconomic concerns. Sound yet innovative approaches to documenting and evaluating socioeconomic elements of ecosystems are essential for developing management strategies and making decisions that weigh all relevant, competing interests and sustain ecosystem functions and economic activities in an acceptable balance. At the heart of the conflict over natural resource management is the difficulty in determining values that different individuals and groups assign to various resources. Information needs in this area include economic and non-economic benefits; demographic measures; formation and modification of values; and costs/pricing techniques.	McNeely (1998) Ziglo (1991) Constanza et al. (1997) Gowdy (1997) Hunt (1997) Pimentel et al. (1997) Bann (1998) Wagner et al. (1998) Emerton (1999, 2000, 2001) Karsenty (2000) Shields et al. (2002)

Table 2. Information and Science Needs for Ecological Approaches to Sustainable Forest Management

#	Topic	Description	References
8	Human dimensions of natural resource use	As we look to the future of natural resource management it is clear that people are at the center of the debate. The needs of people drive the use and the misuse of natural resources. Our efforts to understand how people think about and act on the natural environment have been minimal, and yet most controversies and shortages ultimately arise from human activity. Continued growth in human populations and increases in their production, use and disposal of resources will continue to accelerate pressures on forest management. The opportunity to increase our knowledge and solve problems is great if research on human-natural resource interactions is accelerated and if the social ecology of these resources is better understood.	Machlis and Forester (1996) Vitousek et al. (1997) Clark et al. (1999) Machlis (1999) Colfer and Byron (2001) Uliczka et al. (2004)
9	Ecological restoration technology development	After detecting impairment, effective ecosystem management may restore the impaired function. Research programs in restoration technology and improving the economic arguments associated with restoration of specific ecological functions in high priority ecosystems will help the growth of restoration business opportunities and increase the contributions they can make to sustainable forest management. In many cases restoration efforts have focused only on the restoration of structure and composition and merely infer that essential ecosystem functions will follow. Seldom have restored systems been monitored to confirm that functions are back on line.	Covington et al. (1999) Kenna et al. (1999) Szaro et al. (1999) Urbanska et al. (2000) Lindenmayer et al. (2002) Higgs (2003)
10	Quantifying uncertainty and assessing risk	Science can make major contributions by defining cause-effect relationships along with a measure of that answer's certainty. In communicating scientific data to non-technical managers and the public, however, the measures of certainty are often lost or overlooked. Assessing the relative likelihood of the potential for an adverse ecological impact is critical in making good management decisions. Yet in many crises situations, it is often impractical to invest the time and funding in reducing uncertainty before taking immediate action. Action proceeds on the basis of best professional judgement and limited data but should incorporate opportunities for mid-course correction as new knowledge is generated (see Adaptive Management).	Maquire (1991) Szaro and Sexton (1998) Shrader-Frechette (1998) Haynes and Cleaves (1999) Cleaves and Haynes (1999) Bradshaw and Borchers (2000)
11	Modeling and decision support systems	In order to support prediction, planning and decision-making on an ecosystem basis, scientists and managers require models that are sensitive to the effects of modifying land or water on habitat and ecosystem functions. These models must incorporate a much wider array of factors than are addressed in most current models. They must link landscape changes, changes in water use, observed changes in selected ecological indicators, multiple species responses, and changes in ecosystem condition and function. Field testing is essential to determine their "real-world" applicability.	Oliver and Twery (1999) Reynolds et al. (1999) Scott et al. (2002) Williams et al. (2002) Dale (2003) Angelstam et al. (2004b)

Table 2. Information and Science Needs for Ecological Approaches to Sustainable Forest Management

12	Adaptive management process	Adaptive management is essential because our understanding of ecosystems is not, and may never be, complete (Holling 1978). Since ecological approaches to management must rely upon the best science available, there must be a process by which managers can rapidly incorporate new knowledge as it becomes available in order to modify their management approaches.	Lee (1993) Baskerville (1985) Borman et al. (1999)
13	Criteria and indicators	The 1992 Earth Summit, or United Nations Conference on Environment and Development (UNCED), called upon all nations to ensure sustainable development, including the management of all types of forests. Subsequently, the Third Session of the Commission on Sustainable Development (CSD) decided to establish, under its aegis, an open-ended ad hoc Intergovernmental Panel on Forests (IPF) to pursue consensus and formulation of coordinated proposals for action in an open, transparent and participatory manner. The issue of criteria and indicators for sustainable forest management was one of the main outcomes of the work of the IPF. The development of the C&I remains a crucial step in evaluating and ensuring progress to sustainable forest management.	UNCSD (1996) Canadian Council of Forest Ministers (1997) Lammerts van Bueren and Blom (1997) McDougall et al. (1999) Prabhu et al. (1999) Purvis and Hector (2000) Lindenmayer et al. (2000) MCPFE (2003) Sheil et al. (2004) USDA (2004)
14	Institutions and governance	As management philosophy focuses on sustainability, ecological approaches to management call for a reassessment of how we approach nature, science and politics. Implementation of these approaches to management may require changes in institutional and governance mechanisms and policies.	Gupta (1996) Smythe et al. (1996) Cortner et al. (1998) Watson et al. (1998)

Emerging science themes in developing ecological approaches to management reflect a greater interest by the science community in: (1) biodiversity conservation at multiple levels of definition and scale, assuming it as the broad goal for ecosystem management (Lindenmayer and Franklin, 2002), (2) understanding ecosystem processes including successional dynamics, disturbance, and effects of management actions (Angelstam, 2003), (3) understanding riparian and aquatic processes including the role of riparian protection, stream productivity, and terrestrial and aquatic interactions (Wiens, 2002), and (4) cross- disciplinary science as a tool for answering specific problems (Haynes and Perez, 2001).

Gathering Existing Information and Expertise

Key information for consideration in the planning process can be drawn from three primary sources: (1) assessment and analysis of current scientific information, (2) critical review and analysis of items to be affected, and (3) estimations of risk for various issues and resources through implementation of different management alternatives. Forest resource assessments have to provide reliable, harmonized, politically relevant, cost-efficient and intuitively visible information on the multiple functions of forests in the form of statistics, georeferenced data and thematic cartography (Corona *et al.*, 2004). Sheil *et al.* (2002) eloquently summarized the impetus for the development of multidisciplinary assessments by stating "What is needed is a practical method, or indeed a suite of methods, that can reduce the understanding gap, to provide a comprehensible summary of what actually matters locally: to determine what is important, to whom, how much and why, and a means to make these local preferences more relevant to the decision making process."

A large part of the science follow-up needed for sustainable forest management is not targeted at helping inform the science side of the managing partnership but is actually providing science-based expertise expressed as professional judgments about probable outcomes needed on the governing side (Haynes and Perez, 2001).

Developing and Using New Information

As we enter the 21st century, the list of questions needing scientific investigation has not only changed dramatically, but the character of the questions has changed as well (Szaro *et al.*, 2000; Szaro and Boyce, 2004). Questions are contentious, cover broad scales in space and time, and have a high level of complexity and interdependence. Relevant and credible information about complex systems is increasingly essential to forest policy decisions, and such information covering both natural and human/social sciences is an essential ingredient in policy deliberations in a world where forest management is the focus of intense national and international debate (ICRIS, 1998). The provision of unbiased and objective information to all stakeholders is an important step in informed decision-making. An important element of the priority information needs and other additional information needs is the implementation of an "active adaptive management" feed-back loop to evaluate current plan direction, design monitoring programs to measure effects, and adjust future management activities to better address economic, social, and environmental concerns (Lee, 1993).

This calls for a new model for developing information, one that improves our knowledge as management is implemented (Szaro *et al.*, 2000). A model that:

- recognises uncertainty as an inherent characteristic of all ecosystems and acknowledges that we will never know it all.

- Implements management as part of an experimental design.

- Involves stakeholders at all stages in the research process and in the development of goals and objectives.

- Monitors and evaluates progress towards these goals and objectives.

- Adapts management based on this new information.

Delivering New Information

Choosing from available information and distilling the essential elements to identify potential implications for land and resource management can be overwhelming (Szaro and Peterson, 2004). The generation of new scientific knowledge is necessary but not sufficient for relevance without the communication and application of science findings. Scientific information must be synthesized and integrated to bring focus on important issues. Findings have to be packaged and delivered in ways that facilitate their use in decision-making, including public dialogue and other processes used by the decision-makers. This approach to informing decisions has the potential to reduce conflict by bringing attention to information about options and consequences rather than the advocacy of particular positions. These efforts can help clarify the character and form of the issue. Successful delivery of science means that policy-makers and decision-makers receive tools and information that are understandable and that readily meet their needs (Angelstam *et al.*, 2003).

A Toolbox for Assessing Social-Ecological Systems

To illustrate the need for integrated approaches to natural resource management the landscape concept is useful. In the European Landscape Convention adopted by the Council of Europe's Committee of Ministers in 2000 (Anon., 2000) "landscape" is defined as a zone or area as perceived by local people or visitors, whose visual features and characters are the result of the action of natural and/or cultural (that is, human) factors. Thus a landscape forms a whole, a "social-ecological" system (Berkes *et al.*, 2003), whose natural and cultural components are taken together. With regard to forest ecosystems the landscape concept also reflects the need to expand the spatial scale of management hierarchically from trees and stands, which is the traditional unit for forest management, to landscapes and regions. Additionally, social organizational scales from individual, household or family, to community, county, nation and global need to be included (Manfredo *et al.*, 2004). To understand landscapes as social-ecological systems the following steps are important:

(1) identifying the system;

(2) delimiting the system in time and space;

(3) assessing people involved directly and indirectly, in the past, at present and in the future;

(4) describing subsystems, values, constraints, and relations. Both the ecosystem and institutional dimensions of social-ecological systems are hierarchical regarding the characteristics that can be changed (i.e., be steered).

This means that the landscape concept including abiotic, biotic, social, cultural and administrative dimensions is a very useful common denominator for both the ecosystem and institutional dimensions. To assess the status and trends of sustainability a suite of tools from both natural and social sciences is needed (Angelstam *et al.*, 2003; Lazdinis and Angelstam, 2004).

The Ecological Dimension

To maintain the natural capital of forests, on which economic and socio-cultural values are built, the combined effects on the maintenance of viable populations and ecosystem integrity of protected areas, silvicultural management, traditional agriculture and pastoralism, as well as re-creation of new forests need to be evaluated (Angelstam, 2003). Such integrated evaluations should cover actual landscapes and consider historic changes in the cover of different ecosystems. The assessment and planning problem is usually divided into three sub-processes. The first is strategic planning to decide long-term goals covering an entire rotation from one harvest to the next, the second is tactical planning to select among different alternatives based on the strategic goals at the level of the FMU, but with a finer spatial resolution and with a shorter time horizon. Finally, operational planning is made to administrate the actual operations.

Strategic level – quantitative gap analysis

A gap analysis can be defined as the identification of disproportionate scarcity of certain ecological features within a management unit, relative to the representation to a larger region surrounding the management unit (Perrera *et al.*, 2000). The concept can also be extended quantitatively to scarcity of habitat relative to how much habitat area is required for the maintenance of elements of biodiversity including viable populations of all species in an ecoregion and ecosystem integrity (Angelstam *et al.*, 2001). To estimate the ability of forests to maintain viable populations and ecosystem integrity in an ecoregion one needs: (1) knowledge of the authentic composition, structure and dynamics of forests; (2) the requirements of different species and processes expressed as quantitative targets for the long-term amount of different forest habitats; and (3) an understanding of the extent to which current management regimes contribute to sustaining the ecosystems. With this information, quantitative analyses of representative, long-term goals and area gaps can be undertaken at the strategic level of, say, ecoregions (Table 3).

Table 3. The ABC's of gap analysis for strategic conservation planning.

Explanation	Code
Reference/Benchmark conditions	A
The present situation	B
Science-based threshold (=long-term performance target)	C
Representation	A-B
Long-term goal	A*C
Area gap	B – (A*C)

Given a policy which can be interpreted scientifically, like maintaining viable populations of naturally occurring species, reference conditions (A) such as found in naturally dynamic forests of pre-industrial cultural landscapes, can be quantified. By comparing the present situation (B) with A for different types of forest and wooded grassland, analyses of representation can be made. Finally, with knowledge about the quantitative requirements at the population level, expressed as a proportion of A, long-term targets can be formulated and compared with B, allowing the identification of area gaps for a certain type of vegetation. Next, to assure functional connectivity of the total area, spatially explicit analyses need to be done for the tactical decisions regarding protection, management and restoration.

Tactical level

When gap analysis has been performed, the forest types for which area gaps have been identified also need to be evaluated as to the extent to which they actually provide functional habitat for the specialized focal species. One approach is habitat suitability modeling, which involves combining spatially explicit land cover data with quantitative knowledge about the requirements of specialized species and building spatially explicit maps describing the probability that a species is found in a landscape (Scott *et al.*, 2002). Ideally, focal species should be chosen among the most demanding species for a range of landscape attributes (Roberge and Angelstam, 2004). Since the most demanding species vary among habitats and scales, the suite of focal species should include representatives from a number of different taxa with different ecologies or functional groups. Finally, each model should be validated in order to test how reliably one can predict occurrences of the focal species in real-world landscapes (Scott *et al.*, 2002). With adequate quantitative data on a suite of particular focal species carefully selected to represent all forest types of concern, a series of predictive models can be built to picture landscape functionality. This requires quantitative information on the habitat requirements of the species at different spatial scales. In general, a habitat model for a given species should build on the following variables: land cover type(s) constituting habitat, habitat patch size, landscape-scale proportion of suitable habitat, and habitat duration. Using, for example, neighborhood analysis techniques in Geographic Information Systems, the functionality of the network of each representative habitat (one or several land cover types) can be evaluated (Puumalainen *et al.*, 2002). Because a landscape usually contains a range of types of forest vegetation, a suite of species must be modeled.

Operational level

Maintaining viable populations of species and ecosystem integrity requires an understanding of the range of natural disturbance regimes, the resulting habitats to which species have adapted, and the management regimes that must be used to emulate natural processes (Hunter, 1999; Angelstam, 2003). Natural disturbance regimes include both large-scale and small-scale dynamics associated with abiotic and biotic disturbances. The interaction between natural disturbances and local and regional site conditions can be used to deduce the main types of stand dynamics in an ecosystem (e.g., Bergeron *et al.*, 2002).

Forest management potentially can be used to emulate natural disturbance regimes. Silvicultural systems are usually divided into three groups (even-age, multi-age and uneven-age) and can be arrayed against ecological dimensions to summarize the extent to which different combinations will maintain species that have evolved under different disturbance regimes (Angelstam, 2003). Even-age management for biodiversity conservation and restoration must maintain more successional stages and tree species combinations than is typical when applied to wood production only. Additionally, most traditional management practices are poor at maintaining coarse woody debris in all decay classes, very large and old trees, and other components of naturally dynamic forests. Consequently, conservation areas with both *laissez-faire* and active management strategies will usually be a necessary part of a complete approach to maintain viable populations of species and ecosystem integrity.

The Social Dimension

Thus, if analyses of area gaps, functionality of habitat networks, or choice of management systems would show that the status of ecosystems deviate from the desired, the institutions involved in implementation of policies need to be evaluated. This requires an understanding of temporal and spatial boundaries of the system itself, issues perceived as concerns by the stakeholders in the system, and policy objectives, instruments and organizations addressing these issues.

Clark (2002) defined a practical analytic framework to map a policy process by distinguishing three principal groups of variables for different actors. These are (1) the social process and mapping of the context, (2) the decision process and clarification of the common interest, and (3) problem orientation to find solutions. The policy science approach stresses the need for both participant and observers to understand their stand-points in relation to the policy process, to use multiple methods (Bryman, 2001) and to be guided by democracy and human rights. As opposed to the top-down approach adopted for the evaluation of ecosystems, institutions need to be evaluated from the bottom, i.e. in the actual landscape unit or region chosen for the analysis. The social dimension of a selected actual landscape concerns the implementing actors and institutions and includes:

(1) identification of the actors and mapping of policy networks,

(2) evaluation of the implementation process to learn about the issues of concern, and

(3) evaluation of policy implementation in the defined social-ecological system.

Those whose lives, due to their work, living environment or leisure activities, affect or are affected by some aspect of the forest ecosystem, are actors or stakeholders in the social-ecological system found within an actual landscape. According to Carlsson (1996), policy analyses, studying the network of actors and formal as well as informal institutions, should concentrate on answering two crucial questions: (1) what is (are) the problem(s) to be solved? and (2) who is participating in the creation of institutional arrangements in order to solve them? This evaluation may take place in the framework of a participatory program evaluation approach. Model forests (Besseau *et al.*, 2002) and biosphere reserves (Peine, 1999) are two approaches for combining bottom-up and top-down approaches and to create arenas for integrated natural resources management (Buchy and Hoverman, 2000; Campbell and Sayer, 2003; Sayer and Campbell, 2004).

Integrating Science into the Decision-making Process

It is almost a truism that any important policy decision is better with stronger information behind it (Szaro *et al.*, 1995). Three main factors have inhibited the integration of science into the decision-making process:

(1) decision-makers have not always been aware of how or when research might be useful to them;

(2) in the past, decision-makers have been reluctant to ask researchers for help because it meant acknowledging uncertainty, or worse, relinquishing some power by reducing the range for their discretion; and

(3) basic research is often not designed to answer management and policy questions.

Given the value-laden conflict and increasingly polarized debate concerning the management of natural resources, science should play a larger role in informing the choices made in the decision-making process (Mills and Clark, 2001). Mills and Clark (2001) suggest scientific information can help better inform these difficult decisions in several ways. It can:

- help facilitate productive discussion among different and competing interests;
- help focus the discussion on choices and their consequences rather than on polarized positions;
- highlight the range of available choices, and may even lead to new options that balance competing interests;
- increase the understanding of management decisions and help lead to the expected outcomes.

Using Information to Adapt Management

In an ideal world we would have enough information and be able to predict with sufficient certainty that we could just plan our management activities and be assured of the desired outcome. Unfortunately, this is not the case and adaptive management is essential because our understanding of ecosystems is not, and may never be, complete. There are inherent uncertainties within and among ecological, economic, and social systems. Surprises in the behavior of ecosystems are inevitable and management systems must be designed to adjust to the unexpected rather than act on the basis of a spurious belief in certainties (Gadgil, 1999; Gunderson, 1999; Muradian, 2001). Adaptive management addresses uncertainty by structuring initiatives as experiments in which results are used to continually correct course (Keystone National Policy Dialogue on Ecosystem Management, 1996).

While the concept of adaptive management is relatively straightforward, applying it to complex management strategies requires answers to several critical questions. What new information should compel an adjustment to the management strategy? What threshold should trigger this adjustment? Who decides when and how to make adjustments? What are the definitions and thresholds of acceptable results? Are thresholds feasible to detect given the oftentimes latent effects of impacts? Adaptive ecosystem management depends on a continually evolving understanding of cause and effect relationships in both biological and social systems. Planning for and adapting to surprise will provide an actionary rather than a reactionary basis for more informed decisions.

Feedback between managers and scientists and between the public and scientists is a fundamental component of the adaptive management strategy, and periodic assessment is its operational foundation (Szaro et al., 1995). In adaptive management, models and monitoring are applied within the framework of an assessment protocol, which helps focus monitoring efforts and defines how models will be applied at various stages in management. Ecological indicators are used to evaluate and, when fed into appropriate models, help select among management alternatives. A baseline condition is determined for the same indicators, using monitoring before management strategies are implemented. Then the same indicators, which continue to be monitored after the new management strategies are in place, are used to assess the effect of a management action. To be effective, ecological, economic and social indicators must be practical, sensitive, and capable of being both monitored and modeled (Campbell et al., 2003).

Adaptive management encourages active participation by all stakeholders in the planning, implementation, monitoring, and redirection of ecosystem management initiatives (Keystone National Policy Dialogue, 1996). It depends on negative and positive feedback in the reiterative evaluation of both the continued desirability of management goals and progress toward their achievement (Everett et al., 1993). Social and economic values and expectations are routinely considered along with ecological objectives in continually correcting the course of management. Results from the monitoring of ecological, economic, and social variables are used to track management outcomes. This reiterative approach causes management execution and adaptation systems to make progress towards goals, even if the goals change with time (Baskerville, 1985). It promotes an information-rich environment and a rationale for routinely monitoring and evaluating social, political and biological environments.

Adaptive ecosystem management also depends on an evolving understanding of cause-and-effect relationships in both biological and social arenas. In the social arena, communities interested in the issues must be identified, and their values and expectations understood (Daniels et al., 1993; Montgomery, 1993). Although social and biological components of ecosystems are often ill defined, managers and policy-makers must at least explicitly state hypothesis and proceed via a reiterative process toward developing management models. If a management model operates outside a range of socioeconomic acceptability, the model must be reconsidered, or if the model is constrained by biological realities, society must be informed of the unfeasibility of the goal (Everett et al., 1993).

Scientific Information as a Foundation for Resource Management Decisions

The need for scientific information as a foundation for resource management decisions continues. Science should be expected to contribute technical answers and insights and suggest reasonable solutions that recognise uncertainty so that responsible resource policies and management solutions can be developed and implemented. Science should develop options and scenarios that will help decision- makers make "informed choices" on the ramifications and consequences of any choice, and reduce the critical uncertainties relating to the costs and benefits associated with any avenue of intervention. Much of the debate on sustainability and biodiversity has in the past become uncoupled from objective rigor, developing a blind momentum devoid of good science. While there is real urgency to get things started there need to be systems in place that allow learning and adaptation (see Redford and Sanderson, 1992). For no matter how much is known, the vexing problem persists that management decisions are almost always made with inadequate information (Noss, 2004).

Changing societal expectations and increased public involvement have challenged traditional management policies and practices. Often these public expectations are in conflict. Policy decisions must apply the best science to meet the needs of society. To facilitate this, the interface between social, economic, physical-biological, and ecological models must be improved (Kinzig *et al.*, 2003). The ability to quantify social demands for both consumptive and non-consumptive goods must be perfected. These demands must then be weighed against the need to maintain ecosystems and their attributes. There is a pressing need to assemble and format new and existing research results into packages that are usable by managers and decision-makers. We require innovative ecosystem management approaches and technologies that will accommodate these demands while maintaining healthy ecosystem functioning.

As we move into the future a comprehensive programme of integrated basic and applied ecological, social and economic research should be developed to provide:

- A basis for sustaining ecosystem productivity and biodiversity;

- More adaptive and flexible management systems;

- A broader basis to support the development of a public "will" to lead to a higher likelihood of adoption of ecologically-based management;

- Mechanisms to ensure a wide range of stakeholder participation;

- An improved information base for decision making;

- Techniques for incorporating spatial analysis to link objectives at differing scales into planning and decision-making;

- Methods to predict responses of ecosystems to management activities;

- Methods for integrated planning and management across site, landscape, regional, and perhaps even continental levels;

- Methods to examine the relationships and interdependencies of management actions on one spatial/temporal/biological scale upon actions at other scales, e.g., externalities;

- Participatory techniques to assess the relative values of different components of biodiversity and assess the trade-offs between the costs of conservation, including the opportunity costs incurred by restricting use and the "willingness to pay" of the proponents and beneficiaries of conservation.

Implications for Forest Research

The seriousness and urgency of most forestry and environmental problems are linked to the inability or means of many countries to provide appropriate scientific and technical knowledge, effective policy, regulations and planning frameworks to deal with the problems (Szaro *et al.*, 2000). These factors have many implications for the future of forestry research, the development of its human resources, and its organizational structures, priorities and delivery systems, including:

- The nature of forestry research to be undertaken in support of sustainable forest management is very complex and there is an urgent need to upgrade capabilities at all levels;

- Supporting sustainable management – whether it is with regard to natural forests, plantations or other land uses – should be the key concern of forestry research in all countries;

- Research management has not received adequate attention and in many countries system-wide deficiencies hamper scientific progress;

- Effective priority setting is a process that is under-utilized and should include assessment of the potential benefits, potential for scientific progress, capability to undertake research and research organization;

- Strengthening the capability to access, screen and adapt existing knowledge and skills will be an important step to immediate upgrading of technological capabilities;

- The skill requirements in the future will be drastically different from what they are today; unfortunately insufficient efforts are being made to identify these and to develop the necessary capability;

- Collaborative arrangements within and between countries are generally very weak and need to be strengthened to cost-effectively supplement and complement national and international efforts.

Implications for Forest Management

"Sustainability" is not an all-or-nothing issue. It increasingly reflects a shift to more local and pragmatic concerns (e.g., Gale and Corday 1994; Sheil *et al.*, 2004; Wijewardana *et al.*, 1997). Acceptance of any forest exploitation implies tolerance of some degree of change. Agreeing on what can change and what is to be sustained is, in reality, more of a societal problem than a scientific one. Science and technical ideas play a role, but choices require value judgments.

Different forests have different management needs. Demands, contexts, and abilities vary (Sheil *et al.*, 2004). In a national forest estate, some forests may be managed for specific properties and services (conserving panda bears, protecting water catchments, scenery, or carbon storage, for example), whereas others are focused on production. It helps to be precise, realistic and selective about what needs to be maintained at what cost. Local needs must to be placed within the context of larger scale trade-offs. These aims are not facilitated by uniform prescriptive approaches.

The assumption that "more information equals better management" should be mistrusted (Sheil *et al.*, 2004). Natural resources specialists increasingly recognise that data demands are potentially neverending and all consuming endeavours (Ludwig *et al.*, 1993; Johannes, 1998). If we wait for "perfect" information then we will never make any progress. Research and management must work in concert. Management actions should be designed within a learning context such that future management direction can be improved over time (Bormann and Keister, 2004). This is an evolutionary advance to the concept of adaptive management that starts with the premise that there is no single right decision or direction for management. Rather there are a multitude of choices or possibilities. So rather than making a single decision for a given forest or landscape why not make several choices that are arrayed across the management area. This will increase the likelihood of success for at least a portion of the landscape and help managers make better and more informed choices for future decisions.

The Road to a Sustainable Future

Ecological approaches to forest management are becoming increasingly more sophisticated and adaptive, seeking to achieve balance among multiple products and services while ensuring the sustainability of the forests on which they are based (Floyd, 2002). Good science has a vital role in generating new information that can provide input to managers and the international dialogue on forests through the provision of synthesis of existing information and knowledge; the generation of new policy-relevant information in identified priority areas; and the input of expert technical advice (ICRIS, 1998).

Yet, to be valuable, information should be useful (Sheil, 2001; 2002). Why should limited local resources be used to collect information irrelevant to management? What is the value of counting species (a common theme in monitoring)? Environmental degradation in old-growth forests can lead to increases in species richness as well as declines, and species richness per se has no unambiguous link to ecological viability or system health (Sheil and van Heist, 2000; Sheil *et al.*, 1999). How does such counting improve management response? It is too easy to assume that more data results in a greater understanding and thus better management. Without a clear benefit from such activities how can they be viewed as cost effective or even relevant when financial and human resources are scarce?

Sustainability offers scientists and research institutions the unique opportunity to make more effective use of their limited human resources (Szaro *et al.*, 2000). Improved research effectiveness and capability is crucial as research produces the scientific basis for the development of national science policy and, thereby, more informed international forest negotiations that can lead to improved global governance of forests. Successful integration of training programmes, networking, technology transfer and information dissemination is needed if science is to provide timely inputs to the decision-making process. Moreover, improved linkages among policy-makers, stakeholders and scientific communities are required to make better use of research findings and to ensure that the research being done is relevant to their needs.

4 Global Standards and Locally Adapted Forestry: The Problems of Biodiversity Indicators

Bryan Finegan

Introduction

The last twenty years have seen a rapid increase in the application of forest management as an economically-attractive and environmentally-friendly land use in the tropics. The initial motivation behind this movement was the search for alternative land uses for areas that were unsuitable for many forms of agriculture. More recently, interest has turned to the positive contribution that production forests can make in the conservation of tropical biodiversity and the provision of other environmental services. As a result, several international conservation NGOs have now become supporters of sustainable forest management in the tropics. This rapid evolution of expectations regarding forest has been widely documented of late and it is clear that these changes are consistent with, and to a large extent anticipated, the emergence of the ecosystem management concept in the international policy narrative.

Much of the work related to the conceptualization, communication, implementation and evaluation of sustainable forest management (SFM) has been carried out within the context of efforts to develop standards – sets of Principles, Criteria and Indicators. These standards have usually been defined by participatory processes that have tried to involve all key stakeholders (Lammerts van Beuren and Blom, 1997; Prabhu *et al.*, 2001; FSC, 2004). Well-known standards relevant to forest management throughout the tropics are those of the Forest Stewardship Council (FSC, 2004) and the International Tropical Timber Organization (ITTO, 1998), while many others have been developed at regional and national levels.

The complexities and uncertainties involved in forest management require it to be an adaptive, learning process (Prabhu *et al.*, 2001) and most standards emphasize this requirement. Monitoring is necessary for management to be adaptive and can be defined formally as "a process of information collection used to determine the occurrence, the size, the direction and the importance of changes in key indicators of the quality of management of a resource" (Finegan *et al.*, 2004). Arguably, the term 'adaptive management' simply formalizes a commonsense need for individuals, communities, governments and other levels of societal organization to be aware of changes in their environments and to make adjustments to help ensure that management objectives are attained in spite of those changes, or are themselves adjusted.

Not all elements of standards, however, refer to adaptive management. Many of their elements relate to the contents of management plans and the way in which operations should be carried out (Lammerts van Beuren and Blom, 1997). But adaptive management is enshrined in the FSC Principle 8 – simply titled 'monitoring and assessment'. This establishes that the need to monitor and to use the information so generated as a basis for the revision of management plans is a necessary element of SFM (see Box 1). FSC Principle 9 recognises that some forests are of exceptionally high conservation value and extractive use of them should therefore be more limited. It also states that the

---

Box 1   **Key aspects of the FSC Principle 8: Monitoring and Assessment (extracted from FSC, 2004).**

Principle

Monitoring shall be conducted – appropriate to the scale and intensity of forest management – to assess the condition of the forest, yields of forest products, chain of custody, management activities and their social and environmental impacts.

Criteria:

8.1   The frequency and intensity of monitoring should be determined by the scale and intensity of forest management operations as well as the relative complexity and fragility of the affected environment. Monitoring procedures should be consistent and replicable over time to allow comparison of results and assessment of change.

8.2   Forest management should include the research and data collection needed to monitor, at a minimum, the following indicators: ... b) Growth rates, regeneration and condition of the forest. c) Composition and observed changes in the flora and fauna. d) Environmental and social impacts of harvesting and other operations

8.4   The results of monitoring shall be incorporated into the implementation and revision of the management plan.

8.5   While respecting the confidentiality of information, forest managers shall make publicly available a summary of the results of monitoring indicators, including those listed in Criterion 8.2.

---

characteristics or High Conservation Values (HCVs) that make them special should be monitored (Box 1). Similarly, adaptive management is a central principle of ecosystem approaches such as that of the Convention on Biological Diversity, whose Principle 9 states that management must recognise that change is inevitable (CBD, 2004).

Adaptive management is common sense but major challenges to its implementation arise when the focus moves away from routine forestry operations towards less familiar ones such as biodiversity and ecological processes. Here, many people concerned with forest management are probably unsure about even the right questions to ask, or indeed, why the questions have to be asked. It is unclear how the FSC Principle 8 applies to ecological aspects of forest management in the tropics (Finegan *et al.*, 2004, Appendix B) and further discussion is needed on those aspects of national standards that concern biodiversity and its monitoring (e.g. McGinley and Finegan, 2003). It needs to be more widely recognised that the primary purpose of monitoring is not to determine whether change has occurred, but whether the type and degree of change are acceptable or not (Section 2.2). Many stakeholders, however, are more comfortable defining the contents of conventional management plans and the ways in which forest operations should be carried out than discussing why and how biodiversity should be managed and monitored.

It is hardly surprising that the management of biodiversity and ecological processes in the context of sustainable forest management in the tropics is something of a grey area. Forest operations for polycyclic silvicultural systems – the predominant silvicultural approach for natural tropical timber production forests (Graaf, 1986; Wadsworth, 1997 and see below) – have been evolving for decades and the temperate forest management techniques on which they are based for even longer. On the other hand, FSC´s Principles and Criteria were not defined until 1996 and ecosystem approaches are even more recent. An additional twist is that the relationship between ecosystem approaches and Sustainable Forest Management is still under debate and it is not yet clear from the current debates whether the standards that define SFM are an obstacle to local adaptive management (see chapter 1 of this volume). Independently, Sheil *et al.* (2004) and Bawa *et al.* (2004) have also called for managers to have greater freedom to adapt forest management and conservation to local circumstances.

In this paper I adopt the view that both generality and specificity in standards are necessary for good forest management and that the relative utility of each will depend on local circumstances. I use the example of the ecological basis of forest management to illustrate this point and conclude that ecosystem approaches probably have as much to offer in building on the successes so far achieved under the SFM framework. The particular subject of ecological monitoring (I use the term 'ecological monitoring' in preference to 'the monitoring of biodiversity and ecological processes') is analysed in greater detail as it illustrates some of the most important issues of the forest management debate – the tension between centrally-defined guidelines and local realities and the difficulty of progress towards adaptive management for conservation objectives.

In the light of the preceding observations, the rest of this document will attempt to answer several questions regarding ecological monitoring as a management tool for timber production in natural tropical forests which are certified or seeking certification under the FSC framework.

First, to what extent is it possible to generalize about the ecological basis of the management of tropical forests for timber production? To what extent is it necessary to be specific, and what implications do the answers to these questions have for the ways in which forests should be managed and management impacts monitored? Second, how can biodiversity and ecological processes be monitored in a practical way that is relevant to forest managers seeking certification under the FSC framework or to those aspiring to implement ecosystem approaches? Finally, to what extent do 'centralized' conceptual approaches to management, like FSC certification, promote or inhibit the flexible, situation-specific approaches that are necessary in all individual forest management situations and are fundamental to ecosystem approaches?

Reconciling the Desire for Generality with the Need to be Specific

All tropical forest management units are unique, as forest characteristics vary from one place to another and from one time period to another and are altered by human impacts associated with timber production – which themselves are also subject to change. All general management principles will therefore have to be adapted, to some degree, to the particular conditions at any one time and place. Some principles may not always be applicable and will have to be replaced by local guidelines. These straightforward premises may lead to the conclusion that the adoption of ecosystem approaches for forest management must become a goal. Here we look at the arguments that back up this conclusion, using the ecological dimension of good forest management as our case study.

Changing paradigms in earth and ecological sciences have contributed to the changes in forest management paradigms that have put ecosystem approaches on the agenda. The last two decades of the 20th century saw a hugely important rise in awareness of the need to take into account long time scales and large spatial scales in natural resource management. Landscape ecology became a major discipline (Forman, 1993) and conservation biology, born as a crisis discipline in response to biodiversity loss, has taken on board multiple spatial and temporal scales for evaluation and action (Meffe and Carroll 1997). Among conservation biology's recent products are an important synthesis of multiple-scale, habitat-based approaches to the conservation of forest biodiversity (Lindenmayer and Franklin, 2002) and a pioneer text setting out an ecosystem approach for conservation (Meffe *et al.*, 2003). At the same time, the belief that the biosphere, oceans and atmosphere are in a state of fragile equilibrium disturbed mainly by humans has been replaced by a recognition of the constancy of natural change. We are now aware of the all-pervading role of natural disturbances – hurricanes, fire, landslides, erosion and deposition in floodplains – in the generation and maintenance of biodiversity (Whitmore, 1990; Pickett and Carpenter, 1995). Research on the causes and consequences of climate change has revolutionized our understanding of the planet and has shown that natural forces can bring about massive change in time periods much shorter than a human lifetime (Severinghaus *et al.*, 1998). Overall, uncertainty is a key aspect of current paradigms in earth and ecological sciences – a key contribution from these sciences in promoting ecosystem approaches.

Yet, in emphasising the importance of uncertainty and change in natural systems, it is important to avoid giving the impression that there are no general principles applicable for the guidance of natural resource management in particular local cases. Most ecological scientists would probably accept that there is pattern in nature that can be represented by general principles, that there is also diversity in the sense of departure from principles, and that both are fundamentally important subjects for study. We therefore need awareness of both pattern and diversity in forest management – of the need to balance the application of principles with the development of locally-adapted approaches. To illustrate these points, we can look at pattern and diversity in forest dynamics at scales from the landscape to the individual species population.

All natural systems are dynamic at different scales in space and time. In a small patch of forest, trees grow, die and are replaced. In floodplain landscapes, the huge energy of water destroys forest communities and at the same time creates new land on which new ones arise. The regional distributions of major forest formations shift in response to the variability of climate. These kinds of dynamics operating within natural systems are as important to management as the more traditional characterization of their structure, composition and diversity. Disturbance is often one of the most important drivers of ecosystem dynamics, be it natural disturbance or human-induced through extractive resource use such as timber harvesting (Pickett and Carpenter, 1995). Disturbance and its role must therefore be understood and managed in the context of production forests as well as in any other natural resource management scenario.

Ecologists typically characterize disturbances in terms of their type, their intensity or severity, their frequency and their size and spatial distribution (Pickett and Carpenter, 1995). The characteristics of disturbances will have an important influence on timber production and biodiversity conservation in any forest management situation. Management plans need to identify the natural disturbance regime of a forest, its history of human disturbance and the type, intensity, frequency and size of the disturbances that management will impose. This may sound complex, but it should not be; the disturbances caused by management, for example, are implicitly characterized when plans for timber harvesting are made in terms of estimation of felling cycle length and harvesting intensities. When characterizations of disturbance are carried out, the combination of the natural regime with the history of human intervention and future harvesting plans will give a unique character to each management operation. Nothing can remove the need for managers to start from the principles of the dynamics of natural systems and disturbance, to evaluate local circumstances and to manage accordingly.

To what extent are tropical forests currently being managed in such a way? Certification of timber production operations in natural forest under the FSC framework has made enormous advances in the neotropics and provides a huge amount of material for analysis. Certified forests are found throughout the neotropics, from Belize to Bolivia. A variety of natural disturbance regimes is found over this enormous geographical range. If we describe this variety we can clearly understand why both regional and local specificity are necessary in forest management, and we'll also suggest how and why certification, at least at the moment, is not promoting this specificity. To start with we can follow temperate zone authors (Woodley and Forbes, 1997; Noss, 1999, his Table 1) and organize information using a simple classification of types of disturbance.

'Gap' disturbance regimes are those in which the forest canopy is opened by the death of individual trees or small groups of them. These disturbances are therefore occasional and small-scale within the stand. Gap regimes are currently the predominant natural situation in large areas of the neotropics

(Whitmore, 1990). Yet within this general pattern are regional and landscape-level specifics. One source of this specificity is the history of forest management in different areas. For example, large areas of today´s closed neotropical forest have probably regrown following historical deforestation (see review by Finegan *et al.*, 2001a; Fredericksen and Putz, 2003). Another source of specificity comes from the ecological characteristics of different areas. For example, it seems that the rates at which trees grow, die and are replaced – called forest stand turnover rates by ecologists - are higher in forest of central Mesoamerica (Lieberman and Lieberman, 1987; Finegan and Camacho, 1999) than on the Guiana Shield (Durrieu de Madron, 1994) or in Central Amazonia (Laurance *et al.*, 2004).

'Stand-replacing' disturbance regimes are those in which major natural or human-induced dis-turbances destroy whole forest stands and bring about their replacement by new ones. In contrast to gap regimes, stand destruction and replacement, because of their greater intensity and larger scale; create post- disturbance communities with a different structure and, often, species composition, to those that existed before the disturbance. These post-disturbance communities also differ from other communities in the same landscape or region disturbed at other times, or in which the disturbance regime is the gap type. Natural forces that create this type of disturbance regime in the neotropics include hurricanes, floodplain dynamics and possibly fire (Whitmore, 1990 and Finegan *et al.*, 2001a). Their occurrence varies from place to place bringing specificity regarding management needs at different scales. At the regional scale, hurricanes are limited to the Antilles and part of Mesoamerica, while in Amazonia, very large blowdowns caused by storms are concentrated in a belt in the north of the basin (Nelson *et al.*, 1994). Meanwhile, floodplains and the disturbance regimes that characterize them cover very large areas in two tectonic units in the west of the Amazon basin, but are less important elsewhere in Amazonia (Salo *et al.*, 1986; Dumont *et al.* 1990).

In spite of the diversity of natural disturbance regimes evident at multiple scales in neotropical forests, all the FSC-certified forests are probably being currently managed in basically the same way. Timber is being harvested selectively and future harvesting planned on the basis of trees that are already well-established in the forest – a *polycyclic* silvicultural system. Logging intensities will be determined on the basis of volume legally harvestable in the context of any restrictions imposed by the forest law, a situation that almost invariably means lower volumes of timber are cut in certified forests than in areas logged in a traditional way (Putz *et al.* 2000a). Harvestable volume varies widely between sites, because of variation not only in forest composition or site characteristics, but also in market conditions at local, regional and national scales (Wadsworth, 1997; Putz *et al.*, 2000b). Polycyclic systems prevail at the moment partly because they are appropriate for forests with 'gap' disturbance regimes and partly, I suggest, because their relatively low environmental impacts make them the only option acceptable to many stakeholders. Indeed, they are probably the only silvicultural option permitted by national forest laws in neotropical countries. But there are always 'buts'. Firstly, if silvicultural intervention is necessary to increase the productivity of a forest managed under a polycyclic system, the ecological impact increases enormously and on some sites may be un-acceptable (Finegan and Camacho, 1999; Finegan *et al.*, 2001b). Secondly, polycyclic silviculture is probably not ecologically or economically optimal in the forests of Belize or Bolivia in which the stands being harvested have arisen following severe natural or human disturbance, or on Amazonian floodplains where stands are primarily successional communities on substrates recently deposited by rivers. The ecological resilience of neotropical moist forests means that on some sites, the option exists to convert forests that have 'gap' disturbance regimes to a 'stand-replacing' regime and there may be situations in which this approach has potential advantages both commercially and silvi-culturally (Wadsworth, 1997). However, because this means moving from low-intensity selective harvesting to something resembling clear-felling, it is unlikely that this option will be included within the concept of SFM for the neotropics in the foreseeable future.

In conclusion, earth science and ecology, combined with the factors that determine logging intensities at any given site, provide abundant support for the adoption of ecosystem approaches. On the other hand, evidence from neotropical countries suggests that SFM, as put into practice through national forest laws and the FSC certification process, has so far tended towards a 'one size fits all' approach to timber harvesting and silviculture. Closer examination would probably show that silvicultural approaches are often incompletely adapted to the ecological and economic circumstances of a management operation. At the end of this paper I suggest that this situation is understandable, but that over the medium and long terms, certification and forest laws must take up the challenge of putting greater freedom into the hands of the managers, a freedom that ecosystem approaches provide.

A Proposal for Ecological Monitoring as a Relevant and Practical Management Tool

While the need for adaptive management and monitoring in forest management is widely accepted, the actual implementation of ecological monitoring in tropical timber production forests is still a rarity. A review of on-line forest certification reports from Mesoamerica carried out in 2002 by John P. Hayes (Finegan *et al.*, 2004, Appendix B) found a high level of inconsistency in the ecological monitoring programmes, even though certification requires managers to undertake extensive monitoring.

Box 2 summarises a proposed approach to making ecological monitoring a practical reality. This approach has been recently developed by Finegan *et al.* (2004) and combines general principles with guidelines for the case-by-case development of management tools appropriate to local circumstances.

The proposal outlined in Box 2 is technical and some may object to it because of that. Its use will require the participation of professionals but if the recommended focus on monitoring habitat structure and composition is adopted, any forester who can design, execute and analyse a forest inventory will, with appropriate learning experience, be able to design, execute and analyse a monitoring programme.

A key aspect of the proposal is the process set out for individual programme design. Guidelines for determining whether or not monitoring is necessary, or a priority in relation to other necessities, are offered. Flexibility in programme design is built in but options for local specificity are unavoidably limited because of the small number of indicators whose monitoring is potentially practical. The practicality of indicators depends on, *inter alia*, the cost of their use, their interpretability and their statistical sensitivity (many indicators that managers might be asked to monitor are extremely variable in a statistical sense and would require unacceptably high sampling intensities to reach conclusions regarding management impacts). Habitat structure and composition indicators as proposed by Finegan *et al.* (2004) are holistic and readily interpretable in the cyclic framework of system disturbance and response that is currently widely applied. These indicators have a well-documented, clear and direct relationship to management operations. And for sound practical reasons, indirect indicators like these are used as a basis for conservation planning and assessment in countries where human and financial resources are much more abundant than those of the neotropics (Scott *et al.*, 1991; Duinker, 2001). No single indicator or group of indicators will ever inform us about all or even most biodiversity (Azevedo Ramos *et al.*, 2002; Finegan *et al.*, 2004, Appendix C). The best practical focus for the conservation of biodiversity and ecological processes in neotropical production forests is to control major threats, reduce management impacts and if necessary, monitor a set of habitat structure and composition indicators.

Extractive use of forests changes them in ways that in general terms, are proportional to the intensity of that use (Putz *et al.*, 2000b). If monitoring is determined to be a necessary component of a management operation, its purpose therefore should be to support decisions as to whether the degree of change is acceptable or not. If unacceptable change occurs, the factors behind it must be

<table>
<tr><td>Box 2</td><td>Making Ecological Monitoring a Practical Management Tool for FSC-certified Neotropical Timber Production Forests (as suggested by Finegan et al. (2004)).</td></tr>
</table>

Be general

1. Some impacts are so obviously undesirable that they need to be controlled from the outset, not monitored. Set monitoring in the context of a conservation plan that should give priority to the detection and control of major threats to the forest such as forest conversion, fire, destructive harvesting practices, illegal logging and uncontrolled hunting. Conserve special habitats or known key resources for fauna.

2. Forest managers cannot be held to account for impacts on biodiversity and ecological processes for which they are not responsible. Define clear objectives for monitoring directed towards the detection of change caused by forest management operations and therefore under the forest manager's control.

3. An appropriate reference area, and/or pre-intervention information for managed areas, is a requisite if point 2 is to be attainable. Monitoring involves repeated measurements over time.

4. Monitor at the stand level and the species population level if absolutely necessary. But it is not currently practical to monitor landscape characteristics relevant to large forest management units and conservation at this scale must be catered for by adequate planning of intervention and control of major threats.

5. Species are not necessarily amenable to monitoring. Indicator species or groups lack scientific support as monitoring concepts and interpretable monitoring data are difficult to obtain for most individual species, however important they are from a conservation stand-point – even if they are high conservation value forests. But you must pay attention to the possibility that management threatens the species that you are harvesting with decline or local extinction.

6. Monitor the structure and composition of habitat as a practical and relevant option. These parameters are fundamental to what a forest is besides being correlated with composition and diversity of species. Approaches are readily assimilated by forest and conservation professionals and data collection can, to an extent, be integrated with that for other aspects of management such as growth and yield studies and silvicultural diagnosis.

7. The objective of monitoring is not to determine whether or not change occurs as a consequence of management: it will. Rather, the emphasis must be on the determination of *whether the change observed is within acceptable limits or not.*

Be specific

8. Monitoring programmes need to be designed on a case-by-case basis that reflects the uniqueness of each forest management unit. Three points are emphasised in this context:

    a. recognise and take the option of *not monitoring* where there is no technical or ecological justification for the investment it represents or where lack of human or financial resources means there is currently no practical possibility of carrying it out in any meaningful way.

    b. Use a decision tree or similar approach to support individual monitoring programme design. The type and intensity of management are basic technical criteria to be used in programme design; many of the criteria used will be case-specific.

    c. Besides having the option of designing a monitoring programme using habitat structure and composition indicators, add case-specific indicators to programmes as long as they meet criteria of practicality, relevance and statistical tractability.

9. It is impossible to take decisions regarding the acceptability of change using only scientific criteria. Statistical approaches must be combined with local stakeholder input.

Box 3 **Hypothetical examples of impacts of management on biodiversity**

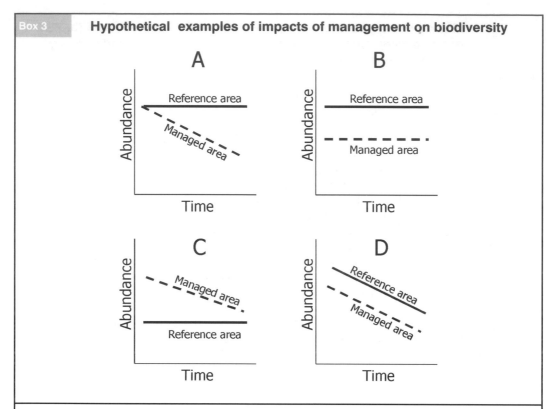

Four hypothetical examples of possible monitoring results. All examples assume that monitoring began before implementation of management activities in an area and continued following implementation of management.

A. This is the simple case where abundance of the species in the reference area and the managed area are the same before management, and management activities result in a decline in abundance in the managed area.

B. In this case, although the managed area has lower abundance of a species than the reference site, the relative difference through time remains the same. The logical conclusion in this case would be that although the managed area is not as good habitat as the reference site, management did not influence species abundance.

C. In this case, the managed area appears to be naturally better habitat than the reference area, as seen from the fact that the abundance was higher in the managed area than the reference area both before and after management. However, relative to the reference area, abundance in the managed area declined following management. The logical conclusion in this case would be that management was a likely cause of the observed declines.

D. In this situation the abundance of the species declined through time in both the managed area and the reference area. Assuming that the reference area is not being indirectly influenced by management, the logical assumption in this situation is that population declines are the result of changes that are not caused by management.

Source: Finegan *et al.* (2004).

identified and procedures modified. Given the fact that forests are managed to satisfy human needs, these decisions on acceptability of change can not be made on a purely scientific basis but will need to include an element of subjective opinion. Finegan *et al.* (2004) propose a combination of general statistical approaches and local stakeholder inputs to address this point, with the statistical approach proposed as the starting point.

Management impacts can only be determined with an acceptable degree of confidence if managed areas are compared with reference areas. The ideal situation is to have pre-disturbance data from the area to be managed, as well as a spatially-separate unmanaged reference area that is monitored at the same time as the managed area. If there are no pre-disturbance data for the management area, then the only way to perform evaluations is to assume that the pre-disturbance values were similar to current values in the reference area. Assuming sampling to be adequate, this assumption is probably reasonable for some indicators, such as forest stand density and basal area. It is problematic for habitat compositional indicators because composition can vary markedly within a structurally quite homogeneous forest. It is also problematic for all individual species indicators. However, evaluations of monitoring results must take into account trends in indicator values and the use of trends overcomes this problem to some extent (Box 3).

Managed areas are compared with reference areas, but on the basis of the assumption that change is inevitable and some degree of change permissible, the approach is not that of a comparison with a null hypothesis of no difference. Rather, it is to determine whether or not indicator values in managed areas lie within the natural range of variation of the indicator, or return to that range within an acceptable time period following disturbance (Noon, 1999; Ghazoul and Hellier, 2000). Finegan *et al.* (2004) describe the simple statistical approach suggested for carrying out evaluations.

Final Comments

In seeking ecological sustainability, should managers be guided (or constrained) by general principles or should they rely on intimate knowledge of local circumstances? Yes and yes. This is not, in my opinion, a debate. What *is* a debate is whether centralized conceptual approaches to forest management – such as SFM as it is evolving under the certification umbrella – promote or inhibit good management at the forest management unit level. In this paper I have argued that SFM is currently falling short in its promotion of locally-appropriate management, particularly in relation to the ecological basis of silviculture and ecological monitoring of management impacts. Key questions in this debate are whether this is because SFM is conceptually inadequate, or because applications of the SFM concept are inadequate, and whether ecosystem approaches bring elements that would be an improvement on SFM. In these concluding comments I discuss these questions in relation to the case of ecological monitoring.

Ecological monitoring tools are needed, not to determine whether or not forests have been disturbed but to track less obvious changes to forest ecosystems as part of good forest stewardship – whether seeking the conservation of as many of the characteristics of the original system as possible (SFM), or more fundamentally, the conservation of system resilience as in ecosystem approaches.

The debate regarding the way in which management impacts on biodiversity and ecological processes should be evaluated seems likely to go on for longer than the debate as to whether monitoring is necessary or not (Sheil *et al.*, 2004). Personally, I favour technical approaches like that described earlier in this paper, because one of the implicit purposes of adaptive management is to reduce the number of mistakes that are made, or at least to reduce the impact of mistakes. The risk of mistakes can never be completely avoided (Steidl *et al.*, 1997) and for the sake of transparency and credibility, professionals need to make clear that even the most rigorous sampling and experiment can occasionally lead to the wrong conclusions. The factors that determine statistical power and how this can limit the value of monitoring data to managers also need to be made clear (Steidl *et al.*, 1997; Finegan *et al.*, 2004). However great the need for local involvement in forest management and conservation, the possibility that a less formal, more participatory decision making process will lead to mistakes seems to be much greater (see Sutherland *et al.* (2004) on "the need for evidence-based conservation"). Keith (1998) compared the use of centrally-defined decision rules for assessing extinction risk in plants with "intuitively-based qualitative schemes in traditional use". He found that the centrally-defined rules fostered greater accuracy and precision in risk classification and were more defensible in the face of challenges.

To be useful, ecological monitoring needs to be applied where necessary and possible, on a case-by-case basis. It should not be a standard hoop that everyone must jump through in order to achieve certification. The certification process has arguably shot itself in the foot by creating Principles and Criteria that (at least as applied at the moment) require managers to monitor at a time when, in the tropics, capacity to do so is still so limited. True, Principle 8 states that monitoring should be appropriate to the scale and intensity of management. But one certification report from Mesoamerica reveals instructions to communities to monitor 54 bird species in concessions with extremely low harvesting intensities (Finegan *et al.*2004, Appendix B). This paper proposes that monitoring should be made operational in relation to the scale and intensity of management, for example by permitting managers to argue for exemption from monitoring if their harvesting intensities are below a certain limit. Principle 9, however, brings up a more difficult situation. It recognises that some forests are more important than others from a conservation point of view and requires that their management be more precautionary and more closely monitored. In this regard, it is a step forward. But its statement that managers must carry out annual monitoring of the effectiveness of measures taken to maintain or increase conservation values flies in the face of reality, as far as biodiversity and ecological processes are concerned. This is particularly so in the case of individual species, which are difficult to monitor in a scientifically and technically meaningful way. Managers will probably find that if species have high conservation value because they are threatened or endangered, they may be impossible to monitor because they are rarely if ever observed. Even full-time researchers working on such species may go for long periods without seeing more than indirect signs (prints, scats) of the animals they are studying. Furthermore, it is a mistake to assume that all species will be negatively impacted by timber production operations. Principle 9, on paper at least, fails to take into account basic aspects of sampling biodiversity and of individualistic species responses to disturbance, not to mention local circumstances. Managers must have the option of deciding that meaningful monitoring is not necessary or possible, either because the high conservation value is unlikely to be impacted by the operations proposed, or because the required human and financial resources are not currently available. And certifiers must evaluate such proposals on their merits, rather than simply imposing monitoring requirements,.

SFM and ecosystem approaches are both conceptual approaches to the management of forests for multiple goods and services. Many forest stakeholders have yet to accept that forests can or should be managed in this way. SFM predates ecosystem approaches but certification as a tool to promote it is less than a decade old. Any process as young, as complicated and as high-profile as certification will be an easy and attractive target for critics. It is true that, while certification has achieved unprecedented advances in the promotion of SFM in the neotropics (see www.fsc-info.org/), much remains to be learned. The Central American situation well-known to this author shows that SFM has been adopted gradually starting, of course, with the basics. In conceptual terms, the basics involved the acceptance by professionals that logged natural stands can produce future harvests and that enrichment planting or conversion to plantations is not necessary. In practical terms, they involved the adoption of plans and controls for harvesting, appropriate forms of community organization, and the strengthening of managerial capacity. Monitoring has not been among the highest priorities during this period. Given abundant evidence that in ecological terms, selective harvesting in an SFM framework is a disturbance well within the capacities of forests to recover (especially with the relatively low harvesting intensities that prevail in SFM in the tropics), we can probably afford this period in which monitoring has been neglected. Stepwise implementation (Nussbaum *et al.*, 2003) and standards for small forest enterprises (Higman and Nussbaum, 2002) are initiatives that recognise some of these realities and show that lessons are being learned. But sooner or later managers in some situations will need to demonstrate that they are not causing adverse impacts on biodiversity and ecological processes or that investments in conservation are producing results. This is when monitoring will cease to be a distraction (Sheil, 2001) and become a necessity (Carrillo *et al.*, 2000).

The fact that forest management for both production and conservation is considered a valid concept in much of the tropics is due to the widespread application of SFM. Still, there is obviously a need for improvements in the use of SFM and this need will continue as SFM applications adapt to changing circumstances. This paper and others in this volume provide arguments in support of ecosystem approaches as a framework to guide future work because it puts local concerns at the forefront.

intu

5 Changing Forest Values in Europe

Per Angelstam, Elena Kapylova, Horst Korn, Marius Lazdinis, Jeffrey A. Sayer, Victor Teplyakov and Johan Törnblom

Introduction

Recent decades have seen a proliferation of innovative approaches to forest management in Europe. Many of these reflect the principles of the "Ecosystem Approach" as elaborated under the Convention on Biological Diversity (CBD). However, although much of the impetus for the development of the concept of Ecosystem Approaches came from Europe, the term "Ecosystem Approach" has not been widely used in relation to forests in Europe. A recent initiative of the Ministerial Conference for the Protection of Forests in Europe – the MCPFE – attempted to compare the CBD principles with the approaches to sustainable forest management that had been agreed under that process. In general the conclusion was that SFM as practiced in Europe is not markedly different from the Ecosystem Approach of the CBD (MCPFE and EFE/PEBLDS Working Group, 2004).

Forestry has a long history in Europe. Sophisticated management systems that allocated rights to different products to different people have been in place since the middle-ages. Many of these traditional forest management systems were widely practiced until recently and some still persist. As populations grew the pressures upon the forests increased and in many parts of Europe destructive over-exploitation of common property forest resources became a major problem. The situation was similar to that found in many tropical developing countries today. Formal forest management emerged in the 18th Century in response to shortages of fuelwood and timber, and in some regions to problems of erosion and avalanches. European forestry has focussed on long-term maintenance of certain resources, usually timber but also hunting and protective functions. This forestry was highly pre-scriptive and based upon a command and control culture. The ruling classes largely dominated the process. Table 1 attempts to categorize these stages in forest history.

Table 1. Stages in European Forest History

1.	Multiple uses of an abundant resource by local people with traditional, experienced-based knowledge – from ancient times through to the middle ages
2.	Multiple "over"-use – a tragedy of the commons situation where resources were depleted and natural values and production potential declined – the late middle ages through to the industrial revolution
3.	The emergence of mono-functional use and landscape segregation which was driven by the introduction of clear land rights and the emergence of specialised production systems for agricultural and forest products. This resulted in the decoupling of ecological and social processes and losses of natural and cultural values – the industrial and agricultural revolutions through to the present day
4.	Widespread adoption of different approaches to age-class rotation forestry – the 19th and 20th Centuries
5.	The development of a new paradigm of sustainable use by integrating ecological, social and economic knowledge and tools in local, cultural contexts – the late 20th Century but with its roots in much traditional forestry practice

There is a long tradition of private forest ownership in Europe and this has had a profound impact on the emergence of new management paradigms. It has been common in many parts of Europe for rural dwellers to own or have rights to small areas of forest that they exploited for multiple products. Firewood, construction timber, hunting, collection of fruits and mushrooms have all been important components of rural economies for generations. There are still four million people in France who own small patches of forest – the average holding is around two hectares. In central Europe 98% of all forest holdings are still private although they only make up 50% of the total area of forest (Rametsteiner and Yadiapalli, 2004). These forest holdings average 11ha but most of the owners are not full-time foresters. They keep the forests to maintain capital but the forests are not a major source of income. In Scandinavia major forest industries obtain much of their raw material from small private forest holdings that are managed under cooperative agreements.

There has been a divergence between the management of large state forest holdings and those of the small private owners. Until recently in most countries the state focussed on intensive management for a small number of products or functions and was quite innovative in introducing new technologies both for management and for the use of forest products. Private forest owners tended to stick with traditional extensive management systems and to use a wider range of products. A minority of private forest owners have led the move towards various forms of "close to nature" forest management. This was partly for aesthetic and cultural reasons and partly because the costs of more intensive management were not justified by the value of the products. These approaches to forest management are based upon the philosophy that by "*mimicking the natural structures and processes it is possible to obtain a high degree of stability of the ecosystem, which leads to high flexibility towards possible future demands and desires from society*" (Emborg *et al.* in press). The overall principle of nature-based forestry is that "T*he principle of management is that the practices are deeply founded in or inspired by the structure and processes that occur in natural forests*". Such an approach to forestry has grown out of a long tradition of relatively low intensity management approaches for multiple products that have existed in many parts of Europe for hundreds of years. A wide range of local conditions has driven its recent re-emergence as a dominant

Fig. 1 Visualization of the transformation from a monoculture to a more nature-based form of forest management.

Traditional spruce plantation (*Picea abies*)

Same stand after conversion to beech with Douglas fir and larch

management paradigm and its manifestations have all been different. Some of the terms that have been used and accounts of the different systems are given in Table 2. Figure 1 shows how nature-based forestry could transform a spruce monoculture into mixed woodland (Larsen, in press).

Table 2. Alphabetically sorted list of different terms in English used for silvicultural approaches in the 'back-to-nature' trend in forestry (developed from Gamborg and Larsen, 2003).

Term suggested	Reference
Alternative silvicultural regimes	Hansen *et al*., 1999
Biodiversity oriented silviculture	Parviainen *et al*., 1995
Biologically sustainable silviculture	Björse and Bradshaw 1998
Close-to-nature silviculture	Dolinšek 1993; Motta *et al*., 1999; Schütz 1999
Close-to-natural silviculture	Schmidt 1998
Continuous cover forestry	Peterken 1996; Kuper 1996
Diversity-oriented silviculture	Lähde *et al*., 1998
Ecological silviculture	Benecke 1996
Ecologically oriented silviculture	Frivold 1992
Ecologically sustainable silviculture	Larsen 1995
Innovative silvicultural systems	Haveraaen 1995
Natural forestry	Peterken 1996
Natural silviculture	Zerbe 1997
Naturally-oriented silviculture	Skovsgaard 1995
Nature-based silviculture	Bradshaw *et al.,* 1994; Emborg *et al*., 2000
Nature-oriented silviculture	Fähser 1995; Koch and Skovsgaard 1999; Nabuurs and Lioubimov 2000
Near-natural silviculture	Tarp *et al*., 2000
Silviculture based on natural dynamics	Bergeron and Harvey 1997; Fries *et al*., 1997; Angelstam 1998
Systemic silviculture	Orazio and Nocentini 1997
Unevenaged silviculture	Gibbs 1978; Schulte and Buongiorno 1998

These innovative approaches to forestry parallel in many respects the goals of the CBD Ecosystem Approach. However, they tend to focus very much on the management unit and on forests where property rights are clear and can be defended under the law. They provide for the public goods values of forests only in an indirect way and they remain focussed on the production of private goods.

There has been a parallel but different process operating at the scale of large public forest lands. Here pressures from environmental and amenity groups have brought about changes in management objectives and methods. These changes were consistent with a stricter interpretation of the Ecosystem Approach. They were built upon public consultation and recognised the principle of societal choice. They integrated the concept of environmental functions and biodiversity having a value to society and that the cost of management should therefore be met by tax-payers. This has been translated into reality in different ways in different countries. In the UK the intensively managed production forests have been privatized but state agencies continue to influence forests through systems of incentive payments and regulations to provide amenity values. A simple characterization of the differences between these approaches and an approach purely aimed at nature conservation is given in Table 3, (Emborg *et al.*, in press). State forest agencies, the corporate sector and private individuals manage forests in each of these categories. The table is useful in showing the extent to which the sorts of goals that are implicit in the Ecosystem Approach are pursued under different forest management paradigms in Europe.

Table 3. Comparison of different management approaches with an indication of their respective fulfilment of different specific management goals. The goal fulfilment is subjectively scored on a scale from 1 to 5 plusses, where '+' = low goal fulfilment and '+++++' = high goal fulfilment. The table shows some basic principles and general features of the three management approaches in question.

Management approach	Plantation approach	Nature-based integrative approach	Nature conservation approach
Specific management goals	Focus on timber production and direct economic outcome	Flexible wood production, nature protection and recreation	Strict forest reserves providing natural structures and processes
Production of timber	+++++	++++	+
Economic outcome, long term	+++	+++++	+
Economic outcome, short term	+++++	+++	+
Production of quality timber	+++	++++	+
Biodiversity protection	+	+++	+++++
Protection of wetlands	+	+++	+++++
Ecosystem integrity and function	+	++++	+++++
Natural-looking landscape	+	++++	+++++
Landscape beauty	++	+++	+++++
Historical and cultural values	+	++++	+++
Space for public life/ recreation	++	++++	++
Place of quietness and meditation	+	+++	+++++
Hunting qualities	+++	++++	+
Robust and stable forests	+	++++	+++++
Flexibility to changing objectives	+	+++++	+

Fig. 2 A conceptual diagram showing how integration of forest functions can be achieved at the level of the management unit or through various forms of landscape mosaic

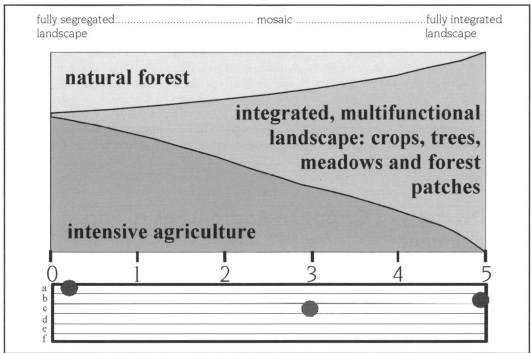

One development in European forestry that is of particular interest is the spreading adoption of "Continuous cover forestry" (Dhubhain and Pommerening, 2004). This is simply the application of shelterwood silvicultural systems; these are selective forms of harvesting that retain seed trees and result in an uneven-aged stand. It avoids the intrusiveness of clear-cut systems that are now very unpopular with amenity and environmental groups. Wales, for instance has set a target of having 50% of its forests under continuous cover management by the year 2020. In suitable sites this approach to forestry is a major advance in ensuring that production forests provide broader environmental functions. However, a lack of dead wood and senescent trees, means that even continuous cover forestry does not provide habitats for all old-growth species.

Many of the principles of the Ecosystem Approach as adopted by the CBD are being addressed in many forest situations in Europe. Perhaps the only points of divergence from the CBD principles concern the processes of decision making which in the case of private forests do not necessarily provide for local stakeholder participation (principle 1) and the issue of off-site effects (principle 3) that are addressed by state and large corporate forest owners but not necessarily by smaller private forest owners or managers of conservation forests. It is, however interesting that in a comprehensive review of nature-based forest management Emborg et al (in press) do not refer once to the Ecosystem Approach.

The remainder of this chapter gives brief summaries of the recent changes in forest practices in a number of European countries to illustrate the diversity of ways in which more integrative approaches to forest management are emerging on the ground. Conceptually the situations in the different countries can be seen as being located at different points on the horizontal axis of the diagram in figure 2. The Ecosystem Principles are silent on the issue of whether the integration of functions should occur within the management unit or through the spatial proximity of cells in a matrix that are dedicated to specialized functions. The application of the Ecosystem Approach does not therefore imply that any position on this axis is better than another. However if a landscape were to be highly segregated in its functions (the left hand end of this axis) then the application of the Ecosystem Principles does strongly suggest that the graininess of the mosaic must be adapted to the range of natural disturbance regimes of the ecosystem. Many European landscapes in the lowland temperate region have for long consisted of a fine-grained mixture of agriculture and forests and are widely appreciated for that quality. Boreal forests, where large-scale disturbances are natural, should in most cases be managed as a coarser-grained mosaic. Public opposition to industrial forestry has often focussed on the "vast monocultures of exotic species" that were a feature of forestry in some countries in the mid-20th Century. In general state forest agencies and forestry corporations have in the past operated in a more segregated landscape context but have tended to move towards more integrated systems in recent decades. Small private forest owners generally operate in more integrated, finer grained systems.

The Diversity of European Approaches to Forest Management

Forests in Europe are under the control of the individual member states of the European Union. However in 1998 the European Union did adopt a Council Resolution on a "Forest Strategy for the European Union" (http://europa.eu.int/comm/agriculture/consultations/forestry/index.en.ht). The pre-ambular paragraph of the Strategy states:

> "*the importance of the multi-functional role of forests and sustainable forest management based on their social, economic, environmental, ecological and cultural functions for the development of society and, in particular, rural areas...*"

The entire policy statement is rich in references to holistic approaches to forestry, of the importance of SFM in creating habitats for biological diversity, of the role of forests in providing incomes, employment and other elements of quality of life and of forests as a renewable source of energy. The Policy also highlights the fact that forests are highly diverse and that different management approaches are needed in different situations. The Policy makes the link with the EU Natura 2000 Ecological Network – a Europe wide network of protected areas that include a large number of forest sites. The Policy also gives official recognition to the definition of sustainable forest management developed by the Ministerial Council for the Protection of Forests in Europe (http://www.mcpfe.org) which is quoted in Chapter 1. It is interesting that the word "ecosystem" does not appear in the EU Forest Policy even though the policy contains much that is consistent with ecosystem approaches.

The diversity of forest situations in Europe and the richness of the recent initiatives towards more integrated forms of management are so great that it is only possible in this chapter to highlight a few examples. In doing so we have attempted to draw upon divergent situations that illustrate how the economic, political and forest resource context have influenced outcomes.

The United Kingdom

At the time of the First World War forests were reduced to 5% of the land surface of the United Kingdom. The country was largely dependent upon imports for timber and shipping blockades threatened to deprive the country of this strategic resource. In 1919 a state forest agency, the Forestry Commission, was established with the mandate to promote reforestation to ensure long-term self sufficiency in timber. The provision of rural employment during a time of economic depression was a secondary objective. The UK thus differed from those continental European countries with extensive forest resources in most of which state forest agencies had already existed for up to a century or more to manage natural forests.

Forests now cover 11% of the UK land area and meet 15% of total timber consumption. Domestic wood production from plantations could be increased further but competition from imported timber, mainly from natural forests, makes it difficult for domestic producers to make a profit. Domestic forestry's importance as a source of raw materials has declined. Indeed forestry is now so unprofitable as to raise issues about the value of commercial plantation forestry (Grundy, 2005).

In contrast there has been a growing demand for outdoor recreation. With the growth of car ownership, leisure time and disposable incomes forests have become more valuable as recreational resources than as sources of wood. The main demand is for access for walking but in addition a wide range of outdoor activities take place on forest land. These include wildlife observation, horse riding, fishing, cross-country cycling, trekking and many others. There has also been an increase in the appreciation of the environmental value of forests. Biodiversity conservation, carbon sequestration and landscape beauty are the object of public demand (Grundy, 2005).

Many of the plantations established by the Forestry Commission were on upland moorlands. Even though these had been forested in historical times the public viewed their openness as "natural" and valued these landscapes. In addition these open upland areas provided habitats for wildlife species that were scarce elsewhere. Opposition to upland plantations of exotic conifers became one of the rallying cries of the environmental movement. Since this occurred at a time when these plantations were becoming economically marginal, the case for a change in policy was overwhelming.

The situation today is that the original reason for afforestation – national security – is no longer relevant. Forestry is only of marginal importance as a provider of employment. But forests, including plantations, are valuable recreational resources and they can be valuable for biodiversity. Environmental pressures have increased the costs of forestry operations and reduced the scope for new commercial plantations.

The creation and restoration of native woodlands, even though they have low timber productivity, is now a major objective of forestry and is favoured by the environmental lobby. Pressures also exist to modify plantations to make them more diverse and thus more suitable for biodiversity and re-creational use. Plantations are managed with structurally and biologically diverse edges that provide wildlife habitat and are visually attractive to recreational users. Old trees and deadwood are retained in parts of the forest to increase "naturalness" and provide wildlife habitat and care is exercised in making large clearcuts in visible locations. However all of this also increases costs and lowers productivity.

As part of general measures to increase economic efficiency the government has been seeking to privatise state operated industries. Plantation forestry has been a target of privatization and official government policy has been that all commercial forestry should be in the private sector. However there was strong opposition to privatization from environmental NGOs, forest users and wood-based industries. There was concern at loss of both access and of the environmental values of plantation forests. The Forestry Commission was perceived as having succeeded in enhancing wildlife and landscape values and it was feared that private owners, driven exclusively by profit motives, would not pursue these management objectives.

The role of the Forestry Commission has now been almost totally reversed. It has moved from being a promoter of commercial forestry to a role of promoting forestry to meet social and environmental objectives. It has become a regulator with the duty of balancing and reconciling conflicting interests and enhancing the environment. It is now administering schemes to provide public access to and enhance wildlife and recreational value of private forests. Private landowners are invited to bid for cash for the provision of access or for the enhancement of biodiversity or landscape values. The Forestry Commission awards grants to those who make the lowest bid for the provision of a public service (Grundy, 2005). These are interesting examples of environmental service payment mechanisms that could have wider application.

The Forestry Commission in the UK has moved from a commodity oriented semi-commercial operation in the 1980s to being an "ecosystem manager" at the turn of the century. This change has been driven in parallel by economic forces and by the effective articulation of new needs by civil society organizations. The lesson from the UK is that when economic and social conditions are right, ecosystem approaches to management will emerge; when conditions are not right it will be difficult to impose them.

The forests of Scotland exemplify these changes, they have had a long history of degradation and loss. Pine-dominated forests previously covered more than 1.5 million hectares of the Scottish Highlands, today only 16,000ha remain. Over half of this consists of very open pine woodland, which is heavily grazed by deer who hamper the natural recruitment of young trees. Clearance of the Caledonian forest started in Neolithic times and progressed slowly until the 17th century, when large-scale harvesting began (Steven and Carlisle, 1959; Aldhous, 1995). Replanting sometimes followed harvesting, with records of selected pine seed being used as early as 1613 (Steven and Carlisle, 1959). Planting and forest restoration occurred on some estates. However, in many cases, the land was converted to sheep pasture or was managed for sport hunting. Large areas of the highlands of Scotland have been managed as "deer forests" since the 19th Century.

During the 20th century the Forestry Commission made major investments in establishing plantations of exotic species in the Highlands of Scotland. Massive afforestation programmes were conducted on open hill areas. These destroyed the habitat of some open ground bird species which are rare in Europe. This process only ended in the 1990s when emphasis shifted to forest management for recreation and biodiversity conservation. From this time on efforts were initiated to restore and expand native woodlands. Tourism is a major industry in Scotland and landscape and biodiversity values are important tourist attractions. The challenge is to move towards a spatial pattern of natural woodlands, plantations and open habitats that can satisfy the conflicting demands of industrial forestry, tourism and wildlife conservation.

Current efforts to maintain biodiversity in the forests of Scotland pursue a twin approach. First, because relict native forests are too small and fragmented to maintain the full range of biodiversity (Moss, 2001) major efforts are being made to restore and expand the forest area. Second, there is an attempt to adapt the management of the existing large plantations to achieve a broader range of benefits. The plantations are being allowed to mature so that in time large trees, deadwood habitats, structural diversity and transitional edge habitats will develop and thus take on some biodiversity and recreational value.

Today virtually all commercial forestry in Scotland has been privatized. In addition significant areas of forest are managed by conservation organizations and there are large areas of open moorland with scattered woods that are managed for recreational hunting. The role of the Forestry Commission is to regulate the private sector, provide technical support and administer grant schemes for the establishment and management of private woodlands and to manage areas for amenity and conservation. It invests considerable resources in convening public participation and in disseminating information to support forest management. Although critics might still find fault with the system the convergence with the principles of the Ecosystem Approach is marked.

Western Russia

The forestry situation in Russia provides a marked contrast with that in the United Kingdom. Russia has abundant forest resources and a long and distinguished history of scientific natural forest management. Morozov already enunciated the basic principles of ecosystem forestry in his seminal work on Russian forestry "On the Foundation of Silviculture" (quoted in Belaenko *et al.*, 1998). However this was a highly sectoral view of forestry; perhaps this was natural where competition for land was not an issue. Russian forestry in the 19th Century was strongly influenced by the intensive multifunctional silviculture developed in Central Europe and especially in Germany. Forests were seen as biological systems whose management consisted of working with natural processes to guide the system towards the desired end. In some ways this was very similar to the close to nature forestry that is re-emerging in Europe today (Teplyakov *et al.*, 1998).

During the Soviet period forests were managed as an industrial resource. The State owned all forest lands and the state determined the objectives of management, principally the sustainable provision of industrial raw materials. Given the vast areas of forest available and the few competing demands upon the land, the concept of multiple-use forestry had little relevance. Other institutions in other parts of the landscape were responsible for conserving biodiversity and the environmental measures applied in production forests consisted of those needed to sustain timber yields.

The economic crisis that followed the breakdown of the Soviet Union deprived the government of the resources that it needed to continue the existing state monopoly on forest management. The regulatory functions of the state were largely abandoned and attempts were made to privatize forestry. Much of the privatization was ill-planned and responded to short-term opportunism. Administrative functions were separated from forest management, the latter traditionally carried out by the Forest Management Units (Leskhozes), was severely curtailed. This led to a rapid decline in both harvesting volumes and timber processing. Serious economic and social problems followed for communities dependent on timber industries.

The newly privatized forest industries sought to maximize their hard currency earnings from exports. In Western Russia they depended for this on exports to Western Europe. Problems arose when importers came under pressure from the environmental lobby to only accept timber from sustainably managed forests. Not only could sustainable forest management not be proven but also evidence began to emerge of the extent of illegal activities in the forest sector. This led not only environmental NGOs but also the European Union and the World Bank to become involved in attempts to improve regulation and governance of the forest sector.

Pressures began to mount from several directions. Citizens of parts of Russia that were heavily dependent on forest industries began to realize the importance of a sustainable and modern forest sector. Entire communities suffered the consequences of the anarchic management of forestry. In addition many of the 220,000 or more employees of the State Forest Service began to express concern. As the economy crumbled, jobs were lost and the forests were degraded, the concern mounted to the highest levels of government. This culminated in an "All Russian Congress of Foresters" in February 2003. The Congress brought together 5500 people from all over Russia. Significant reforms to forestry institutions and regulations occurred at around the time of this Congress. Later that year the President of the Russian Federation made a public statement strongly supporting sustainable forest use and reinforcing the official view of the environmental values of forests.

Throughout the 1990s and through until the year 2004 the forest institutions in Russia were in a constant state of change. The State Forestry Committee (GOSKOMLES) was abolished in 1991 and it was not until 2004 that a Federal Forest Agency was finally established. The intention behind the changes was to bring forests under improved management. The Ecosystem Approach Principles of the

CBD passed largely unnoticed in Russia, but the general ideas of holistic and sustainable management were recognised. The Ministerial Conference for the Protection of Forests in Europe did have an impact and its definitions of sustainable forest management were influential in thinking about forestry. However throughout this period the prime cause of concern was the achievement of short-term economic objectives and the protection of jobs.

The collapse of several foreign investment projects in the forest sector provided additional impetus to the reform process. European investors and importers required evidence that social and environmental concerns were being addressed by logging companies. The issue of the harvesting of old-growth forests in Karelia became a subject of contention in both Russia and Western Europe. Attempts were made to establish a certification system adapted to Russian conditions but in spite of much discussion and the development of criteria and indicators this has never been implemented and until recently there are still no certified forests in Western Russia. Outside pressure did lead to the establishment of new protected areas in some old-growth forest zones in Karelia and financial support for this was provided by the European Union amongst others. A series of model forests have also been established with support from the international model forest network. Some of these model forests are probably the closest that Russia has to any forest management that reflects the Ecosystem Principles.

Russian forestry still has a long way to go to achieve sustainable forest management or an ecosystem approach. The annual timber harvest is well below the annual allowable cut. 70% of the timber harvested in Karelia is exported unprocessed – as compared with only 2% in neighbouring Finland. It is generally accepted that the quality of forests has significantly deteriorated in recent years. Deciduous species are replacing the valuable conifers – especially on the better soils. In Karelia the proportion of mature and over mature forests declined from 61% to 33% in just a few years around 2000.

Some support is being received from Finland to strengthen research capacity and to establish some integrated sustainable forest industries in Karelia. But the case of Russia shows dramatically how difficult it is to manage forests in ways consistent with any recent concepts of sustainability or to apply ecosystem approaches in a situation where institutions are weak and changing, economies are in crisis and the ability to enforce regulations has been diminished (Kopylova and Teplyakov, 2004; Mudahar *et al.*, 1997).

Sweden

The very first Swedish forest law from 1647 was a response to the threat that swidden agriculture and browsing by domestic livestock posed for economically important trees. The first legislation on sustained yield forestry, applying to private land, was passed in 1903. In 1948 a focus on industrial production of wood using intensive management methods was introduced and was the prevailing approach until the mid-1980s (for details see Anon., 2001; Ekelund and Hamilton, 2001). In the 1990s public opposition to clear-cuts, the negative effects of a long history of intensive forest management on a range of specialised species and a wish to deregulate forestry, led to the development of new forest legislation. This determined that sustained forest production and the maintenance of viable populations of all naturally occurring species were of equal importance (Anon., 1993b). At this time the negative effects of acid rain and nitrogen deposition on forest health emerged as an issue (Sverdrup and Stjernquist, 2002).

During the past decade the conservation of biodiversity has dominated the public debate on forestry. This was often narrowly interpreted as the conservation of threatened and red-listed species in the short-term rather than population viability and ecosystem integrity and resilience in the longer term (Angelstam, 2003a,b). There has been considerable development in approaches to stand and landscape planning (Angelstam and Pettersson, 1997), but little attention has been given to assuring the functionality of habitat mosaics at different spatial scales for the long term (Angelstam *et al.*, 2003a). Currently a major effort is being made to increase the area of forest and to develop a network of protected or specially managed forest areas to maintain biodiversity. However, the extent of private forest holdings is such that no more than 2–4% of the forest can be placed in strict nature reserves (Angelstam and Andersson, 2001). There is emerging evidence that the ecosystem processes maintaining not only biodiversity but also the productive functions of forests have been negatively impacted by air pollution (Sverdrup and Stjernquist, 2002).

Some stakeholders see biodiversity conservation as a hindrance to wood production. Recent forest policies are leading to a reduced intensity of forest management and reduced wood production. According to a recent survey made by the National Board of Forestry (Anon., 2001) the main current production problems are: 1) insufficient regeneration after harvesting, 2) insufficient pre-commercial thinning and 3) high levels of browsing damage by wild deer.

Most of the principles of the Ecosystem Approach are now incorporated into forest planning and management. However there is still an unresolved issue of the trade-off between maintaining jobs in the traditional forest sector and the establishment of protected areas for biodiversity. In addition, because of a long history of intensive management there is often a need for intensive management interventions to maintain biodiversity.

The Baltic States

During the first half of the 20th century the Baltic States were independent nations with significant private forest ownership. After annexation to the Soviet Union collective ownership was introduced. For nearly 50 years after World War II, forests in these countries were the exclusive property of the State.

The Baltic States no longer harbour much natural forest, but there are still a few relatively large areas of old semi-natural forests. In Estonia, the forest cover is estimated to have been about 55% around 1700, after which it declined rapidly to a low of *c.*20% in the first decades of the 20th century. It has now increased to today's 52% (Lõhmus *et al.*, 2004). In Latvia, the forest cover 300 years ago was estimated to be 65%, it then declined to a low of 25% in the 1930s, followed by an increase to about 45% in the late 1990s. Finally, in Lithuania, where agriculture is more important, the forest cover in 1700 was about 40%, it reached a low of 17% before World War II and is at present 30%.

At the end of the 20th century when the Baltic States regained their independence the central planning system was replaced by a market economy. Private forest ownership with relatively strong tenure rights was reintroduced. Throughout the transition period, foreign aid has facilitated development of the forest and environmental sectors. Accession to the European Union in 2004 also influenced the institutional context of forest management.

As a consequence, a whole range of management instruments to facilitate conservation of biological diversity has been introduced (Lazdinis and Angelstam, 2004b). Concepts such as "biodiversity trees" (retention of snags, hollow and other trees to provide habitat for species after timber harvesting) and key woodland habitats (small forest areas with high conservation value) were introduced. Larger high conservation value forests were protected within the framework of the European Union NATURA 2000 programme. These concepts and programmes are now incorporated in national forestry laws and regulations. The changes all represent convergence with the principles of the Ecosystem Approach. However it is noteworthy that the pressures to conserve biodiversity came largely from countries that were importing timber products from the Baltic States and not from civil society within the countries themselves.

Germany

Climatically, the German lowlands should be dominated by temperate deciduous forest (Mayer, 1984). These forests have been exploited for wood since the middle ages. In addition they have been used for pasture, litter-collection and the extraction of resin and tannins (Küster, 1998). In the pre-industrial era between the 16th and 18th centuries, wood consumption for the production of salt, charcoal, glass, metal, etc. reached such a level that the continued existence of German forests was jeopardised.

The high demand for wood in the 18th and 19th centuries placed further pressure on the forests. As a consequence, rigorous forestry laws were introduced, and professional forestry education and research began. At this time, research on the growth and yield of Norway spruce and Scots pine demonstrated their high potential productivity. These species performed so well that they were planted both within and beyond their natural range. Forestry was based upon the assumption that if timber yields were maintained then other goods and services would also automatically be sustained.

In recent decades biodiversity, amenity and recreational functions of the forest have assumed greater importance. However, the state forest administrations still obtain 90% of their income from wood sales (BMVEL, 2001). In addition forests continue to be an important source of subsistence income for countless farmers and small forestry enterprises.

Today, almost on third of Germany (30.8% or approximately 10.7 million hectares) is covered with forest. This area has continued to increase during recent decades. Agricultural intensification has led to abandoned fields being afforested or abandoned to natural woodland regeneration. Extensive areas have been reforested for environmental reasons and this has contributed to the growth of the total forest area. In the federal states of former West Germany alone, forests increased by around 500,000 hectares, i.e. approx. 4.9%, from 1950 to 1993 (BMELF, 1998).

However, only about one third of this forested area is now stocked with native broadleaved trees. The other two thirds are predominantly pure or mixed conifer forests. In some parts of Germany forests still exist as large, coherent, and comparatively "close-to-nature" ecosystems. In other areas forests remain only as fragments within predominantly agricultural landscapes. These isolated patches of forest remain important as refuges for many plant and animal species whose habitats elsewhere have been reduced (BMELF, 2000a).

Forests are economically important, particularly in rural regions. In 1999, the timber industry provided about 648,000 jobs, and accounted for sales of more than 87 billion Euros (BMELF, 2000b). The importance of forests as suppliers of renewable and ecologically sound raw materials is likely to increase in future. The wood reserves in German forests have been growing for decades. The average reserves of rough wood amount to approx. 270 m^3 per hectare, and the standing crop nationwide is increasing by about 79 million cubic meters every year (EUROSTAT, 2000). Only 37.2 million m^3 of this is being harvested. It would be possible to increase the harvest by almost 50% without exceeding the annual increment (BMELF, 2000c).

Ownership of forests in Germany is highly diversified. A total of 46% of the total forest area is privately owned, 34% is owned by the federal and states authorities and the remaining 20% is owned by public corporations (BMELF, 2000b). The law leaves owners free to choose amongst a range of management options.

A "National Forest Programme for Germany" (BMELF, 2000a) was developed between 1999 and 2000. This was a multi-stakeholder process. The preamble to the programme states that "*In September 1999, the Federal Ministry of Food, Agriculture and Forestry for the first time invited associations, federations, institutions and representatives of the Laender to participate in an open discussion process on the future orientation of German forestry policy.*" However, some environmental organizations withheld their approval of this programme.

They considered that it had failed to give enough emphasis to nature conservation and had favoured commercial interests (AG WÄLDER, 2001; Häusler and Scherer-Lorenzen, 2002).

Germany has a long history of high quality technical forest management. Forest managers have always addressed a wide range of stakeholder interests. At present Germany is witnessing a general shift towards close to nature forestry both by private forest owners and by state agencies. In the latter case the shift is away from extensive homogeneous conifer plantations towards more broadleaved species. In recent years all state owned forests in Germany have moved to nature-based management. Management is also giving higher priority to amenity and biodiversity values of forests. The private owners have been leaders in Europe in developing the close-to-nature approaches to forestry and significant areas are now under these sorts of management. Both the state agencies and the private owners are moving towards management schemes that are consistent with the principles of the Ecosystem Approach although in neither case do these principles appear to have been responsible for the change. Rather social and economic pressures and the activities of environmental and amenity groups have led to changed objectives for forestry.

The Alps: Switzerland and Austria

The steep terrain and the risk for flooding and avalanches in the Alps have meant that protection has been a dominant driver of management of the mountain conifer forests (Kräuchi et al., 2000; Dorren et al., 2004). More recently, as in Sweden and the Baltic States, there has been an increasing focus on both natural and cultural biodiversity (Duelli and Obrist, 2003; Neet and Bolliger, 2004). Austria and Switzerland, where mountain forests predominate (Dönz-Breuss et al., 2004; Neet and Bolliger, 2004), are good examples of that transition.

In Switzerland laws to protect the environmental values of forests have existed since the mid 19th Century. Today, a national forest biodiversity conservation strategy has been developed and this stresses the new European innovations in close-to-nature silviculture. It also provides for the conservation of important ecological sites and for the establishment of forest reserves (Neet and Bolliger, 2004). Austria has a long history of scientific forestry and a comprehensive nation-wide forest inventory since 1952. In recent years this inventory has emphasised the assessment of biodiversity at genetic, species, and community levels. Biodiversity policies exist in Austria that favour new approaches to forest management (Wohlgemuth et al., 2002).

Bürgi and Schuler (2003) analysed the history of forest regeneration in the Canton of Zürich in Switzerland, and concluded that the driving factors were a complex mix of economy, ecology and politics. They suggested that four major factors were critical to the future development of forest management in this part of Central Europe. These were 1) increased fossil fuel prices making forests more competitive as sources of energy than for timber production; 2) concerns about impacts and adaptation to climate change; 3) international policies encouraging forests to be managed as carbon sinks; and 4) changes in management schemes in response to changes in forest technology and insights from forest ecology.

Forest management in the Alps faces numerous challenges. Mountain forest owners are expected to produce market goods (e.g., timber and game), public environmental goods and services (e.g., protection against natural hazards) and also to maintain biological diversity. In addition, in many alpine communities, forestry is important in providing permanent and seasonal jobs. At present, there is no financial return from the provision of environmental benefits. International competition makes it difficult for forest enterprises to avoid placing short-term economic goals ahead of long-term sustainability (Dönz-Breuss et al., 2004).

Many would claim that the alpine countries have a long tradition of managing forests in ways that are consistent with the principles of the Ecosystem Approach. Forest product prices have always been high enough to offset the costs of maintaining slope protection. Economic constraints and issues of competitivity are now placing some of these management schemes in jeopardy and they will only be able to persist if the environmental values are properly factored in and society at large pays for their costs.

Switzerland's National Forest Programme is interesting in emphasising the problems of the falling competititiveness of commercial forestry. In this it differs from similar policy documents from other European countries that all tend to emphasise a shift towards environmental values. A principle aim of the Swiss NFP is to "…*optimise the three dimensions of sustainability and to improve the economic and social value of the forest as compared with its current relatively high ecological value.*" Of the five priority goals of the NFP three concern the environmental services provided by the forests and two emphasise the need for improved economic performance (www.umwelt-schweiz.ch/buwal/eng/fachgebiete/fg_wald/rubrik3/uebersicht/pr)

Ukraine

Ukraine has a large diversity of forest types ranging from steppes to mountains. Natural forest once covered 50% of the country, the rest being made up of the steppe zone and the swamp areas in Polesie (Hensiruk, 1992). The forests were used by local people for hunting, bee-keeping and for non-wood products. They were also widely cleared for agriculture. Forest ownership records suggest that from the 16th century forest use became more intense. The forest area began to decline and the species composition and structure were altered. Felling led to reduction of beech *Fagus sylvatica*, spruce and mixed beech-spruce-fir forest areas in the Carpathians and destruction of beech and oak *Quercus* spp. forests in central and north-western parts of the country (Hensiruk, 1992; Hensiruk *et al.*, 1995). Increased demand for bread in western European countries in the 18th and 19th centuries drove the expansion of agriculture in eastern Ukraine. The need for new agricultural lands caused disastrous reduction of forest cover in forest-steppes and led to the extinction of many plant and animal species. The forest in this region was reduced by about 80% (Hensiruk *et al.*, 1995).

The first forest conservation legislation was passed in the second part of the 19th century. In the Austro-Hungarian area (Halychyna) a forest protection law was passed in 1852 followed by another in the Russian area in 1888. These laws established control over forest use both on state and private lands. They were the first large-scale attempts at forest restoration in the Carpathians and the first attempt to create protection forests in steppe regions (Vakaluk, 1971).

After a long history of forest clearing for economic and agricultural purposes, the forest cover is now only 15.6% or 9.4 million ha. This forest is concentrated in the northern and western parts of the country. Planted pine and spruce forests occupy more than a half of this area. Mid-age stands (82.9%) prevail, and the areas of young (9.7%) and mature (7.4%) forest stands are small (Anon., 2003b). Forests are state property.

Since the Independence of Ukraine in 1991, deterioration of the standard of living, the collapse of the planned economy and economic stagnation have resulted in negative pressure on natural resources and increased exploitation of forests. Legal and illegal extraction of forest products, both wood and non- timber products have become an important source of income and subsistence for the large rural population (about 15.7 million people or 31.5% of the total). Many of these people live in close proximity to forests and their livelihoods depend upon them (Bihun, 2004; Zibtsev *et al.*, 2004). The 1990s saw an increase in illegal logging and high-grading of valuable hardwood species such as beech and oak. These were intensively exploited by state and private forest enterprises for both export and domestic processing. In 2002, as much as 80% of the wood harvested was exported in the form of roundwood. Pressure for quick income and hard currency meant that regulations were weakly applied and the level of illegal felling increased dramatically. In 2002 65% of wood exports came from illegal harvesting (Bihun, 2004; Maximets, 2004).

In an attempt at reform, a new forestry code has been drafted. It emphasises multi-purpose forest exploitation and the protection of rare plant and animal species and ecosystems. It provides for the development of state and regional programs for forest protection and restoration and for increasing the efficiency and sustainability of exploitation. The code provides for private and communal patterns of forest ownership (Zibtsev et al., 2004).

While the forest sector should be, and still has the potential to become, an engine for economic growth, the combination of past exploitation and the slow pace of economic reform are major obstacles to implementing rational forest policies (Nijnik and van Kooten, 2000). There is no properly functioning market to encourage sustainable use. Forestry is a monopoly of the state and private property rights are not always respected, information is asymmetric and environmental functions are undervalued. The traditional approach of maximizing sustained timber yields is the predominant paradigm in Ukraine, and time will be needed to change this attitude.

Given the right economic incentives and appropriate forest policies, it may still be possible for the Ukraine to improve its future timber supply while enjoying environmental benefits from its forests. However, this would require economic and institutional reforms beyond the forest sector. Nazarov et al. (2001) argue that a change in the mindset of policy makers and the population at large is required in parallel with legal and technical changes. Thus, as pointed out by van Zon (2002), Ukraine faces similar problems to those of many stagnating Third World countries.

Conclusions

Examples of management systems that reflect the principles of the Ecosystem Approach are emerging spontaneously all over Europe. They take many forms and are largely being driven by local processes, in many cases government forest agencies have led the process of innovation, in others they have only changed under pressure from civil society environmental and amenity groups. However, there are also quite a lot of examples where forest management has not progressed as much as would be desirable. In some parts of southern Europe subsidies are still encouraging the planting of monocultures of exotic species that provide neither environmental nor economic benefits. The extent to which the Ecosystem Approach is applied is very much a function of the state of the economy and the degree to which civil society is organised and effective in influencing policies. Amongst the countries reviewed in this chapter the United Kingdom, Sweden and Germany have achieved the closest approximations to the Ecosystem Approach. The Alpine countries are maintaining systems that have always closely reflected the Ecosystem Principles but that are now threatened because they are not economically viable. The economics of forestry in Austria appears to be healthier than in Switzerland. Austria has a thriving forest industry sector and is innovating vigorously. In Switzerland forestry is less profitable and it is proving difficult to maintain the traditional systems.

The economic problems confronting the countries whose economies are in transition are making it difficult to move the forest sector from its traditional command and control paradigm towards more ecosystem approaches. The need to do so is recognised in new legislation in the countries surveyed but institutional weaknesses and the resulting corruption have led to a degree of anarchy in forestry. The Balkan states appear to be managing the transition relatively well but in Russia and the Ukraine performance is patchy and the overall situation is not encouraging. The key lessons that we can learn from experience in Europe are:

- The trajectories of development of forest management that have evolved over several centuries in Europe have in many cases incorporated elements of what are now referred to as ecosystem approaches.

- Civil society organizations and the media have played a prominent role in broadening the forest agenda to encompass environmental and amenity values.

- The technical basis and especially the knowledge of forest ecology and economics in Western Europe has enabled highly targeted and effective forest management and this knowledge has been a resource that was available when the need to broaden the objectives of forestry became an issue.

- Private non-industrial forest owners are major players in the forest sector in Western Europe and in some areas in North and Central Europe they have led the process of innovation towards more nature-based management. This is one of the most exciting developments in relation to ecosystem forestry that we have encountered. However in many parts of Southern Europe forest holdings are too small and they contribute little to household revenues. In these situations there is little innovation and forests are often neglected.

- The Ministerial Conference on the Protection of Forests in Europe and some schemes developed by the European Union have provided strong impetus for more environmentally benign forest policies in Europe.

- An ecosystem approach to forest management in Europe has thus been facilitated by:

  o The adoption of active adaptive management where forest agencies have responded to the changing needs of economies and to the requirements of civil society;

  o Active communication has occurred amongst actors, including civil society, regarding large-scale forestry issues;

  o Zonation has been used to resolve competing issues;

  o There has been extensive international exchange of experiences and a number of technical networks have existed to disseminate improved management practices.

intu

6 Empowering the Forest-Dependent Poor in India

Sushil Saigal, Kinsuk Mitra and Pankaj Lal

Introduction

Recent changes in India reflect the recognition that forests should be sustainably managed as part of the broader social-ecological systems in which they exist. This paper reviews some of the innovations that have taken place in Indian forestry in recent decades and analyses the major drivers behind these changes.

India has seen significant innovations in the involvement of local communities in the management of state forests through the Joint Forest Management (JFM) programme. There has also been greater recognition of the role of local communities in forest conservation in general. This is manifest in ecodevelopment programmes and processes such as the National Biodiversity Strategy and Action Programme and the Bhopal India Process on SFM. All these changes are a reflection of, or are consistent with the Ecosystem Approach of the Convention on biodiversity. However, there are several aspects of the Ecosystem Approach which are not yet reflected in Indian policies and programmes and which require further attention.

The Forest Resources of India

India is one of the 12 mega-biodiversity countries in the world and contains parts of two global biodiversity 'hotspots'. Around 127,000 animal and plant species have been described so far but it is estimated that there could be another 400,000 species yet to be identified (MoEF, 1998). Forestry is the second major land use in the country after agriculture, and a wide variety of forest types are present. These range from alpine forests in the Himalayas to rainforests in the Western Ghats. Around twenty three percent of the country's area is officially classified as forest land (see Table 1).

Table 1. Coverage and categories of forest land

Category	Area (million ha)	Percentage of Total Geographical Area
Total geographical area of India	328.73	100.00%
Officially recorded forests	76.84	23.38%
Actual forest cover*	67.55	20.55%
Dense forests **	41.68	12.68%
Open forests ***	25.87	7.87%

Source: FSI, 2001
* Lands having at least 10% crown cover
** Forests with over 40% crown cover
*** Forests with crown cover between 10 and 40%

Map 1. Distribution of forest cover in India

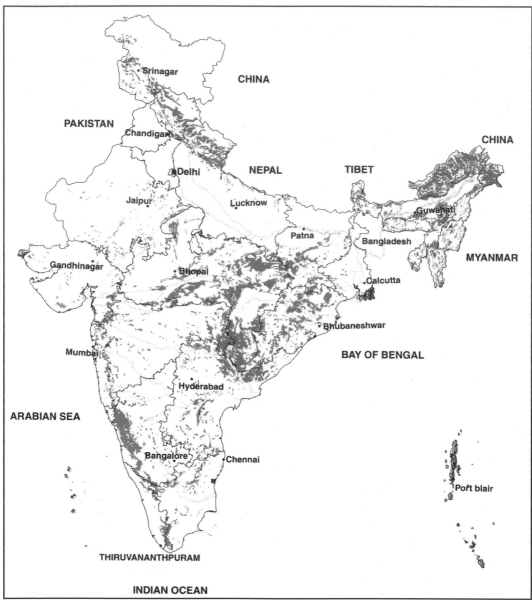

Source: FSI, 1999

However, as Table 1 shows, the actual forest cover is less than the recorded forest area. While some of the officially designated forest lands lack tree cover naturally (e.g. wetlands and snow covered peaks), a significant proportion is degraded.[1] The existing forests are not uniformly spread throughout the country but are concentrated in a few regions such as the Himalayas, northeastern states, central India and the Western Ghats (see Map 1). Although over 23% of the country's geographical area is forest land, the per capita forest area is quite low at about 0.08 ha, one-eighth of the world average.

---

1   The tree cover estimates are for the entire country and include trees on non-forest lands.

Key Players in Indian Forests

Government is a major player in Indian forestry. It controls and manages most of the officially recorded forest lands (ICFRE, 2000). Government also closely regulates forestry on non-forest land. As forestry is on the 'concurrent list' of the Constitution of India, the central as well as the state governments have the power to legislate on forestry-related matters. Each state has its own Forest Department (FD).[2] The command and control type of forest management by the government is often referred to as the 'traditional' system. This has recently given way to a decentralized approach which is more inclusive of other stakeholders. However, effective participation of local communities and other stakeholders is still limited and many key decisions are taken in a top-down fashion. The Ministry of Environment and Forests (MoEF) decides the policy framework and broad guidelines for all states at the national level. In the past, policy making has been a closed-door activity but more recently, efforts have been made to gather feedback on draft policies and to seek inputs from the non-governmental sector at the policy formulation stage.

Local Communities. Forests provide livelihood support to a significant proportion of the population, especially marginalized and vulnerable groups. India has perhaps the largest population of the world's

Map 2. Overlap of forest, poverty and tribal population in India

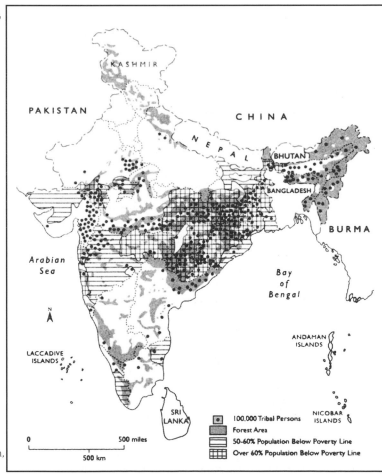

Source: Poffenberger and McGean, 1996

2   India is a federal country consisting of 28 States and seven Union Territories.

poor (c 260 million) and tribal people (c 80 million). Many of these people live within or in close proximity to forests;[3] and as shown in Map 2 there is a clear overlap between the forest, poverty and tribal maps of the country (Poffenberger and McGean, 1996). Most forest-fringe communities, and marginal farmers and landless workers in particular, rely on forests for their basic needs for fuelwood, fodder, small timber, and even food and medicines.[4] For this reason, communities have always protected and utilized forest resources. Building on this traditional relationship, the JFM programme was developed to empower communities to protect and manage forests. This programme formalized the role of local communities in forest management. Experience with JFM has been mixed and several key lessons have been learned in the process. These are discussed in the next section.

Farmers. Farmers, including those living far from forests, now supply about 50% of India's wood from non-forest lands (MoEF, 1999). This has offset the decline in supplies from state forests that has resulted from an increased focus on conservation and the imposition of felling bans in several states. Farmers mainly grow block or field bund plantations of commercially valuable fast-growing species. However, market uncertainty and government control over the harvesting and transport of timber sometimes act as a disincentives for these forest producers.

Development Assistance Agencies. Development assistance agencies play an important role in the forestry sector in India. External assistance has become an important source of funds for forest activities over the past two decades. Between 1981–82 and 1991–92, the percentage share of external assistance in the total budget expenditure for the forestry sector was around 30%. In 1999, 19 externally-assisted forestry projects with a total budget of over Rs. 42 billion were under implementation in 13 states and another five with a total outlay of over Rs. 26 billion were in the pipeline. In 1998-99, the total expenditure of externally-assisted projects was Rs. 8.3 billion, against a total annual expenditure of Rs. 15 billion (MoEF, 1999).

Non Government Organizations (NGOs). The NGO community in India is diverse and vibrant. There is considerable variation in the size of the NGOs and the areas of their operation – from national to village levels. NGO programmes vary widely in the forestry sector and include facilitation, implementation and activism.

The facilitation role includes research, training, policy analysis, documentation and the organization of seminars and workshops. An NGO – Kalpavriksh – is coordinating the National Biodiversity Strategy and Action Plan (NBSAP) process. The implementation role involves execution of projects and programmes in the field, either independently or in collaboration with government agencies. Larger conservation NGOs such as World Wide Fund for Nature (WWF) India and Wildlife Trust of India (WTI) are implementing some programmes that encompass ecosystem approaches to SFM. The activist NGOs generally focus on issues related to environmental degradation, peoples' rights and justice. They often act as pressure groups for changes in policy or practice. For example, a few years ago NGOs such as the Centre for Science and Environment, WWF-India and Society for Promotion of Wastelands Development successfully lobbied against the leasing of state forest lands to industry for plantations.

NGOs have been playing an important role in programmes such as JFM. Information available from six states indicates that 1,061 NGOs are involved in the JFM programme in these states (MoEF, 2002).[5] The level of NGO participation, however, varies considerably from state to state – from very limited participation in states such as Himachal Pradesh and West Bengal to very active participation in Andhra Pradesh where over 250 NGOs are involved in the JFM programme.

---

3   According to one estimate, about 147 million people live in and around forests in India (FSI, 1999).
4   Fuelwood is one of the most important products (in terms of quantity) extracted from India's forests. Of the total demand for wood in the country, it is estimated that over 80% of the demand is just for fuelwood (Saigal *et al.*, 2002).
5   Andhra Pradesh, Manipur, Tamil Nadu, Tripura, Uttar Pradesh and Uttaranchal.

The Corporate Sector. Legal restrictions prevent the corporate sector from playing a significant role in managing forests or raising plantations on state forestlands. However, more than 90% of India's wood-based products are processed by the private sector (MoEF, 1999). Most processing is done in small units, as some 98 % of the 23,000 saw mills have an annual log intake of 3000m³ or less (MoEF, 1999). The total consumption of wood by the processing industries is between 24 to 30 million m³ per year, according to the National Forestry Action Programme (MoEF, 1999), although other estimates of this figure vary widely. As the national policy and legal framework is not favourable to corporate sector involvement on state forest lands, it is unlikely that it will be able to play any significant role in the near future.

The National Forest Policy and Forest (Conservation) Act both actively discourage private sector involvement on state forest lands as is evident from the following extracts from the policy and Act, respectively.

> "Natural forests serve as a gene pool resource and help to maintain ecological balance. Such forests will not, therefore, be made available to industries for undertaking plantation and for any other activities." (paragraph 4.9.) (MoEF, 1988)

> "Notwithstanding anything contained in any other law for the time being in force in a State, no State Government or other authority shall make, except with the prior approval of the Central Government, any order directing that any forest land or any portion thereof may be assigned by way of lease or otherwise to any private person or to any authority, corporation, agency or any other organisation not owned, managed or controlled by Government."(Sub-clause 2 (iii) of the Forest (Conservation) Act, 1980)

A working group of the Planning Commission also examined this issue in 1998 and recommended against the leasing of even degraded forest lands to industry. India does not therefore experience the problems that have been encountered in other tropical countries where industrial forestry concessions have been a major driver of forest change.

The private sector is, however, involved in promoting tree plantations on agriculture and other non-forest lands. Many forest-based industries distribute tree seedlings to farmers. A survey of just 12 companies revealed that they were supplying over 53 million seedlings annually (Saigal *et al.*, 2002). The draft National Environment Policy recently released by the Central Government opens the way for public-private partnerships on issues such as environmental monitoring and more of these kinds of partnerships may develop in the near future.

Policy and Legal Framework

The broad policy framework at the national level is provided by the National Forest Policy, 1988, and the National Conservation Strategy and Policy Statement on Environment and Development, 1992.

The National Forest Policy stresses the management of forests for their environmental and ecological functions and for meeting the subsistence needs of people at the forest margins. It has set a national goal of bringing at least one-third of the country's land area under tree cover. The 'ecosystem' orientation of the policy is clear from the following quotes:

> "The principal aim of forest policy must be to ensure environmental stability and maintenance of ecological balance including atmospheric equilibrium which are vital for sustenance of all life forms,

human, animal and plant. The derivation of direct economic benefit must be subordinated to this principal aim." (paragraph 2.2.)

"The life of tribals and other poor living within and near forests revolves around forests. The rights and concessions enjoyed by them should be fully protected. Their domestic requirements of fuelwood, fodder, minor forest produce and construction timber should be the first charge on forest produce." (paragraph 4.3.4.3.) (MoEF, 1988)

The National Conservation Strategy and Policy Statement on Environment and Development focus on issues related to sustainable development and provide guidelines to "weave environmental considerations into the fabric of our national life and our development process." They provide strategies for dealing with several issues related to conservation of natural resources, including forests. They recognise that *"it is difficult to clearly delineate the causes and consequences of environmental degradation in terms of simple one-to-one relationships. The causes and effects are often interwoven in complex webs of social, technological and environmental factors."* (paragraph 2.13.) The Strategy also recognises the need for people's involvement in the conservation and use of resources such as common lands and degraded forests and supports the use of traditional skills and knowledge in conservation programmes. (paragraphs 5.2.3.1 and 5.2.4.1.) (MoEF, 1992)

These policies reflect elements of the ecosystem approach, and are radically different from the earlier forest policies viz. The National Forest Policy Resolution, 1952 and the Report of the National Commission on Agriculture, 1976. In fact, the new policy environment has reversed the basic approach of management, as the earlier policies were focussed on timber and revenue and considered local communities as a burden on forests. This becomes clear from the following quotes:

"The accident of a village being situated close to the forest doesn't prejudice the right of the country as a whole to receive the benefits of a national asset." (GoI, 1952)

"Production of industrial wood would have to be the raison dᶜ être for the existence of forests. It should be project-oriented and commercially feasible from the point of view of cost and return." (GoI, 1976)

"Free supply of forest produce to the rural population and their rights and privileges have brought destruction to the forest and so it is necessary to reverse the process. The rural people have not contributed much towards the maintenance or regeneration of the forests. Having over-exploited the resources, they cannot in all fairness expect that somebody else will take the trouble of providing them with forest produce free of charge....One of the principal objectives of social forestry is to make it possible to meet these needs in full from readily accessible areas and thereby lighten the burden on production forestry. Such needs should be met by farm forestry, extension forestry and by re-habilitating scrub forests and degraded forests." (GoI, 1976)

The national level legal framework is provided by six main laws. These are: The Indian Forest Act, 1927; The Wildlife (Protection) Amendment Act, 2002; The Forest (Conservation) Act, 1980 (amended 1988); The Environment (Protection) Act, 1986 and The Biological Diversity Act, 2002 and The Constitution (Seventy-third) Amendment Act, 1992.

As with the policy framework, the legal framework has also evolved over time to include elements consistent with ecosystem approaches. The basic Indian Forest Act of 1927 is a colonial legal instrument that mainly deals with the process of reservation of forest lands and their administration by the state. The next set of laws that were introduced in 1970s and 1980s, the Wildlife (Protection) Act, 1972, Forest (Conservation) Act, 1980, and Environment (Protection) Act, 1986, are all conservation-oriented laws. The Wildlife (Protection) Act provides for protection of wild animals and plants by regulating hunting, trade and collection of specific forest products. It governs national parks and sanctuaries in the country.[6] The Forest (Conservation) Act mainly regulates the conversion of forest land for non-forest purposes. It restricts the leasing or assigning of forest lands to any private entity as well as the clearing of naturally-grown trees on forest lands. State governments are required to obtain approval from the central government before carrying out these actions. The Environment (Protection) Act, 1986, empowers the central government to take appropriate measures for the purpose of protecting or improving the environment.

Laws issued in the 1990s, and later, begin to reflect elements of ecosystem thinking. The Wildlife (Protection) Amendment Act, 2002, has a provision for advisory committees for wildlife sanctuaries, which have representation from NGOs as well as Panchayati Raj Institutions (PRIs).[7] The role of the advisory committee is to render advice on measures to be taken for better conservation and management of the sanctuary including participation of people living within and around the sanctuary. Two new categories of protected areas – Conservation Reserves and Community Reserves – have also been introduced. Community Reserves are to be established in areas where the community or an individual has volunteered to conserve wildlife and its habitat. The aim of such community reserves is the protection of fauna, flora and traditional or cultural conservation values and practices.

The Biological Diversity Act, 2002, specifies that a Biodiversity Management Committee should be constituted by every local body within its area for the purpose of promoting conservation, sustainable use and documentation of biological diversity. The Act also provides for the creation of biodiversity heritage sites and the declaration of certain species as 'threatened'.

The Constitution (Seventy-third) Amendment Act, 1992, was introduced to promote empowerment at the grassroots level by establishing democratically-elected three-tier Panchayat Raya Institutions for local self-governance. Schedule XI of the Constitution lists 29 subjects with respect to which PRIs may prepare and implement plans for economic development and social justice for the area under their jurisdiction. This list includes social forestry and farm forestry, minor forest produce, soil conservation, land improvement, watershed development, fuel and fodder, and maintenance of community assets. This Act is a significant attempt to decentralize decision making on several issues, including forestry.[8] India is thus one of the few countries to have elements of ecosystem approaches to forests enshrined in its constitution.

While there are several problems even with these new laws (e.g. community reserves cannot be established on government lands), the overall policy and legislative framework has evolved from a timber-oriented, state-centred view of forests inherited from the colonial period to a much broader and more participative vision of forestry practised today. These changes are all consistent with the global move towards ecosystem-based approaches to forestry and commenced long before the debate on ecosystem approaches was engaged at the inter-governmental level.

---

6   At present, there are 89 National Parks and 500 Wildlife Sanctuaries in the country, covering approximately 156,000km^2 (MoEF, 2003).

7   PRIs are the third tier of government in the country after central and state governments. These are democratically-elected bodies.

8   The Provisions of Panchayats (Extension to the Scheduled Areas) Act, 1996, extends the provisions of the Constitution (Seventy-third) Amendment Act, 1992, to schedule V areas (tribal majority areas outside certain states of northeastern India) and provides extensive powers to gram sabhas (general body of the village panchayat) for management of natural resources in areas under their jurisdiction.

Time Line of Major Events

India has undertaken a number of steps to conserve forests and biodiversity and to safeguard the environment. Taking 1972, the date of the United Nations Conference on the Human Environment (held in Stockholm) as a starting point, Table 2 provides a summary of the major environment and forest-related events.

Table 2. Timeline of major environment and forest related events in India

Year	Event
1972	Wildlife (Protection) Act
1973	Project Tiger
1976	Ratification of Convention on International Trade in Endangered Species (CITES); 42nd Constitutional Amendment (protection of environment, including forests and wildlife, included in directive principles of state policy and fundamental duties of citizens).
1980	Department of Environment; Forest (Conservation) Act
1981	Ratification of Ramsar Convention
1985	Ministry of Environment and Forests; National Wastelands Development Board
1986	Environment (Protection) Act
1988	National Forest Policy
1990	Joint Forest Management Circular
1991	Coastal Regulation Zone Notification
1992	National Conservation Strategy and Policy Statement on Environment and Development; Project Elephant; 73rd Constitutional Amendment
1993	Environment Action Programme
1994	Ratification of CBD
1999	National Programme
1994	Environmental Impact Assessment Notification; Ratification of CBD
1999	Biodiversity Macro-Plan and Strategy
2001	The Coimbatore Charter on Environment and Forests
2002	Wildlife (Protection) Amendment Act; Biological Diversity Act; Wildlife Conservation Strategy; National Wildlife Action Plan; Ratification of Kyoto Protocol
2004	National Biodiversity Strategy and Action Plan (Draft Report)

Major Innovations towards Ecosystem Approaches and Sustainable Forest Management

Joint Forest Management

Perhaps the most significant innovation in Indian forestry has been the ambitious programme known as Joint Forest Management (JFM). This programme involves local communities in the management of state forest lands. Under JFM, the Forest Department and the village community enter into an agreement to jointly protect and manage state forest lands adjoining the village and to share the responsibilities for, and benefits from, these lands. The community gets greater access to a number of non-timber forest products and a share in timber revenue. In return it takes increased responsibility for the protection of forest from fire, grazing and illicit harvesting. In some cases, a Memorandum of

Understanding is signed between the forest protection committee and the Forest Department. In many cases, a forest management plan, that includes village development activities, commonly called a micro-plan is prepared and funds are provided by the Forest Department for its execution. The details vary from state to state as each state has issued its own JFM resolution. In all states, the ownership of the land remains with the government and only management responsibility and a share of the forest offtake belong to the community.

Table 3. Progress of Joint Forest Management (as on September 10, 2003)[9]

State	Number of JFM Groups	Area under JFM (ha)
Arunachal Pradesh	308	80,217.00
Assam	503	79,251.00
Bihar	493	267,240.94
Chhattisgarh	6,881	2,846,762.16
Dadra & Nagar Haveli	NA	NA
Goa	26	13,000.00
Gujarat	1,424	160,525.41
Haryana	875	56,000.00
Himachal Pradesh	835	290,922.80
Jammu & Kashmir	935	49,544.00
Jharkhand	3,358	847,967.93
Karnataka	3,470	232,734.00
Kerala	323	170,712.00
Madhya Pradesh	13,698	5,500,000.00
Maharashtra	5,322	1,411,215.00
Manipur	205	93,941.00
Mizoram	249	10,980.00
Nagaland	306	22,930.00
Orissa	15,985	821,504.00
Punjab	287	56,243.95
Rajasthan	3,667	376,766.00
Sikkim	158	600.00
Tamil Nadu	1,816	445,965.00
Tripura	234	34,154.00
Uttar Pradesh	2,030	112,652.93
Uttaranchal [10]	10,107	859,028.00
West Bengal	3,892	604,334.00
Total	**84,632**	**17,331,955.12**

Source: Bahuguna *et al.*, 2004

JFM is a direct outcome of the forest policy of 1988, which radically changed forest management objectives from timber and revenue to conservation and local communities' needs. Successful experiments with community involvement in protecting state forest lands in the 1970s and 80s, notably at

---

9   The figures in this table indicate the total number of JFM groups that have been created and do not indicate how many of these groups are actually functional.

10 Van Panchayats (forest councils) are also included in the state's JFM figures.

Arabari in West Bengal and Sukhomajri in Haryana, also played an important role in the initiation of the JFM programme in the country. The programme was formally launched in 1990 when the central government issued guidelines for the involvement of communities and voluntary agencies in the protection and management of degraded forestlands.

Over the past two decades JFM has emerged as a major forest management strategy in the country and, by September 2003, there were 84,632 JFM groups protecting and managing over 17 million hectares of state forest lands (see Table 3).

There have been several positive impacts of the JFM programme. Relationships between Forest Department staff and local communities have improved in many places. Participating communities have increased their incomes and the condition of the forests has improved. In a case that illustrates how seriously some communities take their forest protection responsibilities, JFM group members in Botha village in Maharashtra were reported to have postponed a wedding in the village in order to fight a forest fire. This would have been unthinkable in the pre-JFM days (Jha, 2004). In several areas, traditional forest protection practices have also been revived, for example *kesar chhanta* (sacred groves) in Rajasthan (Ghose, 2004).

The increased income of communities participating in the JFM programme, reported in some places, has generally come from the provision of employment and productive assets by the Forest Department; an improvement in the condition of the forest (and thus greater availability of certain forest products) and a greater share in produce/revenue accruing to the communities.

JFM group members have access to significant wage labour opportunities in various forestry operations. These employment opportunities are greatest in areas where externally-assisted projects are in operation. For instance, it is estimated that over 40 million person days of work were created through JFM-related activities during the six years (1994–2000) of the Andhra Pradesh Forestry Project (Mukherji, 2004). In Maharashtra, Rs 973,000 have been spent on the micro-plan of each JFM group covered under the World Bank assisted project (Jha, 2004). A significant proportion of this went as wages to the JFM group members.

In most areas productive assets are provided to the JFM group to enhance people's income and to reduce their dependence on forests. For instance, in Harda Division of Madhya Pradesh, Rs 40.8 million were spent on creating additional irrigation facilities (81 stopdams, 51 lift irrigation systems) in JFM villages, which significantly increased crop yields in several villages (Dubey, 2001).

Regeneration of forests results in increased availability of products such as fuelwood, fodder and non-timber products and these in turn provide income opportunities. For instance, in Gujarat, income from milk has gone up in several villages after the introduction of JFM. It has been reported that income from milk has increased from Rs 100,000 per month to Rs 300,000 per month in Balethi village in Rajpipla (West) Division. In Nisana village (Vyara Division), milk production has increased from 40,000 to 200,000 litres per year (Khanna and Prasad, 2004). In the Joyalbhanga JFM group in Midnapore, West Bengal, each woman is able to earn between Rs 4,500 to 6,000 annually from the sale of *sal* (*Shorea robusta*) leaf plates (Ecotech Services, 2000).

In a few states such as West Bengal, JFM groups have started earning income through intermediate and final harvests. In just four states (Andhra Pradesh, Punjab, Tamil Nadu and West Bengal), JFM groups received Rs 62.59 million through benefit sharing mechanisms in 2000-01 (MoEF, 2002). In West Bengal, although the percentage shared is one of the lowest in the country (25%), it is estimated that each FPC has received about Rs 70,000 per year. In addition, they also earn income from employment in harvesting operations (Palit, 2004). As part of the JFM programme, village community funds have been created in several states. Information available from seven states indicates that the total community funds under JFM at the end of 2000–01 were Rs 557.09 million (MoEF, 2002).[11]

In many places, the forest has regenerated following the protection efforts of the communities. A study in diverse ecological regions of India has demonstrated that JFM has resulted in significant increases in plant diversity and biomass production (Murali *et al*, 2004). At the national level, the 1999 assessment by the Forest Survey of India (FSI) showed that the overall forest and tree cover in the country increased by 3,896km^2 and dense cover by 10,098km^2 , compared to the assessment made in 1997. One of the reasons cited for this improvement was implementation of the JFM programme (FSI, 1999).

In spite of several positive impacts, many challenges still remain to be addressed. Although several provisions in state JFM resolutions safeguard the interests of weaker sections of the population, most JFM groups are dominated by village elites. Weaker groups such as scheduled castes, scheduled tribes and women, are often marginalized and have little say in the group's decision-making process even though they have the greatest dependence on forests and are most directly affected by JFM. An issue closely linked to elite domination is that of inequitable sharing of costs and benefits of forest protection. Under the current JFM model, the community has to forego a part of the current benefits for future usufructuary rights and a share in timber revenue many years later. This has serious equity implications as the decision to 'close' a forest patch to allow regeneration has very different meaning to a large farmer having minimal dependence on forests and to a landless person or artisan (such as a potter or ironsmith) whose livelihood depends on the forest. Women also have to pay a higher cost when forests are protected, as they must walk greater distances to collect fuelwood, shift to smokier fuels such as dry leaves, and/or 'steal' from protected forest patches. Similarly, a grazing ban also affects landless and marginal farmers much more than it does large farmers with irrigation facilities. Many poor families are forced to sell off their goats, which are perceived to be destroyers of forests by the JFM group, and lose an important source of nutrition and income.

While JFM is a partnership between the Forest Department and the community, the Department wields disproportionate powers. In fact, JFM groups are under total control of the Forest Department. In most states, the Forest Department provides the Secretary of the JFM Group. This person plays an important role in convening meetings, keeping records and also implementing physical works. S/he also controls the JFM group's bank account and in many areas also controls the JFM group's common fund.

The Forest Department generally retains the rights to unilaterally dissolve the JFM group or its executive committee. Any appeal against such action usually lies with a senior official of the Department. By and large, JFM microplans are prepared by officials. Cases of exploitation of local communities by these officials have also been reported (Diwan *et al.*, 2001).

In several cases, JFM has resulted in increased inter-community conflicts over boundaries and access rights as customary (and even legal) access rights of different groups are rarely taken into account when initiating JFM. In some cases the introduction of JFM has interfered with the functioning of existing institutions such as *van panchayats* of Uttaranchal and Community Forest Management (CFM) groups in Orissa, Jharkhand and Gujarat.[12]

---

11 The seven states are: Andhra Pradesh, Chhattisgarh, Manipur, Tamil Nadu, Tripura, Uttar Pradesh and Uttaranchal.

12 In several states, notably Orissa, Jharkhand and Gujarat, many communities have started to protect forests on their own without any outside support (from FD or NGOs). This is commonly referred to as community forest management (CFM) to distinguish it from JFM.

One of the biggest shortcomings of the JFM programme is that it lacks a firm legal basis. Except in a handful of states the JFM programme is based on administrative orders that can be withdrawn or changed at any time. JFM groups in most states are also merely registered with the Forest Department and hold no independent legal status. The lack of adequate legal cover for JFM creates several problems. In many states, the terms of partnership between the government and the local community have been changed several times through changes in the JFM resolutions. For instance, in Orissa, JFM groups formed on the basis of 1988 and 1990 government resolutions were declared null and void by the resolution of July 2003 (Pattanaik, 2004). There have also been cases where a forest patch being protected by a particular village under JFM has been allocated to an industry, which may be holding a 'legal' lease. Such examples have been reported from Orissa (Sarin *et al*., 2003) and Gujarat (A. Gupta pers. comm., 8 August 2003).

In spite of all these problems, JFM is an improvement on the earlier situation when local communities were considered a burden on forests and there was very little space for civil society involvement in the forestry sector.[13] Some of the challenges listed above are being addressed by revising the JFM resolutions and in some states such as Andhra Pradesh, there is a move towards providing progressively greater powers to the local community.

Ecodevelopment

The conflict between conservation and communities is pronounced around protected areas. The Ecodevelopment Programme has been established to address such conflicts. Under ecodevelopment, subsistence strategies are developed for the local people through improving productivity and utilization of their lands and enhancing their income. This is intended to help reduce the dependence of these communities on the protected areas. The Ecodevelopment programme has similarities to the Integrated Conservation and Development Programmes operated by many development assistance agencies and NGOs in other countries.

The concept of ecodevelopment was first articulated in a central government document entitled "Eliciting public support for wildlife conservation," published in 1983. In the same year, it also got formal recognition in the National Wildlife Action Plan. Ecodevelopment got much focus in the Eighth Five Year Plan (1992–97), as there was growing realization among national policy makers that the "protection-exclusion" system of wildlife management was not yielding the desired results. There were often increasing conflicts between wildlife managers and local communities and the conservation values of protected areas were getting eroded. In early 1990s, the central government launched an ecodevelopment scheme around selected protected areas, mainly tiger reserves. Ecodevelopment has now become an integral part of wildlife conservation schemes.

The World Bank funded two ecodevelopment projects in the 1990s. The India Ecodevelopment Project began in 1995–96 as a five-year pilot project and covered seven protected areas (Buxa Tiger Reserve, Palamau Tiger Reserve, Ranthambore Tiger Reserve, Gir National Park, Pench Tiger Reserve, Nagarhole Tiger Reserve and Periyar Tiger Reserve). The Forestry Research Education and Extension Project was started in 1994 for a period of five years. It had a sub-project titled Conservation of Biodiversity under which two protected areas *viz*. the Great Himalayan National Park in north India and Kalakkad Mundanthurai Tiger Reserve in south India were selected for experimenting with community-centred biodiversity conservation approaches. In addition to these two projects, support for ecodevelopment activities has also been provided by the World Bank under its general forestry sector projects e.g. Madhya Pradesh Forestry Project.

---

13 Barring a few exceptions like *van panchayats* in Uttaranchal and tribal councils in northeastern states.

Under the ecodevelopment programme, Ecodevelopment Committees are formed at the village level. These work according to the guidelines in the ecodevelopment resolutions of the state governments. The committees are mainly constituted in the fringe areas of national parks and sanctuaries and work for development of alternate livelihoods, which reduce people's pressure on the protected areas and also increase their stake in conservation. Most of the committees have received financial support under ecodevelopment projects or schemes. A number of innovations have taken place under ecodevelopment programme, which have resulted in a shift towards the principles of ecosystem approaches. The following four cases are good examples.[14]

Kanha Tiger Reserve. Kanha Tiger Reserve in Madhya Pradesh has successfully used the core-buffer strategy to balance conservation and community needs. The core area of the reserve, about 940 square kilometres, which is a legally constituted national park, is buffered by a total area of 1,005km² of which about 60% is reserved forests and the rest village land. This zone acts as a two-way buffer between the reserve and the people. While it helps the people in meeting their subsistence needs for forest products, it also acts as a critical habitat for animals dispersing from the core zone and reduces instances of human-animal conflict such as crop raiding.

The integrated management plan covers both the core and buffer zones. Under the Director of the Reserve, there are two Deputy Directors. While one Deputy Director is responsible for protection and wildlife management, the other Deputy Director looks after ecodevelopment and conflict mitigation measures. The forestry operations in the buffer zone are oriented towards meeting subsistence requirements of the local communities and biodiversity conservation even though these forests are quite valuable commercially.

Periyar Tiger Reserve. Periyar Tiger Reserve in Kerala has tried an innovative ecodevelopment strategy under which three different types of ecodevelopment committees have been constituted on the basis of geographic settings, occupational patterns and dependency levels. Neighbourhood committees have been formed at the village level and cover all families in the village. Their micro-plans focus on agricultural improvement and economic upliftment. User Group committees are made up of members who are heavily dependent on the reserve. The focus here is on reduction of the negative impacts of people on the reserve by facilitating alternate livelihoods. The members of such committees are selected based on their link to a particular resource and do not necessarily belong to one settlement.

Professional committees have been constituted for promoting livelihoods that have a potential for long-term positive interaction with the reserve. Membership of these committees is made up of individuals or groups with close interaction with the reserve (even conflicting ones) and those who have intimate local knowledge. In fact, several tribal poachers and smugglers have become trekking and rafting guides for tourists and earn good incomes from ecotourism activities. Other benefits are in the form of drastic reduction of poaching of wild animals such as elephants and smuggling of ivory, sandalwood, cinnamon bark, etc.

Participatory planning methods have been used so that the management plan of the reserve is based not only on scientific inputs but also on the views of fringe communities and other stakeholders. This has resulted in detailed landscape level planning. As an illustration, separate areas are set aside for pil-

---

14 This section is based on the following:
   1. personal communication: S. Upadhyay pers. comm., 22 July 2004; V. Upadhyay. pers. comm., 27 July 2004; M. Mishra pers. comm., 27 July 2004; S. Pandey pers. comm.,30 July 2004.
   2. Websites: http://news.nationalgeographic.com/news/; http://www.periyartigerreserve.org/html/iedp.html; http://www.cseindia.org/dte-supplement/himalayan20040731/himalayan_index.html; http://lnweb18.worldbank.org/sar/sa.nsf; http://projecttiger.nic.in/kalakad.html; http://sdnp.delhi.nic.in/nbsap

grimages (there is a famous temple in the area which attracts many pilgrims), ecotourism and cattle grazing.

Peoples' Protected Areas

Another initiative similar to ecodevelopment is that of the creation of People's Protected Areas in Chhattisgarh. The objective is to remove the conflict between conservation and development. People's protected areas are based on the assumption that development of forest-fringe villages is a prerequisite for forest conservation. It is an attempt to follow a people-centred approach to conservation that lays equal emphasis on poverty alleviation and improvement in the quality of life of the poor.

The People's Protected Area concept encompasses three broad approaches: (1) In-situ conservation; (2) Ex-situ conservation; and (3) Livelihood security. For in-situ conservation, local people are actively involved in protecting forests from excessive cattle grazing, fires and illicit felling. Certain areas in the forest are designated for meeting the basic needs of the local community such as fuelwood, small timber, non-timber products etc. For ex-situ conservation, plantations are raised outside forest lands. Under the livelihood security component, the focus is on economic development, primarily by coordinating the efforts of various line departments working in the area. This model has been tried in the Dhamtari Forest Division since 2001 (Chhattisgarh FD, 2003).

The Wildlife Conservation Strategy, 2002, also focuses on protecting the interests of poor and tribals living around protected areas. It recommends that lands falling within 10km. of the boundaries of national parks and sanctuaries should be notified as eco-fragile zones under the Environment (Protection) Act.

Landscape Level Initiatives

The National Wildlife Action Plan (2002–2016) that aims to bring 10% of the country's area into the protected area network also focuses on landscape level initiatives. There is considerable emphasis on landscape level planning and development of buffer areas and 'corridors' to link different protected areas. There is greater emphasis on stakeholder participation, especially of local communities, as well as greater appreciation of the need to balance conservation and local community needs. There is a proposal to recognise areas within a radius of five kilometres of the boundary of national parks and sanctuaries as special development areas for which the Planning Commission has been requested to allocate separate funds.

There are a number of specific initiatives at the landscape level that incorporate elements of ecosystem approaches. Two key examples of these larger scale conservation programmes are Project Tiger and the Terai Arc Restoration Initiative.[15]

---

15 Other important landscape level initiatives are Asian Rhino and Elephant Action Strategy (AREAS) of WWF India and Wild Lands Programme of Wildlife Trust of India. Under AREAS programme four priority landscapes have been identified for conservation. These are: Nilgiris-Eastern Ghats (elephants) in Karnataka, North Bank (elephants), and Kaziranga-Karbi Anglong (rhinos and elephants) in Assam and Western Terai (rhinos) in Uttar Pradesh. Under Wild Lands Programme, an attempt is being made to create a buffer for the Protected Areas by identifying, prioritising, securing and/or managing privately owned wild lands of critical importance to threatened wild species, thereby contributing to their conservation. The focus of the programme is on maintaining and/or developing wildlife corridors to check fragmentation of wildlife habitats (Source: http://worldwildlife.org and http://wildlifetrustofindia.org).

Project Tiger

Project Tiger, launched in 1973, is one of the oldest conservation programmes in the country. Its aim is the conservation of the threatened tiger population (which had collapsed to less than 2000 individuals) and its habitat. Initially nine tiger reserves were formed but the number had increased to 27 by 2003. The project has resulted in a significant increase in the number of tigers in the country – according to the tiger census, the tiger population rose from 1,827 in 1972 to 3,642 in 2002.

Initially, the project adopted traditional conservation approaches but this is now changing to incorporate ecosystem approaches. There is now an emphasis on managing the landscape and linking different tiger reserves through corridors. There is greater attention to managing the wildlife populations within the carrying capacity of the habitat so that habitat degradation and conflicts with neighbouring communities can be reduced. A minimum core of 300km^2 with a sizeable buffer has been recommended for each project area.[16] Attempts are also being made to bring about greater compatibility between conservation and local community needs, especially in the buffer areas. The recommendations of a workshop co-organized by Project Tiger in 2001 clearly indicate a shift in thinking towards the principles of ecosystem approaches (see Box 1).

Box 1   **Ecosystem approaches adopted by Project Tiger in 2001[17]**

A.   **Incorporation of Ecological Concerns in Landscape/Regional Planning**

- Identify on priority basis, clusters of Protected Areas (PAs) and non-PA areas, which seem contiguous through potential corridors and linkages.
- Consider assemblage of large mammals and patterns of dispersal on the basis of recorded events (scientific and historical) to delineate the landscape.
- Characterize ecological features and attributes such as terrain, topography, hydrology, artifacts, flora and fauna in identified landscapes.
- Superimpose land use features, settlements, and livestock distribution to assess biotic pressures on the landscape.
- Undertake SWOT (Strength, Weakness, Opportunities and Threats) analysis to understand interrelationships between ecological, social, cultural and economic attributes.
- Assign priorities, based on the statement of conservation values and objectives.
- Evolve mechanisms and processes to ensure strategy continuum across Wildlife Management Plans, Forest Working Plans and District and *Panchayat* Plans.

B.   **Building Alliances: Mechanisms for Inter-Agency Cooperation, Inter-State Relations, Trans-Boundary Issues and Ecodevelopment**

- Build an information base through research and monitoring, integrate into the planning process; and integrate local indigenous knowledge and modern scientific knowledge.
- Encourage and strengthen local institutions through appropriate legal and research inputs.
- Pick up commonalties of agenda between different agencies and Government sectors for integrated planning (e.g. water resources, ecotourism, rural development, watershed development, employment and agriculture).
- Assess Tenth Five-Year Plan approach paper and sectional drafts from the biodiversity point of view, and develop strong mechanisms for effective advocacy for Regional Planning.

Cont.

---

16 Source: http://projecttiger.nic.in
17 Regional Planning for Conservation and Development: Recommendations of the National Workshop, 6-8 August, 2001, New Delhi, jointly organised by Wildlife Institute of India and Project Tiger.

Box 1	Ecosystem approaches adopted by Project Tiger in 2001 (cont.)

- Institutionalize dialogue at different levels (PA, State, Village and within FDs) and build alliances with people's initiatives.
- Revitalize institutions/statutory bodies (e.g. State Wildlife Advisory Board, National Board for Wildlife).
- Strengthen inter-sector linkages and evolve planned mechanisms for resource amelioration, including assigning overriding priority to local community needs.
- Identify and use existing fora to build consensus on ecological and economic concerns and also sensitize others (such as through Indian Society of Ecological Economics, and the NBSAP network).
- Build capacity through skill development and attitudinal reorientation of Government organizations, NGOs, *Panchayats* and communities to achieve the objectives of integration of conservation and development at a regional scale.
- Develop regional planning as an integral component of their curricula of existing formal institutions.
- Establish fora and mechanisms for conflict resolution at different levels.
- Set up PA and landscape level bodies comprising primary stakeholders for participatory management.
- Develop demonstration models to promote the concept of integrated regional planning.
- Formulate land/water use plans at local, state, national levels based on the regional approach. These plans should identify critical conservation areas within and across stated levels where human activities should be compatible with conservation values.

Source: National Biodiversity Strategy Action Plan. 2004. Final Technical Report of the UNDP-GEF Sponsored Project. Unpublished.

In 1992, similar approaches were used as a basis for a second major programme to conserve elephants. Project Elephant is being implemented in 12 states of India and 14 elephant reserves had been set up by 2002. There is also an attempt to conserve migratory routes of elephants (MoEF, 2003).

Terai Arc Restoration Initiative[18]

The Terai Arc Restoration Initiative is one of the largest landscape level interventions in South Asia. It was initiated by WWF along with partners in India and Nepal. It is supported by the World Bank/WWF Alliance for Forest Conservation and Sustainable Use. The initiative covers approximately five million hectares of land from Nepal's Bagmati River in the east to India's Yamuna River in the west. The goal is to restore and reconnect eleven national parks in Nepal and India to create one continuous landscape – a green corridor that will allow wildlife to flourish while local people also benefit.

The initiative is based on the concept of *conservation landscapes*, which are defined by WWF as " *areas of land, regional in scale, which can support and maintain a viable metapopulation of animals linked by safe and suitable habitat corridors, together with an adequate natural prey base. On the ground, this will often mean a series of well-managed core protected areas (national parks, wildlife sanctuaries, etc.), together with any buffer zones, linked together by dedicated corridors of suitable habitat or by land-use that is conservation friendly.*"

Terai Arc partners work with all levels of society from local communities, village and district level groups and line agencies. These groups are involved with the planning process at the landscape-level. The development of corridors and of community conservation partnerships to reduce human-animal

---

18 Source: http://www.worldwildlife.org

conflict are the main activities. Along with this, reduction in poaching, improvement in transboundary and international cooperation, and reconciling the needs of animals and people in a mutually beneficial manner are other focus areas.

The Terai Arc ecoregion initiative thus attempts to integrate biodiversity and livelihoods and address these challenges in an integrated way. The initiative is significant because 60% of the people own less than one hectare of land and most of them are below the poverty line. Poverty, seen as the root cause of biodiversity loss, is thus directly targeted.[19]

The Terai Arc initiative is extraordinarily ambitious and it is too soon to say to what extent it will be possible to achieve its objectives. Probably partial success is the best that can be expected. The alleviation of the poverty of the large population of this area will certainly be beyond the scope of conservation organizations alone and will be much more dependent upon general development patterns in the countries of the region. However this is one example where virtually all of the CBD principles of the Ecosystem Approach are being attempted in a single region and it is illustrative of the problems of trying to implement the "full package".

Key Processes Promoting Ecosystem Approaches to Forest Management

In addition to various programmes and projects, two processes have clearly underpinned attempts to achieve ecosystem approaches to forest management in India. These are: Bhopal India Process on SFM and National Biodiversity Strategy and Action Plan.

Bhopal India Process on Sustainable Forest Management

In order to promote the concept of SFM in India, the Central Government constituted a task force and designated the Indian Institute of Forest Management (IIFM), Bhopal, as the lead agency for SFM. IIFM started work on SFM in 1998 and organized a three day meeting entitled "Evolving Criteria and Indicators for SFM in India". This was done in close association with the Madhya Pradesh Forest Department and Madhya Pradesh Minor Forest Produce (Trade and Development) Federation. A set of draft criteria and indicators were identified and over time refined into a set of eight criteria and 43 indicators. This process is commonly referred to as the Bhopal India Process (see Table 4).

Table 4. Criteria and indicators for sustainable forest management developed under the Bhopal India Process

Criteria	Indicators

1. Increase in the extent of forest and tree cover	1.1 Area and type of forest cover under
	  – man-made forest
	  – natural forest
	1.2 Tree cover outside forest area
	1.3 Area of dense and open forest
	1.4 Forest area diverted for non-forestry use
	1.5 Extent of community managed forest areas

19 Nepal Benefits Beyond Boundaries, How to manage protected areas after the WPC 2003: Workshop on 11 December 2003, also at http://www.iucn.org/places/asia

Criteria	Indicators
2. Maintenance, conservation and enhancement of biodiversity	2.1 Area of protected ecosystems 2.2 Area of fragmented ecosystems 2.3 Number of rare, endangered, threatened and endemic species 2.4 Level of species richness, and biodiversity in selected areas 2.5 Availability of medicinal and aromatic plants in various forest types 2.6 Status of non-destructive harvest of NWFP 2.7 Number of keystone and flagship species in various forest types

3. Maintenance and enhancement of ecosystem function and vitality	3.1 Status of natural regeneration
	3.2 Status of secondary forests
	3.3 Incidence of:
	    a) Pests and diseases
	    b) Weed infestation
	    c) Grazing and
	    d) Fire

4. Conservation and maintenance of soil and water resources	4.1 Area under watershed treatment 4.2 Soil erosion status 4.3 Area under ravines, saline and alkaline soils 4.4 Ground water table in the vicinity of forest areas
5. Maintenance and enhancement of forest resource productivity	5.1 Growing stock of wood 5.2 Volume of production of identified important NWFPs 5.3 Increment in volume of identified species of wood 5.4 Level of financial investment in forestry sector 5.5 Extent of seed production areas, seedling orchards, clonal seed orchards
6. Optimization of forest resource utilization	6.1 Aggregate and per capita consumption of wood and NWFPs 6.2 Import and export of non-wood forest products 6.3 Recorded production of wood and NWFPs 6.4 Direct employment in forestry and forest industries 6.5 Contribution of forests to the income of forest dependent people 6.6 Level of processing and value addition in NWFPs and treatment, seasoning and preservation of wood 6.7 Demand and supply ratio of timber, firewood and fodder
7. Maintenance and enhancement of social cultural and spiritual benefits	7.1 Degree of people's participation: Number of committees and area(s) protected by them 7.2 Use of indigenous technical knowledge: identification, documentation & application 7.3 Quality and extent to which rights and privileges are utilized 7.4 Human development index 7.5 Extent of cultural/ sacred – protected landscapes: forests, trees, ponds, streams etc.
8. Adequacy of policy, legal and institutional framework	8.1 Existing policy and legal framework 8.2 Enabling conditions for participation of community, NGOs, civil society, existence of JFM resolutions, transit rules etc. 8.3 Level of investment in research and development 8.4 Human resource capacity building efforts 8.5 Forest resource accounting 8.6 Monitoring and evaluation mechanism 8.7 Status of information dissemination and utilization

Source: IIFM, 2002

Many of the criteria and indicators reflect an ecosystem approach. Under a project funded by the International Tropical Timber Organization, these criteria and indicators are being applied and field-tested by IIFM in eight forest divisions in Madhya Pradesh and Chhattisgarh (IIFM, 2002).[20] A Sustainability Index based on weighted criteria and indicators is also under development (Kotwal and Horo, 2004). On 16 December 2003, the central government issued a letter to all states urging their Forest Departments to adopt SFM using the eight criteria and 43 indicators developed under the Bhopal India process. Even though the actual progress on the ground is quite slow, the Bhopal India Process has initiated a debate in the forestry bureaucracy on the issue of SFM.

National Biodiversity Strategy and Action Plan [21]

India is currently finalising its National Biodiversity Strategy and Action Plan (NBSAP) based on a process carried out by the Ministry of Environment and Forests between 2000–2003. In a unique arrangement, its technical coordination was undertaken by the NGO, Kalpavriksh, which set up a 15-member Technical and Policy Core Group for the purpose. Over a hundred agencies and individuals were key partners in the process, carrying out action planning and expert reviews at various levels. The process involved consultations and planning with thousands of people across the country.

The NBSAP process has resulted in the formulation of about 18 local-level action plans, 32 state-level plans, ten inter-state ecoregional plans, and 13 national thematic plans. All of these feed into the overall national plan. Each action plan contains a comprehensive review of existing programmes, actors and issues. It establishes a time frame for implementation.

The NBSAP draft national plan document strongly advocates ecosystem approaches for biodiversity conservation in the country as is evident from the following extract from the report:

> "The most important and urgent need is to go beyond the artificial boundaries of compartmentalised land/water uses, and conceptualise the conservation and management of entire landscapes/ waterscapes. This 'landscape' (or 'ecoregional' or 'ecosystem') approach provides a comprehensive framework for bringing together a wide range of different approaches to conservation, helping to integrate or coordinate the various sectors with an interest in biodiversity, and regulate those sectors that could harm it."

> "One of the strengths of such an approach would be to consider ecological systems as a whole, attempting to overcome the hurdles often placed by political boundaries."

Using principles of the Ecosystem Approach, ten ecoregions were chosen for planning under the NBSAP, based primarily upon ecological and cultural attributes but also to some extent upon administrative considerations.

The NBSAP national draft action plan recommends formulation of a National Policy and Perspective Plan on Land and Water Use and also setting up of Ecoregional Authorities for monitoring or regulating an entire ecoregion. It suggests that PAs should be managed with local communities' involvement in such a manner that balances conservation and local community needs. It also suggests strengthening of the decentralized natural resource governance structure by empowering the Gram Sabhas (general body) of the panchayats. The NBSAP draft has been submitted to the Ministry of Environment and Forests but has not yet been accepted. If accepted, it could give a major thrust to ecosystem approaches to forest management.

---

20 These are East Mandla, South Seoni, Sheopur, Obedullahgunj and Jhabua in Madhya Pradesh and Dhamtari and North Bilaspur in Chhattisgarh.
21 Source: MoEF, 2003 and NBSAP, 2004.

Drivers of Change

Conflicts and People's Resistance

Increase in conflicts between local communities and the forest bureaucracy over forest management practices has been a major factor that has forced the government to reassess its policies. In the 1970s and 1980s, there was a focus on establishing commercial plantations on state forest lands, often after felling mixed natural forests, while people were expected to meet their forest product requirements from social forestry plantations on non-forest lands. In fact people were considered a burden on forests.

In many places, local communities protested against the restriction of access to forests and their destruction for commercial purposes. In 1975, a World Bank supported project to replace 20,000ha of native mixed *sal* (*Shorea robusta*) forest with tropical pines in the Bastar District of Madhya Pradesh had to be dropped after protests by local tribal communities (Pathak, 1994; Dogra, 1985; Anderson and Huber, 1988, in: Saigal, 1998). In Bihar, there were protests against replacement of natural forests with teak plantations (CSE, 1982, in: Saigal, 1998). In many areas local people tried to assert their rights over forests. In Andhra Pradesh, unrest was caused by shifting cultivators who were left with no legally recognised cultivable land when their lands were declared Reserved Forests. This led to the state government issuing them possession certificates for cultivable land in order to contain the growing militancy in tribal areas (Madhu Sarin, *in litt.*, 9 May 2004).

There was also a general build-up of resentment against the Forest Department's industry and revenue- oriented policies. The illegal forest exploitation by some Forest Department employees and forest contractors further alienated the people (Saigal, 1998). The most well known demonstration of local communities' anger at being marginalized came in the form of the *Chipko* (hug the trees) movement in the Uttaranchal Himalayas.

Similarly, conflicts erupted between protected area managers and local communities when the latter's access to the protected area was restricted or a proposal was mooted to relocate some villages. There are several well-documented cases of such conflicts in almost all protected areas (Kothari et al, 1989; Kothari et al, 1996). A particularly well-known case is that of Rajaji National Park in Uttaranchal.

Concern over Forest Degradation

In the 1970s and 1980s, there was a growing concern about forest degradation, especially among the national policymakers. There was a realization that the existing policies were not effective in curbing the process of forest degradation. It was also apparent that social forestry had not been able to achieve its principal objective of providing fuel and fodder for the people outside government forest areas. It has not reduced people's dependence on forests as most of the plantations raised under social forestry were of fast-growing commercial species such as eucalyptus.

This concern over the state of the country's forest resources was heightened significantly when the National Remote Sensing Agency released its forest cover assessment based on remote sensing data. The data indicated that the forest cover of the country had declined from 16.86% in mid-1970s to 14.10% in 1982 (Rawat, Saxena and Gupta, undated).

The preamble of the new forest policy issued in 1988 clearly states continuing forest degradation as the main reason for change in the policy (see Box 2).

The concern over degradation was also manifested in the creation of the National Wastelands Development Board in 1985. This was mandated to afforest five million hectares of wastelands every

---

Box 2   **Preamble of the National Forest Policy, 1988**

"... over the years, forests in the country have suffered serious depletion. This is attributable to relentless pressures arising from ever-increasing demand for fuelwood, fodder and timber; in-adequacy of protection measures; diversion of forest lands to non- forest uses without ensuring compensatory afforestation and essential environmental safeguards; and the tendency to look upon forests as revenue earning resource. The need to review the situation and to evolve, for the future, a new strategy of forest conservation has become imperative. Conservation includes preservation, maintenance, sustainable utilization, restoration, and enhancement of the natural environment. It has thus become necessary to review and revise the National Forest Policy."

---

year. Subsequently, another body called the National Afforestation and Ecodevelopment Board was created in 1992 with the mandate to restore degraded forests, lands around protected areas and ecologically fragile zones.

The concern over forest degradation is still a major driver for national forest policy as is reflected in the Tenth Five Year Plan (2002–07). There is emphasis on bringing 25% of the area of the country under forest/tree cover by the end of the Tenth Plan period and 33% by the end of the Eleventh Plan period.[22]

The National Forestry Action Programme – a comprehensive strategy and action programme for the forestry sector for 20 years, prepared in 1999 – envisaged an investment of Rs. 1,339 billion (Over US$30 billion) to reach the national target of 33% (MoEF, 1999).

The Forest-Poverty Linkage

Since the 1970s, issues related to forests and environment have been seen by the country's planners as being closely linked to issues of poverty and rural development. This thinking was also reflected in the speech made by the then Prime Minister, Mrs. Indira Gandhi at the Stockholm conference in 1972 (see Box 3).

Since the 1980s, there has been a greater appreciation of the link between rural poverty and environmental degradation in general and forests in particular. Many forestry programmes were initiated in the 1980s mainly to address the issues of poverty and rural development. During the Sixth Five Year Plan (1980–85), government started a number of rural poverty alleviation programmes with a

---

Box 3   **Extract from the Prime Minister of India's statement on poverty at the United Nations Conference on Human Environment, Stockholm, 1972**

"Environment cannot be improved in conditions of poverty. Unless we are in a position to provide employment and purchasing power for the daily necessities of the tribal people and those who live in and around our jungles, we cannot prevent them from combing the forests for food and livelihood; from poaching and from despoiling the vegetation. How can we speak to those who live in villages and slums about keeping the oceans, the rivers and the air clean when their own lives are con-taminated at source."

Source: MoEF, 1998

---

22 It is one of 13 "monitorable targets" under the Tenth Five Year Plan.

substantial forestry component (Vira, 1995). During the Seventh Five Year Plan, 20% of the funds under the rural development schemes were earmarked for the purpose of afforestation, which resulted in the planting of a large number of trees across the country.[23] [24]

Development Assistance Agencies

Many initiatives consistent with ecosystem approaches to forest management have been supported through international development assistance. Ecodevelopment and JFM projects got support from agencies such as the World Bank, the Japan Bank for International Cooperation and the Department for International Development of the UK. The Terai Arc Restoration Initiative is supported by the World Bank/WWF Alliance while the NBSAP process has been supported by funds received from the Global Environment Facility (GEF) through the UNDP.

Donor agencies have also played an important role in bringing about policy changes (e.g. issuance of JFM Resolutions in some states) by making these policy changes a prerequisite for approving the projects. An extract from the Karnataka state's JFM order illustrates this well:

> "The Principal Chief Conservator of Forests has stated that the 'Process Plan' of the Western Ghats Forestry and Environment Project funded by ODA of the U.K. depends mainly on the JFPM, and the ODA authorities have insisted for a Government Order authorising the principles of Joint Forest Planning and Management. Accordingly, he has sent detailed proposal on the above scheme to the Government for consideration." (Notification No. AHFF/232/FAP/86 dated 12.4.93, in: SPWD, 1998)

Judicial Activism

The higher judiciary, especially the Supreme Court, has been a major driver of change in recent years. A spate of judgments, mainly in public interest litigation cases, have virtually set the national policy in respect of matters related to environment and forests.

Many of these cases are what are termed as "continuing mandamus" meaning that the court, rather than passing final judgment, keeps on passing orders and directions with a view to monitoring the functioning of the executive arm. These cases have led to fundamental changes in the pattern of forest governance and decision making in the country. In an ongoing case that is commonly referred to as the forest case,[25] the Supreme Court passed several interim orders that have had far reaching implications for forest management in the country (Divan and Rosencranz, 2001).

On 7 May, 2002 the Supreme Court gave another landmark judgement banning all tree-felling in the Andaman and Nicobar Islands, except for the bona fide use of the local islander populations and directed the shutting down of the Andaman and Nicobar Forest Plantations and Development Corporation that had logged the forests of Little Andaman island for years. It also directed phasing out of existing monoculture plantations of red oil palm, rubber and teak.

---

23 *Source*: The Coimbatore Charter on Environment and Forests. National Conference of Ministers of Environment and Forests, 29–30 January, 2001, Coimbatore.

24 During the Seventh Five Year Plan (1985–1990), 8.86 million hectare area was afforested, which was more than the cumulative total in all previous plan (1951–1984) (MoEF, 1999).

25 T.N. Godavarman Thirumalkpad vs Union of India (CWP. 202 of 1995) in the Supreme Court.

Another Interim Order (dated 14 February 2000) of the Supreme Court has had major impact on protected areas as it prohibited removal of any dead or decaying trees, grasses, drift wood etc. from any area comprising a national park or sanctuary. Many of the Ecosensitive Zones have also been notified after Supreme Court judgements (Divan and Rosencranz, 2001; Sekhsaria, 2002; Sekhsaria, 2004).[26]

Judicial activism is sometimes criticised on the grounds that it may not prescribe scientifically established approaches that lead to sustainable management of forests. Sometimes, it has taken decisions that have alienated local communities. However, there is no doubt that judicial intervention has played a major role in the process of reform of the forest sector.

International Commitments

International commitments (agreements, conventions, etc.) have also played a role in shaping the current policy regime. For instance, the Biological Diversity Act, 2002 is a direct outcome of the CBD. Similarly, trade in all CITES species is prohibited under the Foreign Trade (Regulation and Development) Act, 1992.

In general, however, there seems to be an aversion among national policy makers to accept an international regulatory regime in the forestry and environment sectors as is evident from the National Conservation Strategy and Policy Statement on Environment and Development issued in 1992 (see Box 4).

The position of the Government of India on this matter hasn't changed much in the past decade. The statement made by the Indian Environment and Forests Minister at the UNFF meeting held in 2002 reaffirms India's lack of support for internatioal legal instruments on forests (see Box 5).

The non-binding commitments such as the Rio Forest Principles, the proposals for action of the Intergovernmental Panel on Forests (IPF) and Intergovernmental Forum on Forests (IFF) do not seem to have had any significant impact at the field level. Similarly, as export of wood and wood products in

---

Box 4   **Extracts from the National Conservation Strategy and Policy Statement on Environment and Development, 1992**

"Our economic development cannot be hampered in the name of the global environment, which we have done nothing to damage and can do little to save. Our resources are required to meet our developmental needs such as education, nutrition, health services, drinking water, housing, sanitation, agriculture, industry, infrastructure, even all of which we find it difficult to provide having been behind in the race for development. Without this development, threats to the environment will in any case grow. In the short run, this developmental effort could even add to the discharges and emissions, which cause global problems – but these, are miniscule compared to the quantities, which industrialized countries have already contributed. In any case, such emissions etc. can easily be compensated for a marginal reduction of the same in the industrialized world."

"Regulatory international regimes can be useful in some areas such as ozone depletion or even climate change – provided the special situation of developing countries is fully addressed. But in other sectors – such as forestry – such a regime is neither workable nor acceptable. In such sectors, what is required is a reduction of international economic and commercial pressures which generate unsustainable exploitation, and additional financial resources to tackle the damage already done."

---

26 For example, in cases such as: Rural Litigation and Entitlement Kendra, Dehradun vs. State of Uttar Pradesh and Dahanu Taluka Environment Protection Group vs. Bombay Suburban Electricity Supply Company.

> **Box 5**   **Extract from the statement made by the Indian Minister for Environment and Forests at the ministerial segment of the second substantive session of the United Nations Forum on Forests on March 14, 2002**
>
> "While examining the possibility of the parameters of a legally binding instrument, we would need to assess the sufficiency of the existing mechanisms and instruments and whether there is any requirement of a new instrument. In our view it is not lack of instruments but the lack of implementation of existing instruments/programmes that is hindering the sustainable development of forests."
>
> *Source*: http://envfor.nic.in

the form of logs, timber, stumps, roots, barks, chips, powder, flakes, dust, pulp and charcoal is prohibited, there is little pressure from overseas consumers for changes in forestry practices.

Political Support

Political support from the government of the day has also acted as a very significant driver of change. In states such as Madhya Pradesh and Andhra Pradesh, programmes such as JFM were implemented on a vast scale due to the strong support of the Chief Ministers of these states. The latter saw political advantage in implementing such programmes.

At the national level too, policies have been significantly influenced by the incumbent political party's (or parties') ideological stand on forestry issues. The present United Progressive Alliance (UPA) government's stand on issues such as tribal rights and non-timber products is reflected in the Common Minimum Programme drawn up by the coalition partners (see Box 6).

> **Box 6**   **Extracts from the Common Minimum Programme of the United Progressive Alliance Government, 2004**
>
> The UPA administration will take all measures to reconcile the objectives of economic growth and environmental conservation, particularly as far as tribal communities dependent on forests are concerned.
>
> Eviction of tribal communities and other forest dwelling communities from forest areas will be discontinued. Cooperation of these communities will be sought for protecting forests and for undertaking social afforestation. The rights of tribal communities over mineral resources etc, as laid down by law, will be fully safeguarded.
>
> The UPA will urge the states to make legislation for conferring ownership rights in respect of minor forest produce, including tendu patta, on all those people from the weaker sections who work in the forests.
>
> *Source*: http://sify.com

Conclusions

There has been a marked shift towards the precepts of ecosystem approaches in India in recent decades. This has accelerated recently and many forestry programmes (e.g. JFM and Ecodevelopment) have emphasised people's participation and on the adoption of landscape level planning (e.g. Project Tiger, Terai Arc Restoration Initiative, etc.). Ongoing policy processes such as NBSAP and Bhopal India

Process also strongly advocate adoption of ecosystem approaches. The principles of ecosystem approaches are also reflected in recent forest and biodiversity related legislation as well as the new draft National Environment Policy that was circulated for comments by MoEF in August 2004.

However, progress on the ground has been relatively slow. As discussed in earlier sections, a number of problems plague programmes like JFM and Ecodevelopment. JFM is largely limited to degraded forests and good forests have been kept outside its ambit in most states. The experience with landscape level approaches is also rather limited at present and there is a problem of poor coordination and often contradictions in the plans and programmes of various agencies and sectors.[27] Recommendations of NBSAP are yet to be accepted by the government and criteria and indicators developed under the Bhopal India Process are only being used for monitoring forest management at a handful of sites.

While policies like the National Forest Policy and the draft National Environment Policy focus on ecosystem approaches, they are just guidelines and their provisions are not enforceable. While some new legislation contains elements of ecosystem approaches, there are serious lacunae. For example, while the addition of the new category of community reserves under the new Wildlife Act is a move towards greater community involvement in conservation, its scope is severely limited as these reserves cannot be created on government lands. While the Biological Diversity Act recognises community rights over biodiversity and related knowledge, the rules (the real operational part) passed under the Act seem to be less forthright on these issues.

Similarly, while powers to regulate natural resource management have been given to the Panchayat Raya Institutions (PRIs), the actual progress on the ground is very slow. This is because of different interpretations of the law by different agencies and a lack of capacity within PRIs. There is also an ongoing debate whether all forest related activities should be handled by PRIs or by separate user groups such as JFM groups and ecodevelopment committees. While some feel that creation of user groups is an encroachment on powers granted to PRIs by the Constitution of India, others feel greater involvement of PRIs is not desirable as these are highly politicized bodies and often cover a large area and represent a heterogeneous population. This makes the task of resource management difficult. It will be important to clearly define the role of PRIs for long-term success of any community-based forest management programme.

Many shifts towards ecosystem approaches have been donor driven but over time there appears to have been greater acceptance of these approaches within government. For instance, while many states got funding for JFM from international donors, the central government has now started a new scheme called the "National Afforestation Programme" with a budgetary allocation of over Rs. 10 billion for supporting JFM. Even though this scheme suffers from several serious problems, it does indicate government's commitment towards the JFM programme. States such as West Bengal have successfully continued their JFM programme even after external support ended several years ago.

While the issues related to forest environmental services have not been a major driver in the past, the situation seems to be changing. The forest section of the new draft environment policy focuses on environmental services. The state of Himachal Pradesh imposed an "environmental value tax" in 2002 for use of forest lands for non-forestry purposes based on a green accounting study of the value of the state's forests (Makhaik, 2002). It is likely that there will be greater focus on forest environmental services in the coming years.

---

27 *Source*: NBSAP, 2004.

A number of key lessons emerge from the experience of change in India over the past few decades. Some of these have wide application and are summarised here:

1. Willing, active and informed participation of local communities in decision-making and benefit sharing is essential to achieve sustainable forest management and to implement ecosystem approaches.

2. Given adequate space, encouragement and/or incentives, local communities can effectively contribute towards broad-based sustainable forest management, from the conceptual to the design and implementation phases of programmes.

3. Inequity continues to prevail even in otherwise successful management systems due to the domination by certain more powerful stakeholders.

4. The "cost" of participatory forest management is often heavily skewed with the poorest people suffering the most from "closure" and other such restrictions and from intra and inter-community conflicts.

5. A supportive legal framework is required for long-term success of ecosystem based approaches and India has moved strongly to provide such a framework.

6. Ecosystem based approaches require coordination among different agencies and actors. The strong political will that this requires has been manifest in India although not all politicians subscribe to it.

7. The Indian constitution has been amended to provide enabling conditions for ecosystem approaches but the constitutional mandate of the Panchayats needs to be clearly defined given their role in forest management.

8. Changes in policy statements are not sufficient as practice on the ground does not always fully conform to the stated policy. There is an "implementation gap" and it will be important to develop effective systems to monitor field practices.

intu

7 Balancing Conflicting Values: Ecosystem Solutions in the Pacific Northwest of the United States and Canada

Richard W. Haynes, Robert C. Szaro and Dennis P. Dykstra

Introduction

Ecosystem approaches to sustainable forest management in the Pacific Northwest of the United States and Canada have arisen in response to significant changes that have occurred in these societies over the past century or so (Interagency Ecosystem Management Task Force, 1995). One such change has been rapid population growth along the Pacific Coast, where the mild climate and growing regional economy have induced a high rate of immigration from other parts of the continent. Nearly all of the population growth during the past few decades has been in urban areas, and urban dwellers tend to have different expectations toward large-scale forest management than do rural, resource-dependent populations. Many of the new immigrants come from regions with less abundant natural endowments, and the landscape beauty and opportunities for outdoor recreation in the Pacific Northwest are often cited as major reasons for their immigration.

Another factor contributing to the adoption of ecosystem approaches on public lands is the increasing recognition by managers of public forest lands in the Pacific Northwest that other regions, in both the US and Canada, are increasingly able to meet US demands for softwood lumber. In the past, the perceived need to meet this demand had been a primary motivation for maintaining high levels of timber harvest on public forests in the Pacific Northwest.

The emergence of ecosystem approaches for managing forests in the Pacific Northwest is by no means a sudden event. In the United States, during the latter part of the 19th Century the role of the federal government changed gradually from disposer of land to holder of land, leading eventually to a situation in which federal agencies such as the Forest Service and the Bureau of Land Management became custodians of more than one-third of all US forest land. Much of the federally managed forest is concentrated in the West, and in the Pacific Northwest more than half of all forested lands are under federal ownership. In British Columbia, almost all forest lands are owned by the provincial government and are therefore public property, although they are managed under long-term "tree farm licenses" granted to private companies.

In both Canada and the US, demographic changes during the 20th Century resulted in a gradual evolution in public attitudes toward natural resources that increasingly emphasised stewardship: from single use to multiple use; from extraction to restoration; from disposal to recycling, reuse, and environmental protection. Healthy regional economies and attractive, healthy natural settings have so far gone hand in hand. The need to maintain both a robust economy and the spectacular natural landscape in the face of conflicting pressures has made the PNW a test-bed for the development of operational ecosystem management.

But how can the ecosystem approach be effectively operationalized? How can land managers and policy makers react to the painful dilemmas that arise when decisions must be made that could potentially have devastating impacts on ecosystem stability or on local economies? Land managers find themselves trying to find a balance between maintaining forest ecosystems and at the same time providing the forest products and services needed by society. Trade-offs are inevitable and necessitate formulating and using alternative land management strategies to provide an acceptable mix of commodity production, amenity use, protection of environmental and ecological values, and biodiversity.

The Pacific Northwest has a relatively long tradition of science-based forest management (Meidinger and Pojar, 1991; Kimmins, 1992; Peterson *et al.*, 1997; Duncan, 2000). Since the mid-1980s, forest managers within the region have increasingly become interested in management regimes that are compatible both with commodity production and also with ecological, social, and cultural values (Kohm and Franklin, 1997; Monserud *et al.*, 2003). Because much of the region's forest land is publicly owned, the choice of forest management regimes has been the subject of public debates that have often portrayed management choices as stark tradeoffs between the biophysical and socioeconomic components of ecosystems. This characterization has strongly affected forest management practices throughout the region, both in the United States and Canada.

The evolution of science-based forest management and growing societal concerns about greater balance among the environmental, economic, and social consequences of land management have led to an increasing reliance on managing at the ecosystem level. The Convention on Biological Diversity of 1992, with its emphasis on ecological approaches, has contributed to the development of current strategies for sustainable forest management. This chapter outlines the evolution of these concepts in the Pacific Northwest Region of North America.

The Forests of the Pacific Northwest

The focus of this chapter is on the moist maritime forests of the Pacific Northwest (PNW). Collectively, this is the world's northernmost temperate rain forest (Walter, 1985). Geographically (see Figure 1), the region includes western Oregon and Washington (from the summit of the Cascade Range to the Pacific coast, including the Coast Range and the Olympic Mountains), coastal British Columbia (Coast Mountains), and island-dominated southeastern Alaska as far north as the Kenai Peninsula. It stretches southward almost to San Francisco, California. The east-west extent of this coastal forest varies as a function of climate and elevation; its width extends from a few kilometers at the northern and southern extremes to several hundred kilometers in the middle of its range. Much of the northern half of this range (British Columbia north of Vancouver Island to southeastern Alaska) is in a relatively undisturbed, natural state. The forest southward from Vancouver Island, British Columbia to northern California contains some of the world's most valuable and productive commercial timberlands. An important subset of the PNW is the Douglas-fir subregion (western Washington and Oregon), which is dominated by the fast-growing coastal Douglas-fir (*Pseudotsuga menziesii* (Mirb.) Franco). We refer to this subregion as the Pacific Northwest-Westside, or PNWW.

For the purposes of this chapter we regard the PNW in total as comprising the coastal redwood (*Sequoia sempervirens* (D. Don)) forests of Northern California, the Douglas-fir forests of western Oregon and Washington, and the vast coastal Sitka spruce (*Picea sitchensis* (Bong.) Carr.) and western hemlock (*Tsuga heterophylla* (Raf.) Sarg.) forests of British Columbia and southeastern Alaska. Altogether these coniferous forests contain the highest quality wood-producing lands on the continent, and exhibit some of the greatest biomass accumulations and highest productivity levels of any in the world, temperate or tropical (Franklin and Dyrness, 1973; Fujimori *et al.*, 1976; Franklin and Waring, 1981; Walter, 1985; Franklin, 1988). The forests are valued for their scenery, recreational opportunities,

Fig. 1. The coastal temperate rain forest of the Pacific Northwest.

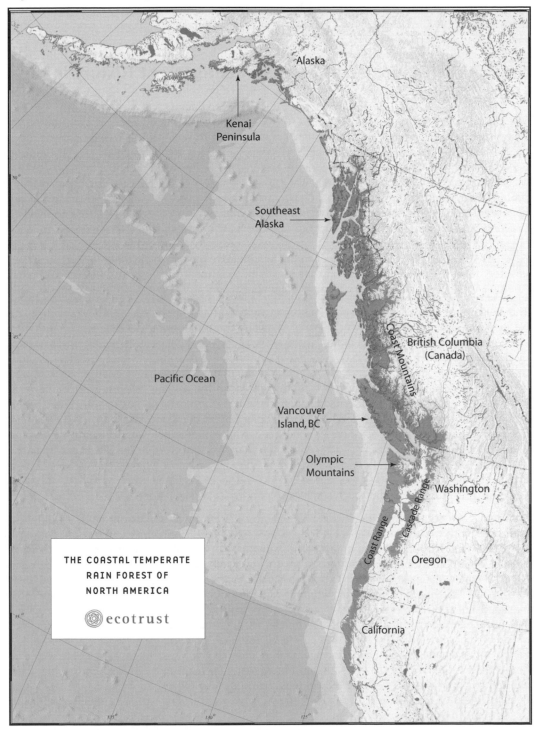

Ecotrust map reprinted by permission (www.ecotrust.org). For similar maps see Schoonmaker et
al. *(1997).*

watershed protection, and fish and wildlife habitat (Peterson and Monserud, 2002). The northern extent of the PNW rain forest (coastal British Columbia and southeastern Alaska) is largely unaltered (Everest *et al.*, 1997).

Setting the Stage, Part 1: Forest Management History in the United States

The USDA Forest Service's legal mandates for forest management have evolved from the original vision espoused by its first Chief, Gifford Pinchot, which was to serve as a significant provider of the nation's timber and wood products (Miller, 2001; Boyce and Szaro, 2004). In actual practice, the Forest Service functioned largely as a caretaker of the Nation's public forests until timber from private lands was in short supply after the end of World War II. The Forest Service, at that time composed mainly of professionally trained foresters, responded to the national need by rapidly increasing the area harvested on the national forests through the late 1960s. As the Forest Service rose to meet the challenge of increasing timber production, negative public pressure grew in response to visible alterations in the landscape and impacts on other resources caused by widespread harvesting activities. This pressure manifested itself in the Multiple Use-Sustained Yield Act (MUSY), which was enacted by the US Congress in 1960 and directed that the national forests were to be administered for "multiple use and sustained yield of the several products and services obtained therefrom".

The heightened environmental consciousness resulted in new environmental laws such as the National Environmental Policy Act (NEPA) of 1969 and the Endangered Species Act (ESA) of 1973. These laws fundamentally changed the way the agency conducted business, requiring specialists from disciplines other than forestry so that the effects of timber harvesting on other resources could be more fully analyzed. By the end of the 20th Century, the knowledge needed to make forest-management decisions in a multiple-use context exceeded the learning and experience of any one individual and pre-harvest analysis had become both time-consuming and extremely costly. Numerous and sometimes conflicting laws and regulations forced decision-makers to rely on planning documents prepared by teams of professionals and, where information was scarce, to rely on their team's technical and professional judgments concerning risks involved in the decisions. Managers, who once had been able to make decisions independently, were now required to base decisions on analyses carried out by teams of specialists. Even so, the decisions were subject to public scrutiny and could be delayed or blocked through administrative appeals and litigation.

Public pressure continued, especially in response to clear cutting practices on the national forests, and in 1974 the Forest and Rangeland Renewable Resources Planning Act (RPA) was passed by Congress, requiring periodic assessment of the status and opportunities for enhanced management of the Nation's publicly held natural resources. This was followed in 1976 with the passage of the National Forest Management Act (NFMA). The NFMA required each forest to develop comprehensive forest plans. Each plan was viewed as a contract with the nation detailing how the resources were to be managed, but at the same time they acknowledged the agency's professional flexibility to manage as it saw fit. Forest plans contained standards (rules that must be followed) and guidelines (suggested practices that should be followed) that specifically outlined how the forest would be managed. As Forest Service managers pushed to meet what they understood to be a national mandate to provide timber in ever-increasing quantities, the environmental movement in the United States relentlessly challenged those practices. Other federal agencies were also trying to fulfill the country's timber demand, but the Forest Service tended to be the primary focus of administrative appeals and litigation by environmental groups.

During the 1990s, Forest Service managers increased scientist involvement by asking for help with forest planning and the ensuing legal battles. Regional natural resource management planning efforts that grew out of increased involved by scientists included the Forest Ecosystem Management Assessment Team (FEMAT, 1993) for northern California, Oregon, and Washington; the Interior Columbia Basin Ecosystem Management Project (ICBEMP) for eastern Washington, Idaho, and western Montana (Quigley and Bigler-Cole, 1997); the Sierra Nevada Ecosystem Project (SNEP, 1996); and the Tongass Land Management Plan (USDA FS, 1997a-1997c).

Setting the Stage, Part 2: Forest Management History in the US Pacific Northwest

The development of ecological approaches to forest management in the Pacific Northwest resulted from decades of conflict over the use and value of forests and their resources. These approaches attempt to involve all stakeholders in defining sustainable alternatives for the interactions of people and the environments in which they live. Similar approaches evolved in a number of places throughout North America but in no place was the process more controversial and contentious than in the Pacific Northwest.

European settlement of the Pacific Northwest began in the mid-1800s, although parts of coastal Alaska had been settled earlier by the Russians. At that time, forests were regarded as unlimited or as impediments to settlement. By the early 1900s, however, the general populace had begun to realize that forests represented a limited resource. One consequence of this was the establishment in the United States of federal forest reserves to protect forest resources, water quality and wildlife habitat. At that time, nearly all timber production came from private timberlands, and the major management issues were protection from fire, regeneration, growth and yield studies, and harvest practices. Until World War II, management of the federal timberlands focused largely on conserving forest resources. Following the war, a deliberate decision was made to increase the level of timber harvesting from public timberlands to help meet the growing demand for forest products as a means of supporting the booming regional population and rapidly expanding economy. From the 1940s until the late 1960s in the United States, there was general agreement among both federal and private land managers that timber production was the primary objective in the management of most forest land (Curtis *et al.*, 1998; Peterson and Monserud, 2002). Basic assumptions were that wood production in old-growth stands was essentially static (no net growth), and that insects and disease were diminishing the amount of usable wood in those stands. It seemed desirable, therefore, to replace old-growth forests with young, rapidly growing stands (USDA FS, 1963; Curtis *et al.*, 1998). In the Douglas-fir region, clearcut logging and broadcast burning were justified as mimicking the catastrophic, stand-replacing fires typical of the region before fire suppression began (Halpern, 1995). This led to adoption of a management system that relied on the financially efficient practice of clearcutting, burning, and replanting. At the same time, public concerns about fire protection and, later, restocking of cutover timberland, led the states of Oregon, California, Washington, and Alaska to adopt forest practice acts in 1971, 1973, 1974, and 1978, respectively. These rely on a combination of best management practices, logger and landowner education, and enforcement activities by state agencies.

Over the years, conflicts over differing forest values have intensified (Cissel *et al.*, 1999; Peterson and Monserud, 2002). The public has become increasingly aware that forests can produce more than wood (Behan, 1990; Beese and Phillips, 1997). Current public debate over management of public forests centers on interactions between wood production and the needs of wildlife, aquatic resources, biodiversity, and social acceptance (Peterson and Monserud, 2002). These debates culminated in the development of the Northwest Forest Plan (USDA and USDI, 1994a-1994b) for western Oregon and Washington, the new Forest Practices Code of British Columbia (1994), and the Tongass Land Management Plan (USDA FS, 1997a–1997c) for the Tongass National Forest in southeastern Alaska. Instead of the traditional goal of economically efficient wood production that relied largely on even-aged management, the focus in these recent efforts is toward "old-growth" and multi-resource ecosystem management, attempting to provide habitat for threatened and endangered species, protect riparian zones to rejuvenate the freshwater and anadromous fisheries, and promote biodiversity (FEMAT, 1993; Clayoquot Scientific Panel, 1995). These changes also increased the interest in and need for science-based silvicultural practices and management regimes that will reduce conflicts among user groups while producing the many values associated with forest lands on a biologically and economically sustainable basis (Curtis *et al.*, 1998; Committee of Scientists, 1999).

Setting the Stage, Part 3: Forest Management History in the Pacific Northwest of Canada

The public ownership of 95% of forestlands in British Columbia is unique in the industrialized world. This predominance of public forests brings a special set of problems for regulating forestry practices (Mitchell *et al.*, 2004). The public has brought considerable pressure to bear for the diversification of silvicultural systems, resulting in the introduction of a results-based forest practices code. Passed in 1994, the code contains provisions for limiting the impact and extent of clearcutting and provides a context for testing the feasibility of partial cutting and "retention" silvicultural systems. The focus on silvicultural practices has resulted in the installation of a number of large-scale experiments in British Columbia (Daigle, 1995; Puttonen and Murphy, 1997). These include Date Creek (Coates *et al.*, 1997), Quesnel Highlands (Armleder and Stevenson, 1994), Lucille Mountain (Eastham and Jull, 1999), Opax Mountain (Klenner and Vyse, 1998), Sicamous Creek (Vyse, 1999) and the Montane Alternative Silvicultural Systems (MASS) Project (Arnott *et al.*, 1995). In total, these experiments represent a major public investment in research relating to the operational, economic and ecological impacts of alternatives to clearcutting.

A premise common to all of these trials is that the amount and the arrangement of retained forest structure will affect ecological values. By retaining diverse structures representative of pre-harvest stand conditions, including dead trees and coarse woody debris, diverse habitats will be conserved for the variety of organisms that underpin ecosystem functions (Franklin *et al.*, 1997; Burgess *et al.*, 2001). Because managing public forests for multiple ecological, social and economic values will require trade-offs, it would be desirable to make decisions based on measurement of the impacts of different silvicultural alternatives on those values. This type of science-informed approach has been taken by Weyerhaeuser Canada in its coastal operations, where research on the operational and economic feasibility of silvicultural alternatives to clearcutting conducted at MASS in part gave the company confidence to proceed with a plan to phase out clearcutting and move toward retention forestry. As the pressure for third-party certification of forestry practices increases, the demand for ecologically based criteria for making decisions about the amount and pattern of overstory retention will likely become more acute. The information needed to develop and apply such criteria is presently quite scanty for most of British Columbia's forest types.

The MASS Project has also contributed to partially resolving some of the clearcutting controversy in which highly active public groups in the nearby urban centres of Vancouver and Victoria have questioned the sustainability of even-aged management associated with clearcutting. The MASS Project demonstrated that partial-cut harvesting systems could be used in coastal forests, contributing to a closer alignment of ecological and economic factors. This helped the industry respond to intense public pressure, resulted in an increased public acceptance of changes in forestry practices, and created a niche for the application of scientific information to inform the debate on managing forests for multiple values.

A further development relating to forest management in British Columbia is an effort by the government to increasingly involve indigenous populations (referred to in Canada as First Nations peoples) in the management of forests. This is reportedly being done partly to increase their participation in economic activities related to lands that the tribes had historically controlled, and partly on the assumption that they will take a more conservative approach (as compared to the forest industry) toward timber harvesting. The approach being taken is to preferentially offer tree farm licenses to First Nations groups that have been certified as competent to manage the forests. In at least one case the government is reportedly negotiating to buy back a large tree farm license currently held by a private timber company and offer it to a qualified First Nations consortium.

Policy Context

The policy context in the Pacific Northwest is set by three converging interests: shifting public recognition of the array of goods and services produced by forests; the growing debate about sustainable forest management; and recognition within the scientific community of the connectiveness among processes and outputs. These interests all shape the emerging concerns about how to achieve good stewardship of our forestlands, both public and private. Key in this is the role that scientific information can play to increase opportunities for producing compatible bundles of goods and services. These goods and services include wood, wildlife habitat, scenery, recreation, water quality (including water as a commodity), and riparian habitat; all provided in a manner that is socially acceptable and economically viable. This is consistent with the emerging emphasis on sustainable forest management and with concerns about ways to meet rising demands for goods and services from the forest in an environmentally acceptable manner. It also emphasizes the need for developing effective partnerships between scientists and managers involved in ecosystem management and decisionmakers charged with the political task of governing (see Lee 1993 for an expanded discussion of the role of civic science).

Contemporary Management Regimes in the Pacific Northwest

The Pacific Northwest is considered one of the premier regions for forest management in both the United States and Canada. Although the US portion comprises less than 5% of US timberland, between 1950 and 1985 it was often responsible for a quarter of the annual softwood harvest. Since World War II it has been a major region for timber management in both countries, as forestry activities were designed to convert the predominately old-growth forests into managed forests dominated by younger trees. Various forest management regimes have evolved as a function of changes in land owner objectives, the development of silvicultural information (including growth and yield information), and changes in the utilization of harvested timber.

Table 1. Forest land area in the US Pacific Northwest-Westside, 1997

Land class	Total	National Forest	Other Public	Forest Industry	Nonindustrial Private
		Million hectares			
Nonreserved					
Timberland	9.425	2.885	1.849	2.768	1.922
Other	0.279	0.016	0.069	0.049	0.146
Reserved – Total	1.255	0.700	0.623	–	0.002
Nonwilderness		0.069			
Wilderness		0.631			
Total forest land	10.959	3.602	2.541	2.817	2.070

Table 1 illustrates the wide diversity of ownerships that characterize the region. It is important to note, however, that unlike most other regions in the US and Canada, the forest ownerships in the PNW tend to be made up of large and relatively contiguous blocks of timberland. This has led to an interest in landscape-scale management approaches. The wide diversity of ownerships, public and private, has led to a patchwork mosaic of management regimes spread across the landscape. The variety of management regimes stems in part from differences in individual owner objectives, market conditions, biophysical productivity, and regulatory conditions within different parts of the region.

Table 2. Private land under various management regimes in the Pacific Northwest-Westside during the late 1990s.

Regime	Forest Industry	Non-industrial Private
	Percent of land base	
No genetic improvements, regenerate only	17	83
No genetic improvements, regenerate + commercial thinning + other [a]	17	0
No genetic improvements, regenerate + precommercial thinning	12	7
Partial cut	2	0
Regenerate with genetically improved stock + other	47	10
Conversion or rehabilitation [b]	0	0
Reserve areas	6	0
Harvest age (years)	43–55	40–60
Area (thousand ha)	2,767	1,924

[a] "Other" may include precommercial thinning and/or fertilization.
[b] Conversion or rehabilitation is replacing an existing understocked or undesired stand with a stand better matched to the site, or of higher commercial value.

Source: Haynes et al. (2003).

Characterization of Current Management Regimes

For much of the past century there has been vigorous debate about the management regimes that are most appropriate for the Pacific Northwest. Much of the debate focused on various individual practices but for the past five decades there has been tentative consensus on the basic set of practices that comprise the core of various management regimes. Given the increasingly diverse objectives among land owners, contemporary forest management is evolving to include greater flexibility both in the application of selected practices and in expected outcomes.

Stand-Level Management Intensities on Private Lands

Since the early 1960s the notion of management intensity has been used to characterize the relative level of investment per hectare made by different landowners. Higher management intensities generally cost more in the short run, but presumably yield a greater return on the investment in the long run. Table 2 summarizes results of a study of management intensities on private forestlands in the PNW-Westside subregion during the late 1990s. Allocations of land to the different regimes, or levels of management intensity, were based on information obtained in some instances by directly questioning landowners and in other cases were developed by knowledgeable experts (see Haynes *et al.*, 2003 for details).

Management intensities differ among landowners. For example, industrial owners' management has consistently involved practices that include regeneration, some form of commercial thinning (CT), and sometimes precommercial thinning (PCT). Recently there has been a decline in intentions to pursue highly complex regimes such as Plant/PCT/Fertilize/CT. These regimes appear to have been replaced by one or two simpler treatment regimes (for example, Plant/PCT or Plant/PCT/fertilize). On nonindustrial private forest (NIPF) lands, management is largely restricted to securing regeneration with only limited use of other treatments. This is consistent with past studies indicating that NIPF lands were in relatively poor management condition (e.g., low conifer restocking after harvest). Recent surveys of NIPF timberlands show a large fraction of the land base in some form of partial cutting or selection management. It is not clear whether this implies a long-term objective of developing a multi-aged selection system or simply a sequence of heavy thinnings to postpone clearcutting.

Rotation age or age of harvest is one of the most closely scrutinised elements of the timber management regime. The limited information on the actual harvest-age behaviour of owners in the PNWW is summarised at the bottom of Table 2.

Federal Land Management in the US Pacific Northwest

Federal land management in the Pacific Northwest since 1993 has been guided by a comprehensive long-term policy for managing habitat for the northern spotted owl, a species protected under the Endangered Species Act (1973). This strategy, which has been called the Northwest Forest Plan (NWFP), was developed from a report prepared by the Forest Ecosystem Management Assessment Team (FEMAT, 1993). The NWFP set in place a connected reserve system with both terrestrial and aquatic components (see Haynes and Perez, 2001 for a summary of the science contributions). The federal land base was allocated among late-successional and riparian reserves, matrix lands (all federal lands outside of reserves, withdrawn areas, and managed late-successional areas), and adaptive management areas (AMAs). The AMAs were included because the plan was an evolutionary strategy using adaptive management to test and modify assumptions, develop opportunities for organizational innovation, and investigate collaborative approaches.

The land management strategy embedded in the NWFP is based on many of the components common among ecosystem management approaches. It uses a connected reserve system to maintain well-distributed habitat on federal lands for two old-growth-dependent bird species, the marbled murrelet and the northern spotted owl, both of which are protected under the Endangered Species Act (1973). The connected-reserve approach is also considered likely to reverse habitat degradation for at-risk fish species or stocks, which is important because in recent years the protection of habitat for native and anadromous fisheries in PNW forests has assumed greater significance. Concern over several species of threatened or endangered salmon, in particular, has been a major focus of the debate over forest management during the past few years.

The approach used in designing the connected reserves was based on consideration of relationships between plant and animal species thought to be closely associated with late-successional forests. The design of the connected reserve system also considered its likelihood of long-term persistence. The management regimes that were applied in both the matrix and late-successional forests were modified versions of those shown in Table 2 but involved extended rotation lengths and greater reliance on partial harvests to increase structural variation within the forests.

In general, three management regimes can be used to describe the present approach being used on the US National Forests (see Mills and Zhou, 2003 for details). The first regime allows a final harvest followed by regeneration, typically by planting seedlings. The second regime uses partial harvesting so that the stand will develop a broader range of structural characteristics over time, including both older and younger trees. Regeneration is accomplished either by underplanting or by favoring natural regeneration. The third regime allows no harvest. These stands are held in reserve, often for development into late successional old-growth habitat.

The Changing Regulatory Environment

One of the significant changes over the past 50 years has been the development of state (or provincial) and federal regulations that influence the design of forest management practices and control the applications of these and other practices. For the most part these regulations reflect the manifestation of public concerns about forest lands or forest conditions.

Early regulations evolved from public concerns, first about fire protection and later about restocking of cutover timberland. Significant regulatory events in the US include the Wilderness Act (1964) that lead to the formal designation of Wilderness on national forest and other federal lands (such designation removes land from the timberland base); the National Environmental Policy Act (1970) that requires analysis of environmental and economic impacts of significant actions; the Oregon State Forest Practices Act (1971) that set minimum standards for a wide variety of management practices; the Endangered Species Act (1973) that required the protection of endangered and threatened species and their habitat; the Washington Forest Practices Act (1974) that regulates practices related to growing, harvesting or processing timber; the National Forest Management Act (1976) that required management plans for each national forest; and the Northwest Forest Plan (FEMAT, 1993) a balanced policy for managing federal lands in the range of the northern spotted owl.

The current management regimes reflect this regulatory environment but there is constant debate about the possible expansion of various regulations, especially those related to forest management in riparian areas. In addition, there are also concerns about how some public policies either directly or indirectly impact forest land use. For instance, a topic currently being debated in Oregon is the issue of whether regulations that restrict certain types of development on private lands constitute a "taking" of land value that should be subject to compensation.

Private timberlands throughout the PNW region (including provincial lands under tree farm licenses in British Columbia) are subject to a wide array of regulations on reforestation, road construction and maintenance, timber harvesting, chemical applications, and slash disposal. Although these regulations vary to some degree because of local political differences, in general they are remarkably similar. The State of Washington has recently moved somewhat beyond the other political subdivisions of the region in that it now requires the development of comprehensive habitat conservation plans where forestry operations cover extensive parts of a single watershed. Such plans must be coordinated among multiple landowners if each has custody over a significant fraction of the watershed area.

Impact of Management Levels on Future Forests

The characteristics of future forests in the PNW will be the consequence, in part, of a myriad of decisions made by a highly diverse array of timberland owners. The forests will also be shaped by the

Fig. 2. Age class distribution by ownership for softwood forest types on timberland in the Pacific Northwest-Westside for 2000 (left), and projected for 2050 (right). The 175-year age class includes all areas with trees whose average age is 170 years or older.

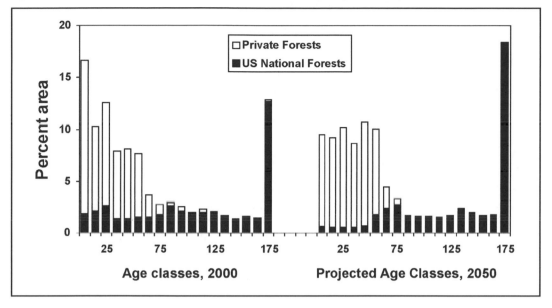

various forest products industries that will arise to utilize the species and sizes of timber available and by public concerns as manifested in various regulations to protect non-market forest benefits.

We expect a resurgence of sawtimber harvest and lumber production in the Pacific Northwest resulting from expanding harvest levels on private timberlands. This expansion is a function of a maturing private timber inventory, large proportions of which will approach minimum harvest age (40 years) after 2010. In the context of total inventories across all ownerships, these changes in private timberlands and the gradual aging of inventories on national forest timberlands will lead to a more pronounced bimodal distribution of age classes as suggested by Figure 2. At the national level, such projections suggest that we "will be able" to meet US demands for softwood products by shifting the harvest onto more intensively managed private timberlands (mostly in the US south) while at the same time preserving large amounts of older western timber stands in the federal ownerships. In the Pacific Northwest, the bimodal forest resource base will exhibit a significant shortage of stands in the 40–80 year range. The majority of younger stands (less than 40 years) will be on private land located typically at lower elevations, and stands older than 80 years will be concentrated on public lands typically at higher elevations and in headwater areas. The bimodal distribution suggested by these projections raises concerns about whether there will be an adequate representation of age classes over the entire region to provide habitat for all forest-dependent species. Equally uncertain is whether such a distribution of age classes is consistent with long-term sustainability of the resource base.

Relationships between Ecosystem Management and Sustainable Forest Management

Sustainable forest management is an enduring issue that in the past decade has taken on increased importance out of concerns about resource overexploitation (Powers, 2001), sustainable development (World Commission on Environment and Development, 1987), and possible climate change effects

(Watson *et al.*, 1995; Schwalm and Ek, 2001). During its 200-year history, the concept of sustainable forest ecosystem management has been the focus of scientific and political discussion, with varying degrees of intensity – it tends to be promoted with vehement fervor during periods of social or economic crisis and less intensely during periods of stability (von Gadow *et al.*, 2000).

Sustainable forestry is difficult to define and quantify (Amaranthus, 1997; Schlaepfer and Elliott, 2000). In its broadest sense, sustainability is a deliberate management goal that implies an ability to maintain the productivity and ecological integrity of the forest in perpetuity (Monserud, in press). This statement includes the interactions among both temporal and spatial scales by expressing the need to consider the timeframe and the spatial extent of management goals. Clearly, measures of sustainability become increasingly complex as the scale increases from stand to landscape to region, and on to national and global scales. Almost all of the work with criteria and indicators of sustainability is at the national scale, or at the scale of an entire forest management unit (e.g., a national forest or a private forest ownership). Forest management, however, is implemented at the stand level, which introduces a profound scale effect (Hall, 2000).

Before the 1990s, most countries managed their forests under the principle of *sustained yield*, with a nearly exclusive focus on timber yield from forest stands or contiguous groups of stands (Tittler *et al.*, 2001). The selection of sustainable forestry practices depends on what one is trying to sustain, a choice often driven by utilitarian principles (Amaranthus, 1997). In response to rising social pressures for a wider variety of goods and services from the forest, the concept of sustainable forestry has expanded to include much larger areas and a broader set of forest uses. Wilson and Wang (1999) define *sustainable forestry* as comprising a host of management regimes to maintain and enhance the long-term health and integrity of forest ecosystems and forest-dependent communities, while providing ecological, economic, social, and cultural opportunities for the benefit of present and future generations. This is a multi-dimensional definition including biological, sociological, political, and economic factors (Perry and Amaranthus, 1997; Wilson and Wang, 1999). Although an all-encompassing definition is appealing, it does not lend itself easily to translation into action, especially at smaller scales.

The shift in attitude from sustained yield to sustainable forestry was triggered internationally by the Brundtland Report on sustainable development in 1987 (World Commission on Environment and Development, 1987) and later consolidated at the Earth Summit in Rio de Janeiro in 1992 with the adoption of the Forest Principles (Tittler *et al.*, 2001). In response, several initiatives and international agreements have attempted to quantify broad-scale sustainability (Mendoza and Prabhu, 2000; Tittler *et al.*, 2001), such as the Montreal Accord (Mihajlovich, 2001). The emphasis in the Montreal Process is on using criteria and indicators for judging if the collective actions of a myriad of land owners and managers represent progress towards sustainable forestry over broad areas, usually at the national scale. There have also been many parallel efforts to apply criteria and indicators for the assessment of the sustainability of individual timber concessions (Mendoza and Prabhu, 2000).

The development of forest certification programs by nongovernmental organizations such as the Forest Stewardship Council and the American Forest and Paper Association is another indicator of the shift in public attitudes and the need for landowners to demonstrate their commitment to responsible forest management. These programs develop principles and objectives or criteria for sustainable forest management that can be applied to a participant's forests. All such certification systems emphasise the use of forest planning, best management practices, and logger and landowner education to achieve sustainable forest management (see AF&PA, 1999).

In practice, much of forest management is conducted at the stand and landscape levels to meet the objectives of individual landowners or managers. Actions designed to promote sustainability of the forest resource seek to simultaneously produce multiple forest goods and services, maintain the ecological integrity of the forest resource, and reduce social conflict regarding management. The net effect of actions by numerous landowners and managers are all complementary to (and likely a subset of) sustainable forest management as a whole.

Conclusions

This examination of the development of ecosystem approaches for forest management in the Pacific Northwest demonstrates the importance of recognizing that any forest management system, especially on publicly owned lands, will be socially acceptable only if it incorporates a thorough understanding of the social context within the region (and possibly even beyond the region, since some of the region's "forest constituents" may live elsewhere). Significantly, this means that forest management actions and outcomes *must* change over time, because society will inevitably change and as it does, its populace will demand changes in forestry objectives and in management practices.

Essentially all of the public forest management agencies within the PNW region have adopted ecosystem approaches to forest management as a guiding principle. Private forest owners, however, are guided more by individual objectives that may vary considerably among the population of owners. Furthermore, private forest owners tend to base management decisions on shorter-term market considerations.

Even so, the collective actions of the various owners within the PNW region appear to be leading to a situation that can generally be described as something close to area regulation. That is, the forests in the Douglas-fir region are becoming roughly evenly distributed across the age classes (and more importantly, across seral stages). As shown in Figure 2 there are differences in the distribution by ownership but in terms of broad forest conditions, the areas are distributed in roughly equal amounts across the various seral stages relevant to Douglas-fir forests. This situation is expected to remain relatively stable, given the expected market and processing options. These conditions also offer opportunities for compatible management systems that combine wood production with biodiversity conservation. This should make it possible to sustain flows of timber while at the same time preserving habitat and the various services derived from the forest's various structural components. At the regional scale, the diversity of ownerships, each with its own set of management objectives, helps provide the degree of variability that is essential in an ecosystem approach to forest management.

As a counterpoint to this generally positive outlook, it should be noted that the increasing reliance on science-based management cannot eliminate uncertainties associated with management outcomes. As one example, the success of the Northwest Forest Plan itself is vigorously debated among land managers and various public groups, each of which defines "success" as seen through its own lens. Perspectives on the success of the Plan are complicated by the extent of the legal battles that have stemmed from its implementation, an ironic outcome given that a major objective of the NWFP was to overcome the legal and administrative gridlock that had constrained management of the US national forests in the years leading up to its development.

A second example of an unanticipated outcome lies in the biophysical realm. Recently it has been determined that the barred owl, a larger and more adaptive bird that is not on the endangered species list, has expanded its range into the eastern part of the Pacific Northwest where it apparently is having a detrimental effect on the recovery of the northern spotted owl.

Such outcomes serve as reminders that forest management is a complex undertaking and that it is embedded in both social and biophysical systems that we only partly understand. Ecosystem approaches offer promise for building consensus and for helping stakeholders come to terms with the many competing demands for forest goods and services. Perhaps even more importantly, they also help retain flexibility so that we can adapt management prescriptions to fit our expanding knowledge and to remain compatible with the ecosystem changes that will inevitably arise over time.

intu

8 Wildlife, Loggers and Livelihoods in the Congo Basin

Jeffrey A. Sayer, Cléto Ndikumagenge, Bruce Campbell and Leonard Usongo

Introduction

The forests of the Congo Basin are remarkable for their global biodiversity values. But these forests face some extraordinary challenges. For more than a decade armed conflicts have been endemic to several of the countries of the region. In addition the countries differ significantly in their history, policy frameworks and current conservation and development programmes. This chapter examines the history of forest management and conservation in the Congo Basin. It identifies some of the reasons for the limited success in applying ecosystem approaches to forest management. The lack of long-term consistent policies and programmes and the relative weakness of forest sector institutions emerge as fundamental problems. The chapter identifies one tool, participatory modelling, that can help stakeholders to get to grips with the complexity of the social-ecological systems of which their forests are part. Such modelling exercises can help enable stakeholders with diverse interests to explore scenarios and negotiate outcomes that are consistent with ecosystem approaches to sustainable forest management.

The historical development of forest management in the Congo Basin

Patterns of forest management in the Congo Basin have been influenced by the policies of the colonial regimes that governed the countries of the region throughout the first 60 years of the 20th Century. The French colonies – present day Republic of Congo, Gabon, and the Central African Republic – had highly centralised forest services primarily concerned with regulating forest exploitation. Units responsible for wildlife and protected areas were located within these departments. Cameroon, which experienced first a German administration and then a joint Franco-British regime, had similar arrangements. In the Democratic Republic of Congo (DRC), the former Zaire, logging occurred in the coastal regions and to a lesser extent in Bandundu and the Kasai but in most of the country timber extraction for export markets, was of very limited importance. There was little high value timber and transport costs to the coast were excessive although the German company Danzer has been running logging operations in the Central Congo Basin for many years. There was little need for a capacity to regulate forest harvesting. However nature conservation was important. The country contains some of Africa's most spectacular forest systems and a very rich fauna of large mammals. An independent agency, the Congolese Institute for Nature Conservation, was established around the time of independence and has remained an effective and influential body to this day. Little attention appears to have been paid to either managing or conserving the forests of Equatorial Guinea by the Spanish colonial authorities and it is only recently that protected areas have been established and some first tentative steps towards regulating industrial logging taken. However, Equatorial Guinea was one of the earlier countries to introduce community forest management and to give rights to local communities.

Table 1. Developments leading to integrated approaches to forestry in the interior of the Congo Basin

Early '70s	Industrial logging begins in Congo and SE Cameroon – based upon "License d'exploitation"
1975	Major expansion of national parks in DRC announced at IUCN General Assembly in Kinshasa
1984–5	Nouabélé-N'Doki National Parks established in Congo
Mid-80s	Rapid expansion of logging in remote parts of Congo Basin countries
	Plans made for a trans-African highway, the "Route du 4ième parallel" from the Atlantic to Bangui although never constructed to the standards originally envisaged
1985–7	End of river transport to Brazzaville – all timber transported by road via Cameroon and Gabon.
1987	Tropical Forestry Action Plan developed in Cameroon – criticised by international conservation groups for advocating major expansion of industrial logging. Also proposes funding of conventional protected areas
1988	Sangha-N'Doki Reserves established in Central African Republic (RCA)
1989	First crash in cacao and coffee prices – triggers expansion of subsistence agriculture into forests
1988–9	First conservation projects in SE Cameroon
1990 onwards	Periods of conflict in DRC, Congo and CAR inhibit attempts to improve forest management – but considerable activity by international agencies in promoting more environmental forestry activities in Cameroon and Gabon. For instance Dutch TROPENBOS Foundation supports research based integrated management of forest areas in Gabon and Cameroon. Canada supports forest management programmes in DRC and Cameroon
1990	Law facilitating the operation of NGOs Cameroon. NGOs become more involved in forest activities
1992	Earth Summit in Rio de Janeiro emphasises links between conservation and development – stimulates more attention to forest conservation in Congo Basin
1992	Ministry of Environment and Forests established in Cameroon bringing forestry and environment into the same ministry. Similar changes subsequently occur in Congo and Gabon
1993–4	World Bank/WWF/McArthur Foundation meeting in SE Cameroon to promote cooperation on tri-national conservation programmes
1995	IUCN convenes CEFDHAC – a multi-stakeholder forum on forests operating at the scale of all the countries of Central Africa
1994–5	Cameroon Forestry Law and Land use framework enacted – provides favourable environment for integrating conservation and development
1995–2000	Demographic explosion SE Cameroon – associate with logging expansion and improved infrastructure – increased pressure on forests and especially bushmeat
1995–2003	Aid agencies provide generous support to NGOs in Cameroon and favour decentralised forest management initiatives.
1999	Yaoundé Summit secures regional political commitment to forest conservation and sustainable management.
1999 +	French GEF supports management planning in forest concessions in the region with objective of securing broad environmental benefits
2000 +	World Bank promotes sectoral forest-environment projects in Cameroon and Gabon and sustainable forest activities through economic stabilization activities in RDC. Bilateral donors agree to place much of their assistance under the World Bank umbrella – NGOs involved in developing projects and in their implementation.
2002	Johannesburg Summit – Congo Basin Forest Partnership launched by countries of the region supported by USA, France and others. Focus is agreed on large landscapes where a balance between forest conservation and sustainable use is to be sought. International NGOs are charged with much of the implementation of this programme.
2002	Initiation of African Forest Law Enforcement and Governance (AFLEG) process in Brazzaville amongst countries of the region and international agencies.
2003	First coordination meeting of the Congo Basin Forest Partnership – CBFP – in Paris
2004	Regional "Convergence plan" adopted by ministers to promote, amongst other things, more integrated approaches to forest management.

Under colonial legislations of the region all forested land belonged to the state. This remained the situation after independence which all of the countries achieved around 1960. Forests were generally perceived to be an abundant resource that was not under any particular threat. Forest exploitation was largely for domestic use – both of timber and wildlife and other non-timber products – and exports were restricted to small quantities of high quality hardwoods that were felled and sawn by hand in the more accessible forests. Total volumes exported were very low up to and after the time of independence. Ecosystem conservation focussed on a few rare species of large mammals or on sites with spectacular scenery or large concentrations of wildlife. Species sought after by sport hunters were generally given more attention than forest wildlife. Some protected areas established in the colonial period did include areas of forest – savannah mosaics.

The forests of the region began to be opened up for logging and agriculture began to expand into forested areas in the 1970s. This period coincided with the wider availability of tracked vehicles and portable chain saws and with a period of high demand for timber to supply the reconstruction efforts in post Second World War Europe. The rate of change of conditions in Congo Basin forests accelerated at this time. The major milestones are presented in Table 1. The conditions in the Congo Basin in the opening years of the 21st Century can perhaps be best understood as a part of this long-term transformation of the region.

The scale of logging activities increased from the 1970s to feed markets for utility grade lumber that could be obtained cheaply from Africa's forests. Cutting licenses and later concessions were authorised and forest departments began investing more resources in regulating harvesting activities. Most of the early logging was by companies from the countries that had recently relinquished colonial control. Logging was still concentrated near the coast and major waterways and only gradually spread inland. Transport difficulties still acted as a major constraint to forest exploitation. However most of the logging operations were linked to processing capacities in Europe and thus created their own demand. This vertical integration of the forest industries from logging through to end product was known in French as the "Filière bois". Forestry operations became increasingly profitable and became closely linked to the political power structures both in the countries of the region and to a surprising extent in the ex-colonial powers. In the late 1970s and 80s, logging spread into remote parts of the Congo Basin although most of the forests of central DRC remained untouched – they contained few commercially valuable species and transport costs were still prohibitive. However, by the 1980s a railway line from Brazzaville to the sea and another that enabled logs to bypass the rapids on the Congo River below Kinshasa allowed logging to spread into both the Congos. Forest departments in all the countries of the region focussed most of their attention on regulating concessions. During this period the French Technical Centre for Tropical Forestry (CTFT, Le Centre Technique Forestier Tropical – later a branch of CIRAD – the International Centre for Agronomic Research for Development) began extensive trials of silvicultural systems adapted to the management of Congo Basin forests and conducted inventories as a basis for forest management planning.

These management trials showed that appropriate pre and post-harvest treatments could greatly improve the growth rates and abundance of commercial timber species for future logging rotations. A great deal of the attention of forest departments began to focus on applying regulations to ensure that concessionaires followed these silvicultural practices. These efforts met with limited success as at this time most of the countries of the region began a period of economic stagnation. This resulted in deterioration of infrastructure and a general decline in efficiency of government services. Forest departments were not immune to this institutional weakening and the general economic climate made commercial logging companies less inclined to make long-term commitments. Various forms of forest crime and associated corruption began to emerge on a widening scale.

In the late 1970s tropical forests began to assume importance in international conservation circles. IUCN – The World Conservation Union – held its 1975 General Assembly at N'Sélé, 60km upstream from Kinshasa and this drew international attention to the conservation problems of the Congo Basin. At that Congress President Mobutu of RDC (then Zaire) declared four major new rainforest national parks – the beginning of a period of rapid growth of the protected area network in the region that continued into the early years of the 21st Century. Also at this time the threats to rainforests posed by a rapidly expanding logging industry began to be seen as a major global conservation problem. The late 1980s was a period when most forest management and conservation effort went into either regulating logging or establishing and protecting parks and reserves. This was a situation that was in many ways the antithesis of ecosystem management. Local communities were largely excluded from any role in forest governance, forest use was sharply segregated into protection and production zones and the central government theoretically controlled everything.

Integrating Conservation and Development

The mid-1980s and early 90s saw the emergence of interest in the complementarity of forest conservation and development. The conceptual basis for this was provided by influential "Ecological Guidelines for the Management of Tropical Forest Lands" (Poore and Sayer1993) produced by IUCN. A second IUCN publication on "Rainforest Buffer Zones" (Sayer 1991) provided further stimulus for the move towards more integrated approaches to forest management. In the Congo Basin pioneering projects in Korup National Park in Cameroon were initiated by WWF and a network of protected areas was established, funded by the European Union under a regional programme known as ECOFAC. These all broke new ground in seeking to better integrate conservation areas into their surroundings and to link forest protection with local livelihood issues.

Most people would now accept that using forests in ways that will improve the livelihoods of people in the Congo Basin should be a priority. The main challenge for ecosystem approaches ought to be to improve the livelihoods of the people that live in the forest zones and depend upon forest resources. However, this has not always been the case. Even today the generation of revenues for the governments and the interests of big-businesses have a predominant influence on policies in the region.

The ECOFAC programme was one of the first major initiatives that explicitly set out to do this. It emerged from a serious dialogue amongst forest conservation and management leaders from the countries of the region and their development assistance partners. Its preparatory phase included thorough diagnostic studies of the problems of conserving forest ecosystems in each of the countries of the region (IUCN, 1989). These studies remain amongst the better accounts of the full range of forest issues that would need to be addressed in any ecosystem approach to conservation. The final project set out to investigate a series of different approaches to forest conservation, with sites located in each of the countries. Each site was to pursue a different theme for conservation-friendly uses of land around a key protected area. The themes ranged from sustainable forest management for timber in CAR, to agroforestry in Cameroon, wildlife farming in DRC and sustainable management of bushmeat in Gabon. Provision was made for annual meetings of the staff of each of the component sites and these meetings were to rotate amongst the sites.

Operating this ambitious and innovative programme proved difficult. EU procedures required that the project be put out to tender and the companies that won the bid were more concerned with responding to the EU's onerous disbursement and reporting requirements than with fostering local ownership of the activities in the field. This programme was implemented largely by commercial companies, a number of whom emerged as important actors in forest conservation and management programmes during this period. The EU selected the protected area authority to lead the project in each of the countries and in most cases this agency lacked the competence or the authority to pursue the development activities in the non-protected parts of the sites. Combining the competencies needed to address the complex development problems of the areas around the ECOFAC core sites in a single technical package also proved difficult. It may have been unreasonable to imagine that this could be achieved in such a project. ECOFAC therefore became a rather conventional channel for institutional support to the core protected areas. The project did not generate much support from the host countries and fell into the common trap of being unable to withdraw its support without the risk of total collapse of the protected areas concerned. The project therefore was drawn into a series of extensions but did eventually begin to engage in activities to support the livelihoods of populations in areas surrounding its sites. However, this process took more than a decade and the project has yet to prove that it can really address conservation problems from an ecosystem perspective.

The WWF Korup project in SW Cameroon also provides interesting lessons on an attempt to conserve a critical forest ecosystem in ways that pre-empted much of the thinking of the ecosystem approach. The project had a very clear objective, the conservation of the species-rich forest on the Nigerian border. From its earliest days the project sought to involve local communities and supported a series of local sustainable development initiatives in the zone surrounding the park. However, it also fell into the classic trap of conservation and development projects in that it failed to establish real links between the development activities and conservation. The project was based upon the unproven assumption that good development in the peripheral zone would diminish pressure on the resources within the park. In reality the project may even have attracted more people into the park's periphery and thus increased pressure on the forests. Since appropriate measures to assess the project's impact were not put into place there is no real way of knowing what the impact of the project was. This criticism applies to many of the integrated projects that proliferated in the 1980s and 90s throughout the developing world and has been well documented by Wells and McShane (2004).

In recent years Cameroon has been at the vanguard of attempts to give communities more control over and benefits from forest resources. A 2002 law (the "Droit de pre-emption) gives communities priority rights to forest resources in their areas. A series of study tours and meetings have been organised to allow other Congo Basin countries to learn from the Cameroon experience and there are now plans for community forestry initiatives in Gabon, DRC and Congo.

Approaches to Sustainable Forest Management

During the late 1980s most of the attention of the mainstream aid donors and the Governments of the region was still focussed on improving the management of production forests. The Tropical Forestry Action Plan, prepared with international donor support for Cameroon in the late 1980s, was typical of a number of similar national studies carried out at that time. It was rooted in a vision of sophisticated large-scale concession management for international markets with silviculture treatments that would greatly increase future yields of commercial timber. It contained the implicit assumption that environmental benefits would be inevitable by-products of good forestry practice. The Cameroon TFAP was vigorously attacked by environmental NGOs on the grounds that it was going to increase logging pressure on natural forests and that it did not address the needs of local forest-dependent communities or of nature conservation. In reality very little donor support materialised to support implementation of the plan and the following years saw a great deal of energy dissipated in discussions about what sort of approach to forestry should be taken. However, the plan did initiate a period of intensive debate about the reorganization of forest management in the country. It also led to the adoption of a new and progressive forestry law in 1994 that provides for approaches to forest management which favour the interests of forest people and biodiversity. Today there are several well-managed forest concessions in Cameroon and a number of promising initiatives to encourage local communities to manage forests. The laws provide considerable benefits to local communities from forestry taxes and from the operation of community concessions. However some critics claim that illegal logging has exploded in and around these community forests. In some cases the larger concessions appear to have withstood pressures from illegal forest activities and agricultural encroachment but here again the record is mixed.

Cameroon remained the main focus of innovation in forestry in the region and although this introduction progress of innovative arrangements was somewhat tortuous, considerable progress was eventually realised on the ground. Intermittent periods of civil conflict in DRC, Congo and CAR inhibited both national and international initiatives in these countries during the 1990s. Congo did eventually enact a new forest law in the early years of the new century and CIRAD – Forêt succeeded in working with a logging company in Ngoto, CAR in developing a management plan.

One isolated example of success was the work of the Wildlife Conservation Society (WCS – the conservation arm of the New York Zoological Society) who pioneered both research and practical interventions to explore options for wildlife conservation in logged forests. WCS managed to maintain its field activities in Congo Basin countries through these periods of civil strife. WCS worked with a German owned concession – the Congolaise Industrielle des Bois (CIB) – in Northern Congo on a programme that was both interesting and controversial. WCS showed that the logged-over forests in the CIB concession were rich in large mammals and still supported viable populations of several rare species. WCS encouraged the concession operators to take measures to improve wildlife habitat, reduce hunting pressure by concession employees and prevent the transport of bushmeat from the concession. Many conservationists familiar with forestry issues in the region believed that the CIB initiative was of major significance in demonstrating the potential of managed forests to make major contributions to biodiversity conservation. However, the project came under attack from environmental activists in Europe who were fundamentally opposed to any logging of tropical forests. This lead to the irony that a project that offered better prospects for the maintenance of important populations of rare animals than many protected areas in the region was singled out for criticism by organizations whose role was precisely to conserve those animals.

The controversy surrounding the CIB concession epitomised the division of opinion that still persists in the Congo Basin – and in other tropical regions – between those who believe that well managed forests should be the core of conservation programmes and those who oppose that view. The opponents of sustainable forestry argue that although good forest management can be compatible with biodiversity conservation, corruption and political meddling compromise its potential. The proponents of this view hold that the only solution to tropical forest conservation lies in establishing ever more protected areas. Those whose experience lies primarily in Latin America hold this view particularly strongly. In that region there is less history of good forest management and protected area establishment has been shown to be successful in diverting development pressures away from forest areas with high conservation values. In the old-world tropics many protected areas in forests have failed to withstand development pressures and have suffered encroachment from loggers and farmers. However, in the old world tropics there is a long tradition of relatively successful post-logging conservation and a commitment to maintaining the "Permanent forest estate". At present protected areas in the Congo Basin are almost totally dependent on international funding, yet they receive very few international visitors. In these circumstances it is difficult to imagine the long-term maintenance of very extensive protected area systems and many observers are more inclined to place confidence in a well managed forest industry to assure the future of forest biodiversity.

A number of regional meetings and initiatives have addressed the issue of wildlife conservation in managed forests and these are reviewed in a report by the Association for the Development of Information on the Environment (ADIE, 2001). This report also proposes rules that should be followed to maintain wildlife populations in forest concessions.

Regional Initiatives to Conserve Forest Ecosystems

Many natural forests with spectacular biodiversity are located in remote border areas of the countries of the Congo Basin – it is their remoteness and inaccessibility that has allowed them to retain their concentrations of large mammals. These areas have been the focus of conservation concern, especially for international conservation NGOs. In a number of these areas problems have occurred because of the movements of poachers and their prey from one country to the next. The need for international cooperation to secure the conservation of the sites has long been recognised. The ECOFAC project began as a plan to use European Union regional funds to support conservation in the forests around the point where CAR, Cameroon and Congo meet in the Dzangha-Sangha area. The special needs of the Dzangha- Sangha area were also one of the concerns that led to the decision by the heads of state of the region to meet in Yaoundé in 1999 to discuss regional collaboration on forest conservation and management. At this meeting the Yaoundé Declaration (Box 1) was adopted and committed the countries to a regional programme that is remarkably consistent with the ecosystem principles that were agreed by the CBD three years later. Subsequently a regional ministerial committee was established (COMIFAC – Comité des Ministres des Forêts d'Afrique Centrale) to oversee the implementation of the declaration. This committee adopted two regional action plans for forests (Le Plan de Convergence et le Plan D'Action Prioritaire) both of which were strong affirmations of ecosystem approaches to forestry. There were concerns that the declaration and the plans would not lead to action on the ground but a review by the ITTO in 2002 concluded that significant progress had been made on many of the commitments made by the heads of state and the ministers (ITTO, 2002).

Box 1   **Proclamation of the Heads of State at the Yaoundé Summit, (Summary translation)**

The Heads of State committed their countries to:

- Biological diversity and sustainable management of ecosystems;
- People's rights to base their social and economic development on forest resources;
- Reaffirmation of the need for regional cooperation for conservation and development;
- The need for an international trust fund to support conservation, management and research on forest ecosystems in the region;
- Accelerate the process of establishment of protected areas and the sustainable development of existing areas;
- Develop fiscal measures to ensure the financing of conservation and management of forest ecosystem;
- Improve management systems and put into place certification systems corresponding to international norms;
- Increase the level of participation of rural communities in planning and management of forest ecosystems whilst ensuring adequate land for socio-economic development;
- Ensure greater involvement of the private sector in sustainable development and conservation of forest ecosystems;
- Ensure better inter-sectoral coordination on issues impacting on forests;
- Increase efforts to control poaching;
- Promote industrialization of the forest sector in ways that increase local value added and create employment;
- Promote national and regional fora and networks to encourage research and development and improve coordination and cooperation on forestry research and development;
- Develop sustainable funding mechanisms for forest development using forest-based revenues and international assistance.

Forest Institutions in the Congo Basin

A number of regional bodies have now been created to address forest issues. The Committee of Ministers of Forests of Central Africa (COMIFAC) and the Conference on Dense Humid Forest Ecosystems of Central Africa (CEFDHAC) provide guidance and cohesion at a political level and at the level of civil society respectively. An African Forest Law Enforcement and Governance initiative was launched in 2002. These initiatives seek to achieve harmonization or at least consistency between national laws and practices and to facilitate the exchange of information amongst the countries of the region. They have also provided the umbrellas for a number of targeted activities that involve more than one country in the region. The Global Environment Facility and a consortium of donors have funded a regional programme to collect and disseminate environmental information in the region. The African Timber Organization has led the process of developing criteria and indicators that might eventually form the basis for an African certification system for sustainable forest management. Hakizumwami and Ndikumagenge (2003) have described these regional processes in detail.

Although a lot of attention has focussed on regional initiatives in recent years it is probably still the national institutions that provide the main determinants of actions on the ground. The legal frameworks for forest conservation and management have been revised for all the countries of the region in the past decade. Development assistance agencies, the World Bank, International conservation NGOs and technical and research institutes have all been strongly associated with this period of legal and institutional reform. Civil society in the countries of the region has also been involved in the process to an uprecendented degree although some would argue that local livelihood interests have been less influential than regional and global environmental and economic concerns. However, there has been a proliferation of environmental NGOs working on forest issues during the 1990s. Box 2 lists the latest forestry laws for the region.

Box 2   **Recent forestry laws in the Congo Basin countries**

Cameroun – Loi numéro 1994 – 01 portant régime des forêts, de la faune et la pêche.

République du Congo 2000 – Loi numéro 16/2000 Portant code forestier.

Gabon – Loi numéro 016/2001, Portant code forestier.

République Démocratique du Congo – Loi numéro 011/2002, Portant code forestier.

République Centrafricaine – Loi numéro 90/2003 Portant Code Forestier Centrafricaine

---

All of these laws reflect a tendency towards a more inclusive – ecosystem – approach to forests. The preamble to the Congolese law refers to "forest ecosystems". Article 17 of the Gabonese law refers to sustainable management as including "*maintaining biological diversity, productivity, regeneration capacity, vitality and capacity to permanently satisfy economic, ecological and social functions without causing negative impacts on other ecosystems*". The legal framework in all of the countries has made considerable progress towards the sorts of objectives for management that are contained in the CBD principles for Ecosystem Approaches.

However, critics argue that the political rhetoric and legal commitments, both at a national and international level are not reflected in progress on the ground. An ITTO report in 2003 (Wehiong 2003) notes that "..... *there still exists a large gap between legal and regulatory measures and realities on the ground. This gap is mainly due to weaknesses in institutional structures and, material, human and financial resources*".

One could argue that it would be unreasonable to expect legal commitments and policy decisions taken so recently to already be having much impact on the ground. The new laws represent major changes in the arrangements for forest management and it seems reasonable that progress will take time and will be patchy. The new commitments to forestry have come at a time when all of the countries of the region are experiencing economic difficulties. Most of the countries have suffered declines in the per capita GNP in recent years. For example in 1999, the only country where the economy grew was Gabon and there it was only by 0.2%. GNP per capita ranges from $104 in DRC to $3,300 in Gabon but the economy of Gabon has been heavily influenced by oil revenues. Even Gabon is now suffering declines as petroleum resources are exhausted. The entire region has only 8,700 kms of asphalted roads (figures cited in Wehiong, 2003). Attempts to change and improve forest management have therefore come at a time when the capacities of the countries to even maintain existing services and functions have been stretched to the limit.

The international community has rallied to support forestry in the region but even this process can be slow and cumbersome. The World Bank has launched ambitious programmes to strengthen the "Forest-environment Sectors" in Cameroon and attempted to do so in Gabon and has included provisions for support to sustainable forestry and conservation in its economic restructuring package for DRC. Discussions have been initiated for World Bank support to the sector in Congo. The Bank has been consistent with its own recent policy in requiring broad approaches to forestry, environmental safeguards and a strong involvement of civil society in determining how the Bank's assistance should be provided. But these processes take time and relatively little has yet been achieved on the ground.

France has intervened more rapidly and in a more focussed way. It has worked at the level of individual concessions to help develop management plans that would ensure that environmental and social issues are addressed at the level of these concessions. A number of such management plans have now been completed but again this has happened at a time when concession operators claim to be facing difficult economic conditions and reports are mixed on the extent to which the plans are being implemented. One cause of concern is that some of the longer-established concessions that had been showing interest in improved forest management and in certification are now abandoning the area. Their concessions are being taken over by entrepreneurs who have little experience in forestry and who many observers fear will not make a long-term commitment to sustainable forestry.

A recent initiative under the Congo Basin Forest Partnership (CBFP) funded by the USA and some European donors is attempting to promote the integration of forest conservation and management at the scale of a number of large landscapes throughout the Congo Basin. The CBFP has only been operational since 2003. It is being executed by international conservation NGOs who have relatively little experience of operating such large scale and ambitious programmes. The objectives of the CBFP will require long-term commitments, yet funding is at present only assured for three years. So far, the most promising results from the CBFP have been in areas where the participating NGOs were already present on the ground and the CBFP was able to increase the resources available to enable them to scale-up their activities.

Some Success Stories from the Congo Basin

There may not be a single location in the Congo Basin where one can truly claim that the principles of ecosystem management are being applied in ways that give reasonable hope for their long-term sustainability. However, there are a number of locations where significant progress is being made. It is perhaps useful to reflect upon the things that appear to be working in these sites and the pre-conditions that seem to have lead to this modest success.

One of the most promising attempts to integrate the biodiversity, social and economic components of ecosystem management in the Congo Basin is in and around the concession of the Congolaise Industrielle des Bois in North Congo. The long-term commitment of the Wildlife Conservation Society to conservation in the area and its close ties to the concession operators has yielded valuable results. The concessionaires have come under considerable pressure from environmental NGOs in Germany, an important market for their timber, to improve their concession management. Most observers consider that they have delivered on their commitment to sustainable management although some technical issues relating to silvicultural treatments to ensure future harvests of high value species are still contested (Wehiong, 2003). In parallel, the Congolese authorities established the Nouabélé-N'Doki protected areas adjacent to the concessions in 1984–85 and WCS has consistently supported conservation in these areas since that time. The concession operators have sought to be transparent in allowing a number of assessments of their operations to be conducted over the years. These outside evaluations have at different times drawn attention to problems of excessive hunting of bushmeat and the use of CIB vehicles to transport it to urban markets. The company has responded by banning transport of bushmeat on its vehicles and has encouraged local rearing of livestock to satisfy local meat demand. Conditions of local people, particularly the Baka pygmies, have been a cause of concern and measures have been taken to improve their livelihoods. Programmes are now in place to monitor large mammal populations. The area is one of the priority landscapes for the CBFP and has received international assistance from a number of sources in support of improved forest conservation and management. The conservation programmes in the area are now being replicated in adjacent parts of Gabon, Cameroon and CAR.

WWF has been active for almost thirty years in the Dzangha-Sangha region in CAR. They have worked closely with concession operators in the area and the parks and concessions have to some extent been managed in compatible ways. The Sangha and N'Doki protected areas were established in 1988 and the infrastructure of the concessions has been useful in protecting the area and facilitating visitor access. WWF has maintained a presence in the area throughout this period. This area is now receiving support from a number of international programmes although the present managers of the conservation programmes are not optimistic about the potential for tourism to ever generate sufficient revenues to cover management costs. Both this area and the adjacent forests in Congo and Cameroon still support large populations of elephants, gorillas and a variety of other forest wildlife and the concessions still operate successfully. However, the concessionaires claim that their operating profits are declining as they face competition from timber from more accessible areas and increased costs of extraction and transport.

A third location where some success has been achieved in the face of very difficult local circumstances is the Ituri Forest in DRC. This area is the home of the rare Okapi – a forest antelope. WCS has maintained a long-term presence and conducted research on this and other species. They gradually built up conservation programmes that were adapted to take account of the presence of a population of pygmies in the area. The programme has been maintained throughout periods of violent conflict that has had direct impacts on the Ituri forest itself. Notwithstanding this conservation and research activities have continued and the forest has now been given special reserve status and is listed under the World Heritage Convention.

These three examples all come from remote, sparsely populated and relatively inaccessible parts of the Congo Basin. Perhaps the real challenge lies in developing successful approaches to ecosystem management in the more densely settled and accessible forest areas. There has been a lot of interest in recent years in helping communities in such areas obtain the benefits of forest management and, where possible, manage forests themselves. These programmes have been particularly well developed in Cameroon where national laws encourage community forestry and where international donors have supported a number of initiatives. Management plans have been developed for a number of community forests and these are now being implemented – although the process of developing and obtaining government approval for the plans has been a challenge for the communities. Observers hold contrasting views on the success and the sustainability of these community concessions. They are often in areas where the most valuable timber has already been extracted in earlier logging cycles. Competition for land with tree crops such as cacao and coffee comes and goes depending on the profitability of these crops. The communities, as everywhere, have internal divisions and conflicts that create problems for the distribution of benefits. The communities also suffer from the fact that they are largely dependent on industrial forest operators for extraction and transport of their logs. In spite of these problems many people see such schemes as the best way forward in the more densely populated forest areas and at least in the short term they can yield multiple environmental and economic benefits.

The Way Forward – Unravelling the Complexity of Congo Basin Landscapes

The CBFP has underlined the challenge of reconciling livelihoods and biodiversity conservation at the scale of large landscapes. One approach to determining the sort of landscape configuration that will be optimal for achieving these two contrasting objectives is the use of simulation models. Modelling approaches are now used routinely in industrialized countries to support decision making on natural resource management problems and their use in the tropics is expanding. WWF has been experimenting with simple models to help plan and monitor its interventions in the landscape known as the Tri-National de la Sangha or TNS. This is the area around the meeting point of CAR, Cameroon and Congo that was referred to earlier and where WWF and WCS have worked for a long time with concession operators.

The objective of the modelling exercise was to work out the relative utility of different mixes of protected areas, logging concessions and community lands. The model was developed at a workshop attended by the WWF staff working in the area. The modelling was undertaken in a participatory manner, so that the model itself provided a framework for discussion and negotiation. The economic benefits to different stakeholder groups and the employment created by different types of land management were quantified. Similarly the costs of protection and the benefits from hunting safaris, bushmeat harvesting and the taxes paid to the government and to local communities from these different activities were calculated.

The model has already yielded some counter-intuitive conclusions. For instance it showed that if concessionaires comply with the law, and especially if they seek to attain international certification standards, then they make considerable contributions to biodiversity conservation. Thus if the proportion of the land under well-managed concessions increases, this would free up conservation funds to increase the intensity of conservation efforts in the national parks. The overall biodiversity outcomes in a landscape with a high proportion of well-managed concessions might therefore be better than in a landscape with a high proportion of the area totally protected.

The economic returns both to the government and to local people from logging and from tree crops (cacao) are about equal at $2000 per km² gross. Protected areas at best might yield an order of magnitude less. Under present conditions protected areas have to be heavily subsidised. So in terms of overall livelihood benefits the allocation of greater part of the landscape to tree crops might seem desirable. However, this would almost certainly encourage in-migration. People's decisions on whether to invest in tree crops are probably determined by their perceptions of the potential returns to their labour. Returns to labour on tree crops will be much higher in more accessible areas – near to main roads or to the coast.

The model was also used to explore the factors that impact on the hunting and trade in bushmeat. So, for example, the in-migration as a result of agricultural expansion and as a result of opening of logging concessions results in significantly increased hunting. It is not only the presence of more people but also their increased disposable income which increases demand for bushmeat. There was no evidence to support the common idea that improved on-farm livelihoods or availability of domestic livestock as protein sources would substitute for bushmeat.

One problem that the model exposed was that the funds generated from taxes on forest concessions and that are intended to be reinvested in the social infrastructure in the concession area are often not used appropriately or efficiently. This led to the conclusion that measures that improved account-ability at the local and national level would contribute to local livelihoods and thus to better forest management. It was thought that greater decentralisation of financial control to the district admin-istrations might encourage such transparency and accountability. Measures by WWF to empower the local civil society and foster local NGOs might help this process. Overall, poor governance and the absence of equitable and transparent application of laws and regulations were seen as major obstacles to achieving ecosystem management.

Perhaps the single most significant conclusion from the modelling exercise was that the interactions within the landscape were much more complex than had previously been thought. Our ability to predict the outcome of any particular intervention was limited. This was especially the case in a landscape that was divided between three countries with different economic, political and regulatory environments. In situations where local institutions are fragile and outside support is limited there are dangers in embarking upon excessively complicated programmes which need high levels of managerial skill and must be based upon agreements amongst highly divergent stakeholders. This led some to conclude that conservation NGOs should continue to channel a significant part of their effort into their area of core competence – protected area management. They should be cautious in expanding into the untried and uncertain worlds of managing large complex systems in which local development activities consume a large proportion of resources. However, at a higher level it is clearly desirable that there should be more coordination between investments in protected areas and those in sustainable forest management and infrastructure development.

It was also concluded that working at the scale of large landscapes required new approaches to measuring the impact of our interventions. A system was developed for the Tri-National de la Sangha that would allow annual assessment of a small number of indicators that would enable the tracking of changes in local livelihoods and biodiversity. It was felt that this would provide system-level tracking and be the basis for periodic adjustments in the balance between the effort applied to local development and that applied to protection.

Conclusions

The overall conclusion for the Congo Basin is that enormous progress has been made in establishing an enabling environment for ecosystem approaches to sustainable forest management. Serious challenges remain in translating this into real achievement on the ground. Synergies and com-plementarity between industrial logging and protected areas are clearly present. Exactly how one accommodates the need to improve local livelihoods with the need to conserve populations of large wild mammals is more problematic. The ultimate outcome will be determined as much by the general development patterns of the country as by interventions directly in the forests. If the population gradually moves to areas that have a comparative advantage for intensive agriculture then clearly there will be less pressure on forests. Many of the environmental values of forests may be maintained in community managed forests and in industrial concessions and these clearly provide more benefits to the economy and to local livelihoods than strictly protected areas. Policies that draw people into intensive agriculture, manufacturing or services and that encourage long-term commitments to industrial concessions and community forests in remote areas are needed. Resources to support strict protection can then be focussed on key biodiversity sites located within a matrix of sustainably managed forests. A number of key lessons can be learned from the experiences in the Congo Basin in recent decades, these can be summarised as follows:

1. All of the countries of the region have committed themselves to international agreements and national laws that are consistent with the principles of ecosystem approaches to forest management – progress on the ground is still lagging behind the commitments.

2. In the past decade there have been numerous projects initiated by international development and conservation organizations that attempt to integrate environmental and development objectives. Many of these are still under implementation and it is too soon to determine the extent of their success and failure although a number of studies have commented on the difficulties of implementing these sorts of activities (e.g. Wehiong, 2003).

3. National forestry institutions have been subject to continuing reorganization over the past decade and much of this change has been consistent with the achievement of ecosystem approaches. However this constant institutional change has not been accompanied by stable or increasing resources on the ground and the actual capacity of forest departments has weakened. The expansion of international assistance has led to the situation where the main role of forest departments is to be brokers and gatekeepers for this assistance and to service the international forestry commitments of their countries (representation at international meetings of the UNFF, CBD etc).

4. The practical difficulties of dealing with the participation of diverse stakeholders, overlapping institutional jurisdictions and conflicting objectives all contribute to the high transaction costs of these projects and account for their inability to deliver practical improvements on the ground, at least in the short-term. However, some smaller projects in the Mountains of Cameroon and at Lossi in North Congo appear to have broken new ground in engaging with communities.

5. Most international donor agencies are still operating on short time horizons and apply too much rigidity in pre-defining the inputs and outputs of their projects. These "project" approaches may not be well adapted to achieving the ambitious and complex goals of ecosystem approaches to forest management.

6. There have been some notable examples of successful attempts at the integration of conservation and development objectives. These have occurred where one or two dominant stakeholders (mainly international conservation NGOs and logging concessionaires) have made a strong commitment to a specific area and have maintained a significant presence on the ground for two decades or more.

7. Participatory modelling is one tool that can be used to come to grips with landscape complexity and to provide a framework for the interaction of diverse stakeholders.

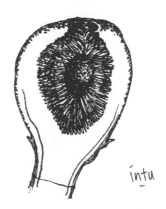

intu

9 Poor Farmers and Fragmented Forests in Central America

José Joaquín Campos Arce, Róger Villalobos and Bastiaan Louman

Introduction

While the ecosystem approach is a relatively new concept in Central America, many of its principles have already been adopted in sustainable forest management (SFM) initiatives in the region. However, implementation of ecosystem approaches and SFM in the short and medium term face many challenges. These include high population growth, high deforestation rates, small and stagnant economies, rural poverty and weak institutions. If ecosystem approaches are to become firmly established in the region, these social, economic and institutional constraints will need to be tackled head-on.

A key driver of ecosystem approaches in Central America has been the legislative changes that have led to decentralized forest management. In Guatemala this can be seen in the form of community forest concessions while in Honduras and Nicaragua it is local governments who have taken on increased responsibility for forest management. Financial mechanisms, particularly in Costa Rica and Guatemala and the development of market instruments (such as payments for environmental services) have also contributed to the spread of ecosystem approaches. In addition, intra-regional integration and the implementation of ecoregional approaches have encouraged conservation programmes to work at larger spatial and temporal scales and have led to more integrated approaches to the management of natural resources. The Mesoamerican Biological Corridor with its many associated initiatives is a good example of this scaling-up.

In this case study, we describe the evolution of ecosystem concepts in forest management in the region. We discuss the observed drivers of change, analyse the main current challenges of ecosystem approaches to forestry, and finally, put forward some conclusions regarding the regional strengthening of forest managment with an ecosystem approach.

Context

Ecosystem approaches are still new concepts in Central America[1] and are relatively unknown known to most stakeholder groups. However, over the past decade many of the ideas contained in the CBD Principles and operational guidelines have already been adopted in sustainable forest management practices in the region.

It is important to realize that the potential for implementing ecosystem approaches in Central America is constrained by some of the region's particular characteristics – not least the high rate of deforestation and ecosystem degradation found in many of its countries. Deforestation was estimated at 341,000ha annually (1.6%) for the decade 1990–2000, leaving only 34.9% of the original forest cover in place (FAO, 2002). The causes of this degradation include policies (both public and private) that have

---

1   Belize, Guatemala, Honduras, El Salvador, Nicaragua, Costa Rica and Panama.

favoured colonization and agricultural development at the expense of sustainable management of forest ecosystems. This trend has been exacerbated by the fact that 51% of the population live in poverty (Campos *et al.*, 2001). The bottom line remains that achieving SFM is extremely difficult in a situation where the population growth rate is high (2.5%), where economies are small and stagnating, where trade is being liberalized and public institutions are weak and unable to control illegal logging and trade of forest products.

Nonetheless, there have been some positive signs in this bleak picture, particularly over the last 10 or 15 years. Back at the end of the 1980s the International Tropical Timber Organization reported that there were no good examples of sound forest management in the region (Poore *et al.*, 1989). And yet today there are 691,346ha of forest certified by the Forest Stewardship Council in 42 forest management units of natural and planted forests (FSC, 2004). The community concessions of the Maya Biosphere Reserve are notable examples of these certified forest areas. FAO (2001) estimates that 13% of forested areas are now under some sort of management regime and that 462,000ha of forest plantations, principally in Costa Rica and Guatemala, currently exist (FAO, 2002).

Progress is also evident in the modernization of the region's central government institutions. Intra-regional integration and the strengthening of municipal governments (particularly in Honduras and Nicaragua) have helped in this regard, as have forestry producer organizations (particularly in Costa Rica and Guatemala) and the mobilization of civil society at large. Overall, there is now much broader participation in forest policy dialogues and the management of forest resources, as evidenced for example by the establishment of community forestry concessions in Guatemala and the development of financial mechanisms that value forest ecosystem services, particularly in Costa Rica.

However, many challenges remain. Despite the fact that some 22% of the region's surface has been allocated to protected areas, the resources and conditions for effective management of these areas are still inadequate. Reconciling conservation objectives with the livelihood needs of neighbouring populations remains a problem in these areas. Protected areas are still not properly integrated into comprehensive landscape-scale strategies although the Mesoamerican Biological Corridor is a major attempt to achieve this. At the same time, the silvicultural knowledge of many forest systems is still weak, notably in mangrove swamps, while their state of conservation is very poor (Paniagua *et al.*, 2001).

On the production side, there is a need for greater efficiency in timber processing and industrialization and for improved managerial skills to enhance the competitiveness of small and medium enterprises. Measures are needed to ensure access to markets and to reward improved environmental and social performance. But above all it will be necessary to establish larger areas of tree plantations and to bring natural forests under sustainable management especially in those countries with more forest cover and high levels of rural poverty such as Nicaragua and Honduras (Valle *et al.*, 2001; Ortiz *et al.*, 2002).

The high degree of fragmentation of the forest landscapes and the small size of the forest management units present additional problems. There has been a lack of coherent management frameworks to address the multiple linkages between the different components of forest landscapes – stakeholders, land uses, scales, and disciplines (Campbell and Sayer, 2003).

It can be seen therefore that the main challenges to implementing ecosystem approaches in Central America are social and economic in nature. Institutional and policy changes are needed to provide an enabling environment for SFM. Forest producers (especially small- and medium-scale ones) need access to technical and financial services and clarity over forest ownership and use rights (Campos *et al.*, 2004).

Mechanisms for payment for environmental services (PES) and other market instruments offer significant potential in helping promote ecosystem approaches. If those in charge of the management and conservation of forest resources receive economic benefits for maintaining the flow of services toward society, better management is likely to follow (Nasi *et al.*, 2002; Rodríguez, 2002). The use of market instruments to reward managers for the economic value of forest ecosystem services is being explored in a number of ways in the region (Rojas and Aylward, 2003). Costa Rica is pioneering these approaches and is serving as an example for other countries both within and outside the region (Campos *et al.*, 2001).

The Application of Ecosystem Approaches to Forest Management in Central America

Stakeholders

The evolution of SFM towards a more ecosystem approach in Central America has involved many different stakeholder groups including academic and scientific bodies, governmental and non-governmental organizations, industry and producer associations and international agencies. The entrepreneurial and industrial sector was probably the last one to become involved with SFM. Historically, the industrial logging sector has been largely indifferent to sustainable management, acting as if it was dealing with an abundant resource. Central American history has shown that SFM will only be accepted, welcomed and respected by society as a whole if all actors have access to information and favourable conditions are put in place (Nilson, 1999; Mora and Salas, 1996).

Schools of forestry were opened in Central American universities mostly during the 1970s, and in several regions they initiated forest management plans and demonstration areas. At the regional level, the Tropical Agricultural Research and Higher Education Center (CATIE) has been a spearhead in research and development for sustainable management of forestry plantations and natural forests. From the start, it adopted a multifunctional approach to forest ecosystems, emphasizing the strengthening of human capital. It established cooperation networks among the various stakeholders in the region (Galloway, 2002), in accordance with principles 11 and 12 of the CBD Ecosystem Approach.

During the 1980s, as SFM concepts began to be promoted by the international academic and scientific sector, these were picked up by local academia, with strong support from international technical cooperation. From this base, SFM concepts began to influence government policies and legislation. At the same time, environmental groups began to apply pressure, drawing attention to the worsening degradation of forest ecosystems. These different influences all played an important role in the development of regulations on the access to and use of forest resources. In parallel, additional pressures were coming from some markets and several business groups started applying sustainable management practices. Meanwhile a small-scale forestry producer sector has emerged, although it has not had the resources to make much progress toward sustainable management.

The ideas of ecosystem approaches were promoted within the framework of Integrated Conservation and Development Projects (ICDP), supported by international cooperation initiatives. One example of such an ICDP was the BOSCOSA project, implemented in Costa Rica from 1989 to 1995 by Fundación Neotrópica, in collaboration with WWF and USAID. In it, SFM was viewed as a tool for conservation of the forest cover and was used to establish a buffer zone for the Corcovado National Park (Donovan and Buschbacher, 1989). Like other ICDPs, its experience showed that addressing rural development is much more complex and slower than undertaking SFM. It also demonstrated the need to provide short- and medium-term incentives to make SFM viable within peasant farmers' production systems. This gave rise to one of the first proposals for a system of payment for environmental services (Campos, 1992). It reinforced the fourth and eighth principles of the Ecosystem Approach and taught us that SFM can make concrete contributions to more comprehensive local development programmes.

Other lessons learned from the ICDPs included the importance of fostering community organizations within a production system such as SFM, to facilitate capacity building efforts. It also became evident that, for SFM to become firmly entrenched in the rural livelihood strategies there is a need for short-, medium- and long-term strategies to tackle the underlying causes of deforestation and forest degradation. Promoting communication and collaboration between local, regional and national stakeholders is particularly important, as is the adoption of a landscape-level, interdisciplinary approach.

The Conservation Project for Sustainable Development in Central America was another ICDP, implemented during the 1990s by CATIE and several local partners, with funding from the Scandinavian countries. This project demonstrated that it is feasible to apply SFM to forest areas under 50 ha, as an integrated component of diversified farming systems based on agriculture and/or livestock production. The project also demonstrated that the feasibility of SFM could be further enhanced if farmers can process the timber before selling it, in order to obtain better prices.

The same project showed that communities in the Maya Biosphere Reserve in El Petén, Guatemala could act as forest conservation agents but that to do so they required more sustainable and profitable agricultural systems and guaranteed legal access to forest resources. The project pioneered community forest concessions and was subsequently reinforced by initiatives such as the CATIE/ CONAP Project. Community groups obtained legal access to the forest by means of concessions that allowed them to protect and use it. Indeed these groups often proved more effective than the State in taking care of protected areas. In the process, they improved their organizational and managerial capacities, their silvicultural ability and their environmental awareness (Monroy, 2001; Reyes and Ammour, 1997; Jiménez and Reyes; 2001; CATIE and CONAP; 2001).

Initiatives such as that in El Petén strengthen SFM as an option for communities. Stakeholders perceive the close interdependence between agricultural and forestry systems and the need for both to be profitable and therefore ecologically and financially well managed. Thus, it is one of the most successful examples of an ecosystem approach to forest management in Central America (Carrera *et al.*, 2002; Carrera *et al.*, 2001).

The German-funded Forestry and Logging Sector Cooperation Project (Cooperación en los Sectores Forestal y Maderero – COSEFORMA) was another important initiative to promote and strengthen SFM in Costa Rica. The project focused on improving industrial efficiency in production and processing and promoting market development and certification of forestry products. And in Honduras, the Broad-leafed Forest Development Project (Desarrollo del Bosque Latifoliado – PDBL), funded by the Canadian International Development Agency, conducted important training and educational activities aimed at better forest management on the Caribbean coast.

Box 1　　**Community forest management in Guatemala**

Official establishment of the Maya Biosphere Reserve in 1990 led to the first community forest concession being granted in 1994. Twelve further community concessions and two industrial ones followed this. The community concessions were given the same rights to timber as the industrial ones and this enabled them to use other products under a land use management plan (Carrera *et al.*, 2002).

Subsequently, the National Council on Protected Areas (Consejo Nacional de Áreas Protegidas (CONAP)) has helped develop a mechanism to monitor these community forestry concessions. This assesses not only the silvicultural techniques and the ecological impact of forest management, but also appropriate administration of financial resources and development of agricultural activities in harmony with forest conservation. This framework also includes the promotion of diversified use of the forest for both timber and non-timber species (Carrera *et al.*, 2001).

In recent years there have been a number of innovative and promising local initiatives in Central America. The Foundation for the Development of the Central Volcanic Range (Fundación para el Desarrollo de la Cordillera Volcánica Central –FUNDECOR) is one such example. This Foundation seeks a fair remuneration for the efforts of SFM in northern and central Costa Rica, in accordance with principle 4 of the Ecosystem Approach. It has made arrangements for the advance purchases of timber, whereby the producer receives income prior to the harvest, thus helping with the cash flow problem inherent in reforestation activities. This financial mechanism is complemented by group certification of small-scale forestry producers. The producers have received technical and logistic assistance and help in obtaining certification and they have had access to incentives such as payment for environmental services (Campos et al., 2004).

These kinds of initiatives foster a new perception among forest-owning farmers, with forests now viewed as valuable production systems, complementary to their agricultural systems and contributing to the sustainability of their farms. This is in contrast to the classical view in the region, where farmers have perceived the forest as a hindrance to development.

The approach of NGOs and international cooperation agencies in promoting the conservation and sustainable management of forests has evolved from one of paternalism to one that aims to strengthen the technical and entrepreneurial abilities of those who use the forest, be they community groups, small farm owners, or even medium to large businessmen. New NGO approaches have also developed thanks to private initiatives by forest owners. For example the Costa Rican Association of Private Reserves (Asociación Costarricense de Reservas Privadas) represents the interests of 120 private owners who voluntarily protect 60,000ha of natural forests. This network has been the basis for the establishment of the Central American Network of Private Natural Reserves (Red Centroamericana de Reservas Naturales Privadas) (Sandí, 2003).

'Environmentalist' groups have also played a key role in promoting SFM by constantly drawing attention to the shortcomings of forestry resource monitoring and management systems. They have also kept constant watch on forestry-related activities and all technical and political initiatives that have an impact on the state of conservation of the forests. For example, they applied pressure to avoid the establishment of a pulpwood plant by the Ston Forestal firm in its plantations in southern Costa Rica, arguing that it would have an ecological impact on the Golfo Dulce bay. These groups have also undertaken some questionable campaigns, such as the one that led to the halting of environmental service payments for forests under SFM in Costa Rica. This restricted the incentive payments to totally protected forests and withdrew support to forests under sustainable management. (Campos et al., 2004).

One of the most significant aspects of the recent evolution of SFM has been the organization of small-scale producers to seek legislation that is more in accordance with their needs. This has been achieved through the promotion of political dialogue. The Forestry Communities Association of El Petén (Asociación de Comunidades Forestales de El Petén – ACOFOP), for example, represents 22 communities in that part of Guatemala and has helped them to obtain and manage forestry concessions. At a regional scale, the Central American Indigenous and Smallholder Association for Community Agroforestry (Asociación Coordinadora Indígena y Campesina de Agroforestería Comunitaria Centroamericana – ACICAFOC), is an important political actor. Since 1994, this grass-roots organization has sought to obtain ready access for its members to technical and financial services, and to "*foster eco-development and empowerment of communities, ...based on their experience, as a practical response to the region's socio-environmental and cultural vulnerability.*"[2]

Producers have also organized themselves to improve production, processing and marketing techniques, for example in the community forestry concessions in El Petén, in Guatemala, or in the regional

---

2   www.acicafoc.net/home.php, accessed on June 30, 2004.

agroforestry cooperative, Cooperativa Regional Agroforestal Colón Atlántida Honduras Limitada, in the Caribbean region of Honduras. Several indigenous groups in the Honduran Mosquitia, and the Forestry Development Commission of San Carlos (Comisión para el Desarrollo Forestal de San Carlos) have taken similar steps. In Costa Rica, a regional organization with over 500 members that fosters SFM, expedites steps to obtain PES and provides technical services. However, many of these small and medium-sized groups are not yet firmly established and would require institutional strengthening to support their work.

Key changes in mentality

Many of the obstacles to more sustainable forest management in the region are cultural and historical in nature. The development models established during the post-colonial period did not consider the forest as a system of production, but rather as an obstacle to agricultural and urban land use. With the exception of a few timber species deemed precious, most timber was burned in the process of converting forests into agricultural lands. The State provided incentives for this conversion by granting 'use or property rights' to those who cut down areas of primary forest. These practices continued to persist until the mid-twentieth century. This under-valuation, together with the real or perceived abundance of timber resources throughout most of the region's history has contributed to low prices for timber. The situation is now changing, especially in the most heavily deforested areas, such as Costa Rica, where scarcity of the more valuable species has allowed a greater variety of species to enter the market. This makes SFM more viable and lowers the pressure on many traditional species that were being over-exploited.

Most importantly, the historical incentives for the conversion of forest into agricultural lands are disappearing, albeit slowly, as the State and society as a whole are becoming increasingly aware that forest systems produce significant goods and services. There are stumbling blocks however. In Costa Rica, for example, while conversion of forest lands into other uses is forbidden, there are provisions that allow conversion for tourist infrastructure. Some forest owners exploit these loopholes to mask the gradual elimination of their forests.

While development of technical and entrepreneurial abilities move forward, forestry producers still face high transaction costs, worsened by complex and excessive official procedures. There has been a shift from policies that fostered deforestation to policies that seek to protect the forest, but when these are poorly applied or regulated, they can encourage corruption and illegal timber extraction. There is a need for efficient oversight mechanisms (for the State and for the producers), in order to eliminate illegal activities.

Recent policies that seek to decentralize oversight of forestry are showing promise. The system of professional forest stewards or 'regentes forestales'[3] in Costa Rica is one example. These are private technical experts officially authorized to monitor SFM. Other initiatives are the Honduran Forest Management Fund (Fondo de Manejo Forestal), the community concessions in northern Guatemala (Carrera *et al.*, 2002) and forest sector cooperation networks in Honduras and Nicaragua.

Payment for environmental services (PES) is an important innovation in the development of incentives for sustainable forest management. The PES system in Costa Rica is particularly innovative (Rojas and Aylward, 2003; Rodríguez, 2002).

A few larger-scale or financially stronger forestry firms have adopted good SFM practices in the region and demonstrated the technical viability of SFM. Precious Woods in Costa Rica and Nicaragua, a firm that develops reforestation following high environmental standards and the Nova Group with a similar approach to reforestation in Panama (ECOFOREST) have been amongst the pioneers. The Pórtico

---

3   Foresters legally responsible for supervising field operations.

Box 2

Improving competitiveness and environmental performance of small- and medium-scale forestry enterprises

CATIE, with support from the Multilateral Investment Fund/Interamerican Development Bank, is strengthening the forestry sector's competitiveness in Guatemala, Honduras and Nicaragua through the Programme on Competitiveness of Small- and Medium-Scale Forestry Enterprises (SMEs) (Programa de Competitividad de las Pequeñas y Medianas Empresas (PYME) Forestales). The programme aims to enhance the visibility and develop the entrepreneurial attitudes of the members of the forestry production chain in each country. The programme targets businessmen who process raw materials from the forest and who depend on a source outside their firm. This is the starting point for a change of entrepreneurial attitude, towards the sourcing of raw material from forests that are managed under standards of sustainability.

In the case of the Petén, most suppliers have sawmills for primary processing of timber; in other cases, such as Honduras, groups of forestry producers depend on middlemen to market the raw material. The programme focuses on the planning and organization of forestry activities and provides information to local processing firms. This strengthens the position of the parties and makes them better able to ensure a financial return on the forest.

In accordance with Principle 4 of the Ecosystem Approach each step-by-step action in this programme establishes and strengthens a network of trade partners that will create a new business environment, based on a culture of sustainable forest management. To continue their productive activity, processing firms need a constant and long-term supply of raw material from the forest. The programme seeks to ensure that the cash flow in the production chain reaches the more entrepreneurial forestry firms, whose investments are based on operational plans (including local workers who are trained and aware of the importance of their work), and on projected income from previously authorized timber volumes.

The programme is consistent with Principle 6 of the Ecosystem Approach in allowing for sharing information.

Alejandro Santos, Personal Communication. August 2004. Project Leader Enhancing Competitiveness and Environmental Performance of Small and Medium-Scale Forest Enterprises in Central America. CATIE-IDB. Managua, Nicaragua.

Box 3

Payment for Environmental Services (PES) in Costa Rica

Conservation of forest ecosystems in Latin America can be feasible and fair if forest residents/owners who practice sustainable management can receive a fair remuneration for the goods and services that they provide to society.

PES were established in Costa Rica by the 1996 Forestry Law and placed under the control of a decentralized institution, the National Forestry Fund (Fondo Nacional de Financiamiento Forestal (FONAFIFO). This Fund manages income from a tax on fossil fuel and from international and national agreements for the sale of environmental services. It is based on the polluter pays principle: those who provide environmental services through conservation of the forest must receive fair payment for them.

The system compensates measures for mitigating greenhouse gases, protecting water sources, protecting biodiversity and ecosystems and maintaining scenic beauty, and has been so successful that the available resources are insufficient to cover the existing demand from forest owners. There are also private PES initiatives in the country by firms that need to ensure conservation of water sources for various purposes (Cordero and Castro, 2001; Nasi et al., 2002; Rodríguez, 2002). In the future, the system needs to increase its fund-raising strategies and ensure that payments go to low-income owners of forests, whose legal and economic status and lack of information make it difficult for them to obtain these incentives.

By 2003, FONAFIFO had issued PES contracts for 63,329ha of protected forests, 3,254 ha for reforestation, and 325 ha of established plantations. Since it began in 1997, PES has covered more than 400,000 ha belonging to 6,000 producers, with a total investment of close to US$100 million.

Source: Data from FONAFIFO on-line [FONAFIFO en línea], August 2004: www.fonafifo.com/

company has set an example by exporting doors made from timber from natural forests on the Caribbean coast of Costa Rica and Nicaragua to markets that require FSC certification.

Forest certification is key, as it generates expectations of a market that will pay for efforts made to conserve forest ecosystems. Although this market premium is not yet firmly established (Louman *et al.*, 2002), the number of certified management units in the region is growing. Technical assistance provided by some local NGOs has been crucial in this regard. Naturaleza para la Vida in Guatemala, FUNDECOR in Costa Rica and international NGOs such as the Worldwide Fund for Nature (WWF) have been particularly important. Carrera *et al.* (2004) provide a detailed discussion of the state and evolution of forest certification in Guatemala.

Joining links

While perceptions of the value of forest management have been gradually changing, there is still a widespread underestimation of the productive potential of forests and this is reflected in many political decisions. Secondary forests have been especially undervalued, even though numerous studies have demonstrated their productive potential (Finegan, 1992). It is not surprising that the sustainable management of secondary forests is still poorly understood by many forest owners and concessionaires. While this concept has been promoted for nearly fifteen years in scientific, academic and political debates, it is in conflict with a culture that has fostered deforestation and which has been in place for some 500 years (Campos *et al.*, 2002).

Real progress in establishing SFM in Central America will require the strengthening of linkages both within the forestry production chain and within the countries of the region.

The post-harvest links in the forestry production chain have received the least attention by institutions in this sector (Louman, 2003). In a manner that is similar to what happened with certain classical Meso-american agricultural products, most of the development of techniques to make the finished products has taken place outside the region. This in turn has inhibited the evolution of a forest management culture, as the raw material coming out of the forest is sold at a very low price, and does not provide a viable economic option for those using the land. Sawmill processing and the development of finished products are often inefficient and few operations provide significant added value. Thus most forest stakeholders remain poor whilst a few get very rich – an outcome that is not consistent with the equity principles of the Ecosystem Approach. Furthermore, processing staff rarely receive formal training and the equipment is often obsolete and inappropriate. Education for all those involved in the production chain is needed to build a more just and equitable society, in accordance with the Ecosystem Approach. It is unfortunate that, although there are several schools of forestry in the region, there are no specialized intermediate-level technical training opportunities.

Integration between the countries of Central America will therefore be important for the training of forest owners, residents and processing staff. But integration is also needed to support other aspects of SFM and ecosystem approaches. Central America is a physiographic unit with common elements and a relatively small size, so in accordance with principles 3 and 7 of the Ecosystem Approach, regional analysis of the interactions and impacts of ecosystem use is especially important. Environmental problems associated with deforestation, for example, should be analysed on a regional scale. Regional organizations play a key role in furthering this vision, as in the case of the Mesoamerican Biological Corridor project or the Central American Commission on Environment and Development (Comisión Centroamericana de Ambiente y Desarrollo – CCAD). This Committee was set up in 1989 and has as one of its main aims *"to promote participatory, democratic, and decentralized environmental management in the countries of the region."* [4]

---

4 www.ccad.ws/antecedentes/antecedenteshistoricos.htm, accessed on June 30, 2004.

Box 4 **Lessons to guide SFM in its evolution toward an Ecosystem Approach**

- An understanding of how forest ecosystems have evolved in Central America requires people to be placed at the focal point of analyses in order to comprehend their culture, history, characteristics and needs.

- Appropriate financial mechanisms for SFM need to be developed to take into account the externalities of SFM.

- The economics of corruption, its motivations and root causes need to be understood before policies can be developed to provide incentives for SFM and make it more competitive.

- An investment approach, rather than a subsidy approach, must be developed, particularly in rural areas.

- Integrated landscape management needs to be given more emphasis and forest resources must be managed on the basis of their interactions with the various components, stakeholders and sectors of the landscape.

- Education, and especially graduate education, must reflect this approach, to ensure the availability of technical staff able to address specific technical topics, but also experienced professionals trained in integrated natural resource management with a systemic view of the territories.

- Participation and the equitable distribution of benefits of conservation need to be promoted.

- Research plays a key role, but it must be relevant and translated into simple and practical tools and decisions at the political level and at the site level.

- Ecological sustainability is a continuous and probably unending process of learning, but good forest management can be implemented with the existing level of knowledge and with a precautionary principle and an adaptive approach.

- Mechanisms to monitor SFM activities must be constantly implemented and updated, as must the description of impacts and the definition of required adjustments (adaptive management).

- Monitoring must not focus exclusively on the forest as the management unit, but rather on the landscape as a whole, in the context of biophysical, ecological or political regions.

In addition, local markets are small and very sensitive to the global context such as imports of timber from other regions. Such problems have become more frequent with new free trade agreements (e.g. imports of radiata pine timber from Chile). Regional marketing strategies might contribute to more stable market management or to strengthening of firms that add value to forestry products established in the isthmus. For example, deforestation in Costa Rica is creating a growing demand for Nicaraguan timber. This shows the need to have regional management and oversight strategies regarding aspects such as illegal logging and trade.

Drivers of change

Before the 1990s neither forest management nor the absolute protection of forests was able to slow down the deforestation and degradation of forests in Central America. Regional rates of yearly deforestation averaged 2.1% from 1980 to 1990 (FAO, 1997). However, questions were raised about the management and protection strategies in place and their polarization, and this led to a re-analysis of the root problems of deforestation and forest degradation. Nevertheless, regional deforestation continues to be high (1.6% for the period between 1990 and 2000; FAO, 2001). Perhaps the most significant recent change has been acceptance of the need to integrate development and conservation. This allows for a greater emphasis on the human aspects of activities and policies geared toward SFM.

Several factors have contributed to this process, many of them pertaining to changes in the relationship between people and natural resources.

A cultural revolution: perceptions of the forest

The first principle of the CBD Ecosystem Approach states that management of resources should be a matter of societal choice. Forest conservation must be considered by Central American society as something that benefits the citizens of the region.

A greater social appreciation of the forest has emerged in recent years, not only because of improved access to education but also as a result of a series of natural disasters. Thus there is more awareness now about the links between forest conservation, water supply and the prevention of natural disasters resulting from drought, excessive rainfall, or hurricanes. Hurricane Mitch caused human and material losses assessed at US$ 6 billion, when it struck in 1998 (Kandel and Rosa, 2000). This disaster had a strong influence on perceptions by the Central American population. The subsequent debates on landscape management and susceptibility to strong rainfall led to a growing number of initiatives for integrated watershed management.

Other recent developments have also fostered better awareness of the real value of the goods and services provided by forests. Societies traditionally linked to the forest, and particularly indigenous ones, are familiar with the range of products it supplies, but few products from this region enter formal regional or international markets. The Yucatan Peninsula, a region that encompasses large areas of Mexico, Belize and Guatemala, has one of the most significant traditions of supplying non-timber forest products (NTFP) to the international market. The gum resin (*Manilkara zapota*), the fruit of allspice (*Pimenta dioica*) and the ornamental leaves of the camedor palm (*Chamaedorea* spp.) are important traded products. Institutionalizing community forestry concessions, as described above, creates more favourable conditions to foster and monitor sustainable management of populations of the harvested species (Carrera *et al.*, 2002; Mollinedo *et al.*, 2002).

Since 1989, the Costa Rican National Biodiversity Institute (Instituto Nacional de Biodiversidad de Costa Rica (INBio)) has negotiated bioprospecting contracts totaling US$2.5 million with major firms or institutions of industrialized countries. The State receives part of this money for management of national parks where the prospecting work is carried out (Laird, 2002). Furthermore, the contracts state that if a chemical principle inspired by or obtained from local biodiversity becomes the basis for a commercial activity, INBio and the National System of Conservation Areas (Sistema Nacional de Áreas de Conservación) will receive a percentage of the profits.

Tourism has become one of the main incentives for forest conservation on non-State lands, and one of the more attractive services provided by the forest to make its conservation more profitable. Sustainable timber production has become a tourist attraction in some areas. Tourists (often students) receive information on SFM while also learning about the ecology of the forest and about the various products supplied by the forest (Otárola, 2001. By remunerating forest owners for their conservation efforts, this type of tourism can help promote the Ecosystem Principle of equitable benefit sharing. However, these small-scale community-based tourist operators find it very difficult to compete with the large hotel firms.

Relations between people and natural resources

Various conditions have hindered the development of more favorable relations between forests and people in Central America. These include:

- A high population growth rate (2.1% year^{-1}; FAO, 2001).

- The fact that in 2001 at least 60% of the rural population was below the poverty line in six of the seven Central American countries (UNDP, 2003).

- High level of dependence on firewood (up to 68% of the population in Nicaragua depends at least in part on firewood for heating and cooking (UNDP, 2003)

- Unequal distribution of land and property rights (Mendieta, 1993; Miller et al., 2001), with 80% of the land in the hands of large landowners in 1976 (Mora-Escalante and Salas, 1996, quoted in IUCN, 2000).

- Low short-term competitiveness of forestry compared to agriculture (Miller et al., 2001).

- Official policies that encouraged the conversion of forests between 1950s and early1990s (Repetto and Gillis, 1988; Sandoval Correa, 2000).

- Downsizing of the State and its services, without a corresponding increase in the private sector provision of basic services such as health and infrastructure, or technical services for the management of forest resources.

- Expansion of unplanned and inappropriate land uses (Miller et al., 2001; PNUD, 2003), including use in areas not appropriate for them. Vargas (1992) has shown that 49% of Central America's land is either under or over-utilized.

One of the main problems is that rural families receive no income for the environmental benefits provided by their forests. There have been many efforts during the last decade to increase the value of forests for their owners and for the communities that depend on them. A number of studies demonstrate the potential of using non-timber products – NTFPs – from primary forests (Godoy et al., 2000; Mollinedo et al., 2002; Villalobos, 2003) and also from secondary forests (Santana et al., 2002). However, according to studies by the World Bank, environmental services account for 72% of the total economic value of forests in the region (Camino et al., 2002).

The system of payment for environmental services (PES) in Costa Rica, described above, seeks to transfer part of the maintenance costs of forest ecosystem services to their ultimate beneficiaries. The Central American, particularly the Costa Rican, experience has been a model for developing similar systems in other countries. However, it has been criticised for not significantly contributing to either the livelihoods of small-scale producers or to conservation in critical areas (Nasi et al., 2002). These criticisms have led to adjustments in the programme and have encouraged research studies on the value of forest services and the identification of high priority areas for landscape-scale conservation. Environmental service payments have been important in establishing biological corridors and protecting strategic watersheds.

A number of recent studies have shown that good forest management can be compatible with the conservation of biodiversity (Aguilar et al., 2000; Delgado et al., 1997; Ordóñez, 2003). This potential synergy can be enhanced by supporting good management with PES and certification (Campos et al., 2004). This provides compelling support for forestry as an environmentally-friendly economic activity with potential to contribute to conservation and rural development (Finegan et al., 1993).

The impacts of the removal of forest vegetation on local water flows have encouraged both local and internationally-supported attempts at landscape-scale management. For example, in Hojancha, Costa Rica, severe loss of forest cover in the 1970s was seen to alter the flow of rivers. Dry season flow decreased and rainy season flow increased. People experienced major floods, reduced harvests and malnourished cattle, as well as a lack of drinking water. When the price of beef fell, people began to encourage natural regeneration of forest vegetation to restore the landscape. They also established forestry plantations and enriched agroforestry systems. This situation was not unique to Hojancha (Camino, 1993). However, the fact that these efforts were supported at a political level and received support from both local and international organizations, together with the use of PES has enhanced the overall impact and replication of the Hojancha experience (Salazar, 2003).

Rural families throughout Central America have suffered severely from the effects of hurricanes, the El Niño phenomenon and extremes of rainfall and drought. Analysis of the effects of hurricane Mitch (Kandel and Rosa, 2000) and individual studies of the role of the forest in rural livelihood strategies have shown that forests may help mitigate the consequences of these extreme events. When climate phenomena destroy houses or cause harvests or markets to fail, forests, even fragmented or secondary ones, can provide people with the resources to overcome periods of hunger and rebuild their dwellings (Vásquez, 1999). These studies also show that the damage caused by hurricanes and forest fires is greatly increased by poor land management practices – and especially poor forest management.

Box 5   **A favourable political environment for landscape restoration and citizen participation**

In Hojancha, Costa Rica, an initial proposal for land use planning was developed in 1970 with support from the local parish priest. Subsequently, a local organization won its struggle to establish the district of Hojancha in 1971, and this improved governance of the area. In 1976 an integrated rural development plan (Plan de Desarrollo Rural Integral – PDRI) was drawn up. This plan focused on strengthening local organizations, creating jobs and improving sustainability. The 1975 law on the establishment of the district-level agricultural centers (Centros Agrícolas Cantonales) as producers' organizations that foster direct participation of the population in local development, allowed them, in 1978, to establish the Centro Agrícola Cantonal of Hojancha (CACH). The CACH was entrusted with implementing the PDRI and it played an important role, among other things, in strengthening local efforts to restore degraded areas. It helped the owners of those lands obtain funds from the government, at first as forestry tax-credit certificates (certificados de abono forestal) and then as PES. These efforts were reinforced by external initiatives, through watershed management and protection projects, technical support for establishment of forestry plantations, and international support to local initiatives for protection, research and production in forestry and coffee growing (Salazar, 2003).

As a result, forest cover has increased substantially and currently covers more than 40% of the land area. Forestry is now the main economic activity in the district and forests have helped improve scenic beauty. Tourism initiatives have followed and tourist attractions now include ecologically friendly agro-industrial projects.

The effects of deforestation and forest fragmentation on biological diversity are viewed as less urgent. Biodiversity currently has little immediate impact on the livelihoods of most of the inhabitants of the region. However, it is estimated that 50 animal species and 200 plant species are in danger of extinction in the region (UNDP, 2003) and forestry and environmental laws have been adapted in some countries to help conserve these species.

A classic case is that of the green macaw (Ara ambigua) in northern Costa Rica. The forest almond tree (Dipteryx panamensis) is important for nest sites and food for this species. A decree in 1996 restricted extraction of this tree to a maximum of 50% of individuals between 70 and 120cm dbh. All trees of this species over 120cm dbh were protected. Despite this restriction the range of the green macaw has declined to 10% of its original extent and the number of macaws observed has also diminished (Chassot et al., 2001). The continued decline of the macau is blamed on continued illegal and legal felling of several tree species and fragmentation of its habitat.

Research studies show that the macau does not cross large open areas. Conservation of the macaw requires continuous forest cover over larger areas and connections between these large forest areas and smaller forest fragments (Ramos, 2004). Emphasis is now shifting to protecting the species in the more extensive forests in neighbouring Nicaragua (Chassot et al., 2003). This example shows the need for conservation action at large landscape scales involving landowners, decision makers and special interest groups (tourism operators, conservationists and farmers). This work has led to the establishment of the Maquenque National Park in Costa Rica and the bi-national Wawashan – La Selva Biological Corridor. Through these initiatives local people have become involved in conservation of private and public forests in the area.

Relations between special interest groups

One of the major changes in recent decades has been the formalized participation of communities in forest management. The Social Forestry System (Sistema Social Forestal) began in 1974 in Honduras. It was subsequently strengthened in the northern part of the country, with support from international aid agencies who encouraged the establishment of the Integrated Management Areas (Areas de Manejo Integral – AMI) (Mendieta, 1993). In several cases this led to good forest management and created a financially-viable alternative that helped contain expansion of the agricultural frontier (Caballero et al., 2002). Another project began in central Honduras in 1992, working with communities and smallholders to foster management of pine forests. The success of this project was due to involvement of forest owners in the management and processing, and through the development of small-scale sawmills (Lazo, 2001; and Scherr, 2000; quoted in Scherr et al., 2004).

Community forestry concessions in northern Guatemala are another example of initiatives that combine conservation and socio-economic development. The agricultural frontier was contained and people were provided with community infrastructure, jobs and greater technical, organizational and administrative capacity (Carrera et al., 2002). Government monitoring and independent certification were linked to the allocation of use rights to the various stakeholders. The objective was to add local value to forest products, increase stakeholders' technical knowledge and access to information, a combination of factors that Poore et al. (1989) identified as crucial to attaining SFM. New remote sensing technologies helped spatial planning and monitoring (Carrera et al., 2002).

Initiatives by communal and indigenous groups in the region are supported by ACICAFOC whose members manage two million hectares of forest. These groups participate in exchanges among organizations to share lessons and cooperate in negotiations with government bodies (Chinchilla, 2002; IUCN, 2000).

In the nineties there were more initiatives to foster communication between various stakeholders. For example, Galloway (2001; 2002) reports on cooperation networks that seek to develop participatory strategic planning of management of natural resources. These networks have been able to coordinate efforts and make better use of the existing knowledge and capabilities in their work areas. They have attained political recognition as a discussion and feedback forum in northern Honduras and southern Nicaragua.

The nineties also saw greater integration between the different countries of the region. This was reflected in the establishment of the Central American Commission on Environment and Development (Comisión Centroamericana del Ambiente y Desarrollo – CCAD) as the official ministerial body responsible for follow-up to the 1992 Earth Summit agreements. More recently, regional cooperation has received further impetus, not least from the effects of hurricane Mitch, which showed that natural disasters do not respect borders and that their effects can only be mitigated by international efforts. CCAD has played an important role in promoting regional conservation projects such as the Mesoamerican Protected Areas System and Biological Corridor. It has supported planning, monitoring

---

Box 6   Catalysts of the Ecosystem Approach to forest management

The case studies from Hojancha and the northern zone in Costa Rica, MAFOR and the Social Forestry Sector in Honduras, operational networks in Nicaragua and Honduras, concessions in the Maya Biosphere Reserve in Guatemala, ACICAFOC and CCAD at the regional level suggest that the following are key catalysts of change towards ecosystem approaches:

- The need to improve resilience against the effects of large-scale natural phenomena.
- The need to deal with the negative hydrological effects of deforestation.
- The need to diversify land use to mitigate climatic impacts and market changes that affect local economies.
- New laws, PES and other incentives, and C&I for good management.
- Political will to improve conditions for SFM.
- Organization of small- and medium-scale producers to improve their participation in a political dialogue and to enhance the visibility of SFM.
- Access to governmental and non-governmental technical and financial services (at the local, national, or international levels).
- Enhanced clarity of use rights and access to the forest and its resources.
- Greater citizen participation made easier by information sharing, strengthening of marginalized groups and pressure from international cooperation agencies.
- Improved knowledge and technology available for key actors.
- Greater proportion of the value of forest goods and services obtained by those who are involved in forest management.

---

and oversight of forest management through the Central American Forestry Action Plan (Plan de Acción Forestal Centroamericano). This gave rise to the Central American Forestry Strategy (Estrategia Forestal Centroamericana), the Lepaterique C&I process and strengthened the legal and political frameworks of all the Central American countries.

Main achievements and challenges

An assessment of the implementation of SFM in Central America over the last two decades reveals some important achievements with regards to the different principles that make up the CBD Ecosystem Approach. Many of these achievements are incomplete and challenges remain in fully attaining a more holistic approach to forest management. Table 1 presents a summary of the main achievements and challenges regarding the 12 principles of the CBD for the Ecosystem Approach.

Table 1. Main achievements and challenges for the Ecosystem Approach to sustainable forest management in Central America.

Principles	Main Achievements	Main Challenges
The objectives of management of land, water and living resources are a matter of societal choice	Participatory management in some regions (e.g. forestry concessions in Peten, Guatemala; landscape restoration in Hojancha, Costa Rica; and land-use planning in El Castillo, Nicaragua). Better access to information and awareness for societal decision-making processes regarding the use of forest lands.	Strengthening existing or development of new participatory decision-making mechanisms (e.g. regional councils in conservation areas, model forests and watershed management committees). Provision of adequate information and environmental awareness for all stakeholders. Comprehensive analysis of forest products and service needs and production options at the national and regional level.
Management should be decentralized to the lowest appropriate level.	County Agricultural Centers and conservation areas in Costa Rica. Technical municipal offices in Honduras.	Capacity building for local organizations. Strengthening or development of producer organizations.
Ecosystem managers should consider the effects (actual or potential) of their activities on adjacent and other ecosystems.	Some examples of forest protection (e.g. mountain forests for water production). Establishment of protected zones within logging areas (e.g. water courses and steep slopes). Zoning of forest uses within watershed management initiatives. Management of biosphere reserves (e.g. Maya – Guatemala and Río Plátano – Honduras).	Decision-making based on better understanding of the interactions between the ecological, social, institutional and economic factors at the landscape level. Development of tools for land-use planning, management and monitoring at the landscape level.
Recognising potential gains from management, there is usually a need to understand and manage the ecosystem in an economic context. Any such ecosystem-management programme should: (a) Reduce those market distortions that adversely affect biological diversity; (b) Align incentives to promote biodiversity conservation and sustainable use; (c) Internalize costs and benefits in the given ecosystem to the extent feasible.	Payment for environmental services and other incentives in Costa Rica and Guatemala. Eco-tourism as an economic alternative for forest management. Availability of information regarding the economic value of the multiple functions of forests. Some successful industries and alliances among producers and industries that have increased profitability and access to markets.	Development and strengthening of mechanisms that provide proper incentives for SFM. Reduce unfair competition from illegal logging and trade. Reduce excessive transaction costs for SFM. Develop local markets that favour sustainable managed sources of a wider variety of forest goods and services (including certified sources). Further organization of alliances among producers to increase competitiveness.

Principles	Main Achievements	Main Challenges
Conservation of ecosystem structure and functioning, in order to maintain ecosystem services, should be a priority target of the ecosystem approach.	Progress in technology and legislation that protects ecosystem structure and functioning. Development of innovative tools to monitor environmental performance of SFM. Better knowledge and understanding of fragmented landscape processes.	Increase the implementation of good forest management practices (e.g. through proper legislation, enforcement and incentives). Consideration of functions and processes at the landscape level in forest management policies and practices. Development of criteria for SFM based on landscape analyses.
Ecosystems must be managed within the limits of their functioning.	Increasing number of examples applying reduced-impact logging and good forest management practices (e.g. certified forests). Formulation and implementation of C&I (i.e. Costa Rica and Guatemala). Better information on growth and yield for timber species.	Better information on growth and yield of timber and non-timber species. Understanding the effects of timber and non-timber species extraction on the functioning of other groups and the ecosystem. Understanding of the carrying capacity and impact of tourism.
The Ecosystem Approach should be undertaken at the appropriate spatial and temporal scales.	Several institutions have addressed conservation at large spatial scales, notably the Mesoamerican Biological Corridor.	Rationalize (simplify) SFM legal requirements and techniques (e.g. GIS) for small-scale forestry (particularly in Costa Rica) bearing in mind the Ecosystem Approach as a framework. Strengthening the application of the Ecosystem Approach within regional and landscape management initiatives (biological corridors, model forests, conservation areas, biosphere reserves and watershed management).
Recognising the varying temporal scales and lag-effects that characterize ecosystem processes, objectives for ecosystem management should be set for the long term.	The use of written management plans as a legal requirement in all countries. Long-term guarantees of forest use rights in community and industrial concessions in Guatemala and community user rights in Honduras. Increasing number of examples of certified forest management and industries.	Long-term vision among forest managers and forest owners. Clear and secure property and use rights. An enabling political and economic environment for long-term investments in forestry.

Principles	Main Achievements	Main Challenges
Management must recognise that change is inevitable.	Use of monitoring systems at the regional and forest management unit levels in Peten, Guatemala and managed forests in other countries.	Adjust or develop effective monitoring systems according to the scale of operation to support adaptive management approaches at the policy and field levels. Better understanding of the nature and dynamics of changes in the forests in the region (hurricanes, fire, pests, logging, and fragmentation).
The Ecosystem Approach should seek the appropriate balance between, and integration of, conservation and use of biological diversity.	Several initiatives have integrated conservation and development objectives (projects, community concessions, certified forests). At some stages the payment for environmental services in Costa Rica promoted the integration of conservation and use of forest goods and services.	Wider awareness and support for initiatives that integrate conservation and use of forests. Adequate policies and incentives for multifunctional forest management. Wider use of payment for environmental services integrating conservation and use of forest products.
The Ecosystem Approach should consider all forms of relevant Information, Including scientific and indigenous and local knowledge, innovations and practices.	Increasing number of publications and other communication tools including wider sources of information. INBio in Costa Rica has made use of local and traditional knowledge	Enhance communications that are effective to diverse audiences (producers, policy and decision-makers). Integration of traditional knowledge with the scientific processes, including further efforts on participatory and action research. Better use of sound knowledge in policy-making processes.
The Ecosystem Approach should involve all relevant sectors of society and scientific disciplines.	Increased opportunities for participation of stakeholders in the policy dialogue and management of forest resources (e.g. formulation of C&I, certification, national forest programmes, networks in Honduras and Nicaragua).	Enhance collaboration among the different actors in SFM. Capacity building and awareness on interdisciplinary and collaborative work.

Conclusions

The social, economic and biophysical conditions in Central America are unique to the region. The implementation of ecosystem approaches must take these special conditions into consideration. The pressing needs of the rural poor and the increasing fragmentation of the remaining forests present major challenges.

A very important pre-condition for ecosystem approaches is the success of the processes and institutions promoting regional integration (such as the Central American Commission on Environment and Development, the Mesoamerican Biological Corridor and ACICAFOC). However, further research will be required to address the complexity of issues and uncertainty affecting ecosystem approaches to forest management. More investment, further capacity-building and better communication will be necessary. Support for producer organizations and increased entrepreneurial capacity will be key to successful implementation of ecosystem approaches.

It is also important to show practical examples of where ecosystem approach initiatives have been applied successfully. Long-term commitments to specific sites that have conditions that require ecosystem approaches are needed. These sites should serve as collaborative learning and demonstration areas for scaling-up and scaling-out lessons and experiences. In order to implement this strategy, much more effective collaboration between policy makers, international agencies, forest industries, NGOs and academic/scientific institutions will be needed.

Monitoring systems to evaluate the progress of current initiatives in the implementation of the ecosystem approach is also needed. These tools should contribute to the emergence of an adaptive management culture for sustainable forestry in Central America.

10 Australian Forestry: "Beyond One Tenure-One Use"

Ian Ferguson

Introduction

This paper reviews the ways in which approaches to the sustainable management of forests are being implemented as part of the broader social-ecological systems in the States of Tasmania, Victoria and Western Australia. These approaches have many parallels with the principles adopted by the Convention on Biological Diversity and are instructive in understanding the issues involved in implementing ecosystem management. The term Ecosystem Approach itself is relatively new in Australia. However, it is consistent with the earlier term of ecologically sustainable forest management arising from the deliberations on Ecologically Sustainable Development by expert Working Groups in the late 1980's e.g. Ecologically Sustainable Development Working Group on Forests Use (1991) and those of the Resource Assessment Commission's (1993) 'Forest and Timber Inquiry'.

The Policy Setting

Australia is a Federation of formerly independent States in which each retains responsibility for land management under the Commonwealth Constitution. For forest policy and management, a clear devolution to the States prevailed until the 1950s, with the exception of special wartime powers in World War II. This was because almost all of the public concerns relating to forest management were confined territorially within individual States. The predominant mode of management was a command and control regime under the State forestry agencies, which also had considerable control over the publicly available knowledge base.

The development of public concern about conservation and, later, the environment, has been accompanied by major changes in the information available to the public. Over the period since the 1950s, and especially since the 1970's, the media have become more concentrated in ownership, more national (and international) in focus and, with the development of television, more pervasive in informing the public about environmental matters both verbally and visually. All State land management agencies have struggled to deal with the change from virtually exclusive control of policy to one of increasing public participation in policy formation.

In contrast to the administrative autonomy in land management provided to the States under the Constitution, the policy role of the Commonwealth government in forestry and environmental matters has greatly increased. Any substantial dispute in the field of forest conservation and the environment quickly became a national matter through the combined influences of the media, especially television, and the national stakeholder groups (principally the forest industry, unions, landholder and environmental non-government organizations).

The Commonwealth Government has no direct powers over land management, so it increasingly uses its indirect powers under the Constitution to influence the outcomes at a State level, often over-riding or confounding the actions of the State concerned. The most important of these powers were those under the Constitution that gave the Commonwealth control of international trade and treaties, and thus of exports and of World Heritage matters. Other important powers derived from Commonwealth legislation on Australian Heritage and environmental protection, enabling the Commonwealth to use their provisions to frustrate proposed State actions using the threat of withholding grants to States. Where the Commonwealth and State government concerned were of different political persuasions, both frequently provoked deliberate disputes, especially over the granting of licenses to export wood chips by the Commonwealth government. Disputes over forests progressively became more frequent and vigorous and involved most States at some stage. Divisions between stakeholders became increasingly polarized, normally with the industry and unions supporting a production view and the environmental non-government organizations taking a conservation view. Most disputes were therefore characterized by arguments suggesting, in simplest form, that a change in tenure from State Forest to National Park was the sole route to achievement of a conservation goal, while retention as State Forest was the sole route to retention of wood production and dependent industries. Dovers (2003) aptly characterized this as a 'one tenure - one use' argument. Because owners of private forests or land were seldom directly involved, they played a lesser role until the recent expansion of plantations on private land.

In 1992, the respective Commonwealth Ministers responsible for resources and the environment had a difference of opinion and the former gave unilateral approval to renewal of a license to export woodchips. This resulted in a massive public protest by stakeholder groups, culminating in a temporary blockade of Canberra by logging trucks. The blockade was the trigger for recognition by the Commonwealth and State governments that this type of interplay was potentially destructive of the standing of both levels of governments, in addition to being counterproductive to all stakeholder interests, and hence the development of a joint Commonwealth-State agreement (Commonwealth of Australia, 1992) that ultimately led to the Regional Forest Agreement process. According to Dovers (2003), the process was 'the most well- funded and intensive resource allocation process undertaken in Australia'. Details of the process are described in official publications (Agriculture, Australia, 2004). However, a brief review of the policies and outcomes in three different States may be useful in putting the processes and associated problems in contexts.

Reference will be made to Tasmania, Victoria and Western Australia because the author has had most involvement in these States and the similarities and differences highlight some issues for an ecosystem approach to sustainable forest management. McKinnell et al. (1991) provide a set of descriptions of forest practices and management in the various major forest types in contention in these States, as they existed prior to the Regional Forest Agreement process. The Regions involved are shown in Figure 1 and span a wide range of forest types and conditions in southern Australia.

In all three States, the forest tenures most under debate have been State Forests and sometimes 'Vacant' Crown Land under the control of the respective State forestry agencies. Trees of the genus Eucalyptus and its recently created sibling subgenus, Corymbia, generally dominate the species distributions in these forests. The dominant tree species and in some cases the forest structures are quite distinct in Western Australia from those in the eastern States of Tasmania and Victoria. Western Australia is dominated by Eucalyptus diversicolor (karri) in the higher rainfall relatively even aged (tall open) forests and E. marginata (jarrah) in the mainly uneven-aged (tall open or open) forests of the intermediate to lower rainfall areas of the South-West Region. Corymbia calophylla (marri) is often a secondary tree species in both forest types. Although seemingly relatively uniform in terms of species and structures, the understorey and ground flora are often very diverse in the E. marginata dominated forest, involving a subtlety that makes ecosystem differences initially difficult to discern (Mattiske Consulting, 2000). Tasmania and Victoria, which were once land linked, have a much more diverse array of dominant tree species and mixtures thereof, reflecting a greater diversity of climatic niches and soil types. The major forest types include higher altitude E. delegatensis (alpine ash) forests; temperate rainforests in Tasmania of Nothofagus cunninghamii (beech), wet eucalypt forests such as

Fig. 1. Forest regions of Australia

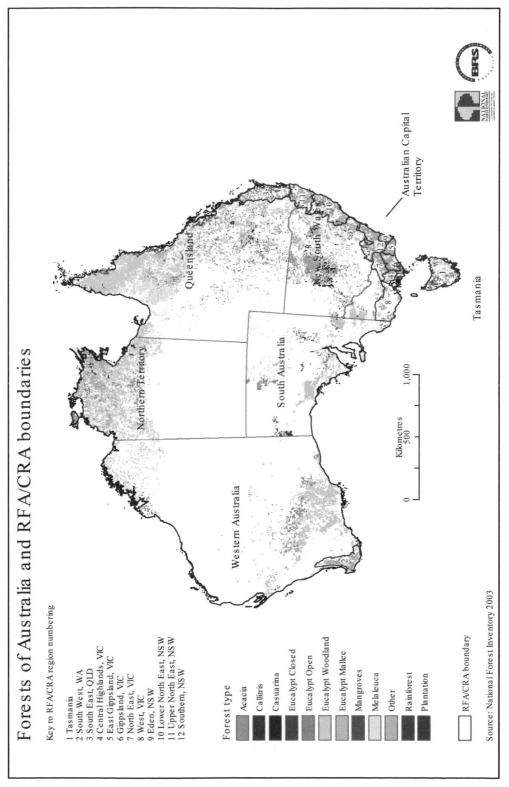

Forests of Australia and RFA/CRA boundaries

Key ro RFA/CRA region numbering

1 Tasmania
2 South West, WA
3 South East, QLD
4 Central Highlands, VIC
5 East Gippsland, VIC
6 Gippsland, VIC
7 North East, VIC
8 West, VIC
9 Eden, NSW
10 Lower North East, NSW
11 Upper North East, NSW
12 Southern, NSW

Forest type

- Acacia
- Callitris
- Casuarina
- Eucalypt Closed
- Eucalypt Open
- Eucalypt Woodland
- Eucalypt Mallee
- Mangroves
- Melaleuca
- Other
- Rainforest
- Plantation

RFA/CRA boundary

Source: National Forest Inventory 2003

Western Australia

Northern Territory

South Australia

Queensland

New South Wales

Australian Capital Territory

Tasmania

Kilometres
0   500   1,000

those dominated by E. *regnans* (mountain ash); intermediate rainfall forests dominated by E. *obliqua*, E. *dives, and* E. *radiata*; and a range of drier forest types that are less important in terms of wood production. Many of the wetter forest structures are naturally mainly even-aged. Victoria has a very large area (circa 120,000 ha) dominated by even-aged E. *regnans* (mountain ash) resulting from a massive wildfire in 1939.

Commonwealth and State Inquiries

Many Commonwealth and State inquiries and policy initiatives have been conducted since 1970 to address forest conservation versus development disputes, culminating in the Regional Forest Agreement process in 1997. Proponents of the Regional Forest Agreement hoped that the process might reduce, if not eliminate, many of the past disputes and for this reason it secured the support of both major parties in the Commonwealth Parliament, despite its considerable expense. The respective histories of the three States show that this hope has not yet been realized.

Tasmania

In Tasmania, the disputes have a long and varied history, reflecting the economic importance of the timber industry to the State economy, as well as the extra-ordinarily concentrated yet varied forest estate, rich in other values. During the past 20 years, the forestry sector has had some 20 separate inquiries into various aspects of forest policy and practices. Among these was a Commonwealth-sponsored inquiry into the Lemonthyme and Southern Forests areas. The inquiry (Helsham *et al.*, 1988) was chaired by a leading judge, assisted by two other commissioners. Legal representation was allowed, leading to a prolonged and very expensive inquiry. The inquiry recommended a balance in terms of conservation and development but it was not well received by conservation or industry interests. Christie (1990) argued that it raised doubts as to the competence of the legal system to deal with scientific and technical evidence in environmental disputes. A newly elected Commonwealth Government increased the area reserved by 'two orders of magnitude above the area recommended in the majority report' of the inquiry (Hickey and Brown, 2003). Disputes continued despite attempts to find agreement through a State Government sponsored Forest and Forest industry Strategy. Its outcomes led to a walkout by conservation interests and the eventual demise of the Green-Labor Parliamentary Accord (Hickey and Brown, 2003).

The Resource Assessment Commission (1993) Australia-wide 'Forest and Timber Inquiry' also invested considerable expert resources in considering Tasmanian forests. Again, it made many recommendations concerning better forest practices, but these received little attention in the media. Its recommendations were not taken up at the time and the Commission was later disbanded. Space does not permit a detailed historical review of the many other inquiries but the sheer volume, cost and uncertainty created by the various Tasmanian inquiries has become a major concern, such that both major political parties wish to avoid further major inquiries and are supportive of Regional Forest Agreement outcomes for that reason, among others.

In terms of process, the Regional Forest Agreement ran reasonably smoothly. Some conservation groups stood outside the process but others participated to varying degrees. Public participation was well handled by the then Public Land Use Commission, (now replaced by a Resource Planning and Development Tribunal), an independent body established to conduct public land use inquiries. This independence was important in diminishing cynicism that would have been generated about the process, had the forestry agency itself conducted it.

The Agreement is currently undergoing a five-yearly review by a joint Commonwealth-State team. Some of the issues currently under dispute stem from recommendations not accepted or observations of earlier working groups in the initial Agreement, including the independence of the Forest Practices Board (now to become an Authority), concerns over the impacts of some forest practices and clearing of cutover native forest for plantation development.

Other issues stem from matters outside the terms of reference of the initial Agreement and relate to the extent of reservation of some forest types; the continuing harvesting of old growth forest, albeit at a lower level than in the past.

The issue of the extent of reservation of forest types stems from the decision of the initial joint Commonwealth-State Committee to consider Tasmania as one Region, rather than dividing it into biologically distinct regions as was done in other eastern Australian States. Conservation groups claim a deliberate bias in that choice, alleging that under the prescribed criteria (to be discussed later), it resulted in a higher reservation of non-commercial forest relative to commercial forest than would otherwise have been the case. It is not possible to gauge the Committee's motives in this respect but my own view is that the choice was more likely to have been driven by the need for simplicity and a relatively short process, rather than a long sequence of separate small regional processes in a State that is suffering acute 'inquiry fatigue'.

Old growth forest remains an iconic issue for conservation groups and one that has been extraordinarily rewarding in the impact of media imagery on urban voters both in Tasmania and the mainland. So much so, that in the recent (October 2004) elections, both major national parties advanced policies that promised substantial reservation of the remaining old growth forest in Tasmania, despite the pleas of the State Labor Government and State Liberal Party to adhere to the Regional Forest Agreement. This illustrates the political power of the 'one tenure-one use' argument (Dovers, 2003) and associated public perceptions of media old growth imagery. The national Labor Party promised virtually complete reservation together with a massive programme of financial assistance. However, this was announced against opposition from the State Labor Government, public opposition by certain of their own Tasmanian candidates in the Commonwealth election, and strong public opposition from the national forestry union. The national Liberal Party followed with a less complete and explicit reservation policy that promised to maintain existing timber industry employment and expand opportunities. While it would be a gross over-simplification to say that the latter policy won national government for the Liberal Party, it certainly had a marked effect on some Tasmanian and mainland electorates.

Victoria

The election of a Labor Government in 1983 saw a desire to defuse the extreme polarization of views expressed by the principal interest groups regarding forest conservation and development. The Government appointed a Board of Inquiry to inquire into all aspects of the timber industry in Victoria.[1] Legal representation was not allowed. The Premier of the day, a solicitor, took some convincing of the merit of this approach but it greatly reduced costs and reduced the personal angst among persons giving evidence that legal representation otherwise often generates. Some 850 written submissions were received and 25 days of public hearings were conducted during the 20-month inquiry, involving evidence on oath about the submissions. The Government accepted a lengthy raft of recommendations (Ferguson, 1985), as did the Opposition, and the recommendations received some media exposure. The Government introduced a major new Timber Industry Strategy, achieving a balance and improvements in forest practices that were, for the next decade, widely accepted.

---

1   The author was the sole Member and Chair.

Nevertheless, certain geographic icons of the conservation movement remained prominent in media debate. One of these was the Otways State Forest, an area heavily logged from 1820 to 1940 and now carrying some fine mature regrowth forest and widely used scenic drives. The forestry agency recognised the local concerns and invested heavily in consultative planning and modelling (Dargavel *et al.*, 1995) to develop an appropriate management plan with respect to timber harvesting in this area. The area was unusual in that the wide spread of ages of the regrowth stands enabled the overall annual harvest to be progressively increased while withdrawing from or greatly modifying harvesting on catchments and other sensitive areas. However, at the conclusion of the planning process in 1992, the plan met considerable opposition from both conservation and industry interests.

After 1992, population changes outstripped the plan and process. The southern coastal strip became an ever more popular holiday area, with a substantial itinerant population of metropolitan residents escaping from the city for weekends and holidays. The farming areas surrounding the forest were also increasingly becoming 'hobby farms' for urban professionals. Forest villages to some degree had become sought after by alternative lifestylers. A strong NIMBY (not in my back yard) attitude to timber harvesting developed in the region. This was reinforced by locally-based conservation groups and concerns over watersheds supplying domestic water. Tourism also became an increasingly important focus, leading to a feasibility study of a treetop walk in a section of the State Forest. The then Labor Government decided to change the State Forest to National Park as part of its election policy in early 2003. The debate was mainly treated by the media as a 'one tenure-one use' argument despite the regrowth nature of the forest, with the future merits of tourism industry employment counterbalancing or outweighing those of employment at risk in the timber industry.

Western Australia

In 1983, following a succession of disputes, the newly elected Western Australian State Government initiated a major policy review by three respected experts that resulted in the formation of a new Department of Conservation and Land Management, CALM, in 1984 (Resource Assessment Commission, 1992). It took over responsibility for all rural public land management, including all the responsibilities of the former Forests Department in the southwest corner of the State. This new department created a highly innovative and statewide approach to conservation, as well as improving standards of forest practice. These initiatives reflected the intellectual flair and vigour of the chief executive, who had been one of the members of the review team. But the conservation movement continued to campaign in support of the reservation of more of the old growth karri forest and, later, a reduced cut and changes to forest practices in the jarrah forest. The chief executive of CALM and CALM itself progressively became identified as impediments to these forest conservation initiatives.

The urban population of Perth, the only large metropolitan centre in Western Australia, located at the northern end of the forest belt, was increasing rapidly in number, mobility and affluence. Access to the forest areas improved dramatically and even parts of the forest distant from Perth became a venue for recreation and tourism. Alternative lifestylers populated some of the old sawmill villages. Academic interest in forest issues grew to unprecedented levels.

By the time the Regional Forest Agreements were initiated in 1997, the forest debate was well and truly polarized. Protest groups occupied or blockaded some harvesting coupes. Free bus tours were arranged for concerned urban residents by conservation groups. Clashes between protestors and forest and timber industry workers became more common. Media coverage was intense and the imagery often dramatic.

CALM was widely viewed as paying only lip service to the public consultation principles involved in the Agreement process and as being committed only to its own strategies that were broadly supportive of the timber industry. Thus there was widespread dissatisfaction with the outcomes of the Agreement

(Conacher and Conacher, 2000), notwithstanding major increases in reservation to achieve the criteria required.

The Liberal Government of the day was aware of the urban unrest concerning the forest issues, prompted in part by the development of a 'Liberals for Forests' political party involving professionals and some former Liberal Party icons. The media debate was mainly conducted on a 'one tenure-one use' basis focussing on the old growth forest. The Government sought a compromise in 1999 by instituting a review of the old growth forest management by a panel of experts chaired by the author (Ferguson *et al.*, 1999). While the outcomes of this review were greeted reasonably favourably by those involved in the extensive consultations, its result was somewhat incoherent in policy terms and it effectively repudiated the Regional Forest Agreement. Thus, at the next election early in 2001, the Labor Party was able to trump this policy by extending reservation to all remaining old growth karri forest and announcing further review of timber harvesting and sustainable yield in the jarrah forest.

The concerns over the jarrah forest were not new but became much more prominent once the old growth forests had been largely, and later fully, reserved. CALM was dismembered, with its timber harvesting functions going to a new Forest Products Commission, policy regulation to a new Conservation Commission. Operational regulatory functions were retained by the new CALM. The Conservation Commission then instituted a major review of the Forest Management Plan for the southwest forests, as required by earlier State legislation. Here the media debate was somewhat more sophisticated. While there were some smaller areas purportedly of high conservation value sought for reservation, much of the concern ranged over timber harvesting issues, including the adequacy of regeneration, dieback (*Phytophthora cinnamomi*) management, fuel reduction burning, water quality and quantity, sustainable yields, and wildlife management. In many respects, the debate and outcomes drew much more on principles akin to those of the Ecosystem Approach but the trade-offs were not clearly identified in the alternative scenarios put forward in the Draft Management Plan (Conservation Commission, 2002).

Regional Forest Agreements process and outcomes

The Regional Forest Agreements led to or were accompanied by major changes in environmental, social and institutional policies that are reviewed in the ensuing sections. While the process spanned all tenures of forest, the greatest controversy related to publicly owned native forests, especially in State Forests and Vacant Crown Lands, and hence most attention will focus on these.

Environmental Changes

Looking back at the changes made over the last thirty years, and especially those made as a result of the Regional Forest Agreements, the improvements in forest practices have been marked. Many of the forest practices now accord closely with the principles underpinning an ecosystem approach to sustainable forest management. The management agencies and the conservation movement are increasingly focusing on these principles and monitoring outcomes with reference to them. There is still scope for further improvement and hence it is useful to review the changes and some of the most important benefits and defects or difficulties. The principal environmental changes involved in the Regional Forest Agreement process relate to the development and implementation of criteria and indicators, codes of forest practice, plans of management, sustainable yields, and environmental management systems.

Criteria and indicators

Australia was a signatory to the Montreal Process on Criteria and Indicators. The Commonwealth took a strong interest in it, funding much of the work involved in developing operational criteria and indicators now in use by the Commonwealth and States for the 'State of the Forests' reporting (Montreal Process Implementation Group, 1997). The principal criteria dealing with all forest resources, global carbon cycles, soil and water protection, ecosystem health, biodiversity, productive capacity, and socio-economic conditions provided the basis for the formal principles underpinning the Regional Forest Agreement process. Operationally, the intent of this approach was to establish a monitoring and reporting system that would enable trends in sustainable forest management to be tracked.

While the use of criteria and indicators has given the reporting mechanisms greater analytical content with respect to the analysis of trends, it suffers from deficiencies (Ferguson *et al.*, 1998). The criteria and indicators approach has the inherent problem of aggregation of the multiple indicators needed to cover complex phenomena. Merely collating multiple sets of data will only provide information on trends if the data can be aggregated or otherwise analysed in an integrated form. The greater the number of data sets, the greater the problem. The problem is especially acute in social data indicators because of the value judgements inherent in appraising the impacts of changes on different socio-economic groups. Even an apparently well-defined statistic such as employment suffers problems because it is generally recorded by place of employment or place of residence, neither of which is necessarily co-incident with the forests.

The aggregation problem highlights a more general issue concerning trade-offs between forest uses or values, whether extractive, non-extractive or a mixture. The fact that different indicators vary independently is not only a difficulty with respect to the so-called intangible uses and values, it is also a difficulty with respect to the various scales in space and in time that these uses span.

Codes of practice

Codes of Practice were first introduced in Tasmania in 1985, then in Victoria in 1988, followed by Western Australia. The Regional Forest Agreements subjected them to detailed review and improvement to provide a regulatory framework for field operations, including fire management. The regulatory framework varies from State to State but spans constraints and requirements with respect to maintaining all other uses that are affected by extractive operations such as wood production.

In many respects, the Codes of Practice simply represented an evolution of past regulatory prescriptions, as Lee and Abbott (2004) describe in their historical review for Western Australia. But the Codes now incorporate the most recent scientific results, the precautionary principle, post-harvest amelioration requirements, and penalties for non-compliance. The fundamental change is that these Codes are publicly available, generally accessible on the web, and subject to a public review process periodically (generally at least every five years). Furthermore, in addition to formal monitoring by the administering agency, they provide a basis for informal monitoring and reporting of performance by environmental non-government organizations, which have been extremely active in monitoring those areas of particular conservation interest.

The Codes of Practice are implemented by a pre-harvest inventory of a proposed harvest coupe that aims to demarcate the boundaries of the area with due regard to prescribed stream buffers, wildlife corridors, habitat trees, rare and endangered species, landscape values and other constraints. This inventory is guided by prior aerial photographic interpretation of forest types, their crown cover and height. In the case of Tasmania and Victoria, the pattern of reasonably homogeneous communities so defined can be quite detailed where ecosystems differ widely in dominant tree species (or mixtures thereof) due to variations in soil or microclimate. In the case of Western Australia, the aerial pattern is less heterogeneous in the E. *marginata* forest although, as noted earlier, the diversity of ground flora is very high. The minimum area for delineation as a distinct community is generally about one hectare (e.g. Forest Practices Board, 2003) but can reach thousands of hectares in size. New aerial mapping techniques greatly assist that process but the human eye and experience are still critical in terms of field implementation.

In all three States, the forester carrying out this work has the authority to exclude additional areas beyond the minima prescribed to give better effect to conserving the ecosystems involved. Some of these variations may reflect a desire to rationalize an otherwise irregular boundary or to encompass local topographic variation that is not evident on the map. In other cases, there may be a need to aggregate habitat trees in clumps and/or to link them with other retained buffers or corridors for protection from wind or fire, where burning forms part of the regeneration or later fuel reduction process. In practice, comparisons of prescribed and actual boundaries show that the additional loss of area to harvesting can be substantial and this has significant implications for sustainable yields that will be discussed later.

On the other hand, there is virtually no scope to vary the prescriptions in the other direction. While this latter provision may seem a sensible safeguard, it is not always so. For example, buffer strips around a third order stream running on relatively flat exposed granite bedrock with shallow soils are not viable for the mature or older trees, which die from exposure or are blown over. Another problem sometimes arises when the conservation of biodiversity is involved; for instance, where owls and watersheds are to be protected. Here, the prescriptions call for protection zones that have sometimes been considered independently and cumulatively, rather than serving a joint purpose. Environmental non-government organizations, acting informally as environmental watchdogs, commonly pillory public agencies over any apparent breaches of the Code, so an overly cautious approach is not surprising. Given the complexity of the trade-offs between uses, however, some scope is needed for the exercise of intelligent judgment in either direction, subject to proper documentation of reasons.

Trade-offs involving little or no cost to either conservation or industry can sometimes be found. One example is the research (Ough and Murphy, 1998) on understorey islands in Victoria's mountain ash (*Eucalyptus regnans*) forests. This established a considerable improvement in the survival of resprouting understorey species with no loss of timber logged, simply by avoiding mechanical disturbance in understorey 'islands' up to 20m x 40m in size within logged coupes. This technique has been recommended for application and/or trialed in other forest types in Victoria (Ough, 2001 and Ough and Murphy, 2004) and Western Australia.

Research studies have greatly aided the development of conservation strategies in these codes of practice but are too numerous to catalogue here. To cite a few recent examples that span a very wide range of issues, Meggs *et al.* (2004) have provided specific conservation strategies for a threatened beetle in Tasmania. Burrows *et al.* (2001, 2002), building on prior research, have developed prescriptions for Western Australian fauna management that are based on the reservation of habitat patches of at least 300ha in area, located relatively closely to large conservation reserves. Recent research in Victoria (Alexander *et al.*, 2002) based on well designed and extensive fauna surveys has assisted the identification of sensitive fauna and habitats and this information has been incorporated into the most recent management plan for Gippsland (Department of Sustainability and Environment, 2004). With respect to research, there can be little doubt that the Regional Forest Agreements have been responsible for a much more rapid implementation of research results.

This research highlights the need for access to specialists. No person can today claim an expert knowledge of all the disciplines involved in making field assessments. We have to rely on a generalist making an initial diagnosis and referring to specialists for expert advice and assessment, just as in medical and other professional fields. The difficulty is that the client is immobile and uncommunicative and that greatly increases the difficulty, cost and time involved in referral. Forest health specialists have already been integrated into the routine of field operations. As the knowledge becomes available, specialists in biodiversity conservation, geomorphology and the like are being integrated into the routine. However, integration tends to be more difficult when specialists are employed in other departments than those responsible of forest management or regulation, as is now often the case – if only because of the financial implications.

Some aspects of research and policy findings remain poorly implemented. The most important of these concerns regeneration systems used in wood production operations. Policy and ecological reviews dating at least from Ferguson (1985) to Dovers (2003) and Lindenmayer (2003), to cite a few of many, have stressed the desirability of tailoring the choice to the particular ecosystem, rather than adopting a uniform system across the entire forest type. Yet that is what is still being done in many of the ash-type (E.*regnans* and kindred species) forests. Commonly, a clearfelling system followed by burning to provide a receptive seedbed and artificial seeding has been adopted. Almost invariably, a long rotation of 80 years is prescribed. While such a regeneration system may be the most cost-effective, and can thus be justified on some of the area, it is not always the most appropriate from the viewpoint of other uses. Some sites are capable of natural regeneration using a variety of tree retention and seedbed preparation systems. Alternative silvicultural systems need to be employed on a significant proportion of the ash-type forests to improve biodiversity management (see Lindenmayer, 2003). Rotation lengths should be varied according to site. Scope exists for cross-site trade-offs if rotation lengths are reduced somewhat on the better sites and lengthened on poorer sites, although setting structural goals (see next section) will make the average length longer than the present prescribed minimum. The reason this is not being done probably reflects the institutional characteristics of the debate, rather than any lack of knowledge on the part of the agencies, and will be taken up again in a later section.

The pre-harvest inventory phase deals with a variety of scales in space and time. In space, these range from micro-site issues of some endangered or rare plants, to the identification of separate ecosystems (not always easy when ecotones exist), to sub-catchment scales. Those run from the timing of the immediate operation or of natural seeding (e.g winter versus summer logging); the timing of regeneration burning, artificial seeding or planting; the timing of post-regeneration treatment, later thinning and health measures, to the timing of the rotation or cutting cycle age – to name a few. The complexity involved, and the need to integrate this level of planning and management with broader scale issues, prompted the Regional Forest Agreement process to adopt an environmental management system framework, that will be summarised in a later section.

Management Plans

The span of scales in time and space is further extended in developing management plans, which form a prescribed part of the planning process. The scope of these plans varies widely in the three Sates. In Western Australia, the legislation requires a single plan for the entire South-west Region. For Tasmania, the plans are based on seven administrative districts. For Victoria, they are based on individual large Regions, although there have been several changes in this scale over the last two decades, each to larger and larger units. These differences and changes reflect the peculiarities of the forests and of the institutional structures.

More importantly, these plans embrace and integrate a broader consideration of scale in space and time that is appropriate to catchment, landscape and biogeographical conservation units. They also deal with the issues of sustainable yield, permissible cut and socio-economic considerations that are the subject of review in the later sections.

Planning at this level also embraces both the broad detail of rationalising boundaries between forest available for harvest and that in conservation and similar reserves. This principally involves decision-making at the Government level, given the nature of the trade-offs and the difficulties and controversy involved. When large changes are involved, they often have more profound impacts that are considered in a later section dealing with social changes.

Hydrological modelling is being used to investigate impacts of harvesting and agricultural pursuits on catchments (Vertessy *et al.*, 2003). As yet, these models have not been well-integrated with harvest scheduling – the primary problem being the coarseness of the hydrological models – a reflection of the sparseness of monitoring data in both space and time.

Harvesting operations potentially impinge on landscape values at several different levels. One is the potentially adverse visual impact of harvest and regeneration operations along roads used relatively intensively by tourists, local recreationists, or local residents. Here strategic planning on a landscape scale is being used to identify sensitive zones and to develop appropriate strategies to reduce or eliminate the visual impact, originally using surveys (e.g. Leonard and Hammond, 1984) and, more recently, computer- based visual impact modelling. Another level is at the local neighbour level or scale, where a particular forest landscape represents a valued visual amenity to an adjacent landholder. This is more often dealt with at the pre-harvest inventory level. Reference will be made in a later section to meta-landscape or whole-of forest scales.

Structural goals (Bradshaw and Rayner, 1997a & b; Bradshaw, 2002) represent a direct planning approach to maintaining a full suite of age and structurally related values, rather than attempting to achieve them using the sustainable yield as a mechanism. Structural goals are also useful in balancing the structural attributes between those found in the reserve system and those in production forests. For example, In the now-current Management Plan for the South-west Region of Western Australia, the predominant rotation lengths were 200 and 100 years, but range from to 220 to 150 years and 250 to 60 years for E. *marginata* (jarrah) and E. *diversicolor* (karri) respectively, reflecting the constraints set by the current structural goals. Thus the 200 and 100-year nominal rotations were only scheduled to be used on about 85 to 90% of the respective areas of those two forest types, most of the remainder being longer. Admittedly this issue has assumed a lesser importance, given the major additions to the conservation reserve system in and after the initial Regional Forest Agreement process. Nevertheless, structural goals represent an explicit attempt to integrate the management of those reserves and the so-called 'off-reserves' on which harvesting and other extractive uses are permitted.

The values for sustainable yield are currently based on rotations that far exceed any purely financial investment decision, being from 80 years to 200 years, depending on species and State. They thus involve harvesting the relatively small proportion of the forest that is available for wood production in any one year (on average 1/80th to 1/200th where clear-felling is used). Nevertheless, the public at large do seem to react adversely to the resulting visual impact on the meta-landscape of publicly owned native forests, especially on slower-growing sites. Thus there is a need to develop lower impact silviculture for these sites. On the other hand, there is a corresponding opportunity to shorten these very long rotations somewhat on the more productive sites. These notions also seem to be at the heart of the Ecosystem Approach in terms of more intelligently tailoring the treatment to the individual ecosystem, its properties and capacities, rather than imposing a uniform rotation length (or regeneration system) across all sites.

In formal reviews of the Ecologically Sustainable Forest Management process by expert committees in the three States, the need for better integration of the management of reserve and off-reserve forests was noted. Some of that attention needed to focus on the reserves because, as was shown in the case of Tasmania, many of the plans for management of reserves (if they existed) were deficient (Public Land Use Commission, 1995a & b). Typically, the plans assumed a direct translation of all of the objectives of the national park or other legislation to that reserve, rather than identifying what conservation or other attributes the particular area was best capable of supplying, focussing on strategies to manage these, and addressing the trade-offs between uses where these were relevant. With some notable exceptions, there has generally been a reluctance or indifference to explicitly identifying objectives, specifying goals, and monitoring outcomes for conservation reserves. Yet the ecosystem approach to sustainable forest management applies just as much to conservation and other reserves as it does to forests in which harvesting and extractive uses are permitted and integration of reserve and off-reserve management cannot be sensibly achieved without it.

Sustainable yield

In all three States, considerable emphasis has been placed on determining the sustainable yield for the forest concerned because it provides a basis for setting the amounts of wood that can be sold in a particular period.

The sustainable yield is based firstly on the estimation of net areas of forest available for harvesting. The term 'net areas' refers to the areas of publicly owned native forest, on which timber production is a permitted activity, i.e. the gross areas minus all those areas of reservations and other exclusions in which timber production is not permitted. Using a Geographic Information System, the net areas are derived by superimposing known reserves and exclusions, such as the prescribed buffers on streams, on a map showing roads, rivers, streams and property boundaries. Additional information on forest types is derived from interpretation of aerial photography, followed by field checking.

The interpretation includes detailed delineation of strata by species mixtures. The species mixtures are broadly applicable but fail to reflect the local variability inherent in these forest types. From the viewpoint of the sustainable yield, these finer distinctions between species are of lesser concern if the field inventory system adequately and representatively samples the strata, because the overall species composition is then adequately reflected in the data for the stratum concerned. To use Western Australia as an example, some 600 strata are recognised in the E. *marginata* (jarrah) State Forests, based on tenure, region, rainfall, height, history of cutting, current structure and whether or not mined. Within each such stratum, there is further subdivision into six silvicultural classes (called cohorts) – thinned, gap creation, shelterwood, temporary exclusion areas, selective logging and dieback. This complexity would be difficult to use in practice without access to Geographic Information Systems.

While reductions in sustainable yield were anticipated to follow the introduction of more stringent Codes of Practice, the impacts have proven larger than expected. Comparison of actual net areas with 'prescribed' areas in Victoria summarized by Vanclay and Turner (2001) suggest reductions of 15 to 24%. Western Australia and Tasmania have had similar experiences. Some of the reductions can be detected with newer aerial photography technology but a number cannot, so that *post facto* comparisons need to be monitored to provide guidance on the total losses to be expected for future harvesting operations.

The technologies used for inventory of the wood volume vary widely in the three States; involving double sampling in Western Australia (Biggs, 1991), model-based sampling in Victoria (Hamilton *et al.*, 1999) or stratified sampling in Tasmania. In all cases, however, the technology is not so much the issue. The difficulty lies in the reconciliation of estimated with actual removals. This is partly because of its relationship to the control of the cut relative to the sustainable yield and partly because of its importance in the audit of valuation, of which we shall say more in a later section. The need for much tighter reconciliation is also important to the issue of efficient utilization between sawlogs, pulpwood and waste.

Finally there is the harvest scheduling, in space and in time, presently largely built around the industrial issues of supplying relatively constant periodic amounts of wood to support processing plants. Most of the sustainable yield systems work on the basis of non-declining flows of sawlogs over extraordinarily long planning horizons. Given the uncertainties and changing technologies and markets in relation to wood use, this is difficult to justify in terms other than political inertia, and it greatly limits the flexibility of planning wood use. A shift to the use of a more realistic planning horizon of say, 50 years, and age-class and other structural goals to be achieved at the end of that horizon may provide a more transparent and accountable basis for planning.

Environmental Management Systems

Reference has already been made to the use of an environmental management system framework to underpin the Regional Forest Agreement process. The ISO 14001 framework was used but there was no compulsion to undertake certification for it. Subsequently, this was also used to underpin the development of a performance-based Australian Forestry Standard (2004), under the aegis of Standards Australia. Forestry Tasmania is seeking certification under this standard. The others are still considering the choice between it and Forest Stewardship Council certification.

Certification has only recently started to have an impact on domestic markets, chiefly through the large retail hardware chains, but is important in relation to exports to Europe and to China for processing and re-export.

Social Change

The debate between two principal sets of stakeholders, the conservation groups on one side and the industry and unions on the other, had become extremely polarised at the time the Regional Forest Agreement process commenced. In the 'one tenure-one use' argument (Dovers, 2003), any gains for one side meant losses for the other. The Regional Forest Agreement process was more sophisticated and was based upon two principal strategies that were intended to assuage conservation and industry interests respectively. The first element of the strategy was concerned with a National Conservation Reserve System and the second concerned resource security for the forest products industry. The two had important implications for social change and attempted to build on public participation in reaching decisions.

National Conservation Reserve System

The first strategy was to create a new National Conservation Reserve System such that the area of reserves was at least 15% of the pre-1750 areas of the major forest types at 1:100,000 scale. This level of 15% was presumably chosen for its political impact, given that the IUCN recommended level was 10%. It was also National only in nominal terms, because the actual tenures had to be granted under State legislation, continuing the process where 'National Parks' are in fact the properties of individual States, not the Commonwealth.

The achievement of a national Conservation Reserve System is widely viewed as the most significant achievement of the Regional Forest Agreements. It achieved a much larger area of reserves under a nationally consistent and tenure-neutral system of criteria. The development of the criteria for this 'comprehensive, adequate and representative' system of reserves (JANIS, 1997) was itself a major feat in achieving agreement between leading forest managers, scientists and non-government organizations, at least for a time. Associated changes also rationalized most of the (often inexplicable) disparities between the environmental and heritage legislation of the Commonwealth and the individual States, as it related to forests.

Resource security

The second strategy was to provide 'resource security' to industry, in order to obviate the uncertainties that had been attached to the previous machinations between industry and conservation interests, and Commonwealth versus State Governments, especially when the governments were of different political persuasion.

Resource security was to be achieved through the 20-year agreement between the Commonwealth and the state concerned in each Regional Forest Agreement. In addition, the Commonwealth waived control over exports of wood from those Regions that had entered into such an agreement. It retained the right to conduct jointly with the state concerned a five-yearly limited review of knowledge and prescriptions.

There were substantial reductions in the industrial timber harvest in all States as an initial result of the Agreements. Adjustment to these was aided by Structural Assistance Grants from the Commonwealth to assist and, where possible, retrain retrenched workers, and encourage greater value adding in the native forest industry through further processing and in some cases to expand plantations. The industry has made these adjustments, albeit slowly. Much of the value-adding change was also driven by the increasingly trade-exposed nature of the timber industry following the reduction of tariffs and abolition of import quotas in the preceding decade, together with increasing competition from plantation grown softwood (P. *radiata* and P. *caribbea*).

As is apparent from earlier sections, the Agreements did not achieve resource security for the industry in Victoria and Western Australia during the first five years. However in Tasmania the Agreement had done so, albeit tenuously. The failure to observe the spirit if not the letter of the Regional Forest Agreements highlights the inability of the Commonwealth to hold individual States to an agreement of this kind when there are no effective sanctions. Parliaments can make or unmake legislation giving effect to policies. Sovereign risk pertains as much to the Commonwealth as to individual States, as recent events show.

Public participation

The Regional Forest Agreement process placed considerable emphasis on public participation. All expert committee reports were publicly available. Some of those committees held various forms of public consultation, ranging from workshops to submissions and later interviews with respondents. Yet the general reaction was that there were insufficient opportunities, time and resources for adequate public involvement.

Tasmania was probably most successful. Arrangements there were conducted by the Public Land Use Commission (now replaced by a Resource Planning and Development Tribunal), an independent body established to conduct public land use inquiries. In Western Australia, the complaints were especially pronounced because there was a widespread perception that the forestry agency was not genuinely interested in public participation (see Mercer, 2000).

In general, public participation was the only initiative involving bottom-up inputs, although brief reference will be made in a later section to a current new experiment involving community management in Victoria.

Plantations

One of the other goals of the Regional Forest Agreement process was to encourage the development of plantations with the goal of trebling the area of plantations by 2020. Considerable progress has been made towards this goal, largely through investment in privately owned hardwood plantations. 'Managed Investment Companies' obtain Australian tax office approval for the issue of a prospectus to raise funds, largely from small investors wishing to take advantage of the avoidance of personal income tax that these offer. Investors can then charge their investment against tax in the year of planting, without waiting until the plantation produces revenues – a provision common to all such primary production ventures.

All three States have also introduced various forms of forestry rights that enable the legal separation of the ownership of the standing trees from the land on which they stand. In the case of softwood plantations in Tasmania and Victoria, this has provided the basis for the sale of the formerly publicly owned softwood trees (and later rights to trees on replanted areas) to private investors.

From a Government perspective, this expansion of plantations also may have the advantage of easing issues of structural adjustment in agriculture as the scale of farming progressively increases, and older or less successful farmers wish to retire. Not surprisingly, however, the rapid expansion of plantations has some adverse social impacts such as those on some small agricultural communities and their dependent businesses; isolation of some of the remaining farmers; and related concerns over roads, social amenities and schools (e.g. Williams *et al.*, 2003; Schirmer and Tonts, 2003).

Indigenous Heritage

The Regional Forest Agreements were probably least successful in addressing the issues of indigenous heritage (Centre for Social Research, 1997), although they at least made a start. The reasons are complex. Indigenous heritage necessarily involves extensive interaction with the Aboriginal community because of reliance on oral history and memories of traditional life. The Aboriginal communities in the forest regions are small, sometimes scattered and often dysfunctional in a community sense. The non-Aboriginal community in the forest (or other) regions is not always sensitive to their plight. Some of the land claims by Aboriginal groups have caused concern for others dependent on the forest for their living. Many of the sites of indigenous heritage are sacred and therefore secret. There are few trained staff and the process of liaison with the communities takes much longer to achieve the necessary levels of trust and involvement. The Commonwealth legislation has been under review for some time and thus rationalization of roles and processes with those of the States has not been effected. Nevertheless, the Commonwealth has recently funded an initiative to prepare an indigenous heritage forest strategy and this may accelerate progress.

Institutional changes

Concurrent with the changes enumerated above, major changes have been taking place in relation to Government agencies engaged in commercial activities, although they focus on the whole-of-government, not just the forestry sector. The Council of Australian Governments, now a Standing Committee comprising the Prime Minister, Premiers of the States and of the two Territories, agreed on a joint National Competition Policy in 1995 (Hilmer *et al.*, 1995). The *Competition Principles Agreement* sets out principles for reforming government monopolies and providing price oversights of government businesses, among other things. The *Conduct Code Agreement* extends the competitive conduct rules to all businesses, including those of government. And the *Implementation Agreement* recommits governments to specific reforms and provides grants contingent on their implementation.

This meant that the commercial activities of any government agency must progressively become competitively neutral, relative to the private sector. In practice, that means that commercial State (and Commonwealth) activities have to charge prices that can be shown to be free of subsidies and hence to pay a contribution to their parent government equivalent to company and other taxes. In this case, there are effective sanctions, so State agencies with commercial activities have progressively been changing course and there is an associated trend towards a greater contracting out of the provision of various operations.

In several States, this change has been caught up in the so-called purchaser-provider approach, in which a forestry agency is seen as simply a commercial entity providing goods commercially to the private sector and therefore to be divorced from a regulatory role and from management of conservation reserves. This view is overly simplistic, not least because the relationship in the case of publicly-owned native State Forest is one of principal (Minister) – agent (forestry agency) due to the inability to shed the joint production of non-commercial goods and services. This renders the relationship with the purchaser much more complex. Nevertheless, the three States now span an array of modes of dealing with this issue and these arrangements mark the complete separation of the management of conservation reserves from those forests used by extractive industries.

Forestry Tasmania is a State-owned corporation but its charter requires it to manage State Forests for non-commercial as well as commercial uses. It also invests in hardwood plantations and holds a 50% share of the Forestry Rights in a joint venture pertaining to the former State-owned softwood plantations. Conservation reserves are managed by a Parks and Wildlife Service reporting to the Minister responsible for parks. Privately owned forests are under the oversight of Private Forestry Tasmania, reporting to the Minister responsible for resources. A separate Forest Practices Authority and Tribunal provide regulatory oversight and reports to the Minister responsible for resources.

In Western Australia, the Forest Products Commission is responsible for the management of all harvesting and extractive operations on State Forests and for State-owned plantations. It is also a major investor and manager of hardwood and softwood plantations. The Department of Conservation and Land Management (formerly CALM) oversees the regulatory aspects, manages conservation reserves and other public land, and oversees private forestry. The Conservation Commission acts as a referee and public sounding-board.

In Victoria, a newly created VicForests is a State-owned corporation within the Department of Primary Industry, with responsibility solely for harvesting and regeneration operations in the most productive State Forests. Community forest management is being tried on some of the less productive or more densely populated State Forests and represents a major experiment in bottom-up management and potential devolution. The Department of Sustainability and Environment is the regulatory agency and that department includes Parks Victoria, which is responsible for managing conservation reserves. Private Forestry is under review but a small Private Forestry Council and branch within the Department of Primary industry currently provides oversight and the regulatory functions are the responsibility of local governments.

Fire management has been a matter of controversy because of recent wildfires and the inability of the managing agencies to meet programs of fuel-reduction burning. These programs are controversial because of the smoke pollution complaints from urban residents, especially in the metropolitan areas of Melbourne and Perth, and a generally negative attitude to fuel-reduction burning by environmental non-government organizations. The agencies responsible for forest fire management vary between the States because of different institutional structures and this raises additional complications.

Finally, the Australian Accounting Standard AASB 1037 for Self-generating and Regenerating Assets complicates financial audits and valuations of State Forests. In addition to the requirements of competitive neutrality under the National Competition Policy, this Standard requires the responsible agencies to value the commercial assets using a current market-determined interest rate reflecting the risks associated with the asset. This implies that criteria of economic efficiency are applied and not sustainability (see Ferguson, 1996). As a result of the various constraints on operations in publicly owned native forests managed and regulated for multiple uses, the future pattern of wood production flows and cash flows do not reflect the entrepreneurial choice that might maximise the value of the forest as a wood producer. Any such valuation is therefore circular in that it simply reflects the planned pattern of regulated wood use of that forest – not the optimum value, if used for wood production alone under minimal constraints that relate only to markets. It does not, therefore, provide any useful guidance as to the return on capital investment for wood production or joint production. Furthermore, the valuation has to exclude those trees or stands that are reserved for other conservation or protective purposes. Therefore it is a very lop-sided evaluation of the total worth of the forest to society. This simply reflects the dilemma that, as yet, the valuation of sustainability and the non-commercial uses and services of forests is not sufficiently precise or established to be incorporated in accounting standards (see Ferguson, 1998). It also explains why even the meta-level choice or trade-off between exclusively conservation use versus extractive and other use is not generally capable of an analytical solution, but must rest with the political process.

Science and Media Roles

International initiatives such as the Montreal Process, Convention on Biological Diversity, World Heritage Convention, the Rio Summit, United Nations Forum on Forests (and its predecessors), and the Kyoto Protocol have all had some influence on the evolution of the ecosystem approach to sustainable forest management as it is now practiced. Of these, only the Kyoto Protocol would be widely known outside the realm of the immediate interest groups.

Much of the focus and momentum for change came from specific concerns arising within Southern Australia and it is therefore more relevant to examine the extent to which the underlying scientific concerns influenced the process versus the media treatment of them?

The scientific community in Australia has both reacted and contributed to those international initiatives and much of the science base owes something to them. Nevertheless, it is not the science that has driven and shaped the public debate, it is the media treatment of it, aided by the 'one tenure - one use' argument that greatly simplifies the media treatment. The Routleys (1973) were one of the first to use visual imagery and a pungent scientific review to great effect to support conservation concerns. But the media has subsequently developed that approach greatly in terms of the impact of visual imagery and accompanying presentations that feed on the polarization that the 'one tenure-one use' argument invites.

The problem with this approach is that it necessarily focuses on the here and now. There is little scope for recognition of the complexities of scale in space and time that are involved in an ecosystem approach to sustainable forest management. Furthermore, as noted earlier, agencies sometimes adopt blanket silvicultural prescriptions across an entire forest type, because to allow variation would require a high degree of discretion to be granted to the field forester. In an environment of 'one tenure -one use' debates, the exercise of such discretion represents an unnecessary concession to the other side by the industry and unions and by the non-government organizations alike, and thus a liability to the agency. By the same token, the public image of 'one tenure-one use' makes it difficult to gain acceptance of the need for more expenditure on data collection for the non-wood uses and for more long term monitoring of ecological trends (Dovers, 2003).

The scientific basis and merits of the Regional Forest Agreement process are not widely appreciated by the general public. While most of the major debates concerning native forest uses may be over, some icons remain and dominate public concerns – especially the continued harvesting of some old growth in Tasmania and Victoria and some conversion of native forest to plantation in Tasmania. These issues will undoubtedly ebb over the next few years, either through political decision or the limitations of ever-decreasing areas. The issues will then turn to advancing ecosystem approaches and whether the financial resources and institutional structures are appropriate to that challenge. Public understanding holds the key to the these requirements and needs to evolve much beyond the 'one tenure-one use' basis if ecosystem approaches are to succeed.

intu

11 | The Political Ecology of the Ecosystem Approach for Forests

Tim Forsyth

Introduction

This paper discusses the politics of the Ecosystem Approach and especially the role of state forestry institutions. To date, most political analysis of ecosystem approaches has focused on their role in international negotiations, or as a means of implementing the Convention on Biological Diversity (Hartje *et al.*, 2003). There has, however, been comparatively little attention to the influence of politics at the national and sub-national level, and in particular to the ways that the ecosystem approaches are defined scientifically, with whose participation, and with access to which type of knowledge. This paper seeks to highlight these factors by discussing the potential ways in which state forestry institutions can influence the formulation of an ecosystem approach, and how localized politics can lead to variations in forest policies between different countries and contexts.

The paper adopts an approach known as 'political ecology.' Academics have used this term since the 1970s to refer to the relationship of ecological science and environmental politics. Initially, much political ecology focused on environmental conflicts between social actors such as the state and non-governmental organizations on topics where environmental impacts were assumed to be clear-cut, such as the establishment of national parks or the location of polluting industries (e.g. Bryant and Bailey, 1997). Increasingly, however, political ecologists are examining the politics of ecological science itself, which looks instead at the political authority of different knowledge claims about environment, or why we have come to assume certain environmental changes are problematic. This approach does not suggest that environmental problems do not exist, or that ecological science cannot help, but acknowledges the greater political controversies about the nature of ecological risk, and the influence of different political actors upon what is seen to be authoritative knowledge (Forsyth, 2003).

The emergence of ecosystem approaches and the role of state forestry departments are both legitimate topics for a political ecology approach. The CBD Ecosystem Approach has been defined as a strategy that 'recognises that humans, with their cultural diversity, are an integral component of ecosystems' (see Convention on Biological Diversity website). Yet, it is important to note that the Ecosystem Approach is a set of guiding principles rather than a specific method to manage ecosystems. To date, little attention has been given to how different social groups or organizations may influence forest policies, and how far the Ecosystem Approach may vary between locations as a result. Similarly, state forest institutions play a fundamental role in formulating and implementing forest policies. There is often an assumption that forest departments are politically neutral bodies simply applying objective science and expertise. The fact that their organizational history and context may have influenced this 'science' is rarely discussed. A growing number of analysts suggest that these questions of political participation and organizational approaches need to be understood in order to make forest policy, including ecosystem approaches, more effective and transparent.

The paper lists some potential ways that political factors may influence forest policies, and how environmental science and politics may be considered 'co-produced.' Second, the paper lists potential impacts of organizational politics and illustrates these with reference to state forestry departments in Thailand and Guinea, West Africa. Third, the paper draws some lessons for understanding the political ecology of ecosystem approaches as scientific approaches, with some suggestions for making them more transparent and socially inclusive in different locations.

Political Influences on the Formulation of the Ecosystem Approach

Ecosystem approaches have been discussed since the mid-1990s as an overarching framework of integrating conservation and development, and particularly as the preferred approach to implementing the Convention on Biological Diversity (CBD). Yet, there is still great uncertainty about the full meaning of this approach, and the extent to which ecosystem approaches represent transferable guidelines for forest management, or an approach to allowing the integration of different objectives from diverse stakeholders.

The definition of the Ecosystem Approach adopted within the CBD highlights some of these uncertainties. The CBD defines the Ecosystem Approach as 'a strategy for the integrated management of land, water and living resources that promotes conservation and sustainable use in an equitable way', and which 'recognises that humans, with their cultural diversity, are an integral component of ecosystems.' In this respect, the Ecosystem Approach seeks to achieve the Convention's three key objectives of conservation, sustainable use of resources and equitable sharing of benefits. Yet, the definitions of terms such as 'sustainable' and 'equitable' are open to interpretation. Plus, the recognition of 'cultural diversity' does not imply how far diverse social perspectives should control ecosystem management, or be developed in consultation with them. Sometimes, political analysis of ecosystem approaches has discussed how far ecosystem managers or the state should consult with different resource users. But the political analysis of ecosystem approaches should not simply rest with asking who should be consulted in implementing policies, but should also include increasing participation in the formulation of locally adapted approaches, and in the scientific assumptions underlying policies and programmes.

The underlying scientific assumptions about ecosystem or forest management may reflect political influences in many ways. First, the concept of ecosystem 'function' is often referred to in factual and universal terms, but without acknowledging the social perspectives that frame concepts of 'function.' Article 2 of the CBD, for example, has stated that 'ecosystem' may be defined as a 'dynamic complex of plant, animal, and micro-organism communities and their non-living environment interacting as a functional unit.' Yet, definitions of 'functional unit' may depend upon the elements of the ecosystem that are particularly valued by different observers. For example, forest systems may have different 'functions' according to whether they are classified as a watershed, wildlife reserve, or site of occasional agricultural production. Each land use would produce different proposals for maintaining ecosystem 'function' at optimal levels. This highlights the way in which professional groups can base their assessments on deeply held assumptions about the nature of the outcomes desired. In scientific terms, academics have called this phenomenon 'problem closure'. It restricts the range of options that are open for debate and encourages the adoption of predefined ways of perceiving an ecosystem. If one specific forest is seen only in terms of (say) its ability to supply year-round water to a lowland area, then much research and explanation of environmental change in this location will be couched in those terms. Seeking to identify a different 'function' for the forest may therefore appear to be counter to existing scientific evidence built upon a different 'function.' Implementing a more diverse, ecosystem approach to forest management may therefore require questioning how far perceptions and empirical information about the forest have been shaped by past definitions of its function by only a few social groups.

Second, the question of ecosystem function also raises important questions of the temporal and spatial scale of inquiry. Frequently, the definition of ecosystem 'function' may simultaneously define, and be defined by, the spatial area under consideration, and the social groups within this area. For example, the categorization of land as a watershed forest must necessarily be based upon the existence of water users outside the zone who wish to gain access to water from inside it (Barham, 2001). This combination of consultation and problem closure may exclude social groups who live inside the allotted watershed forest who may wish to use the land and forest for purposes other than protecting the supply of water outside. Similarly, the definition of ecosystem extent may change if the objective is protection of specific species. The spatial scales of ecosystems and problem closure are therefore closely linked, and both may change if the social consultation about problem closure changes.

Indeed, the assumption that ecological functions are fixed in space has caused much political commentary. For example, the early writings on ecological politics in the 1960s urged attention to the necessary limits posed by ecosystems to human activities without necessarily identifying the social divisions in how ecosystem functions were defined. For example, Eugene Odum, one of the most influential early ecologists, wrote: *The new ecology is thus a systems ecology ... [it] deals with the structure and function of levels of organization beyond that of the individual and species* (Odum, 1964). Later critics have suggested that this ready association of 'communities' with ecosystems was generated more by a concern about the state of society and politics, rather than about the needs for specific communities to live within ecological boundaries. Moreover, others have suggested that making generalizations about the cohesiveness of social groupings was a recipe for excluding social groups such as indigenous people, or for avoiding the differences within society based on factors such as age and gender (Agrawal and Gibson, 1999).

Third, it is also clear that forest policies rarely develop in a vacuum, and frequently have relationships, seen and unseen, with other political objectives. Forest departments are rarely independent from other sections of the state, and often forest policies are seen to be ways to enact a variety of complementary political objectives. For example, the classification of land as protected or non-protected may often overlap with strategic concerns about land in border regions, or where insurgency has been experienced in the past. Moreover, state forestry policy may reflect the desire of the state to win support from social groups outside the state such as growing numbers of middle classes. For example, the protection of land seen as 'wilderness' may be partly to win political alliance with urban populations who are increasingly worried about rapid forest loss (e.g. see Neumann, 1998). Academics have often described how governments may 'depoliticize' complex strategies for control and legitimization by ascribing these decisions to the supposedly neutral 'scientific' world of forest departments or development agencies (for a discussion of this process in Lesotho, see Ferguson, 1990). Moreover, the overlapping interests of allying political actors may result in the adoption of scientific explanations or problem closures as means of cementing these interests. Academics have called this phenomenon 'discourse coalitions' (Hajer, 1995), because they occur when different viewpoints and objectives overlap, and consequently reinforce the belief that these views are the only way of seeing things. An alliance of a state, which seeks to gain control over strategic land, and middle classes, who want to see more action on protecting wilderness, may therefore result in the perceived function of that land in being classified as untouchable by localized agriculture.

Hence, as a consequence of these factors, the scientific assumptions underlying many approaches to ecosystem management may reflect the political participation in how such management has been framed, for what spatial area, and for which purposes. Analysts have frequently referred to repetitive patterns of environmental explanations as 'environmental narratives' because they are commonly repeated explanations of how an ecosystem works, or how it may be degraded. They are often seen as 'fact', but are based in social discourse that has accumulated over some years (see Roe, 1991). It is important to acknowledge that some powerful political actors may support these narratives, but the narratives do not necessarily reflect the potential framing (or problem closures) of different social groups. Indeed they may avoid the insights of alternative knowledge claims from actors who have not been involved in the creation of narratives. Frequently, state forestry institutions have strongly influenced the creation of narratives about forest management, and yet their role is often left unchallenged.

Political Influences of State Forest Departments

State forestry departments, of course, may influence, or be influenced by the kinds of political factors described above, and these may be less visible than their stated policy objectives. In particular, the history, and original terms of reference may influence the 'functions' and problem closures ascribed to ecosystems by forest departments. It is well known, for example, that many forest departments in developing countries were established during colonial administrations, and hence had objectives that reflected those of colonial authorities rather than diverse stakeholders. Indeed, analysts have argued that the very identification and mapping of forest areas by forestry departments simplified diverse forest ecosystems into the single function of 'timber farms' (Scott, 1998:263). The techniques used by forestry departments, such as cadastral mapping, and the pre-identification of different trees as 'timber' or trash' species in effect defined what was seen to be viable forest according to particular 'problem closures', and did not highlight how other methods of measurement may indicate alternative functions.

The policies of colonial forestry departments also, obviously, reflected partial social consultation. In Bengal in India during the nineteenth century, teak and sal production was given priority, and the practices of shifting cultivators were seen to be inimical to the objectives of the foresters. Hill forest areas were identified as less valuable for timber production and therefore were burnt to encourage the cultivation of less valuable products such as sabai grass (Sivaramakrishnan, 2000). The objectives of forestry departments have changed over time to reflect a higher prioritization of biodiversity conservation but not all organizations can change attitudes or have the ability to adopt new policies as quickly as some would want (Dove, 1992).

Forest departments are not, usually, overt political bodies in the sense that they take formal political stances on topics of citizenship, public accountability of the government, or law formulation that are usually the responsibility of legal or parliamentary sections of the state. Yet, the search for alternative forms of forest management may increasingly require forestry departments to consider such questions as citizenship or rights for minorities. If the Ecosystem Approach really does call for a greater recognition 'that humans, with their cultural diversity, are an integral component of ecosystems', then this also calls for a diversification in the means of managing forests. Such transitions may challenge historic practices within forestry departments in order to start acknowledging forest uses instead of log production alone. Yet, these changes also require forestry departments to be aware of practical problems of access to land, land tenure, and political representation that may prevent some minority groups from influencing how ecosystem management may proceed.

Furthermore, many forest department actions have implicit political motives that require greater scrutiny. Forestry departments are often called upon to provide expertise in their role as a scientific agency. Yet, analysts are increasingly proposing that scientific advice in this context should not be seen as neutral and an independent prelude to policymaking, but as a further manifestation of dominant environmental narratives developed by the state and its allies. Indeed, forestry departments occupy an influential position of being able to determine how far scientific information about forests and ecosystems connect with the policy world. This influence, and the boundaries used between so-called 'science' and 'politics' (and who defines them) are increasingly seen to be important in revealing the tacit assumptions underlying scientific advice. Academics have used the term 'boundary organization' to describe such social organizations or collectives that can be accessed equally by members of each world without losing identity (Guston, 2001). According to this line of thinking, we should not look to see how forest departments may use science to influence other parts of the state and public, but instead see how the organization may remain stable (or successful) while building consensus in both constituencies of forest ecologists and overt policymakers. Instead of the science being communicated as it 'exists', the concept of boundary organizations suggests we should look at how far the scientific information is shaped, and pre-shaped to find areas of agreement between these constituencies. Frequently, such areas of agreement may also be called 'discourse coalitions' as discussed above.

Consequently, seeking to reform state forestry departments may throw up challenges to various ways in which the departments have previously established authority, and this includes the notion that forest departments are the arbiters of scientific approaches to ecosystem management. The concept of 'scientific forestry' – or the maximized production of logs or watershed protection functions through application of forestry and ecological science – may be challenged on the social grounds that it excludes various alternative framings of ecosystem purpose (Scott, 1998). It is incomplete because it proposes that the science used is without social and political contextualization. In some cases, challenging the tacit assumptions of scientific principles underlying forest institutions may also challenge the political purpose of the institution. At times, this may refer to international or non-governmental organizations as well as state forestry departments. For example, the 'Alternatives to Slash and Burn' initiative overseen by the Consultative Group on International Agricultural Research (CGIAR), has been criticized for defining ecosystem management in a way that automatically, and without negotiation, defines some forms of shifting cultivation as problematic (Forsyth, 2003). Similarly, some authors (e.g. Jeanrenaud, 2002; Fairhead and Leach, 2003) have detected a backlash to the entire conservation-with-development enterprise from conservationists who advocate a return to the values and practices of strict nature protection. Such advocates have often promoted a purely biophysical and spatial basis of defining ecosystem 'functionality' (e.g. Oates, 2000; Terborgh, 1999). These critics have written:

> In this context, eco-regional approaches [i.e. those that specify an ecosystem function according to the regional extent, rather than by the views of people who live within it] have become more than mere ways to set priorities for conservation, coming to represent a new era of biologically-led and supra-national initiatives responding to the urgency of biodiversity protection, overcoming the problems of inefficient or failed states, and justifying major funding through scientifically-led strategic plans (Fairhead and Leach, 2003).

Thus, there still remain two main interpretations discernible in discussions concerning ecosystem approaches: a focus on managerialism and predefined notions of ecosystem function; and an alternative focus on adaptation, negotiation and open-ended governance as a means of achieving ecosystem management. The first tends to be rooted in the typical history of state forestry departments, and recently some larger conservation organizations as managers and advisers about forest areas; the second is an attempt to achieve the wording of the Ecosystem Principles in recognising cultural diversity and local human uses of resources. The role of state forestry departments is crucial in either approach, or if direct managerialism is to be replaced by more open-ended discussion. Yet, of course, there are significant organizational barriers to achieving these changes in practice.

The Case of the Royal Forestry Department of Thailand

The Thai Royal Forestry Department (RFD) was established in 1896 to oversee the logging of Thailand's teak forests. Thailand was never colonized by a European power, and so the RFD cannot be described as a 'colonial' forestry department, but the department is representative of state forestry institutions that have adapted from a primarily exploitative function to one that deals increasingly with conservation. This paper cannot summarise the entire history or structure of the RFD (see Anat *et al.*, 1988), but will focus on the relationship of the RFD to recent political debates concerning the proposed Community Forestry Bill, which has been discussed in Thai politics since the 1990s. The Bill in many ways reflects the concerns of the Ecosystem Approach, as it involves defining how far forests can be managed in diverse and decentralized ways, with recognition of cultural perceptions.

Thailand's legal framework for forestry and forestland is complicated, and dates from times when the current population distribution and economic activity of Thailand was very different. The Forest Act of 1941 defined 'forest' as 'the land area which no one has authority to occupy or use' (Anat *et al.*, 1988). Consequently, the indications of such land at the time defined vast quantities of the country as state-owned forestland, even if there were technically no forest there, or if local customs about settlement and land occupation implied that land could be settled through usufruct or regular cultivation. Most deforestation occurred in Thailand in the mid-twentieth century, with total forest area falling from 53% of the kingdom in 1961, to just 29% in 1985 (Anat *et al.*, 1988). Illegal logging, urbanization, agricultural expansion (especially in the north), and the extension of aquaculture in previous-mangrove forests in the south have accounted for this loss. In 1989 Thailand implemented a total ban on logging as a response to the problem, and discussions since have attempted to reform this total ban into a more flexible form of 'community forestry' to allow some limited forms of forest use.

The RFD produced the first official draft of community forestry legislation in 1990, yet this was criticised by non-governmental organizations for maintaining the strong role of the state in forest management. In response, a coalition of activists and NGOs such as the Project for Ecological Recovery developed a new 'people's' draft bill that asserted the rights of local villagers to enter and use forests. Discussion on community forestry was delayed because of the re-emergence of a military government (1991–1992), and the attempts of this and successive governments to regain control of land in north-eastern Thailand through large-scale plantation and resettlement of villages in land claimed by the state. But in 1996, the government requested the National Economic and Social development Board (NESDB), a policymaking body composed of government and public figures, to develop a new Community Forestry Bill. This Bill has yet to be passed by parliament but has been rewritten following criticisms from conservationist NGOs, and pro-business politicians (such as the one-time Prime Minister, Chavalit Yonchaiyudh), who wanted to open forests to logging and mining concessions. The RFD, in particular, opposed decentralization of governance to the village level, with a previous Director General once stating in emotional terms that people and forests cannot co-exist. One key debate, for example, refers to the definition of 'community.' The 'people's' version proposes, in accordance with the 1997 Constitution, that a local community is defined as a 'social group' living in the same locality and having the same cultural heritage, and who can apply for that status after a minimum of five years experience in safeguarding forest land. By contrast, the alternative government version proposes that a 'community' may comprise at least 50 individuals living in proximity to forest, regardless of how long they have been there or how the forest is managed (see Johnson and Forsyth, 2002).

It is important to note that the specific discussion of the Community Forestry Bill is not explicitly a discussion of an ecosystem approach, but that many parallels exist between the two concepts, and on occasions, ecosystem approaches have been discussed in the context of community forestry. The debate in Thailand also paralleled many of the general political themes outlined above. Most fundamentally, the implications of defining ecosystem 'function' in specific ways have resulted in different policy proposals for a supposedly 'sustainable' forest ecosystem. The government and RFD, for example, have defined forest ecosystems in the mountainous north of Thailand as predominantly watersheds for the lower plains and cities, and as sites for log production via teak and pine plantations.

Yet, the 'people's' version of community forestry frames forests instead as sites of rural livelihoods, where poor villagers require access to forests in order to gather fuelwood and make limited use of land for agriculture. Both of these perspectives, however, have invoked political rhetoric of ecological fragility and potential devastation, on the one hand, with democratization and human rights on the other. The portrayal of ethnic minorities in the north of Thailand has also been shaped by this debate. Much discussion in Thailand represents the Karen people, on the Thai-Myanmar border, as classically closer to the type of localized forest management intended under the Community Forestry Bill. This is because the Karen have usually lived in settlements for decades or even centuries, and have generally adopted forms of shifting cultivation that allow for field rotation and fallow periods. This is seen in contrast to new, more migratory, ethnic groups in Thailand such as the Hmong and Akha, who have typically relocated villages every 10–20 years, without concern for field rotation. Some critics have suggested that the romantic image often afforded to the Karen in the context of community forestry discussions is more the result of current political perceptions, and the desire to find examples of positive local forest users, rather than a deeper understanding of how all groups may, or may not, adopt ecosystem approaches (Walker, 2001). In other words, one dominating 'narrative' (that shifting cultivation is necessarily damaging to upland watersheds) is now being amended by reference to another narrative that refers to a popular idea of how upland villages should be.

Yet, political debate about forests is also limited by who is allowed to participate. The Thai government clearly cannot give formal citizenship to all people who cross international borders from China, Laos and Myanmar. But local academics in Thailand have estimated that 40–50% of Thailand's one million ethnic minority people in the north do not have formal citizenship, and consequently have fewer rights of political participation or land tenure. In May 1999, some 5,000 hill farmers from both Thai and ethnic- minority groups congregated outside the provincial hall in the northern capital of Chiang Mai, requesting citizenship and an end to plantations on agricultural land. The police and RFD forcibly broke up this demonstration.

Moreover, there is also growing concern that the underlying assumptions about the impacts of upland agriculture on lowland water supplies are flawed or simplistic. Long-term research on water patterns has suggested that the presumed influence of upland land-use-cover change on the discharge of major rivers may have been overstated. It seems likely that increases in lowland demand for water resulting from urbanization, industrialization and irrigation may be more immediate causes (Alford, 1992; Walker, 2002). Indeed, these results have been claimed in other locations, and there is also evidence to suggest that teak plantations may increase soil erosion and runoff because of their influence on the impact of rainfall on the soil surface (Calder, 1999). Much RFD literature and public statements, however, continue to make the link between upland agriculture and lowland water shortages.

The Case of Guinea, West Africa

The country of Guinea in West Africa is quite different to Thailand because it is a much poorer country, with a relatively more arid climate, and of course with a different political history and diversity of cultures. One further difference is that Guinea was a French colony. Yet, Guinea is worth describing alongside Thailand because forest policies have been highly contested here, and the role of formal forestry institutions such as the state forestry department can be examined.

Formal concern about forest resources in Guinea by the colonial authorities dated to the late nineteenth century, when local administrators sought to establish financial and military security for the region (see Fairhead and Leach, 1996). Surveyors noted that the landscape of Guinea was characterized by 'forest islands' that frequently surrounded villages, and a wider savannah ecosystem in-between such islands. These forest islands were often maintained by villages as a means of military defence against potential raiders. At the time, the colonial surveyors, and particularly the botanist, Chevalier, assumed that local agricultural practices and population increase were threatening both the forest islands and savannah by degrading forest and accelerating soil erosion. As in Thailand, much concern to protect the forests was because of a belief that the forests were a key factor in maintaining high levels of rainfall. Moreover, the forest islands were seen to be relics of a previously much larger closed-forest area. One colonial administrator, Nicolas, wrote in 1914: *...the effects of this de-wooding are disastrous; one will soon see nothing more than entirely naked blocks of granite... Now there rests no more than a little belt of trees around each village and that is all* (Fairhead and Leach, 1996).

These views had important consequences for how forestry was seen at the time, and on how ecosystem function and equitable sharing of benefits have been defined since, such as under the Ecosystem Approach. In colonial times, various administrators were concerned about the perceived relationship between land use and forest loss, and its impact on other potential land uses such as plantations for export crops such as rubber, coffee and oil palm. But the first, formal state forestry department was created only in 1931 with the national Service des Eaux et Forêts, as a separate unit from the agricultural service. The initial forest policy was to create a 'curtain' of reserves to halt southwards savannization, and two ridges were identified for reforestation and restricted land use. In 1935, a new decree distinguished between 'wild' and 'useful' fire, which sought to ban the former and restrict the latter to controlled circumstances. There was also more state regulation of farmers' land and tree management. These strategies were partly inspired by the desire to ensure that the flow of the River Niger was not adversely affected by land-use practices. It reflected the belief found in Thailand and elsewhere that lowland water shortages could be explained largely through upland vegetation change (Calder, 1999).

Such views, however, have been criticised by recent research in Guinea about the origin of the forest islands. Fairhead and Leach (1996, 1998, 2004), for example, have used historic photographs, land-cover transects, and oral histories of villagers to argue that the 'forest islands' should not be seen as relics of a previously-larger forest, but as units of forests that have been created largely by the villages themselves. Moreover, the assumptions about savannization and human land use have been questioned by more general research that has highlighted the role of longer-term changes in climate, and the vegetation dynamics within savannah ecosystems themselves. This may explain the progression and regression of land classified as savannah (e.g. Bassett and Zuéli, 2000; Cline-Cole and Madge, 2000).

According to such critics, the belief that rural land use contributed to landscape degradation can be described as another narrative that reflected the historic functions ascribed to the ecosystems and the selective knowledge at the time. *Ostensibly concerned with the environment and the sustainability of resource use, this landscape interpretation in policy has had the instrumental effect of appropriating resource control and revenue from villagers, and of extending state bureaucracy into rural areas* (Fairhead and Leach, 1996). These views suggest that outdated scientific narratives may already jeopardise the Ecosystem Approach's objectives of integrating the perspectives of diverse stakeholders into forest management. These narratives reflect historic views of ecosystem functions, and the long-term objectives of the state to control rural areas. Implementing ecosystem approaches may therefore require revising accepted 'truths' about the causes of forest degradation, rather than seeking to implement forest management without challenging such beliefs.

It is unclear still how far these scientific narratives inform current environmental policies. International aid for Guinea has increased since independence from France in 1958, and some attempts to support local biodiversity or forestry policies have reflected older beliefs. For example, Fairhead and Leach (2003) cite one expatriate forestry official in Guinea as saying. *In village forests, biodiversity has no role. It does not interest villagers. In the forest reserve, the biodiversity aim must necessarily reduce the extent of participation; the more one has a goal of biodiversity conservation, the less one has participation.* Such views, of course, run counter to the definition of the Ecosystem Approach discussed above. To achieve the objectives of the Ecosystem Approach, it may be necessary to diversify approaches to biodiversity in order to acknowledge the historic ways in which villagers have protected forest islands, or manipulated the growth of different species of use to them, rather than adhere to certain specific definitions of biodiversity. Moreover, this statement suggests that the speaker sees expertise as lying mainly within formal organizations rather than with resource users, again counter to the intentions of the Ecosystem Approach.

Some international land-cover monitoring agencies have also apparently adopted the view that forest islands are still relics of wider forest areas. Taking a controversial position, Fairhead and Leach (1998) have estimated that total forest loss in six West African countries since 1900 may have been 9.5–10.5 million hectares, rather than commonly stated estimates of 25.5–30.2 million hectares. But some agencies, such as the World Conservation Monitoring Centre, have placed deforestation in this region even higher, at 48.6 million hectares. These criticisms do not suggest that rural land use is without impacts on forest cover, or that there is no need for formal forest policy. Instead, they indicate that there is a need to reconsider the driving forces behind land-cover change in order to make forest policies more relevant, and to prevent them from restricting rural livelihoods in unnecessary ways. In Guinea, it seems, implementing ecosystem approaches – in the terms discussed under the CBD – depends on challenging certain beliefs about the extent and causes of forest loss, and in working alongside (rather than criticising) the perspectives and expertise within local populations. Thus Principle 11 of the CBD that calls for "all relevant information, including scientific and indigenous and local knowledge" to be used is highly pertinent.

Conclusion

This chapter has summarised various ways in which national political structures and institutions shape the implementation of ecosystem approaches. It uses the examples of state forestry departments in Thailand and Guinea, West Africa, to indicate how specific organizations may shape forest policies, and how political factors may influence state forest departments. But what are the general conclusions for questions concerning ecosystem approaches?

First, it can be suggested that the Ecosystem Approach – as defined under the CBD – underestimates the role of local institutions and politics in determining how it may be interpreted and implemented. There is a tendency within the CBD discussions to portray the Ecosystem Approach as a single approach that may be applied in different locations. Instead, it is important to note that the Ecosystem Principles should really be seen as a set of guiding principles, from which different institutions may 'pick and choose' in order to suit strategic goals. While the essence of the Ecosystem Approach could be better seen as a negotiable, and culturally sensitive approach to ecosystem management that can be adopted in diverse locations, it is important to note how local contexts and politics will result in different policy outcomes.

Second, the nature of forest policy adopted formally by state institutions frequently reflects political concerns of a wide-ranging nature, and which are not always specifically the domain of forest management or of people living in zones affected by forest policies. In Thailand, for example, much forest policy has been influenced by the treatment of "ecosystem function" as being synonymous with the protection of watersheds for the lowland plains and cities. Similarly national security concerns are equated with issues of citizenship and state control over lands close to national borders. In Guinea, forest policies have similarly been linked to attempts at state expansion into rural areas and also to attempts of international conservation organizations to highlight forest loss in these areas.

Third, the scientific basis of forest policy may be based on so-called 'narratives' of explanation that reflect historic framings of how ecosystems should be seen (or so-called 'problem closures'), and the experiences of only a selected number of people. Frequently, such narratives are repeated and reinforced by state forestry departments because these are seen to be the underlying purpose of such bodies, or because they open the way for political alliances or funding from other actors. In Thailand, the narrative that shifting cultivation or upland agriculture is responsible for lowland water shortages has found support from the military (who have sought to control upland areas for security reasons) and urban middle classes (who are concerned about lost wilderness and who may also not be willing to regulate water shortages by reducing water demand). In Guinea, the underlying narrative that historic rural land uses cause savannization found initial support from the French authorities who wanted to regulate lowland water flow, and more recently from some international conservation organizations. But it is also important to note that critiques of such entrenched positions may also reflect counter-narratives of their own. For example, in Thailand, critics have suggested some proponents of community forestry have portrayed one minority (the Karen) in ways that are romantic and detrimental to ways of identifying effective ecosystem management (Walker, 2001). These sorts of problems are common to many of the more pluralistic approaches to forest and natural resources management.

Fourth, forest departments may frequently use 'science' as a means to define themselves with authority and legitimacy within political debates about forest policy. Yet, frequently such science is based on narratives that are increasingly challenged – such as that concerning the relationship of upland agriculture and lowland water supply, or the relationship of rural agriculture with savannization. This tendency has implications for the ability to implement the Ecosystem Approach in terms that allow for pluralistic visions of ecosystem management. The Ecosystem Approach urges forest departments to 'recognise that humans, with their cultural diversity, are an integral component of ecosystems.' Yet, this statement effectively means that predefined scientific explanations that blame environmental degradation on the practices of ethnic minorities should be challenged. Forest departments in Thailand and Guinea have shown themselves to be highly resistant to attempts to accept decentralized expertise, and this has partly reinforced the presentation of departments as scientific expert bodies in order to reduce the possibility for influence from other sources.

These conclusions, however, should not be interpreted simply as reasons to dismiss state forestry departments, but instead as reasons to view their influence more critically. It is clear from the examples of Thailand and Guinea that forestry departments are frequently prejudiced by broad political influences. They are often allied with external actors such as other government departments and middle class activists within countries, or with international organizations. There is still a crucial need for state forestry departments to act as coordinating units for forest policy, and to enforce policies where needed. There is also a need to make their influence more transparent, and to enhance their ability to consult and include alternative perspectives and explanations of ecosystem function and impacts. This has fundamental implications for the organization and management culture of forest departments and these are further discussed in the concluding chapter of this book.

Two important steps may enable forestry departments to adopt the Ecosystem Principles more effectively. First, it is important to see the Ecosystem Approach as a new form of diversified forest governance rather than another uniform code of ecological guidelines. The objective of the Ecosystem Principles is to enhance biodiversity and ecosystem protection. But it must seek to do this on the basis of greater awareness of cultural diversity and of the need to avoid using environmental policies to restrict local livelihood options. This cannot be achieved by centralized power within state forestry departments that may still be influenced by wider political concerns and narratives based on controlling rural lifestyles. There must be greater ability to make forest governance more diversified, yet in such ways that still harnesses the political power and analytical expertise usually contained within state institutions.

The second step is to analyse state forestry departments, and reform them, in ways that reflect their ability to influence the production of knowledge about forest management. This paper has called upon debates in political ecology to suggest various ways in which forestry departments can be analysed: the concepts of problem closure and narratives help to identify the structured way in which debate about forests may be foreclosed in advance. The concepts of boundary organizations and discourse coalitions indicate ways specific forestry departments may interact with other actors and organizations to reinforce those debates. Showing how forestry departments use science and narratives to reinforce their resistance to reform is necessary to enabling the adoption of the Ecosystem Principles. Such analysis should then be followed up by the reform of departments, or the creation of alternative arenas, that allow the discussion of biodiversity and ecosystem management without such predefined ideas.

12 Forests in Landscapes: Expanding Horizons for Ecosystem Forestry

Jeffrey A. Sayer and Stewart Maginnis

Negotiating Standards for Forestry

The latter part of the 20th Century was a period when there was a preoccupation with developing or negotiating standardized "cookie-cutter" approaches to forest management. This process was driven by civil society dissatisfied by the performance of forestry operators and by forestry agencies attempting to reflect the broader concerns of society. The last decade of the 20th Century saw the emergence of numerous sets of Criteria & Indicators defining a newer, broader, view of sustainable forest management. They addressed the multiple attributes of forests that needed to be the objects of modern forest management. "Model" approaches to forestry were promoted at an international level with strong impetus from Canada. These sought to replicate solutions to achieving balance between industrial forestry and environmental and social concerns that had worked in Canada and apply them elsewhere. Many development assistance projects sponsored "models" for sustainable, community or social forestry, seeking to promote broad adoption of approaches that had succeeded in one locality.

During the debates that led up to the United Nations Conference on Environment and Development in Rio de Janeiro in 1992 there was a strong lobby for a forest convention. Advocates of a convention saw it as providing a globally applicable set of rules governing how forests should be managed. The pro-convention lobby was made up of northern environmental groups seeking some form of international regulation of forestry and countries such as Canada that wanted a level playing field for international trade in industrial forest products. Opponents of the convention were mainly southern countries who resented any international intrusion on their sovereign right to manage forests – and especially their right to convert forest lands to other uses to achieve their development goals.

The non-binding principles adopted at the Rio conference were a compromise. They provided a global set of "norms" for sustainable forest management but they anticipated some of the principles of the CBD Ecosystem Approach by recognising the legitimacy of managing forests for local and national benefits. A consensus was beginning to emerge that forest management practices have to be situation specific and that global or national norms could only be useful at a very broad level of generalization. The major conclusion of this book is that we need to back off even more from this tendency towards "normalizing" forestry and more fully embrace the idea of pluralism and locally adapted solutions to forest problems.

The CBD definitions of Ecosystem Principles and the different C&I for SFM can be seen either as further attempts to establish norms or "cookie-cutter" approaches to forest management or they can be seen as general frameworks or approaches to management within which the locally adapted management solutions are developed. We emphatically see them as the latter and view them as just a subset of a large number of attempts to convey the idea that forests have to be managed as part of the dynamic social-ecological systems of which they are fundamental components.

Global Failure but Local Success

The dominant discourse at international gatherings about forests is that we are still facing something of a crisis. We hear that forests are being managed badly, deforestation is rampant, illegal activities are ubiquitous and that climate change and sheer demand for land and resources jeopardise the future of our forests. However one also observes that there are large numbers of places on the planet where things are going quite well for the forests. Some of these are at the scale of countries, some of big corporations and the majority at the level of communities. The interesting question is whether all of these good things are happening because of the level of international attention that they get or in spite of it! The global policy narrative may have created the conditions under which positive local initiatives can prosper but in many cases it appears more probable that these successes came because people confronted with a "forest problem" organized themselves to deal with it. In the case of companies it may have been mainly the threat of loss of access to markets that required certified timber. They also feared losing market share to substitute products such as steel and cement because they were failing to make the case that wood was an environmentally benign product. In the case of communities it may have been the concern that unsustainable forestry was leading to a decline in supplies of a broad range of forest products. The review of the 1992 World Bank Forest Policy conducted towards the end of the '90s showed that forestry projects and loans to countries with low forest cover had in general performed much better than those to rich forest countries. Once forests become scarce resources people respond by seeking recognition of their forest rights and taking initiatives to restore or improve their forests. As long as forests are perceived as super- abundant it is difficult to convince people of the need for improved husbandry.

The World Bank has been a significant and controversial actor in the global forestry debate. Its earlier forestry loans in the 1970s and 80s were accused of being overly sectoral and commodity oriented. The World Bank was a major sponsor of the Tropical Forestry Action Plan in 1985. This plan was criticised for not addressing the interests of forest dependent people or the environment and for not encouraging civil society involvement in forestry. Instead of calling for changes in forestry projects it was seen as calling simply for more forestry projects. Notwithstanding these criticisms the Tropical Forestry Action Plan did contain elements that were innovative at the time and did make tentative steps in the direction of what we now call ecosystem approaches. The negative reaction to the TFAP was one factor that led the World Bank to develop a new forest policy in 1992. The debate surrounding the issuance of this policy was strongly rooted in a northern rich-country preservation agenda and of a "single best way" of managing forests. Environmental concerns, especially biodiversity, and concerns for forest dwelling indigenous people were the central elements of the policy. Unlike the TFAP the 1992 World Bank Forest Policy gave the development benefits of forestry a low profile. Contrast this with the new forest policy developed by the World Bank in the early years of the new century. The new policy is more balanced, stressing not only poverty reduction but also economic development and the maintenance of environmental values and promoting a more pluralistic vision of how forestry should be tackled. The new World Bank forest policy was based upon far broader consultation with the full diversity of forest actors and was less prescriptive – instead it placed value on local processes in determining the forest agenda. This is consistent with ecosystem approaches and the case studies in this volume all argue that in the 21st Century we should be seeking a much greater diversity of approaches to forestry. In the following sections we attempt to capture some of the messages that emerge from the case studies that are presented in chapters 5 to 10 of this book.

Europe

Many European foresters would argue that the basic concepts of ecosystem approaches to forestry have been part of mainstream forestry in the continent ever since forestry emerged as a formal scientific pursuit in the 18th Century. This is true, up to a point. European forestry has always been rooted strongly in knowledge of the ecology of the forests. It has also been very much a reflection of a central government, technical approach to forest management. The opportunities for civil society to seriously question the overall objectives of forestry have only emerged quite recently. Countries with few forest resources may have moved more rapidly towards ecosystem approaches than those with abundant forests. In the former, civil society mobilized itself more rapidly, the shortage of amenity and environmental forest values was felt more acutely. In forest rich countries these shortages were not apparent and forest agencies were stronger and more conservative.

The past decade has seen a very rapid and significant move towards more holistic, broader-based approaches to forests. This has been reflected in policy statements and institutional changes at all levels from local to national to the European Union itself. Civil society is now firmly in the driving seat in determining how forests are managed in most countries in the region. Environmental and social values are clearly the main drivers of forest management programmes. Ambitious programmes to improve the contribution of forests to multi-functional landscapes are now emerging both at the national and the EU levels. Ecosystem approaches to forests are now well established as the prevailing forest management paradigm in most of the European Union.

The development of ecosystem approaches in Russia and the Ukraine is still in its infancy, although some progress has been made over the last two decades. The 'command and control' approach to forest management, firmly in place up until the early 1990s, was a classic version of SFM that focused on timber production, while largely ignoring any social or off-site environmental concerns. The transition to market economies, the collapse of state-run systems and the privatization of most industrial forest enterprises created a situation of great uncertainty. Harvesting volumes dropped sharply, social tensions erupted and illegal forestry activities soared. Recent years have seen some serious attempts at reorganizing the forest sectors to achieve broader-based and more sustainable approaches. The impact of these on the ground is still limited.

The potential impact of public debate, seen in other country case studies as a driver of ecosystem approaches, is beginning to emerge. One such debate started in the 1990s and centred on the fate of the virgin taiga forests on the border of Karelia (Western Russia) and Finland. Local authorities and environmental groups took strongly opposing positions, national and international stakeholders became involved and European importers called for a boycott of timber shipments. A productive dialogue was finally established and national parks were established to protect old growth forests. Model forests have now been established in several parts of Russia and these espouse the principles of ecosystem approaches. However, these successes are the exception to the norm and examples of integration of environmental and social concerns within Russian and Ukrainian forest management regimes are still hard to find.

Australia: Politics and Polarity

The debate on forest management in Australia has been shaped by simplistic media treatment that has led to two polarizations: State governments versus the Commonwealth (Central) government and rural forest users versus largely urban conservationists. The heat of the forest dialogues has also been turned up by strong national stakeholder groups (including the forest industry, unions, landholder and environmental NGOs) and by Commonwealth and State governments intent on making political capital from the issues. Typically the Commonwealth government's position has been that a change in tenure from State Forest to National Park is the sole route to achieving effective conservation, while the State governments have argued that retaining State Forests is the only way to maintain wood production and dependent industries and employment.

This polarized debate has been termed one of 'single tenure-single use', with any gains for one side translated as losses for the other. Things came to a head in 1992 after a massive public protest over a politically motivated renewal of a wood chip export license. Both the Commonwealth and State governments recognised that this type of political posturing was counterproductive to all stakeholder interests. In response the government introduced the concept of negotiated Regional Forest Agreements. This process introduced many elements of ecosystem approaches, seeking a balance between conservation and forest production and attempting to ensure broad public participation in decision-making. Regional Forest Agreements were developed across the country, reflecting principles in their codes of forest practice, management plans, sustainable yield calculations, and environmental management systems. While the Regional Forest Agreements have also had their weaknesses, particularly in achieving resource security for wood-using industries and in taking account of indigenous heritage concerns, they represent a major step towards a more rational, balanced approach to forest management. The need for ecosystem approaches to forests in Australia was met through the Regional Forest Agreement process.

USA Pacific Northwest: Old Growth and Owls

Here is an excellent example of how a more demanding public, seeking broader forest benefits, has led managers of publicly-owned forests to adopt ecosystem approaches. The rapidly urbanizing society of the Pacific Northwest (PNW), whose ranks have swelled in the last few decades by immigrants attracted by the area's environment and economy, has quite different expectations of forest functions to those of the resource-dependent rural communities. Landscape beauty and recreational opportunities are top priorities for these urban populations, and forest managers have had to respond to these demands by providing an acceptable mix of commodity production, amenity use, and environmental and biodiversity protection. Balance has had to be sought between reconciling conservation concerns (including the endangered northern spotted owl, dependent on the area's old growth forests) and employment with economic objectives.

The approach to managing publicly-owned forests until the 1980s, was dominated by clearcutting, burning and replanting, with timber extraction as a primary objective (although within a multiple-use context). Strong public reactions to the visual and environmental impacts of this system, and the ensuing conflicts between the different stakeholder groups in the 'jobs versus owls' debate, resulted in the PNW becoming a test-bed for the development of operational ecosystem management, as the Forest Service sought ways of building consensus and defusing conflict. Similar ecosystem approaches have evolved elsewhere in North America but nowhere was the process as controversial and contentious as in the PNW.

The ecosystem approach is reflected in the area's natural resource management plans developed during the 1990s, that now focus on 'old-growth' and multi-resource ecosystem management to provide habitat for threatened and endangered species (notably the northern spotted owl and wild salmon), protect riparian zones and promote biodiversity. State regulations for forest management also include many of the principles behind the ecosystem approach. It is particularly interesting that the Northwest Forest Plan, developed in 1993 as a long-term policy for managing northern spotted owl habitat, includes the designation of Adaptive Management Areas to allow for the testing and modification of conservation management assumptions and approaches. The forests of the PNW are now managed as part of a large social-ecological system.

India: Beyond Joint Forest Management

The watershed event in the development of ecosystem approaches in India was the 1988 U-turn in government policy that saw commercial timber interests subordinated to conservation and local communities' needs as the primary objectives of forest management.

Conflicts between local communities and the forest bureaucracy, and public protests against the earlier policy contributed to this important re-orientation of forest policy. Based on the new policy, and the encouraging results from some pioneering experiments in community-based forest management, the government started the ambitious Joint Forest Management (JFM) programme that shares many of the same principles as the Ecosystem Approach.

Over the past two decades, JFM has emerged as a major forest management strategy in the country. The positive impacts of the JFM programme have included an improvement in the relationship between the Forest Department staff and local communities, increased income for participating communities and an improvement in the condition of forests. On the other hand, JFM has had several shortcomings, including a lack of a firm legal basis, domination of JFM groups by the village elite, inequitable sharing of benefits within communities, and in some cases the programme has led to inter-community conflicts. A key challenge has also been the limited empowerment of the JFM groups in real terms and the *de facto* control that the Forest Department still retains over them. Despite these problems, JFM still represents a significant improvement in forest management.

Alongside JFM, other initiatives have also promoted ecosystem approaches, including the Ecodevelopment programme and People's Protected Areas, both of which seek to address the conflicts between conservation and communities in and around protected areas. The Sustainable Forest Management work of the Indian Institute of Forest Management, which began in 1998 and the current preparation of the National Biodiversity Strategy and Action Plan, which strongly advocates an ecosystem approach, are further landmarks on the road to acceptance of this approach in India. With its huge population and limited forest resources India was a country where there was an urgent need for broader, more equitable and multi-functional approaches to forests. It is therefore not surprising that the basic principles of ecosystem approaches have emerged in multiple independent manifestations in response to a range of forest "problems" in India.

Central America: Changing a Relationship

Historically, the relationship between people and forests in Central America has been a difficult one. Local people have seen little benefit in forest conservation. They were often competing with the state for access to forest lands. As a result forest landscapes have been highly fragmented and forest management units have been small. The region's high levels of poverty and population growth, small and stagnating economies and weak public institutions present additional barriers to achieving an optimal distribution of forests and availability of forest products and services.

Yet, in the face of these huge challenges, there are encouraging signs of progress. At the end of the 1980s the International Tropical Timber Organization reported that there were no good examples of sound forest management in the region, while today, the Forest Stewardship Council records show 691,346 hectares of certified forest in 42 units of natural and planted forests, including the community concessions of the Maya Biosphere Reserve in Guatamala. This move towards sustainability has been driven not by the region's forest industries, but by its research institutes. In particular, the Tropical Agricultural Research and Higher Education Center (CATIE) has spearheaded research and development for sustainable forest management based on ecosystem concepts. The ideas underlying ecosystem approaches have found ready acceptance amongst governments and other actors throughout the region. Ecosystem approaches found strong support from international donors and began to emerge in new policies and projects.

At the same time, there has been a gradual shift in how the region's peoples and governments view forests, following several natural disasters. Hurricane Mitch in particular revealed the link between climate, natural resources and people and forced Central American governments and international cooperation agencies to re-orient their development strategies to address social and ecological vulnerability, transparency, participation, and local development. These natural disasters also emphasised the important role of forests in reducing and mitigating the impacts of such events and helped to promote the development of integrated watershed management policies.

An important example of government reform, favouring ecosystem approaches, is the recent de-centralization and reorientation of natural resource management in Costa Rica, which has put eco-regions as the basis for the country's national conservation area network.

The growing awareness among Central American states and societies that forest systems produce significant goods and services has helped reduce the historical incentives for forest conversion, and this has been the key to creating an enabling environment for ecosystem approaches.

Congo Basin: Improving Policies

The history of forest management in the Congo Basin did not provide a promising start for the development of ecosystem approaches. In the 1970s and early '80s, most forest management and conservation efforts went into either regulating logging concessions or establishing and protecting parks and reserves. This situation was in many ways the antithesis of ecosystem management, as local communities were largely excluded from forest governance, forest use was sharply segregated into protection and production zones and the central government controlled everything.

Even in the late 1980s, international donor support for forest management in the region paid very little attention to social or environmental objectives. The Tropical Forestry Action Plan (TFAP) for Cameroon, prepared with donor support, was rooted in a vision of sophisticated large-scale con-cession management for international markets with silvicultural treatments that would greatly increase future yields of commercial timber. The TFAP contained the implicit assumption that environmental benefits would be inevitable by-products of good forestry practice. The Cameroon TFAP was vigorously attacked by environmental NGOs for its pro-logging stance and its failure to address the needs of conservation and of forest-dependent communities. The debate that followed influenced the development of a new and progressive forestry law in 1994, which contains many innovations that favour the interests of forest people and biodiversity.

Cameroon remains the main focus of innovation in forestry in the region, as intermittent periods of civil conflict in the Democratic Republic of Congo, Congo-Brazzaville and the Central African Republic have inhibited similar innovations in those countries. However, despite the civil unrest and declining or stagnant economies in the region, a raft of recent policy decisions and international commitments by governments is pointing towards a more inclusive approach to forests. The preamble to the Congolese forest law of 2002, for example, refers to "forest ecosystems", and the legal frameworks in all countries of the Congo Basin now show considerable progress towards the integration of ecosystem approach objectives. Progress on the ground is still very patchy, though it is still early days since these legal commitments have only recently been made. Economic difficulties across the region mean that their forest management capacities are stretched to the limit and innovation is difficult.

Still, there are a few success stories for forest ecosystem management. These include the work of the Wildlife Conservation Society (WCS) in and around the concession of the Congolaise Industrielle des

Bois in northern Congo. Significant steps have been taken by this, and other concessionaires, towards sustainable forest management, including the provision of livelihood support for the resident Baka pygmy communities and the monitoring of large mammal populations. Other successful efforts include the work of WWF in the Dzangha-Sangha region of the Central African Republic and the work of WCS in the Ituri Forest of the Democratic Republic of Congo. The legal and policy commitment to ecosystem approaches to forests is in place. Some practical examples exist but the Congo Basin countries are far from the point where ecosystem approaches are mainstreamed throughout their forest management programmes.

Cross-cutting Issues

Societal Choice and Decentralization

Two of the key principles of the Ecosystem Approach as advocated by the Convention on Biological Diversity are that forest management must be a matter for societal choice and that management must be devolved as far as possible to local stakeholders. These principles are a reaction to the historical situation where the management and conservation of natural resources has often been a source of tension between powerful, centralized state authorities (the ruling elite) and less powerful local communities. The history of forest governance and forestry as a profession has been a reflection of the underlying tension between the "centre" and the "local". In theory centralized forest institutions were established as the guarantors of the public goods and intergenerational values of forests on the assumption that local forest users would be more concerned with immediate and private benefits. The reality was often a struggle for land and valuable timber and wildlife resources between different sectors of society.

The way in which rights and assets have traditionally been partitioned has been a reflection of the power structures existing in the societies concerned. A model for forestry which evolved in Central Europe in the 18th Century subsequently formed the basis of much forest law in the Asian and African tropics. This gave the ownership of land, timber and high value game animals to the aristocracy or the state and rights to lower value products such as dead timber, mushrooms, pasture etc. to the peasantry. The nature conservation movement that emerged when people began to attach value to dramatic landscapes, rare animals and plants and wilderness in the 19th Century sought to add these additional values to those over which the state tried to exercise control (Rackham, 2001; Scott, 1998; Schama, 1995).

The modern nature conservation movement began with the establishment of National Parks and similar protected areas where outstanding natural features were placed under permanent state control. During most of the first hundred years of formal, planned nature conservation, natural areas were transferred from local control to State control. The prevailing paradigm was to conserve nature in centrally managed areas. The number and extent of such protected areas was often the principal criteria for the success of conservation programmes. Until recently, inclusion in the United Nations list of protected areas required that an area be placed under the jurisdiction of the "highest competent authority" of the state. Protected areas were expected to have clearly defined boundaries, management plans etc. Until the relatively recent past most governmental and non-governmental conservation organizations focussed their efforts on the establishment of new national parks and equivalent reserves or on supporting the improved management of those that existed.

The "set-aside" approach to conservation remains strong in some quarters. Environmental groups still advocate setting aside a minimum of 10% of all forests as inviolate protected areas, while some more preservationist-oriented groups would like to see all remaining near-natural forests given total protection. The World Parks Congress in Durban, South Africa in 2003 celebrated the fact that the 10%

target had been exceeded. Over 12% of terrestrial ecosystems worldwide are now included in some sort of formal protected area. In the final decades of the 20th Century a number of international conventions and processes have been developed to give global stewardship to important natural areas. The World Heritage Convention, adopted in 1972, is a significant manifestation of the tendency towards "Global governance". Many people still advocate the designation of the world's high conservation forests as World Heritage Sites under a form of global protection (Sayer *et al.*, 2000).

Set against this tendency to centralize control and ownership of forests has been a tradition, deeply rooted in history, for the development of local rules and institutions to conserve and ensure equitable access to forests. Arrangements for conserving forests, water and other natural resources are said to have been amongst the forces that drove the emergence of local governments and democratic processes. In many parts of the world traditional arrangements for managing forests have functioned successfully for centuries. Modern foresters and conservationists have ignored these local forest stewardship arrangements and in many cases have sought to weaken or disempower traditional local forest managers. Government forest agencies and even conservation NGOs have often undermined local management traditions.

The past few decades have seen a reversal of this historic tendency towards centralization. Numerous initiatives have been taken to devolve more management responsibility to local communities. In some cases these processes were driven by the desire for "smaller government", in other cases they were in response to economic crises and in yet others they represented a genuine desire to move to more pluralistic and equitable forms of resource management. The most significant moves in this direction that are documented in this book are those from India and Central America. Both development and conservation organizations generally consider experience with decentralized and devolved forest management over recent decades to have been very positive. Problems have occurred but these have often been caused by the way in which decentralization was handled – they do not undermine the basic principles. In many cases decentralization has occurred too rapidly and has been subject to multiple and conflicting pressures. Central authorities may have de-localized some decision making but they have often retained control of the most valuable assets. Hasty or opportunistic de-centralization has often left institutional vacuums and an absence of accountability. Some attempts to "turn the clock back" have failed. One cannot assume that local communities will be able to re-establish traditional systems of forest management overnight after years of central government interference. The conclusion from many recent experiences of devolved management in Africa and Asia is that they often did not really work, but we now understand why. If it had been done right then better outcomes would have been achieved.

A lot of the experience of decentralization has occurred in situations where all governance institutions, both central and local, are weak. Decentralization or devolution alone will not solve these problems. The experience in the Congo Basin (chapter 9) contrasts with that in India and Central America. The principle of decentralized management has been accepted (at least in some of the countries) in the Congo Basin but the capacity of both central and local institutions to handle the process has been lacking. When institutions are weak and the rule of law does not prevail then neither centralized nor decentralized systems have much chance of succeeding.

Most programmes to devolve forest management to communities and local authorities have been driven by the need to improve local livelihoods and were initiated by development NGOs or local communities themselves. Conservation organizations have often become involved after the process was already engaged. There seem to be few situations where baseline data on environmental values is adequate to evaluate the extent to which decentralized forest management conserves the broad range of natural forest values. For instance we know that locally managed forests can be rich in biodiversity but we do not really know if they can conserve the full biodiversity values that a protected area can provide. We have information on the presence or absence of forest cover but we know little about the biodiversity values of that forest. Conservation groups have tended to take the position that any forest is better than no forest and that decentralized management has been the best option for maintaining some degree of forest cover.

There are many situations in less developed countries where central forest institutions have had great difficulty in conserving forest environments. In many tropical countries forests are continuing to disappear rapidly. However there are many examples where natural forests have spread as a consequence of the institution of local management arrangements (Sayer *et al.*, 2004). This is the basis of the optimism of conservation organizations regarding local forest management. However it is somewhat surprising that the CBD has embraced decentralization so enthusiastically in its principles. In all of the case studies in this book countries have opted for central control of the key protected areas that are the cornerstone of conservation programmes. Practical demonstrations that devolved management systems are the best option for biodiversity conservation are lacking. Devolved management systems do have a vital role to play in achieving the complementary patchwork of different forest types in multi-functional landscapes that are essential to address broad conservation goals. But most countries still appear to favour central control for those sites whose biodiversity is truly of national or global value. The general conclusion of this overview is that in certain circumstances decentralization is a positive force for conservation while in other situations it poses dangers. The key issue is often not whether to decentralize or not, it is about how and what to decentralize. The following general guidelines emerge from a review of this issue (Sayer *et al.*, 2004 and this volume):

The Conditions under which Decentralization Supports Ecosystem Approaches to Management

1. Devolved and decentralized management schemes have often led to the maintenance or extension of areas of species-rich indigenous forests and have thus provided biodiversity benefits. There are many situations where local management has proved more successful in achieving this than centralized management.

2. Decentralization must be a planned and negotiated process – decentralization in response to economic crises risks leaving an institutional vacuum and may result in rapid resource depletion.

3. When the benefits of protected areas and other conservation measures accrue mainly at a broad public or global level it may be unwise and unrealistic to assume that decentralized management will be effective. This will only be true if an effective regulatory or incentive framework is in place to encourage local users to forego many of their prior entitlements. This suggests that most strictly protected areas will need to be retained under central government control.

4. Local managers must have legitimacy and be representative of local resource users; a large degree of local downward accountability may be a pre-requisite for any sort of decentralization to work (Ribot, 2002 and 2003).

5. Assets, rights, power and entitlements to invest in developing and retaining resources must be transferred to local managers, not just responsibility.

6. Resources to support conservation programmes must be available to decentralized institutions.

7. Economic benefits must accrue to decentralized managers and these must be equal to or exceed the opportunity costs foregone to ensure biodiversity conservation.

8. When the value of conservation activities accrues mainly to external constituents then some form of regulatory or financial incentive must be provided for decentralized managers.

9. Direct environmental payments will often be necessary to offset local costs and opportunity costs of programmes to conserve biodiversity whose value accrues to the "global community" and not directly to local people. However it has proved difficult to make environmental payment schemes work in countries with weak institutions.

Ecosystem Approaches and Managing Natural Ecosystems

The Ecosystem Principles of the CBD make it clear that ecosystem approaches need to be applied to any social-ecological system no matter how much it may have been altered by man. Most of the principles, with the exception of principles 5 and 6, stress the need to maintain ecological, social and economic functions of the area under management. It is however clear from our case studies, and particularly from the European examples, that ecosystem approaches are being interpreted as those approaches that seek to preserve biodiversity by maintaining conditions as close as possible to those of the natural ecosystem. A movement in Europe to promote "Close to Nature Forestry" is a good example of this. In this study we have interpreted ecosystem approaches to mean any approach to management that seeks to maintain those ecological functions that are considered desirable. We recognise that in many situations the best way of ensuring that ecological services are maintained may be to retain natural ecosystems but this will not always be the case. It will often not be consistent with the principles of societal choice and decentralization. We prefer to interpret the ecosystem principles in the sense of seeking to modify ecosystems in ways that will favour the best combination of social and ecological outcomes. The ecosystem approach can thus be applied to highly degraded systems and may involve engineering works to restore ecological functions. The following section takes the special case of plantation forestry as an example of where ecosystem approaches can be applied in highly artificial landscapes.

The exact nature of the ecosystem approach adopted will depend upon the objectives of management. There are many situations where managing for the maintenance or re-establishment of natural ecosystems will not be appropriate. Thus many wetland and grassland nature reserves in the United Kingdom and elsewhere have to be maintained in a highly artificial state in order to provide habitat for rare species. Once again our case studies show that the solutions are very situation-dependent. In countries like Australia, USA, Canada and Russia the best way of reconciling economic and conservation objectives may be through large scale land allocation. Large blocks of forest may be intensively managed for production whilst conservation areas may be subject to minimum disturbance and allowed to develop old-growth conditions. In more densely settled and modified landscapes such as those found in Western Europe, India and Central America a finer grain integration of production and conservation functions may be appropriate with more active management of conservation areas to compensate for their small size and prior history of modification. The concept of old-growth forest may have less relevance in these highly fragmented and modified landscapes.

Ecosystem Approaches and Plantation Forestry

Forest plantations are expanding rapidly and are producing an ever increasing proportion of the world's timber and wood fibre. Some projections see plantations producing most of the world's timber and fibre in the future with natural forests only being maintained for amenity and environmental purposes. These extreme scenarios are the antithesis of ecosystem approaches.

Plantations are defined as "forest stands established by planting and/or seeding in the process of afforestation or reforestation..." Despite the high losses of the world's natural forests at the global level, new forest plantation areas are being established at a rate of 4.5 million hectares per year, with Asia and South America accounting for more new plantations than the other regions. Only about 70% of new plantations, or 3.1 million hectares per year, are successful, as on large areas that are planted the trees are neglected and subsequently die or burn. Of the estimated 187 million hectares of plantations worldwide, Asia had by far the largest area, accounting for 62% of the world total. In terms of composition, Pinus (20%) and Eucalyptus (10%) remain the dominant genera worldwide, although the diversity of species planted is increasing. Industrial plantations (producing wood or fibre for supply to wood processing industries) accounted for 48% of the global forest plantation estate and non-industrial plantations (e.g. for provision of fuelwood or soil and water protection) for 26%.

The extent of plantations in industrialized countries is harder to measure than in developing countries. Many industrialized countries make no distinction between planted and natural forests in their inventories. In Western Europe most forests have been planted or enriched at some time in their history and the distinction between plantations and other forests is blurred.

The FAO Forest Resources Assessment 2000 identified the ten countries with the largest plantation development programmes (as a percentage of the global plantation area) as China, 24%; India, 18%; the Russian Federation, 9%; the United States, 9%; Japan, 6%; Indonesia, 5%, Brazil, 3%; Thailand, 3%; Ukraine, 2% and the Islamic Republic of Iran, 1%. These countries account for 80% of the global forest plantation area.

Trees outside forests also have significant environmental values and are an integral part of the ecosystems that need to be managed to meet the environmental and social objectives of ecosystem approaches and sustainable forest management. Despite the fact that trees outside forests often play an important role in the livelihoods of the rural population, especially of women, they are often overlooked, both in forest resource assessments and in policy and decision-making processes. Little is known about their broader environmental benefits, for instance for biodiversity. The consequent scarcity of information makes it difficult to draw conclusions on the importance of the resource. Complicating the collection of data on trees outside forests is the fact that neither traditional forest inventories nor modern remote sensing technology are very useful for conducting quantitative assessments. Most of the information on trees outside the forest is site specific and scattered among different institutions and sectors, including informal sectors.

During the meetings that have been held during the present study of ecosystem approaches and sustainable forest management many people have questioned the logic of applying the principles of ecosystem approaches or sustainable forest management to plantations and trees outside forests. Given the growing significance of planted trees, the fact that plantations can be important for biodiversity and that many are established with environmental objectives we conclude that ecosystem approaches apply just as much to planted trees and forests as to natural stands. The potential for plantations to contribute to biodiversity conservation objectives has often been under-estimated (Carnus et al., 2003). In all of our case studies, planted trees and forests have been important in expanding the options for providing ecosystem services and contributing to local livelihoods. Yet again, the way in which they contribute is situation-specific but we conclude that plantations will often be important parts of the social-ecological landscapes that ecosystem approaches and sustainable forest management seek to promote.

Some European countries are beginning to manage maturing plantations for biodiversity and amenity values. Countries like Denmark and the United Kingdom originally established most plantations for purely commercial objectives. These plantations cannot now produce timber at prices that are competitive with those for equivalent imported timber. But civil society in both countries now values the plantations for their amenity and environmental values. Management is now focussing on allowing the plantations to develop towards more structurally and biologically diverse systems with timber production a distant secondary objective (Hahn *et al.*, in press, Grundy, 2005). The Global Partnership for Forest Landscape Restoration is a manifestation of an emerging view of the multi-functional role of plantations as part of conservation landscapes: (www.unep-wcmc.org/forest/restoration/ globalpartnership/).

Knowledge and Information for Ecosystem Approaches and Sustainable Forest Management

As the objectives of forestry broaden so the needs for forest information change. In the past a lot of attention has been given at an international level to the amassing of statistics on the extent of forest cover and the rate of its loss. Global statistics on standing timber volumes and annual timber increments are widely available. Some effort has been made to evaluate the amount of carbon stored in forests and sequestered both by standing forests and through reforestation schemes. Data on fuel wood are also compiled by FAO. Many of these categories of information on forests have been shown to be subject to large errors and to be of dubious utility in taking decisions on forestry. They often extrapolate from small samples or make assumptions about per capita consumption, homogeneity of forest types etc. Now that we are attempting to manage forests for an even larger range of products and services the difficulties of global assessments are even more apparent. The Millennium Assessment (www.millenniumassessment.org) has attempted an overview of forest resource information but has found it hard to provide insights that go beyond those provided by the Forest Resources Assessment team at FAO. The new insights emerging from the Millennium Assessment, at least on forests, are from the integrated sub-regional assessments (www.MAweb.org/en/subglobal.overview.aspx). It is becoming apparent that there are only a few attributes of forests that are amenable to assessment at the global level and FAO adequately monitors these. The real challenge for ecosystem approaches and sustainable forest management is to assess the multiple-functions of forests at the local and landscape levels. These are the levels at which management decisions are taken and for which information on status and trends are required.

One problem with many comparisons of global forest resource information is that different definitions are being used and the trends and patterns that people claim to detect are often more a function of these differences than of realities on the ground. The problems of assessment are even further complicated where management is seeking to achieve multiple functions across a mosaic of forest and non-forest land. One of the problems of conservation and development projects and of some current approaches to landscape-level conservation planning is that there are no widely agreed methods for assessing the performance of large systems with multiple objectives. These issues are extensively discussed in Sayer and Campbell (2004). Essentially assessment and monitoring schemes where trade-offs are inherent in management require multi-dimensional tools and progress cannot be measured along a single axis of variation. Chapter 5 of this book demonstrates the weaknesses of even relatively simple performance measurement techniques applied at the stand level to monitor some ecological attributes of forests. Measurement systems to cover the complexity of ecosystem approaches still represent a major challenge.

New Types of Institutions for Ecosystem Approaches and Sustainable Forest Management

Many forest practitioners are becoming impatient with the proliferation of meetings that they are required to attend, however these meetings are where learning occurs and innovations are communicated. Meetings are where networks of specialists are established. These networks may be the beginning of the new forms of institutions that will manage our forests. As we devolve more and more control over forests to private individuals, corporations and communities the role of centralized forest agencies has to change. Some of their functions are being taken up by the informal networks that allow individual managers to access new technologies, markets and to exploit or influence incentive mechanisms such as subsidies, tax breaks etc. The proliferation of meetings of people concerned with forests cannot be seen outside of the context of new institutional arrangements for forests in general. Some of the attributes of the new arrangements that are needed for forests are well articulated by Carley and Christie (1992):

> As the notion of self-sufficient organizations gives way to more complex networks, organizational and managerial skills in joint working become critical to environmental management and sustainable development, often as important as the substantive nature of any environmental issue. The development of localised management skills, entrepreneurial abilities and modes of partnership is therefore a critical but largely un-addressed aspect of environmental management. A key constraint in human resource terms, then, is insufficient skills in newer integrating styles of management. This is true both for lower and higher income countries, because where higher income countries gain in sophistication of training they often lose in terms of long-term entrenched compartmentalization in bureaucracies.

It is interesting to note that some relatively weak developing country forest institutions have been more amenable to change than some of their stronger counterparts in developed economies. This is especially true in developing countries with low forest cover. Whenever forests become scarce commodities people mobilize to conserve them and government forestry agencies operating in this environment have far more acceptance amongst the population than those who simply apply silvicultural laws in forest-rich situations.

Forest systems have always changed, but the nature and rate of change that we are likely to see in coming decades has no precedent. Climate change will have huge impacts on forests. It will test the ecological tolerance of forest species, it will introduce new threats from pest, diseases and invasive species, it will severely test conservation paradigms rooted in the maintenance of the status quo. But other changes will impact forestry. One can only speculate about the nature and intensity of these changes. At the same time that urban populations engaged in the knowledge or service economy may require forests for their amenity and environmental values so the reduced availability of fossil fuels may give greater prominence to forests as a source of fuel, fibre and industrial raw materials. Renewable energy could come from forests or from intensified agricultural systems but the latter would compete for land with forests and provide fewer other environmental values. These sorts of changes will create dilemmas that traditional forestry will struggle to resolve.

The role of forestry departments will no longer be one of developing expert-driven management prescriptions and then regulating their enforcement. Forest departments will be steering rather than rowing – working with society to establish broadly accepted visions of forest futures and then providing the technical supporting services to help attain these. Several of the case study chapters in this book illustrate the progress that many forest departments have already made in this direction. Some of these more progressive forest departments are assuming new roles. They are increasingly working with civil society to:

- Facilitate a dialogue amongst all forest stakeholders to establish a vision for their forests and to determine the limits within which forest owners and managers may operate.
- Establish and maintain multiple-resource databases on forests to enable trends and patterns to be detected and adjustments to management to be made.

- Provide a problem-solving research capacity to deal with emerging problems of pest and diseases, to determine management requirements for specific targets – the maintenance of an endangered species for example.

- Develop an early warning capacity so that emerging threats and issues can be detected and adaptive management measures brought to bear to deal with them – the early signs of climate change impacts are a good example. This implies a "radar" function – being alert on broader extra-sectoral developments that may impact on forests.

- Provide the overview, analysis and verification needed to make environmental service payments effective in supporting the production of the public goods values of forests.

- Facilitate and contribute to development of criteria and indicators as they emerge as a sort of civil society soft law mechanism by which regulation of forestry activities is subject to broader scrutiny by civil society.

- Notwithstanding the above, forest departments will still have to defend forest rights and enforce regulations.

- Defend forest interests in the various governmental and civil society arenas where important decisions about the environment, natural resources and land-use are taken.

The nature of the interactions between forest departments and civil society are destined to continue to change. We are seeing the emergence of a new form of collective action to manage forests within large-scale multi-functional landscapes. This has parallels in community forestry but it is forestry where the community includes distant and urban populations and where values include "existence values" etc.

Conclusions: Implementing Ecosystem Approaches and Sustainable Forest Management – the Ten Tenets of Good Practice

The final message from this volume is that forestry has an exciting future. The numerous goods and services that humanity derives from forests will be in even greater demand in the future. We will have more people, higher consumption of natural resources, more disposable income and leisure and less land available for forests. The stewards of tomorrow's forest lands will have to get more products and services out of a smaller area. They will have to deploy the best technologies together with the skills of the political, economic and social sciences. The demands upon them will change constantly. However we hope that they will take care of some 40% of the world's land area and that some of the ideas and experiences explored in this book will help them to do so in a sustainable and equitable manner. Critically it will be important that foresters do not feel obliged to apply any particular articulation of SFM or of ecosystem principles in a stereotyped manner to all forests. Tomorrow's managers must base their management arrangements on the local interpretation and application of the Ecosystem Principles and the SFM paradigms. They will have to borrow and adapt from these concepts and other related philosophies for broad-based, holistic management to assist the societies to whom they are accountable in making good choices about forests in a changing and dynamic world.

We conclude by suggesting the following ten tenets for best practice in forest management:

1. There is no single approach to the management of forest ecosystems, but multiple approaches – elements of the CBD Ecosystem Principles and SFM concepts – will need to be adapted and applied pragmatically in each situation.

2. People are part of ecosystems – jobs, livelihoods and wealth generation are as important as the broader environmental values.

3. All environmental management must be adaptable: we manage, experiment, learn and re-direct our management arrangements.

4. Ecosystem approaches and SFM require tools that measure the performance of the whole system – both environmental gains and people's livelihood improvements.

5. Clear and defendable land rights, democratic institutions and the rule of law are important elements of an enabling environment for best practice in managing forests.

6. Forestry professionals must be eclectic, have excellent inter-personal skills, must stand back from the fray and earn the respect of all stakeholder groups.

7. Science does not provide the answers but it helps us to learn from mistakes, adapt and explore innovative options.

8. The soft side of the Ecosystem Principles and the various definitions of SFM are more important than the hard side. These approaches are not just another formula – they entail a new attitude, approach, set of competencies and a broadened range of skills.

9. Many elements of ecosystem and SFM approaches are not directly under the control of forest departments, so these agencies have to learn to exert influence and broker deals.

10. Ecosystem approaches and the C&I that underpin SFM will not make conflicts disappear; win-win situations remain rare. Ecosystem approaches and C&I make trade-offs more explicit but there will always be winners and losers. Good practice can help reduce the power differentials between stakeholders and lead to more equitable outcomes, ensuring that society in general and specific stakeholder groups in particular are winning more and losing less.

The difficulty lies not so much in developing new ideas,
as in escaping from the old ones

References

Chapter 1

Berkes, F., Colding, J. and Folke, C. (Eds). 2003. *Navigating Social-Ecological Systems: Building resilience for complexity and change*. Cambridge University Press, Cambridge, UK.

Ellenberg, H. 2003. *"Ecosystem approach" versus "Sustainable forest management" – attempt at a comparison*. Federal Research Centre for Forestry and Forest Products and University of Hamburg, Hamburg, Germany.

Elliott, C. 2000. *Forest certification: a policy perspective*. Center for International Forestry Research, Bogor, Indonesia.

Ferguson, I.S. 1996. *Sustainable Forest Management*. Oxford University Press, Oxford, UK.

Forsyth, T. 2003. *Critical Political Ecology: The politics of environmental science*. Routledge, London, UK and New York, USA.

Gunderson, L.H., Holling, C.S. and Light, S. (Eds). 1995. *Barriers and Bridges to the renewal of ecosystems and institutions*. Columbia University Press, New York, USA.

Johnson, N.C., Malk, A.J., Szaro, R.C. and Sexton, W.T. 1999. *Ecological Stewardship: A common reference for ecosystem management*. Elsevier Science, Oxford, UK.

Lee, K.L. 1993. *Compass and Gyroscope; Science and Policy for the Environment*. Island Press, Washington DC, USA.

Sayer, J.A., Elliot, C., Barrow, E., Gretzinger, S., Maginnis, S., McShane, T. and Shepherd, G. 2004. *The Implications for Biodiversity conservation of Decentralised Forest Resources Management*. Proceedings of UNFF workshop on decentralised forest management, Interlaken, Switzerland. CIFOR, Bogor, Indonesia.

Schlaepfer, R. 1997. *Ecosystem-based management of natural resources: a step towards sustainable development*. IUFRO Occasional paper 6. IUFRO, Vienna, Austria.

Sedjo, R., Coetzl, A. and Moffat, S.O. 1998. *Sustainability of Temperate Forests*. Resources for the Future, Washington DC, USA.

Shepherd, G. 2004. *The Ecosystem Approach: five steps to implementation*. IUCN, Gland, Switzerland and Cambridge, UK.

Smith, R.D. and Maltby, E. 2003. *Using the Ecosystem Approach to Implement the Convention on Biological Diversity: Key issues and case studies*. IUCN, Gland, Switzerland.

White, A. and Martin, A. 2002. *Who own the world's forests? Forest tenure and public forests in transition*. Forest Trends/Center for International Environmental Law, Washington, DC, USA.

Wilkie, M.L., Holmgren, P. and Castaneda, F. 2003. *Sustainable Forest Management and the Ecosystem Approach: Two concepts one goal*. FAO Working paper FM25, Rome, Italy.

Chapter 2

Abelson, P. 1996. *Project Appraisal and Valuation Methods for the Environment with Special Reference to Developing Countries*. Macmillan, New York, USA.

Adger, W.N., Brown, K., Cervigni, R. and Moran, D. 1995. Total Economic Value of Forests in Mexico. *Ambio* **24(5)**: 286–296.

Amelung, T. 1991. Tropical deforestation as an international economic problem. Paper presented at the Egon-Sohmen-Foundation Conference on Economic Evolution and Environmental Concerns, Linz, Austria, 30-31 August.

Amelung, T. and Diehl, M. 1992. *Deforestation of Tropical Forests: Economic Causes and Impact on Development.* Kieler Studien No. 241, Institut fur Weltwirtschaft an der Universitat Kiel. J.C.B. Mohr, Tubingen, Germany.

Andersen, L.E., Granger, C.W.J., Reis, E.J., Weinhold, D. and Wunder, S. 2002. *The dynamic of deforestation and economic growth in the Brazilian Amazon.* Cambridge University Press, Cambridge, UK.

Angelsen, A. and Kaimowitz, D. (Eds) 2001. *Agricultural technologies and tropical deforestation.* CABI and the Center for International Forestry Research, Wallingford, UK.

Aylward, B., Echevarría, J., Fernández González, A., Porras, I., Allen, K. and Mejías, R. 1998. *Economic Incentives for Watershed Protection: A Case Study of Lake Arenal, Costa Rica.* CREED Final Report. International Institute for Environment and Development, London, UK.

Barbier, E.B. 1999. The effects of the Uruguay Round tariff reduction on the forest product trade: A partial equilibrium analysis. *The World Economy* **22(1)**: 87–115.

Barbier, E.B. and Aylward, B.A. 1996. Capturing the Pharmaceutical Value of Biodiversity in a Developing Country. *Environmental and Resource Economics* **8(2)**: 157–191.

Barbier, E.B., Burgess, J.C., Bishop, J. and Aylward, B. 1994. *The Economics of the Tropical Timber Trade.* Earthscan, London, UK.

Bass, S., Thornber, K., Markopoulos, M., Roberts, S. and Grieg-Gran, M. 2001. *Certification's Impacts on Forests, Stakeholders and Supply Chains.* International Institute for Environment and Development, London, UK.

Bateman, I., Brainard, J. and Lovett, A. 1999. Developing a Benefits Transfer Model of Woodland Recreation: A GIS Approach. In: Roper, C.S. and Park, A. (Eds). *The Living Forest: Non-Market Benefits of Forestry. Proceedings of an International Symposium, Edinburgh 24–28 June 1996.* Forestry Commission. H.M. Stationery Office, London, UK.

Baumol, W.J. and Oates, W.E. 1988. *The Theory of Environmental Policy.* 2nd edition. Cambridge University Press, New York, USA.

Bennett, C.P.A. and Byron, R.N. 1997. *Valuing Resource Valuation: Exploring the Role of Quantitative Valuation of Indonesia's Forest Resources.* Center for International Forestry Research, Bogor, Indonesia.

Boardman, A. Greenberg, D. Vining, A. and Weimer, D. 2001. *Cost-Benefit Analysis: Concepts and Practice.* 2nd edition. Prentice Hall, NJ, USA.

Bourke, I.J. and Leitch, Jeanette. 1998. *Trade restrictions and their impact on international trade in forest products.* Food and Agriculture Organization of the United Nations (FAO), Rome, Italy.

Browder, J. 1985. *Subsidies, deforestation, and the forest sector of the Brazilian Amazon.* World Resources Institute, Washington, DC, USA.

Brown, Chris. 1997. The implications of the GATT Uruguay Round and other trade arrangements for the Asia-Pacific forest products trade. Forestry Planning and Statistics Branch, working paper No: APFSOS/WP/03, FAO, Rome, Italy.

Brown, K. and Pearce, D.W. (Eds). 1994. *The Causes of Tropical Deforestation.* University College London Press, London, UK.

Calder, I. 1999. *The Blue Revolution: Land Use and Integrated Water Resource Management.* Earthscan, London, UK.

Chomitz, K. and Gray, D. 1996. Roads, Lands, Markets, and Deforestation: a Model of Land Use in Belize. *World Bank Economic Review*: 487–512.

Chomitz, K.M. and Kumari, K. 1998. The Domestic Benefits of Tropical Forest Preservation: A Critical Review Emphasizing Hydrological Functions. *World Bank Research Observer* **13(1)**: 13–35.

Chomitz, K.M., Thomas, T.S. and Brandão, A.S. 2003. Creating Markets for Habitat Conservation when Habitats are Heterogenous. Paper presentation to the 4th BioEcon conference on Economic Analysis of Policies for Biodiversity Conservation, 28-29 August 2003, Venice (April).

Clark, D. and Downes, D. 1995. What Price Biodiversity? Economics and Biodiversity Conservation in the United States. Center for International Environmental Law, Washington, DC, USA. (reprinted in *Journal of Environmental Law and Litigation* **9(11)**, 1997).

Daily, G.C. 1997. *Nature's Services: Societal Dependence on Natural Ecosystems*. Island Press, Washington, DC, USA.

Daily, G.C. and Ellison, K. 2002. *The New Economy of Nature and the Marketplace: The Quest to Make Conservation Profitable*. Island Press, Washington, DC, USA.

De Koning, F., Olschewski, R., Veldkamp, E., Benítez, P., Laclau, P., López, M., de Urquiza, M. and Schlichter, T. 2002. *Evaluation of the CO_2 sequestration potential of afforestation projects and secondary forests in two different climate zones of South America*. TOEB Tropical Forest Research Publication No. TWF-37e, Deutsche Gesellschaft für Technische Zusammenarbeit, Eschborn, Germany.

Dixon, J.A., Scura, L.F., Carpenter, R.A. and Sherman, P.B. 1994. *Economic Analysis of Environmental Impacts*. Earthscan, London, UK.

Easterly, William. 2001. The effect of IMF and World Bank Programmes on Poverty. U.N. University, Wider Discussion Paper No. 2001/102, October.

Eba'a Atyi, R. and Simula, M. 2002. *Forest Certification: Pending Challenges for Tropical Timber*. Background Paper. ITTO: Yokohama, Japan.

Federal Register. 1999. Office of the United States Trade Representative, Council on Environmental Quality, 64(122, Friday, 25 June) 34304–34306.

Ferraro, P.J. and Kiss, A. 2002. Direct Payments to Conserve Biodiversity. *Science* **298** (29 November): 1718–1719.

Ferraro, P.J. and Simpson, R.D. 2002. The Cost-effectiveness of Conservation Performance Payments. *Land Economics* **78(3)**: 339–353.

Freeman, A.M., III. 1993. *The Measurement of Environmental and Resource Values: Theory and Methods*. Resources for the Future, Washington, DC, USA.

Garrod, G. and Willis, K. 1992. The Environmental Economic Impact of Woodland: A Two-Stage Hedonic Price Model of the Amenity Value of Forestry in Britain. *Applied Economics* **24**: 715–728.

Grundy, D. 2005. From Plantation Developer to Steward of the Nation's Forests: the UK. In: Garforth, M. and Mayers, J. *Plantations, Privatization, Poverty and Power. Changing Ownership and Management of State Forests*. Earthscan, London, UK.

Gutman, P. (Ed.) 2003. *From Goodwill to Payments for Environmental Services: A Survey of Financing Options for Sustainable Natural Resource Management in Developing Countries*. Danida and WWF, Washington, DC, USA.

Hanley, N. and Spash, C. 1994. *Cost-Benefit Analysis and the Environment*. Edward Elgar, Cheltenham, UK.

Hanley, N., Willis, K., Powe, N. and Anderson, M. 2002. *Valuing the benefits of biodiversity in forests. Social and Environmental Benefits of Forestry Phase 2, Report to UK Forestry Commission*. Centre for Research in Environmental Appraisal and Management (http://www.newcastle.ac.uk/cream/), University of Newcastle upon Tyne, UK.

Hardner, J. and Rice, R. 2002. Rethinking green consumerism. *Scientific American* **287**: 89–95.

Hearne, R.R. 1996. Economic Appraisal of Use and Non-Use Values of Environmental Goods and Services in Developing Countries. *Project Appraisal* **11(4)**: 255–260.

IIED. 2003. *Valuing Forests: A review of methods and applications in developing countries*. Environmental Economics Programme, International Institute for Environment and Development, London, UK.

Johnson, N., White, A. and Perrot-Maître, D. 2001. *Developing Markets for Water Services from Forests: Issues and Lessons for Innovators*. Forest Trends with World Resources Institute and the Katoomba Group, Washington, DC, USA.

Kaimowitz, D., Erwidodo, Ndoye, O., Pacheco, P. and Sunderlin, W. 1998. Considering the impact of structural adjustment policies on forests in Bolivia, Cameroon, and Indonesia. *Unasylva* **49(194)**: 57–64.

Kopp, R. and Smith, V.K. (Eds). 1993. *Valuing Natural Assets: The Economics of Natural Resource Damage Assessment*. Resources for the Future, Washington, DC, USA.

Kramer, R.A., Sharma, N. and Munasinghe, M. 1995. Valuing Tropical Forests: Methodology and Case Study of Madagascar. *Environment Paper* **No. 13**. The World Bank, Washington, DC, USA.

Kumari, K. 1995. Mainstreaming Biodiversity Conservation: A Peninsular Malaysian Case. *International Journal of Sustainable Development and World Ecology* **2**: 182–198.

Laird, S.A. and ten Kate, K. 2002. Linking Biodiversity Prospecting and Forest Conservation. In: Pagiola, S., Bishop, J. and Landell-Mills, N. (Eds). *Selling Forest Environmental Services: Market-Based Mechanisms for Conservation and Development*. Earthscan, London, UK.

Landell-Mills, N. and Porras, I. 2002. *Markets for Forest Environmental Services: Silver Bullet or Fool's Gold?* International Institute for Environment and Development, London, UK.

Lecocq, F. 2004. *State and Trends of the Carbon Market 2004*. World Bank, Washington, DC, USA.

Loomis, J.B. and Walsh, R.G. 1997. *Recreation Economic Decisions: Comparing Benefits and Costs*. 2nd Edition. Venture Publishing, State College, PA, USA.

Mallaby, S., 2004. THE WORLD'S BANKER: A *Story of Failed States, Financial Crises and the Wealth and Poverty of Nations*. Council on Foreign Relations Book, The Penguin Press, New York, USA.

Mantua, U., Merlo, M., Sekot, W. and Welcker, B. 2001. Recreational and Environmental Markets for Forest Enterprises: A New Approach Towards Marketability of Public Goods. CABI Publishing, Wallingford, UK.

Margulis, S. 2004. Causes of Deforestation of the Brazilian Amazon. World Bank Working Report No. 22. The World Bank, Washington, DC, USA.

Munasinghe, M. and Lutz, E. 1993. Environmental Economics and Valuation in Development Decision Making. In: Munasinghe, M. (Ed.) *Environmental Economics and Natural Resource Management in Developing Countries*. World Bank, Washington, DC, USA.

Munasinghe, M. (Ed.) 2001. *Macroeconomics and the Environment*. Edward Elgar Publ., UK.

Munasinghe, M. and Cruz, W. 1995. Economy-wide Policies and the Environment: Lessons from Experience. World Bank Environment Paper # 10, The World Bank, Washington, USA.

National Research Council. 2001. *Compensating for Wetland Losses under the Clean Water Act*. Committee on Mitigating Wetland Losses, Board on Environmental Studies and Toxicology, Water Science and Technology Board, Division on Earth and Life Studies, National Research Council. National Academy Press, Washington, DC, USA.

OECD. 2002. *Handbook of Biodiversity Valuation: A guide for policy makers*. Organisation for Economic Co-operation and Development, Paris, France.

Orlando, B., Baldock, D., Canger, S., Mackensen, J., Maginnis, S., Socorro Manguiat, M., Rietbergen, S., Robledo, C. and Schneider, N. 2002. *Carbon, Forests and People: Towards the integrated management of carbon sequestration, the environment, and sustainable livelihoods*. IUCN, Gland, Switzerland and Cambridge, UK.

Ozório de Almeida, A.L. and Campari, J. 1995. *Sustainable Settlement in the Amazon*. The World Bank, Washington, DC, USA.

Pagiola, S. 2002. Paying for Water Services in Central America: Learning from Costa Rica. In: Pagiola, S., Bishop, J. and Landell-Mills, N. (Eds). *Selling Forest Environmental Services: Market-Based Mechanisms for Conservation and Development*. Earthscan, London, UK.

Pagiola, S., Bishop, J. and Landell-Mills, N. (Eds). 2002. *Selling Forest Environmental Services: Market-Based Mechanisms for Conservation and Development*. Earthscan, London, UK.

Pandey, Kiran D. and Wheeler, David. 2001. *Structural adjustment and forest resources: The impact of World Bank operations*. Development Research Group, World Bank, Washington, DC, USA. <http://econ.worldbank.org/view.php?id=1693>

Pearce, D.W. and Turner, R.K. 1990. *Economics of Natural Resources and the Environment*. Harvester Wheatsheaf, Hemel Hempstead, UK.

Pearce, D.W., Putz, F. and Vanclay, J. 2002. Is sustainable forestry economically possible? In: Pearce, D.W., Pearce, C.G. and Palmer, C.E. (Eds). *Valuing the Environment in Developing Countries: Case Studies*. Edward Elgar, Cheltenham, UK.

Powe, N.A., Garrod, G.D. and Willis, K.G. 1995. Valuation of urban amenities using a hedonic price model. *Journal of Property Research* **12**: 137–147.

Powell, I., White, A. and Landell-Mills, N. 2001. *Developing Markets for Ecosystem Services of Forests*. Forest Trends, Washington, DC, USA.

Rausser, G. and Small, A. 2000. Valuing research leads: bioprospecting and the conservation of genetic resources. *Journal of Political Economy* **108(1)**: 173–206.

Reed, D. (Ed.) 1992. *Structural Adjustment and the Environment*. World Wildlife Fund (WWF) International. Westview Press, Boulder, USA.

Reed, D. (Ed.). 1996. *Structural adjustment, the environment, and sustainable development*. Earthscan Publications/World Wildlife Fund, London, UK.

Repetto, R. and Cruz, W.1992. *The environmental effects of stabilization and structural adjustment programs: The Philippine case*. World Resource Institute, Washington, DC, USA.

Repetto, R. and Gillis, M. (Eds). 1988. *Government Policies and the Misuse of Forest Resources*. Cambridge University Press, Cambridge, UK.

Ricketts, T.H., Daily, G.C., Ehrlich, P.R. and Michener, C.D. 2004. *Economic value of tropical forest to coffee production*. Proc. Natl. Acad. Sci. USA, 10.1073/ pnas. 0405147101.

Scherr, S., White, A. and Khare, A., with Inbar, M. and Molnar, A. 2004. *For Services Rendered: The current status and future potential of markets for the ecosystem services provided by tropical forests*. ITTO Technical Series No 21, International Tropical Timber Organization, Yokohama, Japan.

Scherr, S.J., White, A. and Kaimowitz, D. 2001. *Making Markets Work for Forest Communities*. Forest Trends, Washington, DC, USA.

Sedjo, Roger A. and Simpson, R. David. 1999. Tariff liberalization, wood trade flows and global forests. Report prepared for the Forest Service. RFF discussion paper 00-05, December.

Simpson, D., Sedjo, R. and Reid, J. 1996. Valuing biodiversity for use in pharmaceutical research. *Journal of Political Economy* **104(1)**: 163–185.

Smith, J. and Scherr, S.J. 2002. *Forest Carbon and Local Livelihoods: Assessment of Opportunities and Policy Recommendations*. Occasional Paper No. 37. Center for International Forestry Research and Forest Trends, Bogor, Indonesia.

Snider, A.G., Pattanayak, S.K., Sills, E.O. and Schuler, J.L. 2003. Policy Innovations for Private Forest Management and Conservation in Costa Rica. *Journal of Forestry* **(July/August)**: 18–23.

Stavins, R. 2003. Market-Based Environmental Policies: What Can We Learn from U.S. Experience and Related Research? Faculty Research Working Papers Series, No. RWP03-031, John F. Kennedy School of Government, Harvard University: Cambridge, MA (available at: http://ssrn.com/abstract=421720).

Stoneham, G., Chaudhri, V., Ha, A. and Strappazzon, L. 2003. Auctions for conservation contracts: an empirical examination of Victoria's Bush Tender trial. *Australian Journal of Agricultural and Resource Economics* **47(4)**: 477–500.

Sunderlin, W.D., Angelsen, A. and Wunder, S. 2003. Forests and Poverty Alleviation. In: FAO. *State of the World's Forests*. Food and Agriculture Organization of the United Nations, Rome, Italy.

Sunderlin, W. D., Ndoye, O., Bikié, H., Laporte, N., Mertens, B. and Pokam, J. 2000. Economic crisis, small-scale agriculture, and forest cover change in southern Cameroon. *Environmental Conservation* **27(3)**: 284–290.

Swingland, I. (Ed.) 2002. *Capturing Carbon and Conserving Biodiversity: The Market Approach*. Earthscan, London, UK.

Tietenberg, T. 2002. *The Tradable Permits Approach to Protecting the Commons: What Have We Learned?* Nota di Lavoro 36.2002, Fondazione Eni Enrico Mattei, Venice, Italy.

Upton, C. and Bass, S. 1995. *The Forest Certification Handbook*. Earthscan, London, UK.

van Bueren, M. 2001. *Emerging markets for environmental services: Implications and opportunities for resource management in Australia*. Publication No. 01/162, Rural Industries Research and Development Corporation, Barton and Kingston (November).

Vincent, J. R. and Gillis, M. 1998. Deforestation and Forest Land Use: A Comment. *The World Bank Research Observer* **13(1)**: 133–140.

Vincent, J.R., Crawford, E.W. and Hoehn, J.P. (Eds). 1991. *Valuing Environmental Benefits in Developing Economies*. Proceedings of a seminar series, February–May 1990, at Michigan State University. Michigan State University, East Lansing, USA.

Warford, J.J., Schwab, A., Cruz, W. and Hansen, S. 1994. The Evolution of Environmental Concerns in Adjustment Lending: A Review. Environment Department Working Paper No. 65. World Bank, Washington, DC, USA.

White, H. 1992. The macroeconomic impact of development aid: A critical survey. *Journal of Development Studies* **28(2)**: 163–183.

White, A. and Martin, A. 2002. *Who Owns the World's Forests?* Forest Trends, Washington, DC, USA.

Wilkinson, J. and Kennedy, C. 2002. *Banks and Fees: The status of off-site wetland mitigation in the United States*. Environmental Law Institute, Washington, DC, USA.

Willis, K.G. 2002. *Benefits and costs of forests to water supply and water quality. Social and Environmental Benefits of Forestry: Phase 2*. Report to UK Forestry Commission. Centre for Research in Environmental Appraisal and Management (http://www.newcastle.ac.uk/cream/), University of Newcastle upon Tyne, UK.

Willis, K.G., Garrod, G., Scarpa, R., Macmillan, D. and Bateman, I. 2000. *Non-Market Benefits of Forestry: Phase 1*. Report to the UK Forestry Commission. Centre for Research in Environmental Appraisal and Management, University of Newcastle upon Tyne, UK.

Wunder, S. 2003. *Oil Wealth and the Fate of the Forest: A Comparative Study of Eight Tropical Countries*. Routledge, Taylor & Francis Group, New York, USA.

Chapter 3

Allen, T.F.H. and Hoekstra, T.W. 1993. *Toward a Unified Ecology*. Columbia University Press, New York, USA.

Angelstam, P. 2003. Reconciling the linkages of land management with natural disturbance regimes to maintain forest biodiversity in Europe. In: Bissonette, J. A. and Storch, I. (Eds). *Landscape ecology and resource management: linking theory with practice*. Island Press, Covelo, CA and Washington, DC, USA.

Angelstam, P. and Andersson, L. 2001. Estimates of the needs for forest reserves in Sweden. *Scandinavian Journal of Forest Research* **Supplement No. 3**: 38–51.

Angelstam, P., Anufriev, V., Balciauskas, L., Blagovidov, A., Borgegård, S-O., Hodge, S., Majewski, P., Ponomarenko, S., Shvarts, E., Tishkov, A., Tomialojc, L. and Wesolowski, T. 1997. Biodiversity and sustainable forestry in European forests – how west and east can learn from each other. *Wildlife Society Bulletin* **25(1)**: 38–48.

Angelstam, P., Mikusinski, G., Rönnbäck, B.-I., Östman, A., Lazdinis, M., Roberge, J-M., Arnberg, W. and Olsson, J. 2003. Two-dimensional gap analysis: a tool for efficient conservation planning and biodiversity policy implementation. *Ambio* **33(8)**: 527–534.

Angelstam, P., Ek, T., Laestadius, L. and Roberge, J-M. 2004a. Data and tools for conservation, management and restoration of forest ecosystems at multiple scales. In: Stanturf, J.A. and Madsen, P. (Eds). *Restoration of boreal and temperate forests*. Lewis Publishers, Boca Raton, USA.

Angelstam, P., Persson, R. and Schlaepfer, R. 2004b. The sustainable forest management vision and biodiversity – barriers and bridges for implementation in actual landscapes. *Ecol. Bull.* **51.**

Anon. 2000. *European Landscape Convention*. European Treaty Series No. 176, Council of Europe.

Bailey, R.G. 2002. Ecoregion-based design for sustainability. Springer-Verlag, New York, USA.

Bann, C. 1998. *The economic valuation of tropical forest land use options: a manual for researchers*. Economy and Environment Program for Southeast Asia, Singapore.

Bartuska, A., Alexander, R., Boling, T., Breed, B., Griffis, R., Hamilton, K., Lawrence, D., Mangold, R. and Young, S. 1995. Institutional Approaches. In: *The Ecosystem Approach: Healthy Ecosystems and*

Sustainable Economies, Volume II – Implementation Issues. Report of the Interagency Ecosystem Management Task Force, Washington, DC, USA.

Baskerville, G. 1985. Adaptive management: wood availability and habitat availability. *The Forestry Chronicle* **61(2)**: 171–175.

Basset, Y., Novotny, V., Miller, S.E. and Pyle, R. 2000. Quantifying biodiversity: experience with parataxonomists and digital photography in Papua New Guinea and Guyana. *BioScience* **50**: 899–908.

Bergeron, Y., Leduc, A., Harvey, B. D. and Gauthier, S. 2002. Natural fire regime: a guide for sustainable management of the Canadian boreal forest. *Silva Fennica* **36**: 81–95.

Berkes, F., Colding, J. and Folke, C. 2003. *Navigating social-ecological systems: Building resilience for complexity and change.* Cambridge University Press, Cambridge, UK.

Besseau, P., Dansou, K. and Johnson, F. 2002. The international model forest network (IMFN): elements of success. *The Forestry Chronicle* **78**: 648–654.

Bormann, B.T., Martin, J.R., Wagner, F.H., Wood, G.W., Algria, J., Cunningham, P.G., Brooks, M.H., Friesema, P., Berg. J. and Henshaw, J.R. Adaptive Management. In: Sexton, W.T., Malk, A.J., Szaro, R.C. and Johnson, N.C. (Eds). *Ecological Stewardship: A Common Reference for Ecosystem Management.* Vol. III. Elsevier Science Ltd., Oxford, UK.

Bormann, B.T. and Keister, A.R. 2004. Options Forestry: Acting on Uncertainty. *J. Forestry* **102(4)**: 22–27.

Boyce, D.A., Jr. and Szaro, R.C. 2004. An Overview of Science Contributions to the Sustainable Management of the Tongass National Forest, Alaska. *Landscape and Urban Planning* [In press]

Boyle, T.J.B. and Boontawee, B. 1995. *Measuring and monitoring biodiversity in tropical and temperate forests.* Center for International Forestry Research (CIFOR), Bogor, Indonesia.

Bradshaw, G.A. and Borchers, J.G., 2000. Uncertainty as information: narrowing the science-policy gap. *Conservation Ecology* **4(1)**: 7. [online] URL: www.consecol.org/vol4/iss1/art7

Bryman, A. 2001. *Social Research Methods.* Oxford University Press, Oxford, UK.

Buchy, M. and Hoverman, S. 2000. Understanding public participation in forest planning: a review. *Forest Policy and Economics* **1**: 15–25.

Busch, D.E. and Trexler, J.C. 2003. *Monitoring ecosystems: interdisciplinary approaches for evaluating ecoregional initiatives.* Island Press, Washington DC, USA.

Byron, N. and Turnbull, J. 1998. New arrangements for Forest Science to Meet the Needs of Sustainable Forest Management. In: Enters, T., Nair, C.T.S. and Kaosa-ard, A. (Eds). *Emerging Institutional Arrangements for Forestry Research.* Forestry Research Support Programme for Asia and the Pacific, FAO, Bangkok, Thailand.

Campbell, B.M. and Sayer, J.A. (Eds). 2003. *Integrated natural resource management: linking productivity, environment and development.* CABI Publishing and Centre for International Forestry Research (CIFOR), Wallingford, UK.

Campbell, B.M., Sayer, J.A., Frost, P., Vermeulen, S., Pérez, M.R., Cunningham, A. and Prabhu, R. Assessing the performance of natural resource systems. In: Campbell, B.M. and Sayer, J.A. (Eds). *Integrated natural resource management: linking productivity, environment and development.* CABI Publishing and Centre for International Forestry Research (CIFOR), Wallingford, UK.

Canadian Council of Forest Ministers. 1997. *Criteria and indicators of sustainable forest management in Canada.* Technical Report 1997. CCFM, Ottawa, Canada.

Christensen, N.L., Bartuska, A.M., Brown, J.H., Carpenter, S., D'Antonio, C., Francis, R., Franklin, J.F., MacMahon, J.A., Noss, R.F., Parsons, D.J., Peterson, C.H., Turner, M.G. and Woodmansee, R.G. 1996. The Report of the Ecological Society of America Committee on the Scientific Basis for Ecosystem Management. *Ecological Applications* **6**: 665–691.

Clark, R.N., Stankey, G.H., Brown, P.J., Burchfield, J.A., Haynes R.W. and McCool, S.F. 1999. Toward an ecological approach: integrating social, economic, cultural, biological, and physical considerations.

In: Sexton, W.T., Malk, A.J., Szaro, R.C. and Johnson, N.C. (Eds). *Ecological Stewardship*: A *Common Reference for Ecosystem Management. Vol.* III. Elsevier Science Ltd., Oxford, UK.

Clark, T.W. 2002. *The policy process.* A *practical guide for natural resource professionals.* Yale University Press, New Haven, USA and London, UK.

Cleaves, D.A. and Haynes, R.W. 1999. Risk management for ecological stewardship. In: Sexton, W.T., Malk, A.J., Szaro, R.C. and Johnson, N.C. (Eds). *Ecological Stewardship*: A *Common Reference for Ecosystem Management. Vol.* III. Elsevier Science Ltd., Oxford, UK.

Colfer, C.J.P. and Byron, Y. (Eds). 2001. *People managing forests. The links between human well-being and sustainability.* Resources for the future, Washington DC, USA.

Corona, P., Kšhl, M. and Marchetti, M. (Eds). 2004. Advances in Forest Inventory for Sustainable Forest Management and Biodiversity Monitoring. *Forestry Sciences* **76**. Kluwer Academic Publishers, Dordrecht, The Netherlands.

Cortner, H.J., Wallace, M.G., Burke, B. and Moote, M.A. 1998. Institutions matter: the need to address the institutional challenges of ecosystem management. *Landscape and Urban Planning* **40(1–3)**: 159–166.

Costanza, R., Cumberland, J., Daly, H., Goodland, R. and Norgaard, R. 1997. An *introduction to ecological economics.* St. Lucie Press, Boca Raton, USA.

Covington, W.W., Niering W., Starkley, E. and Walker, J. 1999. Ecosystem restoration and management: scientific principles and concepts. In: Sexton, W.T., Malk, A.J., Szaro, R.C. and Johnson, N.C. (Eds). *Ecological Stewardship*: A *Common Reference for Ecosystem Management. Vol.* III. Elsevier Science Ltd., Oxford, UK.

Dallmeier, F. (Ed.) 1992. Long-term monitoring of biological diversity in tropical forest areas: methods for establishment and inventory of permanent plots. MAB D*igest* **11**. UNESCO, Paris, France.

Daniels, S.E., Walker, G.B., Boeder, J.R. and Means, J.E. 1993. Managing ecosystems and social conflict. In: Jensen, M.E. and Bourgeron, P.S. *Eastside Forest Health Assessment, Volume* II, *Ecosystem Management: Principles and Applications.* USDA National Forest System and Forest Service Research, Washington, DC, USA.

Emerton, L.A. 1999. *Economic tools for environmental planning and management in Eastern Africa.* Biodiversity and Economics Programme, IUCN Eastern Africa Regional Office, Nairobi, Kenya.

Emerton, L.A. 2000. *Economic measures for biodiversity planning: an annotated bibliography of methods, experiences and cases.* IUCN, Nairobi, Kenya.

Emerton, L. A. 2001. *The use of economic measures for biodiversity planning: an annotated bibliography of methods, experiences and cases.* IUCN, Gland, Switzerland and Cambridge, UK.

Everett, R., Oliver, C., Saveland, J., Hessburg, P., Diaz, N. and Irwin, L. 1993. Adaptive Ecosystem Management. In: Jensen, M.E. and Bourgeron, P.S. *Eastside Forest Health Assessment, Volume* II, *Ecosystem Management: Principles and Applications.* USDA National Forest System and Forest Service Research, Washington, DC, UK.

Floyd, D.W. 2002. *Forest Sustainability: the history, the challenge, the promise.* Forest History Society, Durham, USA.

Gadgil, M. 1999. *Deploying Funds to Nurture Biodiversity*: A *Proposal.* The Norway/UN Conference on the Ecosystem Approach for Sustainable Use of Biological Diversity. Trondheim, Norway. http://ces.iisc.ernet.in/ hpg/cesmg/susfor/Complete.html

Gibbons, M., Limoges, C., Nowotny, H., Schwartzman, S., Scott, P. and Trow, M. 1994. *The new production of knowledge: the dynamics of science and research in contemporary societies.* Sage, London, UK.

Goebel, J.J., Schreder, H.T., House, C.C., Geissler, P.H., Olsen, A.R., and Williams, W.R. 1998. *Integrating surveys of terrestrial natural resources: the Oregon demonstration project.* Inventory and Monitoring Report No. 2. USDA Forest Service, Portland, USA.

Gowdy, J.M. 1997. The value of biodiversity: markets, society and ecosystems. *Land Economics* **73(1)**: 25–41.

Graham, R.T., Jain, T.B., Haynes, R.L., Sanders,J. and Cleaves, D.L. 1999. Assessments for ecological stewardship. In: Sexton, W.T., Malk, A.J., Szaro, R.C. and Johnson, N.C. (Eds). *Ecological Stewardship*: A *Common Reference for Ecosystem Management*. *Vol*. III. Elsevier Science Ltd., Oxford, UK.

Grumbine, R.E., 1994. What is ecosystem management? *Conservation Biology* **8(1)**: 27–38.

Gunderson, L. 1999. Resilience, flexibility and adaptive management – antidotes for spurious certitude. *Conservation Biology* **3(1)**: 7. [online] URL: http://www.consecol.org/ vol3/iss1/art7

Gupta, A.K. 1996. Incentives, institutions and innovations: golden triangle of sustainable conservation. Workshop on Incentives for Biodiversity: Sharing Experiences, 4th Global Biodiversity Forum, Montreal, Canada, 30 August–1 September 1996.

Haufler, J. B., Crow, T. and Wilcove, D.1999. Scale considerations for Ecosystem Management. 1999. Ecosystem restoration and management: scientific principles and concepts. In: Sexton, W.T., Malk, A.J., Szaro, R.C. and Johnson, N.C. (Eds). *Ecological Stewardship*: A *Common Reference for Ecosystem Management*. *Vol*. II. Elsevier Science Ltd., Oxford, UK.

Hawksworth, D.L., Kirk, P.M. and Clarke, S.D. (Eds). 1997. *Biodiversity information: needs and options*. *Proceedings of the* 1996 *International Workshop on Biodiversity Information*. CAB International, Wallingford, UK.

Haynes, R.W. and Cleaves, D.A. 1999. Uncertainty, risk and ecosystem management. In: Sexton, W.T., Malk, A.J., Szaro, R.C. and Johnson, N.C. (Eds). *Ecological Stewardship*: A *Common Reference for Ecosystem Management*. *Vol*. III. Elsevier Science Ltd., Oxford, UK.

Haynes, R.W. and Perez, G.E. (Tech. Eds). 2001. Northwest Forest Plan research synthesis. *Gen. Tech. Rep*. PNW-GTR-498. U.S. Department of Agriculture, Forest Service, Pacific Northwest Research Station, Portland, USA.

Heyer, W.R., Donnelly, M.A., McDiarmid, R.W., Hayek, L.A.C. and Foster, M. (Eds). 1994. *Measuring and monitoring biological diversity: standard methods for amphibians*. Smithsonian Institution Press, Washington DC, USA.

Higgs, E. 2003. *Nature by Design: People, Natural Process, and Ecological Restoration*. MIT Press, Cambridge, USA.

Hunt, C. 1997. *Economic instruments for environmental and natural resource conservation and management in the South Pacific*. Working Paper in Ecological Economics No. 9706. Center for Resource and Environmental Studies, Australian National University, Canberra, Australia.

ICRIS. 1998. *Proceedings of the International Consultation on Research and Information Systems in Forestry* (ICRIS), 7–10 *September* 1998, *Gmunden, Austria*. Federal Ministry of Agriculture and Forestry, Vienna, Austria.

Jakobsen, C.H., Hels, T. and McLaughlin, W.J. 2004. Barriers and facilitators to integration among scientists in transdisciplinary landscape analyses: a cross-country comparison. *Forest Policy and Economics* **6**: 15–31.

Johannes, R.E. 1998. The case for data-less marine resource management: examples from tropical nearshore fisheries. *Trends in Ecology and Evolution* **13**: 243–246.

Johnson, N.C., Malk, A.J., Sexton, W.T. and Szaro, R.C. 1999. *Ecological Stewardship*: A *Common Reference for Ecosystem Management*. Elsevier Science, Oxford, UK.

Karr, J.R. 2000. Health, integrity and biological assessments: the importance of measuring whole things. In: Pimentel, D., Westra, L. and Noss, R.R. (Eds). *Ecological integrity: integrating environment, conservation and health*. Island Press, Washington, DC, USA.

Karsenty, A. 2000. *Economic instruments for tropical forests: the Congo Basin case*. IIED Forestry and Land Use. CIFOR, CIRAD.

Kates, R.W., Clark, W.C., Corell, R., Hall, J.M., Jaeger, C.C., Lowe, I., McCarthy, J.J., Schellnhuber, H.J., Bolin, B., Dickson, N.M., Faucheux, S., Gallopin, G.C., Grubler, A., Huntley, B., Jager, J., Jodha, N.S., Kasperson, R.E., Mabogunje, A., Matson, P., Mooney, H., Moore, B., O'Riordan, T. and Svedlin, U. 2001. Sustainability science. *Science* **292**: 641–642.

Kenna, J.G., Robinson, G.R., Jr., Pell, B., Thompson, M.A. and McNeel, J. 1999. Ecosystem restoration and management: scientific principles and concepts. In: Sexton, W.T., Malk, A.J., Szaro, R.C. and Johnson, N.C. (Eds). *Ecological Stewardship: A Common Reference for Ecosystem Management. Vol. II.* Elsevier Science Ltd., Oxford, UK.

Keystone National Policy Dialogue on Ecosystem Management (KNPDEM). 1996. *Final Report.* The Keystone Center, Keystone, Colorado, USA.

Kinzig, A., Starrett, D., Arrow, K., Aniyar, S., Bolin, B., Dasgupta, P., Ehrlich, P., Folke, C., Hanemann, M., Heal, G., Hoel, M., Jansson, A., Jansson, B.O., Kautsky, N., Levin, S., Lubchenco, J., Maler, K.G., Pacala, S.W., Schneider, S.H., Siniscalco, D. and Walker, B. *et al.* 2003. Coping with uncertainty: A call for a new science-policy forum. *Ambio* **32**: 330–335.

Lackey, R.T. 1998. Seven Pillars of Ecosystem Management. *Landscape and Urban Planning* **40(1–3)**: 21–30.

Lammerts van Bueren, E.M. and Blom, E.M. 1997. *Hierarchical framework for the formulation of sustainable forest management standards.* The Tropenbos Foundation, Wageningen, The Netherlands. Lazdinis, M. and Angelstam, P. 2004. Connecting social and ecological systems: an integrated toolbox for hierarchical evaluation of biodiversity policy implementation. *Ecological Bulletin* **51**.

Lee, Kai N. 1993. Compass and gyroscope: integrating science and politics for the environment. Island Press, Washington, DC, USA.

Lessard, G. 1998. An adaptive approach to planning and decision-making. *Landscape and Urban Planning* **40(1–3)**: 81–87.

Lessard, G., Archer, S., Probst, J. and Clark, S. 1999. Understanding and managing the assessment process. In: Sexton, W.T., Malk, A.J., Szaro, R.C. and Johnson, N.C. (Eds). *Ecological Stewardship: A Common Reference for Ecosystem Management. Vol. III.* Elsevier Science Ltd., Oxford, UK.

Lindenmayer, D.B. and Franklin, J.F. 2002. *Conserving forest biodiversity. A comprehensive multiscaled approach.* Island Press, Washington DC, USA.

Lindenmayer, D.B., Margules, C.R. and Botkin, D.B. 2000. Indicators of biodiversity for ecologically sustainable management. *Conservation Biology* **14**: 941–950.

Lindenmayer, D.B., Manning, A.D., Smith, P.L., Possingham, H.P., Fischer, J., Oliver, I. and McCarthy, M.A. 2002. The focal-species approach and landscape restoration: a critique. *Conservation Biology* **16**: 338–345.

Ludwig, D., Hilborn, R. and Walters, C. 1993. Uncertainty, resource exploitation, and conservation lessons from history. *Science* **262**: 17 and 36.

Machlis, G.E. and Forester, D.J. 1996. The Relationship between Socio-Economic Factors and the Loss of Biodiversity: First Efforts at Theoretical And Quantitative Models. In: Szaro, R.C. and Johnston, D.J. *Biodiversity in Managed Landscapes.* Oxford University Press, New York, USA.

Manfredo, M. J., Vaske, J.J., Bruyere, B.L., Field, D.R. and Brown, P.J. (Eds). 2004. *Society and natural resources. A summary of knowledge.* Modern Litho, Jefferson, USA.

Maquire, L.A. 1991. Risk analysis for conservation biologists. *Conservation Biology* **5**: 123–125.

McDougall, C., Isbadi, I.R., Santoso, L., Corless, M. and Purnomo, H. (Eds). 1999. *The CIFOR Criteria and Indicators Resource Book Database.* C&I Tool No. 4. Center for International Forestry Research (CIFOR), Bogor, Indonesia.

McNeely, J. 1988. *Economics and biological diversity: developing and using economic instruments to conserve biological diversity.* IUCN, Gland, Switzerland.

MCPFE (Ministerial Conference on the Protection of Forests in Europe). 2003. *Improved Pan-European Indicators for Sustainable Forest Management.* MCPFE Liaison Unit, Vienna, Austria.

Mills, T.J. and Clark, R.N. 2001. Roles of research scientists in natural resource decision-making. *Forest Ecology and Management* **153(1–3)**: 189–198.

Mills, T.J., Smythe, R.V. and Diaz-Soltero, H., 2002. *Achieving science-based national forest management decisions while maintaining the capability of the research and development program.* Washington, DC, U.S.D.A. Forest Service.

Montgomery, C.A. 1993. Socioeconomic risk assessment and its relationship to ecosystem management. In: Jensen, M.E. and Bourgeron, P.S. *Eastside Forest Health Assessment, Volume II, Ecosystem Management: Principles and Applications*. USDA National Forest System and Forest Service Research, Washington, DC, USA.

Muradian, R. 2001. Ecological thresholds: a survey. *Ecological Economics* 38: 7–24.

Noble, I.R. and Dirzo, R. 1997. Forests as human-dominated ecosystems. *Science* **277**: 522–525.

Noon, B.N., Spies, T.A. and Raphael, M.G. 1999. Conceptual basis for designing an effectiveness monitoring program. In: Mulder, B.S., Noon, B.R., Spies, T.A., Raphael, M.G., Palmer, C.J., Olsen, A.R., Reeves, G.H. and Welsh, H.H. (Tech. Coords). *The strategy and design of the effectiveness monitoring program for the northwest forest plan*. Gen. Tech. Rep. PNW-GTR-437. USDA Forest Service, Portland, USA.

Noss, R.F. 1996. Conservation of biodiversity at the landscape scale. In: Szaro, R.C. and Johnston, D.W. (Eds). *Biodiversity in managed landscapes: theory and practice*. Oxford University Press, Oxford, UK.

Noss, R.F. 2004. Conservation targets and information needs for regional conservation planning. *Natural Areas Journal* **24**: 223–231.

Oliver, C.D. and Twery, M.J. 1999. Decision support systems/models and analyses. In: Sexton, W.T., Malk, A.J., Szaro, R.C. and Johnson, N.C. (Eds). *Ecological Stewardship: A Common Reference for Ecosystem Management. Vol. III.* Elsevier Science Ltd., Oxford, UK.

Peine, J.D. 1999. *Ecosystem management for sustainability. Principles and practices illustrated by a regional biosphere reserve cooperative*. Lewis Publishers, Boca Raton, USA.

Pimentel, D., Wilson, C. McCullum, C., Huang, R., Dwen, P., Flack, J. Tran, Q., Saltman, T. and Cliff, B. 1997. Economic and environmental benefits of biodiversity. *Bioscience* **47**: 747–757.

Poiani, K.A., Richter, B.D., Anderson, M.G. and Richter, H.E. 2000. Biodiversity conservation at multiple scales: functional sites, landscapes, and networks. *Bioscience* **50**: 133–146.

Prabhu, R., Colfer, C.J.P. and Dudley, R.G. 1999. *Guidelines for Developing, Testing and Selecting Criteria and Indicators for Sustainable Forest Management*. C&I Tool No. 1. Center for International Forestry Research (CIFOR), Bogor, Indonesia.

Purvis, A. and Hector, A. 2000. Getting the measure of biodiversity. *Nature* **405**: 212–219.

Puumalainen, J., Angelstam, P., Banko, G., Brandt, J., Caldeira, M., Estreguil, C., Folving, S.,Garcia del Barrio, J.M., Keller, M., Kennedy, P., Köhl, M., Marchetti, M., Neville, P., Olsson, H., Parviainen, J., Pretzsch, H., Ravn, H.P., Ståhl, G., Tomppo, E., Uuttera, J., Watt, A., Winkler, B. and Wrbka, T. 2002. *Forest Biodiversity Assessment Approaches for Europe*. EUR Report 20423. Joint Research Centre, Ispra, Italy.

Redford, K. and Sanderson, S. 1992. The brief barren marriage of biodiversity and sustainability? *Bulletin of the Ecological Society of America* **73**: 36–39.

Reynolds, K., Bjork, J., Hershey, R.R., Schmoldt, D., Payne, J., King, S., eCola, L., Twery, M. and Cunningham, P. 1999. Decision support for ecosystem management. In: Sexton, W.T., Malk, A.J., Szaro, R.C. and Johnson, N.C. (Eds). *Ecological Stewardship: A Common Reference for Ecosystem Management. Vol. III.* Elsevier Science Ltd., Oxford, UK.

Ricketts, T.H., Dinerstein, E., Olson, D.M., Loucks, C.J., Eichbaum, W.M., DellaSala, D.A., Kavanagh, K.C., Hedao, P., Hurley, P.T., Carney, K.M., Abell, R.A. and Walters, S. 1999. *A conservation assessment of the terrestrial ecoregions of North America. Volume I. The United States and Canada*. Island Press, Washington, DC, USA.

Roberge, J-M. and Angelstam, P. 2004. Usefulness of the umbrella species concept as a conservation tool. *Conservation Biology* **18**: 76–85.

Sayer, J.A. and Campbell, B.M. 2004. *The Science of Sustainable Development: local livelihoods and the global environment*. Cambridge University Press, Cambridge, UK.

Sayer, J.A. 1999. *Ecosystems, timber and biodiversity*. Paper presented at Session 8 of the Trondheim Conference on Ecosystem Approaches to Biodiversity Conservation. Ecosystem Approaches in Forest Resource Use, Trondheim, Norway.

Scott, J.M., Tear, T.H. and Davis, F.W. (Eds). 1996. *Gap Analysis: A landscape approach to biodiversity planning*. American Society for Photogrammetry and Remote Sensing, Bethesda, USA.

Scott, J.M., Heglund, P.J., Morrison, M., Haufler, J.B., Raphael, M.G., Wall, W.A. and Samson, F.B. (Eds). 2002. *Predicting species occurrences: issues of scale and accuracy*. Island Press, Covelo, CA, USA.

Sexton, W.T. and Szaro, R.C. 1998. Implementing ecosystem management: Using multiple boundaries for organizing information. *Landscape and Urban Planning* **40 (1–3)**: 167–172.

Sexton, W.T., Dull, C.W. and Szaro, R.C. 1998. Implementing ecosystem management: A framework for remotely sensed information at multiple scales. *Landscape and Urban Planning* **40(1–3)**: 173–184.

Sexton, W.T. and Szaro, R.C. 1998. Implementing Ecosystem Management Concepts at Multiple Organizational Levels. In: *North American Science Symposium: Toward a unified framework for inventorying and monitoring forest ecosystem resources*, November 1–6, 1998, Guadalajara, Jalisco, Mexico.

Sheil, D. 2001. Conservation and biodiversity monitoring in the tropics – realities, priorities and distractions. *Conservation Biology* **15(4)**: 1179–1182.

Sheil, D. 2002. Why doesn't biodiversity monitoring support conservation priorities in the tropics? *Unasylva* **209**: 50–55. http: //www.fao.org/forestry/foris

Sheil, D. and van Heist, M. 2000. Ecology for tropical forest management. *International Forestry Review* **2(4)**: 261–270.

Sheil, D., Ducey, M.D., Sidiyasa, K. and Samsoedin, I. 2003 A new type of sample unit for the efficient assessment of diverse tree communities in complex forest landscapes. *Journal of Tropical Forest Science* **15(1)**: 117–135.

Sheil, D., Nasi, R. and Johnson, B. 2004. Ecological criteria and indicators for tropical forest landscapes: challenges in the search for progress. *Ecology and Society* **9(1)**: 7. [online] URL:www.ecologyandsociety.org/vol9/iss1/art7

Sheil, D., Puri, R.K., Basuki, I., van Heist, M., Wan, M., Liswanti, N., Rukmiyati, Sardjono, M.A., Samsoedin, I., Sidiyasa, K., Chrisandini, Permana, E., Angi, E.M., Gatzweiler, F., Johnson, B. and Wijaya, A. 2002. *Exploring biological diversity, environment and local people's perspectives in forest landscapes: Methods for a multidisciplinary landscape assessment*. Center for International Forestry Research, Bogor, Indonesia.

Sheil, D., Sayer, J.A. and O'Brien, T. 1999. Tree Species Diversity in Logged Rainforests. *Science* **284(5420)**: 1587.

Shields, D.J., Martin, I.M., Martin, W.E. and Haefele, M.A. 2002. *Survey results of the American public's values, objectives, beliefs, and attitudes regarding forests and rangelands*. Rocky Mountain Research Station GTR-RMRS-95. USDA Forest Service, Fort Collins, USA.

Shrader-Frechette, K. 1998. What Risk Management Teaches Us about Ecosystem Management. *Landscape and Urban Planning* **40(1–3)**: 141–150.

Smythe, K.D., Bernabo, J.C. and Carter, T.B. 1996. Focusing biodiversity research on the needs of decision makers. *Environmental Management* **20**: 865–872.

Szaro, R.C. 1995. Biodiversity Maintenance. In: Bisio, A. and Boots, S.G. (Eds). *Encyclopedia of Energy Technology and the Environment*. 1st Edition. Wiley-Interscience, John Wiley & Sons, Inc., New York, USA.

Szaro, R.C., Berc, J., Cameron, S. Cordle, S., Crosby, M., Martin, L., Norton, D. O'Malley, R. and Ruark, G. 1998. The Ecosystem Approach: Science and Information Management Issues. *Landscape and Urban Planning* **40 (1–3)**: 89–102.

Szaro, R.C. and Boyce, D.A., Jr. 2004. The Challenges Associated with Developing Science-based Regional Scale Management Plans. *Landscape and Urban Planning*. [In press]

Szaro, R.C., Carroll, R., Hendriks, R. and Blank, M. 1999. Ecosystem sustainability and condition. In: Johnson, N., Malk, A., Szaro, R.C. and Sexton, W.T. (Eds). *Ecological Stewardship: A Common Reference for Ecosystem Management*, Volume 1: *Key Findings*. Elsevier Science, Oxford, UK.

Szaro, R.C. and Johnston, D.W. (Eds.) 1996. Biodiversity in Managed Landscapes. Oxford University Press, New York, USA.

Szaro, R.C., Langor, D. and Yapi, A.M. 2000. Sustainable forest management in the developing world: science challenges and contributions. *Landscape and Urban Planning* **47(3–4)**: 135–142.

Szaro, R.C., Lessard, G.D. and Sexton, W.T. 1996. Ecosystem Management: An Approach for Conserving Biodiversity. In: Di Castri, F. and Younès, T. (Eds). Biodiversity: Science and Development – Towards a New Partnership. CAB International, Wallingford, UK and International Union of Biological Sciences, Paris, France.

Szaro, R.C. and Peterson, C.E. 2004. Evolving approaches toward science-based forest management. *Forest Snow and Landscape Research* **78(1/2)**: 9–20.

Szaro, R.C., Sayer, J.A., Sheil, D., Snook, L., Gillison, A., Applegate, G., Poulsen, J. and Nasi, R. 1999. *Biodiversity Conservation in Production Forests*. Center for International Forestry Research, Jakarta, Indonesia and International Union of Forest Research Organizations, Vienna, Austria.

Szaro, R.C. and Sexton, W.T. 1998. Ecosystem Management as an Approach for Sustaining Forests and their Biodiversity. In: Sassa, K. (Ed.) *Environmental Forest Science: Proceedings of International Union of Forestry Research Organizations-Division 8 Conference, Kyoto University, Kyoto, Japan*. Kluwer Academic Publishers, Dordrecht, The Netherlands.

Szaro, R.C., Sexton, W.T. and Malone, C.R. 1998. The emergence of ecosystem management as a tool for meeting people's needs and sustaining ecosystems. *Landscape and Urban Planning* **40(1–3)**: 1–8.

Szaro, R.C., Thulstrup, E.W., Bowers, W.W., Souvannavong, O. and Kone, I. 1998. Mechanisms for Forestry Research Capacity Building. In: *International Consultation on Research and Information Systems in Forestry* (ICRIS), 7–10 *September* 1998, *Gmunden, Austria*. Federal Ministry of Agriculture and Forestry, Vienna, Austria.

Turner, M., Gardner R.H. and O'Neill, R.V. 2001. *Landscape Ecology in Theory and Practice: Pattern and Process*. Springer-Verlag Telos, New York, USA. Bk&CD-Rom edition.

UNCSD (United Nations Commission on Sustainable Development). 1996. *Scientific Research, Forest Assessment and Development of Criteria and Indicators for Sustainable Forest Management*. Programme element III.1 (a): Assessment of the multiple benefits of all types of forests. E/CN.17/IPF/1996/6, 20 February 1996. Report of the Secretary General prepared for Ad Hoc Intergovernmental Panel on Forests, Second session. 11–22 March 1996.

UNCSD. 1997. National mechanisms and international cooperation for capacity building in developing countries. In: *Overall progress achieved since the United Nations Conference on Environment and Development*, Report of the Secretary General. E/CN.17/1997/2/Add.27.

Urbanska, K.M., Webb, N.R. and Edwards, P.J. (Eds). 2000. *Restoration Ecology and Sustainable Development*. Cambridge University Press, Cambridge, UK.

USDA (United States Department of Agriculture). 2004. *National Report on Sustainable Forests – 2003*. FS-766. Forest Service, Washington DC, USA.

Vale, V.H. (Ed.) 2003. Ecological modeling for resource management. Springer-Verlag, New York, USA.

Vitousek, P.M., Mooney, H.A. Lubchenko, J. and Melillo, J.M. 1997. Human domination of earth's ecosystems. *Science* **277**: 494–499.

Wagner, J.E., Luzadis, V.A. and Floyd, D.W. 1998. Economic Evaluations for Ecosystem Management. *Landscape and Urban Planning* **40(1–3)**: 151–158.

Watson, V., Cervantes, S., Castro, C., Mora, L., Solis, M., Porras, I. and Cornejo, B. 1998. *Making space for better forestry: Costa Rica study*. IIED Forestry and Land Use, Junaforca, Centro Cientifico Tropical.

Wear, D.N. and Gresis, J.G. 2002. Southern forest resource assessment. Southern Research Station GTR-SRS-53. USDA Forest Service, Asheville, USA.

Wiens, J. 2002. Riverine landscapes: taking landscape ecology into the water. *Freshwater Biology* **47**: 501–515.

Williams, B.K., Nichols, J.D. and Conroy, M.J. 2002. *Analysis and management of animal populations*. Academic Press, New York, USA.

Wilson, E.O. (Ed.) 1988. *Biodiversity*. National Academy Press, Washington, DC, USA.

Wong, J.L.G., Thornber, K. and Baker, N. 2001. *Resource assessment of non-wood forest products: experience and biometric principles*. FAO, Rome, Italy.

World Resources Institute (WRI), The World Conservation Union (IUCN), and United Nations Environment Programme (UNEP). 1992. *Global Biodiversity Strategy: Guidelines for Action to Save, Study, and Use Earth's Biotic Wealth Sustainably and Equitably*. World Resources Institute, Washington, DC, USA.

Wright, P.A., Colby, J.L., Alward, G., Hoekstra, T.W., Tegler, B. and Turner, M. 2002. *Monitoring for forest management unit scale sustainability: the local unit criteria and indicators development* (LUCID) *test*. Inventory and Monitoring Institute Report No. 5. USDA Forest Service, Fort Collins, USA.

Ziglo, E. 1991. The Delphi method and its contribution to decision-making. In: Ziglo, M.A. and E. (Eds). *Gazing into the oracle: the Delphi method and its application to social policy and public health*. Jessica Kingsley Publishers, London, UK.

Chapter 4

Azevedo-Ramos, C., Carvalho Jr., O. de and Nasi, R. 2002. Animal indicators, a tool to assess biotic integrity after logging tropical forests? Centre for International Forestry Research. Report.

Bawa, K.S., Seidler, R. and Raven, P.H. 2004. Reconciling conservation paradigms. *Conservation Biology* **18**: 859–860.

Carrillo, E., Wong, G. and Cuarón, A.D. 2000. Monitoring mammal populations in Costa Rican protected areas under different hunting restrictions. *Conservation Biology* **14**: 1580–1591.

Convention on Biological Diversity (CBD). 2004. Ecosystem Approach: Principles. [online] URL: www.biodiv.org/programmes/cross-cutting/ecosystem/principles.asp

Duinker, P.N. 2001. Criteria and indicators of sustainable forest management in Canada: progress and problems in integrating science and politics at the local level. In: Franc, A., Laroussinie, O. and Karjalainen, T. (Eds). *Criteria and Indicators for Sustainable Forest Management at the Forest Management Unit Level*. European Forestry Institute Proceeding no. 38.

Dumont, J.F., Lamotte, S. and Kahn, F. 1990. Wetland and upland forest ecosystems in Peruvian Amazonia: plant species diversity in the light of some geological and botanical evidence. *Forest Ecology and Management* **33/34**: 125–139.

Finegan, B. and Camacho, M. 1999. Stand dynamics in a logged and silviculturally treated Costa Rican rain forest, 1988–1996. *Forest Ecology and Management* **121**: 177–189.

Finegan, B., Palacios, W., Zamora, N. and Delgado, D. 2001. Ecosystem-level forest biodiversity and sustainability assessments for forest management. In: Raison, R.J., Brown, A.G. and Flinn, D.W. (Eds). *Criteria and Indicators for Sustainable Forest Management*. CAB International, Wallingford, UK.

Finegan, B., Delgado, D., Camacho, M. and Zamora, N. 2001. Timber production and plant biodiversity conservation in a Costa Rican rain forest: an experimental study and its lessons for adaptive sustainability assessment. In: Franc, A., Laroussinie, O. and Karjalainen, T. (Eds). *Criteria and Indicators for Sustainable Forest Management at the Forest Management Unit Level*. European Forestry Institute Proceeding no. 38.

Finegan, B., Hayes, J.P, Delgado, D. and Gretzinger, S. 2004. Ecological monitoring of forest management in the humid tropics: a guide for forest operators and certifiers with emphasis on High Conservation Forests. WWF Central America.
[online] URL: www.wwfca.org/photos/libros/Guia%20y%20Monitoreo.pdf (in Spanish).

Forest Stewardship Council (FSC). 2004. FSC Principles and Criteria of Forest Stewardship. [online] URL: www.fsc.org/fsc/how_fsc_works/policy_standards/princ_criteria

Forman, R.T.T. 1993. *Landscape and Regional Ecology*. Cambridge University Press, Cambridge, UK.

Fredericksen, T.S. and Putz, F.E. 2003. Silvicultural intensification for tropical forest conservation. *Biodiversity and Conservation* **12**: 1445–1453.

Ghazoul, J. and Hellier, A. 2000. Setting critical limits to ecological indicators of sustainable tropical forestry. *International Forestry Review* **2**: 243–253.

Graaf, N.R. de. 1986. *A silvicultural system for natural regeneration of tropical rain forest in Suriname.* Agricultural University, Wageningen, The Netherlands.

Higman, S. and Nussbaum, R. 2002. *How standards constrain certification of small forest enterprises.* ProForest, Oxford, UK.

International Tropical Timber Organization (ITTO). 1998. Criteria and Indicators for Sustainable Forest Management. [online] URL: www.itto.or.jp/live/PageDisplayHandler?pageId=201

Keith, D.A. 1998. An evaluation and modification of World Conservation Union Red List Criteria for classification of extinction risk in vascular plants. *Conservation Biology* **12**: 1076–1090.

Lammerts van Beuren, E. M. and Blom, E.M. 1997. *Principles, Criteria, Indicators: Hierarchical Framework for the Formulation of Sustainable Forest Management Standards.* Tropenbos Foundation, The Netherlands.

Laurance, W.F., Nascimento, H.E.M., Laurance, S.G., Condit, R., D´Angelo, S. and Andrade, A. 2004. Inferred longevity of Amazonian rainforest trees based on a long-term demographic study. *Forest Ecology and Management* **190**: 131–143.

Lieberman, D. and Lieberman, M. 1987. Forest tree growth and dynamics at La Selva, Costa Rica (1969–1982). *Journal of Tropical Ecology* **3**: 347–358.

Lindenmayer, D.B., Margules, C.R. and Botkin, D.B. 2000. Indicators of biodiversity for ecologically sustainable forest management. *Conservation Biology* **14**: 941–951.

Lindenmayer, D.B. and Franklin, J.F. 2002. *Conserving forest biodiversity: a comprehensive multiscaled approach.* Island Press, Washington, USA.

McGinley, K. and Finegan, B. 2003. The ecological sustainability of tropical forest management: evaluation of the national forest management standards of Costa Rica and Nicaragua, with emphasis on the need for adaptive management. *Forest Policy and Economics* **5**: 421–431.

Meffe, G.K. and Carroll, C.R. 1997. *Principles of conservation biology.* Second edition. Sinauer Associates, Sunderland, USA.

Meffe, G.K., Nielson, L.A., Knight, R.L. and Shenborn, D.A. 2003. *Ecosystem management: adaptive, community-based conservation.* Island Press, Washington, DC, USA.

Nature editorial, 2004. Ignorance is not bliss. *Nature* **430**: 385.

Nelson, B.W., Kapos, V., Adams, J.B., Oliveira, W.J. and Braun, O.P.G. 1994. Forest disturbance by large blowdowns in the Brazilian Amazon. *Ecology* **75**: 853–858.

Noon, B.R. 1999. Scientific framework for effectiveness monitoring of the Northwest Forest Plan. In: Mulder, B. S., Welsh, H.H., Spies, T.A., Reeves, G.H., Raphael, M.G., Palmer, C. and Olsen, A.R. (Technical Coordinators). *The strategy and design of the effectiveness monitoring program for the Northwest Forest Plan.* USDA Forest Service General Technical Report PNW-GTR-437.

Noss, R.F. 1999. Assessing and monitoring forest biodiversity: a suggested framework and indicators. *Forest Ecology and Management* **115**: 135–146.

Nussbaum, R., Gray, I. and Higman, S. (Compilers). 2003. *Modular implementation and verification* (MIV): *a toolkit for the phased application of forest management standards and certification.* Proforest, Oxford, UK.

Pickett, S.T.A. and Carpenter, S.R. 1995. Overview of disturbance. In: Heywood, V.H. and Watson, R.T. (Eds). *Global Biodiversity Assessment.* Cambridge University Press for UNEP, Cambridge, UK.

Prabhu, R., Ruitenbeek, H.J., Boyle, T.J.B. and Colfer, C.J.P. 2001. Between voodoo science and adaptive management: the role and research needs for indicators of sustainable forest management. In: Raison, R.J., Brown, A.G. and Flinn, D.W. (Eds). *Criteria and Indicators for Sustainable Forest Management.* CAB International, Wallingford, UK.

Putz, F.E., Redford, K.H., Robinson, J.G., Fimbel, R. and Blate, G.M. 2000. *Biodiversity conservation in the context of tropical forest management.* World Bank Environment Department Papers no. 75. World Bank, Washington, DC, USA.

Putz, F.E., Dykstra, D.P. and Heinrich, R. 2000. Why poor logging practices persist in the tropics. *Conservation Biology* **14**: 951–956.

Salo, J., Kalliola, R., Hakkinen, I., Makinen, Y., Niemela, P., Puhakka, M. and Coley, P. 1986. River dynamics and the diversity of Amazonian lowland forest. *Nature* **322**: 254–258.

Severinghaus, J.P., Sowers, T., Brook, E.J., Alley, R.B. and Bender, M.L. 1998. Timing of abrupt climate change at the end of the younger Dryas interval from thermally fractionated gases in polar ice. *Nature* **391**: 141–146.

Scott, J.M., Csuti, B., Smith, K., Estes, J.E. and Caicco, S. 1991. Gap analysis of species richness and vegetation cover: an integrated biodiversity conservation strategy. In: Kohm, K.A. (Ed.) *Balancing on the Brink of Extinction: The Endangered Species Act and Lessons for the Future.* Island Press, Washington, DC, USA.

Sheil, D. 2001. Conservation and biodiversity monitoring in the tropics: realities, priorities and distractions. *Conservation Biology* **15**: 1179–1182.

Sheil, D., Nasi, R. and Johnson, B. 2004. Ecological criteria and indicators for tropical forest landscapes: challenges in the search for progress. *Ecology and Society* **9**: 7. [online] URL: www.ecologyandsociety.org/vol9/iss1/art7

Steidl, R.J., Hayes, J.P and Schauber, E. 1997. Statistical power in wildlife research. *Journal of Wildlife Management* **61**: 270–279.

Sutherland, W.J., Pullin, A.S., Dolman P.M. and Knight, T.M. 2004. The need for evidence-based conservation. *Trends in Ecology and Evolution* **19**: 305–308.

Wadsworth, F.H. 1997. *Forest production for tropical America.* USDA Forest Service Agriculture Handbook 710.

Watt, A.D. 1998. Measuring disturbance in tropical forests: a critique of the use of species-abundance models and indicator measures in general. *Journal of Applied Ecology* **35**: 467–469.

Whitmore, T.C. 1990. An Introduction to Tropical Rain Forests. Clarendon Press, Oxford, UK.

Woodley, S. and Forbes, G. (1997) *Forest Management Guidelines to Protect Native Biodiversity in the Fundy Model Forest.* Greater Fundy Ecosystem Research Group, UNB Faculty of Forestry and Environmental Management, Fredricton, Canada. [online] URL: www.unb.ca/web/forestry/centers/cwru/opening.htm

Chapter 5

AG WÄLDER (Forum Umwelt und Entwicklung). 2001. Appell für ein Nationales Waldprogramm Deutschland. Unpublished.

Aldhous, J. R. (Ed.) 1995. *Our pinewood heritage.* Proceedings of a conference at Culloden Academy, Inverness. – Forestry Commission, The Royal Society of the Protection of Birds, Scottish Heritage. Bell and Bain, Glasgow. UK.

Angelstam, P. 1998. Maintaining and restoring biodiversity by simulating natural disturbance regimes in European boreal forest. *Journal of Vegetation Science* **9**: 593–602.

Angelstam, P. 2003. Reconciling the linkages of land management with natural disturbance regimes to maintain forest biodiversity in Europe. In: Bissonette, J. A. and Storch, I. (Eds). *Landscape ecology and resource management: linking theory with practice.* Island Press, Covelo, CA and Washington, DC, USA.

Angelstam, P. and Andersson, L. 2001. Estimates of the needs for forest reserves in Sweden. *Scandinavian Journal of Forest Research* Supplement No. **3**: 38–51.

Angelstam, P. and Pettersson, B. 1997. Principles of present Swedish forest biodiversity management. *Ecol. Bull.* **46**: 191–203.

Angelstam, P., Bütler, R., Lazdinis, M., Mitusinski, G. and Roberge, J-M. 2003a. Habitat thresholds for focal species at multiple scales and forest biodiversity conservation – dead wood as an example. *Annales Zoologici Fennici* **40**: 473–482.

Angelstam, P., Mikusinski, G., Rönnbäck, B.-L., Östman, A., Lazdinis, M., Roberge, J-M., Arnberg, W. and Olsson, J. 2003b. Two-dimensional gap analysis – improving strategic and tactic conservation planning and biodiversity policy implementation. *Ambio* **33**: 526–533.

Angelstam, P., Dönz-Breuss, M. and Roberge, J-M. (Eds). 2004. Targets and Tools for the Maintenance of Forest Biodiversity. *Ecological Bulletin* **51**.

Angelstam, P., Roberge, J-M., Ek, T. and Laestadius, L. 2005. Data and Tools for Conservation Management and Restoration of Forest Ecosystems at Multiple Scales. In: Stanturf, J.A. and Madsen, P. (Eds). *Restoration of Boreal and Temperate Forests*. CRC Press, Boca Raton, USA.

Anon. 1993b. *Swedish Forestry Act 1979*. With complementary regulation from 1993; SFS 1979:429 and 1993:553, in Swedish.

Anon. 2001. *Skogsvårdsorganisationens utvärdering av skogspolitikens effekter* (SUS 2001). Skogsstyrelsens förlag, Jönköping, in Swedish.

Anon. 2003. *Consequences on forestry and forest industry from land use restrictions in northern Sweden*. Jaakko Pöyry Consulting, Finland.

Belaenko, A.P., Borisov, V.A. and Giryaev, D.M. 1998. 200*th Anniversary of the Forest Department*. Vol. 2 (1898–1998). Federal Forest Service of Russia. Moscow, Russian Federation.

Benecke, U. 1996: Ecological silviculture: the application of age-old methods. *New Zealand Forestry* **August**: 27–33.

Bergeron, Y. and Harvey, B. 1997. Basing silviculture on natural ecosystem dynamics: an approach applied to the southern boreal mixed wood forest of Quebec. *Forest Ecology and Management* **92**: 235–242.

Bihun, Y. 2004. Principles of sustainable forest management in the framework of regional economic development. Unpublished article presented at the Fulbright Seminar "The Pathways of Sustainable Development of the Ukrainian Carpathians" (Lviv-Skole, 2004).

Björse, G. and Bradshaw, R. 1998. 2000 years of forest dynamics in southern Sweden: suggestions for forest management. *Forest Ecology and Management* **104**: 15–26.

Bjørnlund, L., Vestergard, M., Johansson, S., Nyborg, M., Steffensen, L. and Christensen, S. 2002. Nematode communities of natural and managed beech forests – a pilot survey. *Pedobiologia* **46(1)**: 53–62.

BMELF (Bundesministerium für ernährung, landwirtschaft und forsten). 1998. *Waldbericht der Bundesregierung*. Bonn, Germany.

BMELF. 2000a. *Nationales Forstprogramm Deutschland – Ein gesellschaftspolitischer Dialog zur Förderung nachhaltiger Waldbewirtschaftung im Rahmen einer nachhaltigen Entwicklung* 1999/2000. Bonn, Germany.BMELF. 2000b. *Aufkommen und Verwendung von Nadel- und Laubrohholz in der Bundesrepublik Deutschland*. AZ Nr. 532–7440 vom 11.8.2000. Bonn, Germany.

BMELF. 2000c. *Land- und Forstwirtschaft in Deutschland: Daten und Fakten*. Bonn, Germany.

BMVEL (Bundesministerium für verbraucherschutz, ernährung und landwirtschaft). 2001. *Gesamtwaldbericht der Bundesregierung*. Bonn, Germany.

Bradshaw, R., Gemmel, P. and Björkman, L. 1994: Development of nature-based silvicultural models in Southern Sweden: The scientific background. *Forest and Landscape Research* **1**: 95–110.

Bürgi, M. and Schuler, A. 2003. Driving forces of forest management – an analysis of regeneration practices in the forests of the Swiss Central Plateau during the 19th and 20th century. *Forest Ecology and Management* **176**: 173–183.

Dhubhain, A.N. and Pommerening, A. 2004. Transformation to continuous cover forestry. *European Forest Institute News* **12:2**. EFI, Joensuu, Finland.

Dolinšek, H, 1993. Forty years of close-to-nature silviculture in Slovenia. In: *Proc. 1st European Congress of Pro Silva*. Besancon: Centre Régional de la Propriété Forestière de Franche Comte.

Dönz-Breuss, M., Maier, B. and Malin, H. 2004. Management for forest biodiversity in Austria – the view of a local forest enterprise. *Ecol. Bull.* **51**: 109–115.

Dorren, L.K.A., Berger, F., Imeson, A.C., Maier, B. and Rey, F. 2004. Integrity, stability and management of protection forests in the European Alps. *Forest Ecology and Management* **195**: 165–176.

Duelli, P. and Obrist, M. K. 2003. Biodiversity indicators: the choice of values and measures. *Agriculture, Ecosystems and Environment* **98**: 87–98.

Ekelund, H. and Hamilton, G. 2001. *Skogspolitisk historia.* Rapport 8A, Skogsstyrelsen, Jönköping, in Swedish.

Emborg, J., Christensen, M. and Heilmann-Clausen, J. 2000. The structural dynamics of Suserup Skov, a near-natural temperate deciduous forest in Denmark. *Forest Ecology and Management* **126**: 173–189.

Emborg, J., Hahn, K., Larsen, J.B. and Diaci, J. [In press] Principles of nature-based management. In: Mountford, E., Emborg, J. and Standovar, T. (Eds). *Beech Forests in Europe: Their history, ecology and nature-based management.* CABI Publishing, Wallingford, UK.

EUROSTAT. 2000. *Forststatistik 1992–96.* Direktion F. Luxemburg.

Fähser, L. 1995. Nature-oriented forestry in Luebeck. *International Journal of Ecoforestry* **11(7)**: 7–11.

Fries, C., Johansson, O., Pettersson, B. and Simonsson, P. 1997: Silvicultural models to maintain and restore natural stand structures in Swedish boreal forests. *Forest Ecology and Management* **94**: 89–103.

Frivold, L. H. 1992: *Ecologically oriented silviculture in the boreal coniferous forest zone.* IUFRO Proc. Centennial, Berlin-Eberswalde, Germany, 31 August–4 September.

Gamborg, C. and Larsen, J.B. 2003. 'Back to nature' a sustainable future for forestry? *Forest Ecology and Management* **179**: 559–571.

Gibbs, C.B. 1978: Uneven-aged silviculture and management? Even-aged silviculture and management? Definitions and differences. In: *Uneven-aged silviculture and management in the United States.* WO-24. USDA Forest Service Timber Management Research, Washington DC, USA.

Grundy, D. 2005. From plantation developer to steward of the nation's forests: the UK. In: Garforth, M. and Mayers, J. *Plantations, Privatization, Poverty and Power: Changing ownership and management of state forests.* Earthscan, London, UK.

Hansen, A.J., Garman, S.L., Weigand, J.F., Urban, D.L., McVomb, W.C. and Raphael, M.G. 1999. Alternative silvicultural regimes in the Pacific Northwest: simulations of ecological and economic effects. *Ecological Applications* **5**: 535–554.

Häusler, A. and Scherer-Lorenzen, M. 2002. *Nachhaltige Forstwirtschaft in Deutschland im Spiegel des ganzheitlichen Ansatzes der Biodiversitätskonvention.* BfN – Skripten 62. Bundesamt für Naturschutz, Bonn, Germany.

Haveraaen, O. 1995. Silvicultural systems in the Nordic countries. In: Bamsey, C.R. (Ed.) *Innovative silvicultural systems in boreal forests.* Canadian Forest Service, Natural Resources Canada.

Hensiruk, S. 1992. *Forests of Ukraine.* Naukova dumka, Kiev, Ukraine.

Hensiruk S., Furdychko, O. and Bondar V. 1995. *The history of forestry in Ukraine.* Svit, Lviv, Ukraine.

Koch, N.E. and Skovsgaard, J.P. 1999. Sustainable management of planted forests: some comparisons between Central Europe and the United States. *New Forests* **17**: 11–22.

Kopylova, E. and Teplyakov, V.K. 2004. Recent changes in social welfare of the forest sector of the Russian Federation. In: *Proceedings of Human Dimensions of Family, Farm, and Community Forestry International Symposium.* Washington State University, Pullman, USA. Washington State University Extension MISC0526.

Kräuchi, N., Brang, P. and Schönenberger, W. 2000. Forests of mountainous regions: gaps in knowledge and research needs. *Forest Ecology and Management* **132**: 73–82.

Kuper, J.H. 1996. Uneven ages in silviculture: instrument or objective? *Continuous Cover Forestry Group Newsletter* **8**: 4–5

Küster, H. 1998. *Geschichte des Waldes. Von der Urzeit bis zur Gegenwart.* Verlag C.H. Beck, München, Germany.

Lähde,E., Laiho, O. and Norokorpi, Y. 1998. Diversity-orientated silviculture in the boreal zone of Europe. *Forest Ecology and Management* **118**: 223–243.

Larsen, J.B. 1995. Ecological stability and sustainable silviculture. *Forest Ecology and Management* **73**: 85–96.

Larsen, B. Functional Forests in Multi-functional landscapes – restoring the adaptive capacity of landscapes with forests and trees. [In press] Proceedings of the International conference on Forest Landscape Restoration, Hameenlinna, Finland, October 2004. To be published by the European Forest Institute, Joensuu, Finland.

Lazdinis, M. and Angelstam, P. 2004a. Maintenance of forest biodiversity in a post-Soviet political system: conservation needs as perceived by local stakeholders in Lithuania. In: Lazdinis, M. PhD Thesis, Swedish University of Agricultural Sciences, Sweden.

Lazdinis, M. and Angelstam, P. 2004b. Connecting social and ecological systems: an integrated toolbox for hierarchical evaluation of biodiversity policy implementation. *Ecol. Bull.* **51**: 385–400.

Lõhmus, A., Kohv, K., Palo, A. and Viilma, K. 2004. Loss of old-growth, and the minimum need for strictly protected forests in Estonia. *Ecol. Bull.* **51**: 401–411.

Maximets, O. 2004. Unpublished dissertation. Section Two: Current Status of Wood Products Markets and Trends for its Development. Ukrainian State University of Forestry and Wood technology. Lviv, Ukraine.

Mayer, H. 1984. *Wälder Europas*. Gustav Fischer Verlag, Stuttgart, Germany. In German.

MCPFE and EFE/PEBLDS Working Group, 2004. Development of the Pan-European understanding of the relation between the Ecosystem Approach and Sustainable Forest Management. MCPFE Secretariat, Krakow, Poland. (Available from MCPFE website).

Moss, R. 2001. Second extinction of capercaillie (*Tetrao urogallus*) in Scotland? *Biological Conservation* **101**: 255–257.

Motta, R., Nola, P. and Piussi, P. 1999. Structure and stand development in three subalpine Norway spruce (*Picea abies* (L.) Karst.) stands in Paneveggio (Trento, Italy). *Global Ecology and Biogeography* **8**: 455–471.

Mudahar, Mohinder S., Wagner, H., Foellmi, H. *et al.* 1997. *Russia: Forest Policy during Transition. The World Bank Country Study*. World Bank, Washington, DC, USA.

Nabuurs, G.J. and Lioubimov, A.V. 2000: Future development of the Leningrad region forests under nature-oriented forest management. *Forest Ecology and Management* **130**: 235–251.

Nazarov, N., Cook, H.F. and Woodgate, G. 2001. Environmental issues in the post-communist Ukraine. *Journal of Environmental Management* **63**: 71–86.

Neet, C. and Bolliger, M. 2004. Biodiversity management in Swiss mountain forests. *Ecol. Bull.* **51**: 101–108.

Nijnik, M. and van Kooten, G.C. 2000. Forestry in the Ukraine: the road ahead? *Forest Policy and Economics* **1**: 139–151.

Orazio, C. and Nocentini, S. 1997. The forest and man: the evolution of forestry thought from modern humanism to the culture of complexity. Systemic silviculture and management on natural bases. In: Ciancio, O. (Ed.) *The forest and man*. Accademia Italiana di Scienze Forestali, Florence, Italy.

Parviainen, J., Schuck, A. and Bückling, W. 1995. A Pan-European system for measuring biodiversity, succession and structure of undisturbed forests and for improving biodiversity-oriented silviculture. In: Bamsey, C.R. (Ed.) *Innovative silvicultural systems in boreal forests*. Canadian Forest Service, Natural Resources Canada.

Peterken. G.F. 1996. *Natural woodland. Ecology and conservation in northern temperate regions*. Cambridge University Press, Cambridge, UK.

Rametsteiner, E. and Yadlapalli, L. 2004. Fostering Innovation and Entrepreneurship. *European Forestry Institute News* **12:2**. EFI, Joensuu, Finland.

Schmidt, P.A. 1998. Potential natural vegetation as an objective of close-to-natural forest management? *Forstwissenschaftliches Centralblatt* **117**: 193–205.

Schulte, B.J. and Buongiorno, J. 1998. Effects of uneven-aged silviculture on the stand structure, species composition, and economic returns of loblolly pine stands. *Forest Ecology and Management* **111**: 83–101.

Schutz, J-P. 1999. Close-to-nature silviculture: is this concept compatible with species diversity? *Forestry* **72**: 359–366.

Skovsgaard, J.P. 1995. *Challenges for the modelling of growth and yield in mixed stands with a naturally-oriented silviculture, based on experiments in pure even-aged stands and on evidence from non-intervention forest types: The present situation in Denmark.* Deutscher Verband Forstlicher Forschungsanstalten, Sektion Ertragskunde (Ed.) Proceedings of 1995 Meeting.

Steven, M.M. and Carlisle, A. 1959. *The native pinewoods of Scotland.* Oliver and Boyd, Edinburgh, UK.

Sverdrup, H. and Stjernquist, I. (Eds). 2002. *Developing principles and models for sustainable forestry in Sweden.* Kluwer Academic Publications, Dordrecht, The Netherlands.

Tarp, P., Helles, F., Holten-Andersen, P., Larsen, J.B. and Strange, N. 2000. Modelling near-natural silvicultural regimes for beech – an economic sensitivity analysis. *Forest Ecology and Management* **130**: 187–198.

Teplyakov, V.K., Kuzmichev, E.P., Baumgartner, D. and Everett, R.L. 1998. A *History of Russian Forestry and its Leaders.* Washington State University, Pullman, USA.

Vakaluk, P. 1971. *Improving of forest seeds and afforestation – the main task of Ukrainian foresters.* Forestry, Paper and Woodwork Industry, Kiev, Ukraine.

van Zon, H. 2002. Alternative scenarios for Ukraine. *Futures* **34**: 401–416.

Wohlgemuth, T., Bürgi, M., Scheidegger, C. and Schütz, M. 2002. Dominance reduction of species through disturbance – a proposed management principle for central European forests. *Forest Ecology and Management* **166**: 1–15.

Zerbe, S. 1997: Can potential natural vegetation (PNV) be a meaningful objective in natural silviculture? *Forstwissenschaftliches Centralblatt* **116**: 1–15.

Zibtsev, S., Sviridenko, V., Kremenetski, E. and Tokareva, O. 2004. Monitoring of the structure and phytodiversity of a 160 year-old natural Scots pine forest in the Central Region of Ukraine. Document in preparation for Proceedings from the International Conference and Excursion. Muckachevo, Transcarpathia, Ukraine. Natural Forests in the Temperate Zone of Europe – Values of and Utilisation. Swiss Federal Research Institute, Birmensdorf, Switzerland.

Chapter 6

Bahuguna, V.K., Mitra, K., Capistrano, D. and Saigal, S. (Eds). *Root to Canopy.* Winrock International India and Commonwealth Forestry Association, New Delhi, India.

Chhattisgarh Forest Department. 2003. *Dhamtari Model.* Chhattisgarh Forest Department, Raipur, India.

Divan, S. and Rosencranz, A. 2001. *Environmental Laws and Policy in India.* Oxford University Press, New Delhi, India.

Diwan, R., Sarin, M. and Sundar, N. 2001. Summary Report of Jan Sunwai (Public Hearing) on forest rights at village Indpura, Harda District on 26th May, 2001. Unpublished.

Dubey, A.P. 2001. Letter to Ministry of Environment and Forests. 6th July.

Ecotech Services. 2000. Study on Management of Community Funds and Local Institutions. Ecotech Services, New Delhi, India. Unpublished.

FSI (Forest Survey of India). 1999. *The State of Forest Report.* FSI, Dehradun, India.

FSI. 2001. *The State of Forest Report.* FSI, Dehradun, India.

Ghose, A. 2004. Rajasthan. In: Bahuguna, V.K., Mitra, K., Capistrano, D. and Saigal, S. (Eds). *Root to Canopy.* Winrock International India and Commonwealth Forestry Association, New Delhi, India.

GoI (Government of India). 1976. *Report of the National Commission on Agriculture: Forestry, Vol. IX*. Ministry of Agriculture and Irrigation, GoI, New Delhi, India.

GoI. 2002. *Joint Forest Management: A Decade of Partnership*. Ministry of Environment and Forests, New Delhi, India.

ICFRE (Indian Council of Forestry Research and Education). 2000. *Forestry Statistics India – 2000*. ICFRE, Dehradun, India.

IIFM (Indian Institute of Forest Management). 2002. *Manual for Operationalising Criteria and Indicators for Sustainable Forest Management at Forest Management Unit Level in India*. IIFM, Bhopal, India.

Jha, M. 2004. Maharashtra. In: Bahuguna, V.K., Mitra, K., Capistrano, D. and Saigal, S. (Eds). *Root to Canopy*. Winrock International India and Commonwealth Forestry Association, New Delhi, India.

Kothari, A., Singh, S., Pande, P. and Variava, D. 1989. *Management of National Parks and Sanctuaries in India: A Status Report*. Indian Institute of Public Administration, New Delhi, India.

Kothari, A., Singh, N. and Suri, S. (Eds). 1996. *People and Protected Areas in India: Towards Participatory Conservation*. Sage Publications, New Delhi, India.

Kotwal, P.C. and Horo. N.V. 2004. Developing sustainability index for forestry resources and their management. *IIFM Newsletter* **2(2)**.

Makhaik, R. 2002. HP imposes environmental value tax. The Hindustan Times, 23 August.

MoEF (Ministry of Environment and Forests). 1988. *National Forest Policy Resolution*. MoEF, New Delhi, India.

MoEF. 1992. *National Conservation Strategy and Policy Statement on Environment and Development*. MoEF, New Delhi, India.

MoEF. 1998. *Implementation of Article 6 of the Convention on Biological Diversity in India – National Report*. MoEF, New Delhi, India.

MoEF. 1999. *National Forestry Action Programme – India*. MoEF, New Delhi, India.

MoEF. 2001. *India's Second National Report to the Convention on Biological Diversity in India*. MoEF, New Delhi, India.

MoEF. 2002. *Joint Forest Management: A Decade of Partnership*. MoEF, New Delhi, India.

MoEF. 2003. *Annual Report 2002–2003*. MoEF, New Delhi, India.

Mukherji, S.D. 2004. Andhra Pradesh. In: Bahuguna, V.K., Mitra, K., Capistrano, D. and Saigal, S. (Eds). *Root to Canopy*. Winrock International India and Commonwealth Forestry Association, New Delhi, India.

Murali, K.S., Murthy, I.K, Nagaraj, B.C. and Ravindranath, N.H. 2004. A decade of JFM and its ecological impacts. In: Bahuguna, V.K., Mitra, K., Capistrano, D. and Saigal, S. (Eds). *Root to Canopy*. Winrock International India and Commonwealth Forestry Association, New Delhi, India.

NBSAP (National Biodiversity Strategy Action Plan). 2004. Final Technical Report of the UNDP-GEF Sponsored Project (Draft). Unpublished.

Palit, S. 2004. West Bengal. In: Bahuguna, V.K., Mitra, K., Capistrano, D. and Saigal, S. (Eds). *Root to Canopy*. Winrock International India and Commonwealth Forestry Association, New Delhi, India.

Poffenberger, M. and McGean, B. (Eds). 1996. *Village Voices, Forest Choices: Joint Forest Management in India*. Oxford University Press, New Delhi, India.

Protected Area Update. 2004. No. 49, June. Kalpavriksh, Pune, India.

Rawat, J.K., Saxena, A. and Gupta, S. (undated). Monitoring India's forest cover through remote sensing. Paper posted at www.gisdevelopment.net/application/nrm/forestry/mi04178pf.htm

Saigal, S. 1998. Participatory Forestry in India: Analysis and Lessons. MSc Dissertation, Oxford Forestry Institute. Unpublished.

Saigal, S., Arora, H. and Rizvi, S.S. 2002. *The New Foresters: Role of Private Enterprise in the Indian Forestry Sector*. International Institute for Environment and Development, London, UK.

Sarin, M., Singh, N.M., Sundar, N. and Bhogal, R.K. 2003. Devolution as a threat to democratic decision-making in forestry? Findings from three states in India. In: Edmunds, D. and Wollenberg, E.

(Eds). *Local Forest Management: The Impacts of Devolution Policies*. Earthscan, London, UK and Sterling, USA.

Sekhsaria, P. 2002. To Save an Archipelago. *Frontline* **19(12)**, June 8–21.

SPWD (Society for Promotion of Wastelands Development). 1998. *Joint Forest Management Update*. SPWD, New Delhi, India.

Vira, B. 1995. *Institutional Change in India's Forest Sector, 1976-94: Reflections on State Policy*. Oxford Centre for the Environment, Ethics and Society (OCEES) research paper no. 5. OCEES, Oxford, UK.

Chapter 7

Alaska Forest Resources and Practices Act. 1978. AS 41.17. Juneau, Alaska.

Amaranthus, M.R. 1997. *Forest Sustainability: An Approach to Definition and Assessment*. General Technical Report PNW-GTR-416. US Department of Agriculture, Forest Service, Pacific Northwest Research Station, Portland, USA.

American Forest & Paper Association [AF&PA]. 1999. *Sustainable Forestry Initiatives Standard: Principles and Objectives*. American Forest & Paper Association, Washington, DC, USA.

Armleder, H.M. and Stevenson, S.K. 1994. Silviculture systems to maintain caribou habitat in managed British Columbia forests. In: Bamsey, C. (Ed.) *Innovative Silviculture Systems in Boreal Forests Symposium*. Oct. 2–8, Edmonton, Alberta. Natural Resources Canada, Canadian Forest Service.

Arnott, J.T., Beese, W.J., Mitchell, A.K. and Peterson, J. (Eds). 1995. *Proceedings of Montane Alternative Silviculture Systems (MASS) Workshop, Courtenay, B.C., June 7–8, 1995*. FRDA Report 238. Canadian Forest Service and B.C. Ministry of Forests, Victoria, Canada.

Beese, W.J. and Phillips, E.J. 1997. Harvesting costs and impacts of alternative silvicultural prescriptions in old growth. In: *Forest Management into the Next Century: What Will Make it Work?* Publication 7276, Forest Products Society, Madison, USA.

Behan, R. 1990. Multiresource forest management: A paradigmatic challenge to professional forestry. *Journal of Forestry* **88(4)**: 12–18.

Boyce, D.A., Jr. and Szaro, R.C. An overview of science contributions to the management of the Tongass National Forest, Alaska. *Landscape and Urban Planning*. [In press]

Burgess, D., Mitchell, A.K. and Puttonen, P. 2001. Silvicultural Systems for Boreal and Temperate Forests. Agricultural and Natural Sciences. In: El Tayeb, M., Kochetkov, V. and Huynh, H. (Eds). *Encyclopedia of Life Support Systems* (EOLSS), [Online] Eolss Publishers, Oxford, UK. [www.eolss.net], [accessed September 2004].

California (Z'Berg-Nejedly) Forest Practice Act. 1973. California Public Resources Code, Sections 4511–4628. Sacramento, USA.

Cissel, J.H., Swanson, F.J. and Weisberg, P.J. 1999. Landscape management using historical fire regimes: Blue River, Oregon. *Ecological Applications* **9(4)**: 1217–1231.

Clayoquot Scientific Panel. 1995. *Sustainable Ecosystem Management in Clayoquot Sound: Planning and Practices*. Report 5, Scientific Panel for Sustainable Forest Practices in Clayoquot Sound, Victoria, Canada.

Coates, K.D., Banner, A., Steventon, J.D., LePage, P. and Bartemucci, P. 1997. *The Date Creek silvicultural systems study in the interior cedar-hemlock forests of northwestern British Columbia*. B.C. Ministry of Forests Land Management Handbook 38.

Committee of Scientists. 1999. *Sustaining the People's Lands: Recommendations for Stewardship of the National Forests and Grasslands into the Next Century*. US Department of Agriculture, Washington, DC, USA. Retrieved April 1999 from http://www.fs.fed.us/news/science/

Curtis, R.O., DeBell, D.S., Harrington, C.A., Lavender, D.P., St. Clair, J.B., Tappeiner, J.C. and Walstad, J.D. 1998. *Silviculture for Multiple Objectives in the Douglas-fir Region*. General Technical Report

PNW-GTR-435, US Department of Agriculture, Forest Service, Pacific Northwest Research Station, Portland, USA.

Daigle, P.W. 1995. PARTCUTS: A *Computerized Annotated Bibliography of Partial Cutting Methods in the Northwest* (1995 *Update*). Canada-British Columbia Forest Resource Development Agreement, FRDA Handbook 101.

Duncan, S. 2000. *Closer to the Truth: 75 years of Discovery in Forest & Range Research*. Miscellaneous publication, US Department of Agriculture, Forest Service, Pacific Northwest Research Station, Portland, USA.

Eastham, A.M. and Jull, M.J. 1999. Factors affecting natural regeneration of *Abies lasiocarpa* and *Picea engelmanni* in a subalpine silvicultural systems trial. *Canadian Journal of Forest Research* **29**: 1847–1885.

Endangered Species Act of 1973 [ESA]; 16 U.S.C. 153–1536, 1538–1540.

Everest, F.H., Swanston, D.N., Shaw, C.G. III, Smith, W.P., Julin, K.R. and Allen, S.D. 1997. *Evaluation of the Use of Scientific Information in Developing the 1997 Forest Plan for the Tongass National Forest*. General Technical Report PNW-GTR-415, US Department of Agriculture, Forest Service, Pacific Northwest Research Station, Portland, USA.

Forest Ecosystem Management Assessment Team (FEMAT). 1993. *Forest Ecosystem Management: An Ecological, Economic, and Social Assessment*. US Department of Agriculture, Forest Service; US Department of Commerce, National Oceanic and Atmospheric Administration; US Department of Interior, Bureau of Land Management, US Fish and Wildlife Service, and National Park Service; and Environmental Protection Agency, Washington, DC, USA.

Forest Practices Code of British Columbia Act. 1994. Statutes of B.C., Bill 40. Queen's Printer, Victoria, Canada. Retrieved April 4, 2003 from www.legis.gov.bc.ca/1994/3rd_read/gov40-3.htm

Franklin, J.F. 1988. Pacific Northwest forests. In: Barbour, M.G. and Billings, W.D. (Eds). *North American Terrestrial Vegetation*. Cambridge University Press, New York, USA.

Franklin, J.F. and Dyrness, C.T. 1973. *Natural Vegetation of Oregon and Washington*. General Technical Report PNW-GTR-8, US Department of Agriculture, Forest Service, Pacific Northwest Research Station, Portland, USA.

Franklin, J.F., Berg, D.R., Thornburgh, D.A. and Tappeiner, J.C. 1997. Alternative silvicultural approaches to timber harvesting: variable retention harvest systems. In: Kohm, K.A. and Franklin, J.F. (Eds). *Creating a Forestry for the 21st Century: The Science Of Ecosystem Management*.

Franklin, J.F. and Waring, R.H. 1981. Distinctive features of the northwestern coniferous forest: development, structure, and function. In: Waring, R.H. (Ed.) *Forests: Fresh Perspectives from Ecosystem Research*. Oregon State University Press, Corvallis, USA.

Fujimori, T., Kawanabe, S., Saito, H., Grier, C.C. and Shidei, T. 1976. Biomass and primary production in forests of three major vegetation zones of the northwestern United States. *Journal of Japanese Forestry Society* **58**: 360–373.

Hall, P. 2000. The issue of scale in the aggregation of data on indicators of sustainable forest management from subnational to national levels. *Forestry Chronicle* **76(3)**: 419–422.

Halpern, C.B. 1995. *Response of Forest Communities to Green-Tree Retention Harvest: A Study Plan for the Vegetation Component of the Demonstration of Ecosystem Management Options* (DEMO) *Study*. College Forestry Resources, University of Washington, Seattle, USA.

Haynes, R.W. (Technical Coordinator) 2003. An *Analysis of the Timber Situation in the United States: 1952 to 2050*. Technical document supporting the 2000 USDA Forest Service RPA Assessment. Gen. Tech. Rep. PNW-GTR-560, US Department of Agriculture, Forest Service, Pacific Northwest Research Station, Portland, USA.

Haynes, R.W. and Perez, G.E. (Eds). 2000. *Northwest Forest Plan Research Synthesis*. Gen. Tech. Rep. PNW-GTR-498, US Department of Agriculture, Forest Service, Pacific Northwest Research Station, Portland, USA.

Interagency Ecosystem Management Task Force. 1995. *The Ecosystem Approach: Healthy Ecosystems and Sustainable Economies. Volume I – Overview*. Office of Environmental Policy, Washington, DC, USA.

Kimmins, H. 1992. *Balancing Act: Environmental Issues in Forestry*. University of British Columbia Press, Vancouver, Canada.

Klenner, W. and Vyse, A. 1998. The Opax Mountain Silvicultural Systems Project: Evaluating alternative approaches to managing dry Douglas-fir forests. In: Vyse, A., Hollstedt, C. and Huggard, D. (Eds). *Managing the Dry Douglas-fir Forests of the Southern Interior: Workshop Proceedings*. Working Paper 34. B.C. Ministry of Forests, Victoria, Canada.

Kohm, K.A. and Franklin, J.F. (Eds). 1997. *Creating a Forestry for the 21st Century: The Science of Ecosystem Management*. Island Press, Washington, DC, USA.

Lee, Kai N. 1993. *Compass and Gyroscope: Integrating Science and Politics for the Environment*. Island Press, Washington, DC, USA.

Meidinger, D. and Pojar, J. (Eds). 1991. *Ecosystems of British Columbia*. Special Report Series 6, British Columbia Ministry of Forests, Victoria, Canada.

Mendoza, G.A. and Prabhu, R. 2000. Qualitative multi-criteria approaches to assessing indicators of sustainable forest resource management. *Forest Ecology and Management* **131**: 107–126.

Mihajlovich, M. 2001. Does forest certification assure sustainability? *Forestry Chronicle* **77(6)**: 994–997.

Miller, C. 2001. *Gifford Pinchot and the Making of Modern Environmentalism*. Island Press, Washington DC, USA.

Mills, J.R. and Zhou, X. 2003. *Projecting National Forest Inventories for the 2000 RPA Timber Assessment*. Gen. Tech. Rep. PNW-GTR-568, US Department of Agriculture, Forest Service, Pacific Northwest Research Station, Portland, USA.

Mitchell, A.K., Vyse, A., Huggard, D.J. and Beese, W.J. 2004. Long-term silviculture experiments contribute to science-based forest management in British Columbia's public forests. *Forest, Snow and Landscape Research* **78(1/2)**: 139–150.

Monserud, R.A. Evaluating forest models in a sustainable forest management context. Forest Biometry, Modelling and Information Sciences (FBMIS). [In press] To be available online at www.fbmis.info/

Monserud, R.A., Haynes, R.W. and Johnson, A.C.. 2003. The search for compatibility: What have we learned? In: Monserud, R.A., Haynes, R.W. and Johnson, A.C. (Eds). *Compatible Forest Management*. Kluwer Academic Publishers, Dordrecht, The Netherlands.

Multiple Use-Sustained Yield Act of 1960 [MUSY]. 1960 16 USC 528–531.

National Environmental Policy Act of 1969 [NEPA]. 42 USC 4321 *et seq.*

National Forest Management Act of 1976 [NFMA]. Act of October 22, 1976; 16 USC 1600.

Oregon State Forest Practices Act. 1971. ORS 527.610 to 527.770. Salem, Oregon.

Perry, D.A. and Amaranthus, M.P. 1997. Disturbance, recovery, and stability. In: Kohm, K.A. and Franklin, J.F. (Eds). *Creating a Forestry for the 2lst Century*. Island Press, Washington, DC, USA.

Peterson, C.E. and Monserud, R.A. 2002. *Compatibility between Wood Production and other Values and Uses on Forested Lands. A Problem Analysis*. General Technical Report PNW-GTR-564, US Department of Agriculture, Forest Service, Pacific Northwest Research Station, Portland, USA.

Peterson, E.B., Peterson, N.M., Weetman, G.F. and Martin, P.J. 1997. *Ecology and Management of Sitka Spruce, Emphasizing its Natural Range*. University of British Columbia Press, Vancouver, Canada.

Powers, R.F. 2001. Assessing potential sustainable wood yield. In: Evans, J. (Ed.) *The Forestry Handbook. Applying Forest Science for Sustainable Management, Vol. 2*. Blackwell Science, Oxford, UK.

Puttonen, P. and Murphy, B. 1997. Developing silvicultural systems for sustainable forestry in British Columbia. In: Hollstedt, C. and Vyse, A. (Eds). *Sicamous Creek Silvicultural Systems Project: Workshop Proceedings, April 24–25, 1996*. Working Paper 24/1997. Kamloops, British Columbia, Canada. Research Branch, B.C. Ministry of Forests, Victoria, Canada.

Quigley, T.M. and Bigler-Cole, H. 1997. *Highlighted Scientific Findings of the Interior Columbia Basin Ecosystem Management Project*. Gen. Tech. Rep. PNW-GTR-404, US Department of Agriculture, Forest Service, Pacific Northwest Research Station; US Department of the Interior, Bureau of Land Management, Portland, USA.

Schlaepfer, R. and Elliott, C. 2000. Ecological and landscape considerations in forest management – The end of forestry? In: von Gadow, K., Pukkala, T. and Tomé, M. (Eds). *Sustainable Forest Management*. Kluwer Academic Publishers, Dordrecht, The Netherlands.

Schoonmaker, P.K., von Hagen, B. and Wolf, E.C. (Eds). 1997. *The Rain Forests of Home: Profile of a North American Bioregion*. Island Press, Washington DC, USA.

Schwalm, C. and Ek, A.R. 2001. Climate change and site: relevant mechanisms and modeling techniques. *Forest Ecology and Management* **150**: 241–257.

Sierra Nevada Ecosystem Project Science Team and Special Consultants [SNEP]. 1996. *Status of the Sierra Nevada: Assessment Summaries and Management Strategies*. Wildlands Resource Center Report 36, Vol. 1. University of California, Davis, Centers for Water and Wildland Resources, Davis, USA.

Tittler, R., Messier, C. and Burton, P.I. 2001. Hierarchical forest management planning and sustainable forest management in the boreal forest. *Forestry Chronicle* **77(6)**: 998–1005.

US Department of Agriculture, Forest Service. 1963. *Timber Trends in Western Oregon and Western Washington*. Research Paper PNW-5. Pacific Northwest Forest and Range Experiment Station, Division of Forest Economics Research, Portland, USA.

US Department of Agriculture, Forest Service. 1997a. *Land and Resource Management Plan: Tongass National Forest*. R10-MB-338dd, Alaska Regional Office, Juneau, USA.

US Department of Agriculture, Forest Service. 1997b. *Tongass Land Management Plan Revision: Final Environmental Impact Statement* [FEIS]. Part 1: Summary, Chapters 1 through 3 (Physical and Biological Environment). R10-MB-338b. Alaska Regional Office, Juneau, USA.

US Department of Agriculture, Forest Service 1997c. *Tongass Land Management Plan Revision: Record of Decision* [ROD]. R10-MB-338a. Alaska Regional Office, Juneau, USA.

US Department of Agriculture, Forest Service and US Department of the Interior, Bureau of Land Management. 1994a. *Final Supplemental Environmental Impact Statement on Management of Habitat for Late-Successional and Old-Growth Forest Related Species within the Range of the Northern Spotted Owl, Vol. 1 and 2*. Washington, DC, USA.

US Department of Agriculture, Forest Service and US Department of the Interior, Bureau of Land Management. 1994b. *Record of Decision for the President's Forest Plan*. Washington, DC, USA.

von Gadow, K., Pukkala, T. and Tomé, M. (Eds).. 2000. *Sustainable Forest Management*. Kluwer Academic Publishers, Dordrecht, The Netherlands.

Walter, H. 1985. *Vegetation of the Earth and Ecological Systems of the Geobiosphere*. 3rd Edition. Springer-Verlag, New York, USA.

Washington Forest Practices Act. 1974. *Chapter 76.09 of the Revised Code of Washington*. Olympia, WA, USA.

Watson, R.T., Zinyowera, M.C. and Moss, R.H. (Eds). 1995. *Climate Change 1995: Impacts, Adaptations and Mitigation of Climate Change: Scientific-Technical Analyses*. Contribution of Working Group 2 to the second assessment of the Intergovernmental Panel on Climate Change. Cambridge University Press, Cambridge, UK.

Wilderness Act of 1964. 16 U.S.C. 1121 (note), 1131–1136.

Wilson, B. and Wang, S. 1999. Sustainable forestry – the policy prescription in British Columbia. In: Yoshimoto, A. and Yukutake, K. (Eds). *Global Concerns for Forest Resource Utilization – Sustainable Use and Management*. Kluwer Academic Publishers, Dordrecht, The Netherlands.

World Commission on Environment and Development. 1987. *Our Common Future: Report of the World Commission on Environment and Development*. Oxford University Press, New York, USA.

Chapter 8

ADIE (Association pour le Développement de l'Information Environmentale), 2001. *Comment minimiser l'impact de l'exploitation forestière sur la faune dans le Bassin du Congo*. Série Forêt No. 1. ADIE, Libreville, Gabon.

Hakizumwami, E. and Ndikumagenge, C. 2003. *Initiatives et processus sous-régionaux de conservation et de gestion forestière en Afrique Centrale*. Actes du 12ième Congrès Forestier Mondial, Quebec, Canada.

International Tropical Timber Organization. 2002. *Plan de Convergence sur la conservation et la gestion durable des forêts dans le bassin du Congo*. ITTO, Yokohama, Japan.

IUCN. 1989. *La conservation des écosystèmes forestiers d'Afrique Centrale: un plan d'action*. IUCN, Gland, Switzerland.

Poore, D and Sayer, J. 1993. *La gestion des régions forestières tropicales humides; Directives écologiques*. IUCN, Gland, Switzerland.

Sayer, J.A. 1991. *Rainforest Buffer Zones: Guidelines for protected area managers*. IUCN, Gland, Switzerland.

Wehiong, Makon. 2003. *Bilan et analyse des expériences de partenariat en gestion forestière dans le Bassin du Congo*. IUCN, Yaoundé, Cameroon and ITTO, Yokohama, Japan.

Wells, M. and McShane, T. 2004. *Making Conservation Projects Work*. Columbia University Press, New York, USA.

Chapter 9

Aguilar-Amuchastegui, N., Finegan, B., Louman, B. and Delgado, D. 2000. Patrones de respuesta de Scarabaeinae a las actividades de manejo en bosques naturales tropicales. *Revista Forestal Centroamericana* **30**: 40–45.

Caballero, M., Cardona, L., Sánchez, A. and Isidro, C. 2002. Manejo forestal con participación comunitaria en la costa norte de Honduras. In: Sabogal, C. and Silva, J.N.M. (Eds). *Aplicando resultados de pesquisa, envolvendo atores e definindo políticas públicas*. Embrapa Amazonia Oriental and Ministerio de Agricultura, Pecuaria e Abastecimiento, Belém, Brazil.

Camacho, M. and Finegan, B. 1997. *Efectos del aprovechamiento forestal y el tratamiento silvicultural en un bosque húmedo del noreste de Costa Rica. El crecimiento diamétrico con énfasis en el rodal comercial*. Serie Técnica, Informe Técnico No. 295. CATIE, Turrialba, Costa Rica.

Camino, R. de, 1993. El papel del bosque húmedo tropical en el desarrollo sostenible de América Central: desafíos y posibles soluciones. *Revista Forestal Centroamericana* **6**: 7–16.

Campbell B. and Sayer, J.A., 2003. *Integrated natural resources management. Linking productivity, the environment and development*. CABI Publishing, Wallingford, UK.

Campos A, J.J. 1992. Incentives and *campesino* participation in forestry development: the case of the Osa Peninsula. Invited Paper at the Central American Workshop on Forest Incentives. World Wildlife Fund (WWF) and the Nicaraguan Forestry Action Plan. Managua, Nicaragua. August, 26–27, 1992.

Campos A., J.J, Ortiz, R., Smith, J., Maldonado, T. and Camino, T. de. 2000. *Almacenamiento de carbono y conservación de biodiversidad por medio de actividades forestales en el Área de Conservación Cordillera Volcánica Central, Costa Rica. Potencialidades y limitantes*. Serie Técnica, Informe Técnico No. 314. CATIE, Turrialba, Costa Rica.

Campos A., J.J., Finegan, B. and Villalobos, R. 2001. Management of goods and services from neotropical forests biodiversity: diversified forest management in Mesoamerica. In: *Assessment, conservation and sustainable use of forest biodiversity*. CBD Technical Series No. 3. Secretariat of the Convention on Biological Diversity. Montreal.

Campos A., J.J., Camacho, M., Villalobos, R., Rodríguez, C.M. and Gómez, M. 2002. Tala ilegal en Costa Rica: problemática y propuestas de solución. *Biocenosis* **16(1–2)**: 40–46.

Campos A., J.J., Louman, B., Locatelli, B., Garay, M., Yalle, S., Villalobos, R., López, G. and Carrera, F. *Efectos del pago por servicios ambientales y la certificación forestal en el desempeño ambiental y socioeconómico del manejo de bosques naturales en Costa Rica*. Serie Técnica. Informe Técnico. [In press]

Carrera, F. and Pinelo, G. 1995. *Prácticas mejoradas para aprovechamientos forestales de bajo impacto*. Serie Oficial, Informe Técnico No. 262. CATIE, Turrialba, Costa Rica.

Carrera, J.R., Campos A., J.J., Morales, J. and Louman, B. 2001. Evaluación de indicadores para el monitoreo de concesiones forestales en Petén, Guatemala. *Revista Forestal Centroamericana* **34**: 84–88.

Carrera, F., Morales, J. and Galvez, J. 2002. Concesiones forestales comunitarias en la Reserva Biosfera Maya, Petén, Guatemala. In: Sabogal, C. and Silva, J.N.M. (Eds). *Aplicando resultados de pesquisa, envolvendo atores e definindo políticas públicas*. Embrapa Amazonia Oriental and Ministerio de Agricultura, Pecuaria e Abastecimiento, Belém, Brazil.

Carrera, F., Stoian, D., Campos A., J.J., Pinelo, G. and Morales, J. Forest certification in Guatemala. In: Forest Certification in Developing Countries and Countries in Transition. Paper presented at the Symposium "Forest Certification in Developing Countries and Countries in Transition" held at the University of Yale on June 10–14, 2004. [In press]

CATIE, and CONAP. 2001. *Plan general de manejo forestal diversificado de la concesión comunitaria de San Miguel La Palotada*. Serie Técnica, Informe Técnico No. 320. CATIE, Turrialba, Costa Rica.

Chassot, O., Monge, G., Powell, G., Palmintiri, S., Alemán, U., Wright, P. and Adamek, K. 2001. Lapa verde, víctima del manejo forestal insostenible. *Ciencias Ambientales* **21**: 60–69.

Chassot, O., Monge, G., Ruiz, A. and Mariscal, T. 2003. Corredor Biológico Costa Rica–Nicaragua pro lapa verde. *Ambientico* No.114. On Line: www.una.ac.cr/ambi/Ambien-Tico/114/chassot.html

Chinchilla, A. 2002. Central America: ACICAFOC, an on-going proposal. WRM bulletin no 63. Consultado en internet 30 junio 2004 en: /www.wrm.org.uy/bulletin/63/Acicafoc.html

Clark, D.A. 1998. Deciphering landscape mosaics of neotropical trees: GIS and systematic sampling provide new views of tropical rainforest diversity. *Annals of the Missouri Botanical Garden* **85(1)**: 18–33.

Comisión Nacional de Certificación Forestal. 1999. *Estándares y procedimientos para el manejo sostenible y la certificación forestal en Costa Rica*. Comisión Nacional de Certificación Forestal, Costa Rica.

Cordero, D. and Castro, E. 2001. Pago por servicio ambiental hídrico. *Revista Forestal Centroamericana* **36**: 41–45.

Delgado, D., Finegan, B., Zamora, N. and Meir, P. 1997. *Efectos del aprovechamiento forestal y el tratamiento silvicultural en un bosque húmedo del noroeste de Costa Rica*. Serie Técnica, Informe Técnico No. 298. CATIE, Turrialba, Costa Rica.

Donovan, R. and Buschbacher, R. 1989. *The forest conservation and management project (Boscosa) of the Osa Peninsula, Costa Rica. Annual Report and Work plan*. Fundación Neotrópica, World Wildlife Fund.

FAO. 1997. *State of the World's Forests 1997*. Food and Agriculture Organization of the United Nations, Rome, Italy.

FAO. 2001. *State of the World's Forests 2001*. Food and Agriculture Organization of the United Nations, Rome, Italy.

FAO. 2002. *Evaluación de los recursos forestales mundiales 2000. Informe principal*. Estudio FAO Montes 140. Organización de las Naciones Unidas para la Agricultura y la Alimentación, Roma, Italia.

Finegan, B. 1992. *El potencial de manejo de los bosques húmedos secundarios neotropicales de las tierras bajas*. Serie técnica, Informe Técnico No. 188. CATIE, Turrialba, Costa Rica.

Finegan, B., Sabogal, C., Reiche, C. and Hutchinson, I. 1993. Los bosques húmedos tropicales de América Central: su manejo sostenible es posible y rentable. *Revista Forestal Centroamericana* **6**: 17–27.

Forest Stewardship Council. 2004. Forests certified by FCS-accredited certification bodies. Consulted June 23rd 2004. International Center, Bonn, Germany. www.fscoax.org

Galloway, G. 2001. Redes operativas: un mecanismo efectivo para promocionar el manejo de bosques tropicales. *Revista Forestal Centroamericana* **33**: 33–37.

Galloway, G. 2002. Las redes operativas y su papel en la política forestal. Experiencias prometedoras en Honduras y Nicaragua. *Revista Forestal Centroamericana* **37**: 26–32.

Godoy, R., Wilkie, D., Overman, H., Cubas, A., Cubas, G., Demmer, J., McSweeney, K. and Brokaw, N. 2000. Valuation of consumption and sale of forest goods from a Central American rain forest. *Nature* **406(6791)**: 62–63.

IUCN. 2000. *Comunidad y gestión de bosques en Mesoamérica*. Perfil regional del grupo de trabajo sobre participación comunitaria en el manejo de los bosques. CICAFOC/UNOFOC/IUCN, San José, Costa Rica.

Jiménez, J. and Reyes, R. 2001. *Experiencias sobre la introducción de alternativas productivas en una concesión forestal comunitaria de Petén, Guatemala.* Serie Técnica, Informe Técnico No. 316. CATIE, Turrialba, Costa Rica.

Kandel, S. and Rosa, H. 2000. Después del Mitch: temas y actores en la agenda de transformación de Centroamérica. In: EIRD/OPS (Estrategia Internacional para la Reducción de Desastres/Organización Panamericana de la Salud)(Compiladores). *Huracán Mitch: una mirada a algunas tendencias temáticas para la reducción del riesgo*. EIRD, San José, Costa Rica.

Laird, S. (Ed.) 2002. *Biodiversity and traditional knowledge. Equitable partnerships in practice.* Earthscan, London, UK.

Lazo, F. 2001. El papel forestal en la mitigación de la probeza; Perfil de Honduras. Background paper for inter-agency forum on "The role of forestry in poverty alleviation", Tuscany, Italy, September 2001. FAO, Rome, Italy.

Louman, B., Campos A., J.J., Schmidt, S., Zagt, R. and Haripersaud, P. 2002. Los procesos nacionales de certificación forestal y su relación con la investigación forestal. Interacciones entre políticas y manejo forestal, casos de Costa Rica y Guyana. *Revista Forestal Centroamericana* **37**: 41–46.

Louman, B. 2003. Cadena forestal: Cuándo funciona y por qué no funciona siempre. In: *Cadenas de producción para el desarrollo económico local y el uso sostenible de la biodiversidad. Internacional Seminar. Managua, 17–19 March, 2003.*

Louman, B., Garay, M., Yalle, S., Campos A., J.J., Locatelli, B., Villalobos, R., López, G. and Carrera, F. Environmental and socioeconomic effects of the payment of environmental services and forest certification of natural forest management in Costa Rica. Draft paper to be submitted to *Journal of Forest Policy and Economics*. [In prep.]

McGinley, K. and Finegan, B. 2002. *Evaluations for sustainable forest management.* Serie Técnica, Informe Técnico No. 238. CATIE, Turrialba, Costa Rica.

Mendietta, M. 1993. Manejo sustentable del bosque húmedo tropical en Honduras: experiencias de la región forestal Atlántida. *Revista Forestal Centroamericana* **6**: 28–37.

Miller, K., Chang, E. and Johnson, N. 2001. *En busca de un enfoque común para el corredor biológico mesoamericano.* World Resources Institute.Washington DC, USA.

Mollinedo, A., Campos A., J.J., Kanninen, M. and Gómez, M. 2002. *Beneficios sociales y rentabilidad financiera del manejo forestal comunitario en la Reserva de la Biosfera Maya, Guatemala.* Serie Técnica, Informe Técnico No. 327 CATIE, Turrialba, Costa Rica.

Monroy, H. 2001. *Manual de planificación y ejecución de aprovechamientos forestales en las concesiones comunitarias de Petén.* Serie Técnica, Manual Técnico No. 47. CATIE, Turrialba, Costa Rica.

Mora-Escalante, J. and Salas, A. 1996. Contexto regional para el uso sostenible de los recursos naturales en América Central (documento para la discusión). IUCN Regional Office for Mesoamerica (IUCN-ORMA).

Nasi, R., Wunder, S. and Campos A., J.J. 2002. Forest ecosystem services: can they pay our way out of deforestation? Discussion paper presented for the forestry roundtable of GEF and UNFF II, Costa Rica, March 11, 2002. New York.

Nilsson, M. 1999. *Conceptos básicos en el trabajo con bosques y comunidades.* Serie Técnica, Boletín Técnico No. 307. CATIE, Turrialba, Costa Rica.

Ordoñez, Y. 2003. Validación de indicadores ecológicos para la evaluación de sostenibilidad en bosques bajo manejo forestal en el trópico húmedo, con énfasis en bosques de alto valor para la conservación. Tesis Mag. Sc. CATIE, Turrialba, Costa Rica.

Ortiz, S., Carrera, F. and Ormeño, L.M. 2002. *Comercialización de productos maderables en concesiones forestales comunitarias en Petén, Guatemala.* Serie Técnica, Informe Técnico No. 326. CATIE, Turrialba, Costa Rica.

Otárola, M. 2001. Análisis de preferencias para la evaluación de la compatibilidad de actividades turísticas y silvícolas en robledales de la parte alta y media de la cuenca del Río Grande de Orosí, Costa Rica. Thesis Mag. Sc. CATIE, Turrialba, Costa Rica.

Paniagua, C., Cajina, O. and Marmillod, D. 2001. *Primer caso de manejo forestal comunitario en manglares de Nicaragua: Experiencias de la cooperativa 28 de julio.* Serie Técnica, Informe Técnico No. 318. CATIE, Turrialba, Costa Rica.

Poore, D., Burgess, P., Palmer, J., Rietbergen, S. and Synnott, T. (Eds). 1989. *No Timber Without Trees: Sustainability in the Tropical Forest.* Earthscan, London, UK.

Ramos, Z. 2004. Estructura y Composición de un Paisaje Boscoso Fragmentado: Herramienta para el Diseño de Estrategias de Conservación de la Biodiversidad. Thesis Mag. Sc. CATIE, Turrialba, Costa Rica.

Repetto, R. and Gillis, M. 1988. *Public policies and the misuse of forest resources.* Cambridge University Press, Cambridge, UK.

Reyes, R. and Ammour, T. 1997. *Sostenibilidad de los sistemas de producción en la concesión counitaria de San Miguel, Petén, Guatemala.* Serie Petén No. 1. CATIE, Turrialba, Costa Rica.

Rodríguez, J. 2002. Los servicios ambientales del bosque: el ejemplo de Costa Rica. *Revista Forestal Centroamericana* **37**: 47–53.

Rojas, M. and Aylward, B. 2003. *What are we learning from experiences with markets for environmental services in Costa Rica? A review and critique of the literature.* International Institute for Environment and Development. London, UK.

Sabogal, C., Castillo, A., Carrera, F. and Castañeda, A. 2001. *Aprovechamiento forestal mejorado en bosques de producción.* Serie Técnica, Informe Técnico No. 323. CATIE, Turrialba, Costa Rica.

Sabogal, C., Castillo, A., Mejía, A. and Castañeda, A. 2001. *Aplicación de un tratamiento silvicultural experimental en un bosque de La Lupe, Río San Juan, Nicaragua.* Serie Técnica, Informe Técnico No. 324. CATIE, Turrialba, Costa Rica.

Salazar, M. 2003. Evaluación de la restauración del paisaje en el Cantón de Hojancha, Costa Rica. Thesis Mag. Sc. CATIE, Turrialba, Costa Rica.

Sandí, C. 2003. Conservación privada en Centroamérica. *Ambientico* No. 120. On line: www.una.ac.cr/ambi/Ambien-Tico/120/Sandi.htm

Sandoval, R. 2000. *Honduras: su gente, su tierra y su bosque. Tomo I.* Graficentro editores, Tegucigalpa, Honduras.

Santana, R., Montagnini, F., Louman, B., Villalobos, R. and Gómez, M. 2002. Productos de bosques secundarios del Sur de Nicaragua con potencial para la elaboración de artesanías de Masaya. *Revista Forestal Centroamericana* **38**: 85–90.

Scherr, J.S. 2000. A downward spiral? Research evidence on the relationship between poverty and natural resource degradation. *Food Policy* **25**: 479–498.

Scherr, J.S., White, A. and Kaimowitz, D. 2004. *A new agenda for forest conservation and poverty reduction: making markets work for low-income producers.* Forest Trends/CIFOR/IUCN, Washington DC, USA.

UNDP. 2003. Segundo informe sobre desarrollo humano en Centroamérica y Panamá. San José, Costa Rica. Disponible en http://www.estadonacion.or.cr – consultado el 20 de junio 2004.

Valle, L.F., Cruz, A. and Centeno, G.A. 2001. *Estado actual del manejo forestal en Honduras*. Consultores Forestales de Honduras FORESTA. Proyecto Información y Análisis para el Manejo Forestal Sostenible. Santiago de Chile.

Vargas, U.G. 1992. Estudio de uso actual y capacidad de uso de la tierra en América Central. *Anuario de Estudios Centroamericanos* **18(2)**.

Vásquez, A.A. 1999. Determinación de la contribución del bosque secundario a la economía de familias rurales de la zona Norte y Sur de Honduras. Thesis Mag. Sc. CATIE, Turrialba, Costa Rica.

Villalobos, R. 2003. El comercio de productos no maderables: estímulo o escollo para la promoción del manejo forestal sostenible. In: *Cadenas de producción para el desarrollo económico local y el uso sostenible de la biodiversidad. International Seminar. Managua, Nicaragua.* 17–19 March, 2003.

Chapter 10

Agriculture, Australia. Regional Forest Agreements. www.daff.gov.au

Alexander, J.S.A., Scotts, D.J. and Loyn, R.H. 2002. Impacts of timber harvesting on mammals, reptiles and nocturnal birds in native hardwood forests of East Gippsland, Victoria: a retrospective approach. *Australian Forestry* **65(3)**: 182–210.

Australian Forestry Standard. 2004. Background Papers. www.forestrystandard.org.au

Biggs, P.H. and Spencer, R.G. 1990. New approaches to extensive forest inventory in Western Australia using large-scale aerial photography. *Australian Forestry* **53(3)**.

Bradshaw, F.J and Rayner, M.E. 1997a. Age structure of the karri forest: 1. Defining and mapping structural development stages. *Australian Forestry* **60(3)**: 178–187.

Bradshaw, F.J and Rayner, M.E. 1997b. Age structure of the karri forest: 2. Projections of future forest structure and implications for management. *Australian Forestry* **60(3)**: 188–195.

Bradshaw, F.J. 2002. *Forest Structural Goals: Recommendations to the Department of Conservation and Land Management*. The author, Manjimup, Australia. www.calm.wa.gov.au/forest_facts/index.html

Burrows, N., Christensen, P., Hopper, S., Ruprecht, J. and Young, J. 2001. *Ministerial Condition 11: Panel Report Part 1*. Report to the Department of Conservation and Land Management. Conservation and Land Management, Perth, Australia.

Burrows, N., Christensen, P., Hopper, S., Ruprecht, J. and Young, J. 2002. *Towards Ecologically Sustainable Forest Management in Western Australia: A Review of Draft Jarrah Silviculture Guideline 1/02*. Panel Report Part 2. Report for the Conservation Commission. Conservation Commission, Perth, Australia.

Centre for Social Research. 1997. *Aboriginal Consultation Project*. Vols 1 & 2. Report for Western Australia Regional Forest Agreement Committee. Centre for Social Research, Edith Cowan University, Perth, Australia.

Christie, E. 1990. Environmental legislation, sustainable resource use and scientific terminology: issues in statutory interpretation. *Environmental and Planning Law Journal* **7**: 262–270.

Commonwealth of Australia, 1992. National Forest Policy Statement: A New Focus for Australia's Forests. The author, Canberra, Australia.

Conacher, A. and Conacher, J. 2000. *Environmental Planning and Management in Australia*. Oxford University Press, Melbourne, Australia.

Conservation Commission, 2002. *Draft Forest Management Plan*. Conservation Commission, Perth, Australia.
www.conservation.wa.gov.au/downloads.htm?subCatID=5&TLCN=Forest+Management+Plan& SLCN=Draft+Forest+Management+Plan

Dargavel, J. 1995. *Fashioning Australia's Forests*. Oxford University Press, Melbourne, Australia.

Dargavel, J., Holden, J., Brinkman, R. and Turner, B. 1995. Advanced forest planning: reflections on the Otways Forest Management Planning Project. *Australian Forestry* **58(2)**: 23–30.

Department of Sustainability and Environment, 2004. *Forest Management Plan for Gippsland*. Department of Sustainability and Environment, Melbourne, Australia.

Dovers. S. 2003. Are forests different as a policy challenge. In: Lindenmayer, D.B. and Franklin, J.F. (Eds). *Towards Forest Sustainability*. CSIRO Publishing, Collingwood, Australia.

Ecologically Sustainable Development Working Group on Forest Use, 1991. *Final Report – Forest Use*. Australian Government Publishing Service, Canberra, Australia.

Ferguson, I.S. 1985. *Report of the Board of Inquiry into the Timber Industry in Victoria*, 2 Vols. Victorian Government Printer, Melbourne, Australia.

Ferguson, I.S. 1996. *Sustainable Forest Management*. Oxford University Press, Melbourne, Australia.

Ferguson, I.S. 1998. Valuing different forest uses. Invited paper. In: *Outlook 98. Commodity Markets and Resource Management, Volume 3, February 1998*. Bureau of Agricultural and Resource Economics, Canberra, Australia.

Ferguson, I., Adams, M., Bradshaw, J., Davey, S., McCormack, R. and Young, J. 2003. *Sustained Yield for the Forest Management Plan (2004-2013) STAGE 3 Report*. Report for the Conservation Commission of Western Australia by the Independent Panel, June, 2003. Conservation Commission, Perth, Australia. www.conservation.wa.gov.au/files/docs/125.pdf

Ferguson, I., Dargavel, J., Conley, K., Kanowski, P.and Bhati, U.N. 1998. Socio-Economic Indicators for Sustainable Forest Management: Issues and Possible Solutions. In: Prasad, R., Raghaven, S., Phuka, B.R. and Joshi, B. (Eds). *Proceedings of National Workshop on Evolving Criteria and Management for Sustainable Forest Management in India*. Indian Institute of Forest Management, Bhopal, India.

Forest Practices Board. 2003. Forest Botany Manuals. 9 modules. www.ftb.tas.gov.au/docs/botany_manuals_drafts.htm

Hamilton, F., Penny, R., Black, P., Cumming, F. and Irvine, M. 1999. Victoria's Statewide Forest Resource Inventory. *Australian Forestry* **62(4)**: 353–359.

Helsham, M., Hitchcock, P. and Wallace, R. 1988. *Report of the Commission of Inquiry into the Lemonthyme and Southern Forests*. 2 Vols. Australian Government Publishing Service, Canberra, Australia.

Hickey, J. and Brown, M. 2003. Towards ecological forestry in Tasmania. In: Lindenmayer, D.B. and Franklin, J.F. (Eds). *Towards Forest Sustainability*. CSIRO Publishing, Collingwood, Australia.

Hilmer, F., Tapperel, G. and Rayner, M. 1993. *National Competition Policy: Report of the Independent Committee of Inquiry*. Australian Government Publishing Service, Canberra, Australia.

JANIS. 1997. Nationally Agreed Criteria for the Establishment of a Comprehensive, Adequate and Representative Reserve System for Forests in Australia. A Report by the Joint ANZECC/MCFFA National Forest Policy Statement Implementation Sub-committee. Commonwealth of Australia, Canberra, Australia.

Lee, K.M. and Abbott, I.A. 2004. Precautionary forest management; a case study from Western Australian legislation, policies, management plans, codes of practice and manuals for the period 1919–1999. *Australian Forestry* **67(2)**: 114–121.

Leonard, M. and Hammond, R. 1983. *Landscape Character Types of Victoria with Frames of Reference for Scenic Quality Assessment*. Forests Commission, Victoria, Australia.

Lindenmayer, D. 2003. Integrating wildlife conservation and wood production in Victorian montane ash forests. In: Lindenmayer, D.B. and Franklin, J.F. (Eds). *Towards Forest Sustainability*. CSIRO Publishing, Collingwood, Australia.

Mattiske Consulting. (2000). *Vegetation Mapping of South-west Forest Regions of Western Australia*. Report prepared for CALMScience. Department of Conservation and Land Management and Environment, Perth, Australia.

McKinnell, F.H., Hopkins. E.R. and Fox, J.E.D. 1991. *Forest Management in Australia*. Surrey Beatty & Sons Pty Ltd, Chipping Norton, Australia.

Meggs, J., Munks, S., Corkrey, R. and Richards, K. 2004. Development and evaluation of predictive habitat models to assist conservation planning of a threatened lucanid beetle, *Hoplogonus simsoni*, in north-east Tasmania. *Biological Conservation* **118(2004)**: 501–511.

Mercer, D. 2000. A *Question of Balance*. The Federation Press, Annandale, Australia.

Montreal Process Implementation Group. 1998. A *framework of regional (sub-national) level criteria and indicators of sustainable forest management in Australia*. Department of Primary Industries and Energy, Canberra, Australia.

Ough, K. 2001. Regeneration of Wet Forest flora a decade after clearfelling or wildfire – is there a difference? *Australian Journal of Botany* **49**: 645–664.

Ough, K. and Murphy, A. 1998. *Understorey islands: a method of protecting understorey flora during clearing operations*. VSP Internal Report No. 29, Department of Natural Resources and Environment, Melbourne, Australia.

Ough, K. and Murphy, A. 2004. Decline in tree-fern abundance after clearfell logging. *Forest Ecology & Management*. [In press]

Public Land Use Commission. 1995a. *Inquiry into Tasmanian Crown Land Classifications Background Report March 1995*. Public Land Use Commission, Hobart, Australia.

Public Land Use Commission. 1995b. *Inquiry into Tasmanian Crown Land Classifications Final Recommendations Report 15 November 1995*. Public Land Use Commission, Hobart, Australia.

Resource Assessment Commission. 1992. *Forest and Timber Inquiry, Final Report*. 3 Vols. Australian Government Publishing Service, Canberra, Australia.

Routley, R. and Routley, V. 1973. The Fight for the Forests. ANU Research School of Social Science, Canberra, Australia.

Schirmer, J. and Tonts, M. 2003. Plantations and sustainable communities. *Australian Forestry* **66(1)**: 67–74.

Vertessy, R.A., Zhang, L. and Dawes, W.R. 2003. Plantations, river flows and salinity. *Australian Forestry* **66(1)**: 55–61.

Williams, K.M., Nettle, R. and Petheram, J.P. 2003. Public response to plantation forestry on farms in south-western Victoria. *Australian Forestry* **66(2)**: 93–99.

Chapter 11

Agrawal, A. 1995. Dismantling the divide between indigenous and scientific knowledge. *Development and Change* **26(3)**: 413–439.

Agrawal, A. and Gibson, C. 1999. Enchantment and disenchantment: The role of community in natural resource conservation. *World Development* **27(4)**: 629–649.

Anat Arbhabhirama, Dhira Phantumvanit, Elkington, J. and Phaitoon Ingkasuwan. 1988. *Thailand: Natural Resources Profile*. Oxford University Press, Oxford, UK.

Barham, E. 2001. Ecological boundaries as community boundaries: The politics of watersheds. *Society and Natural Resources* **14**: 181–191.

Bassett, T. and Zuéli, K. 2000. Environmental discourses and the Ivorian Savanna. *Annals of the Association of American Geographers* **90(1)**: 67–95.

Bryant, R. and Bailey, S. 1997. *Third-World Political Ecology*. Routledge, London, UK.

Calder, I. 1999. *The Blue Revolution: Land Use and Integrated Water Resources*. Earthscan, London, UK.

Cline-Cole, R. and Madge, C. (Eds). 2000. *Contesting Forestry in West Africa*. Ashgate, Aldershot, UK.

Convention on Biological Diversity website http://www.biodiv.org/

Dove, M. 1992. Foresters' belief about farmers: A priority for social science research in social forestry. *Agroforestry Systems* **17**: 13–41.

Fairhead, J. and Leach, M. 1996. *Misreading the African Landscape: Society and Ecology in a Forest-Savanna Mosaic*. Cambridge University Press, Cambridge, UK.

Fairhead, J. and Leach, M. 1998. *Reframing Deforestation: Global Analysis and Local Realities: Studies in West Africa*. Routledge, London, UK.

Fairhead, J. and Leach, M. 2003. *Science, Society and Power: Environmental Knowledge and Policy in West Africa and the Caribbean*. Cambridge University Press, Cambridge, UK.

Ferguson, J. 1990. *The Anti-Politics Machine: Development, Depoliticization, and Bureaucratic Power in Lesotho*. University of Minnesota Press, St. Paul, USA.

Forsyth, T. 2003. *Critical Political Ecology: The Politics of Environmental Science*. Routledge, London, UK and New York, USA.

Guston, D. 2001. Boundary organizations in environmental policy and science: an introduction. *Science, Technology and Human Values* **26(4)**: 399–408.

Hajer, M. 1995. *The Politics of Environmental Discourse*. Clarendon, Oxford, UK.

Hartje, V., Klaphake, A. and Schliep, R. 2003. *The International Debate on the Ecosystem Approach: Critical Review, International Actors, Obstacles and Challenges*. Bundesamt für Naturschutz, Bonn, Germany.

Jeanrenaud, S. 2002. Changing people/nature representations in international conservation discourses. *IDS Bulletin* **33(1)**: 111–122.

Johnson, C. and Forsyth, T. 2002. In the eyes of the state: Negotiating a 'rights-based approach' to forest conservation in Thailand. *World Development* **30(9)**: 1591–1605.

Neumann, R. 1998. *Imposing Wilderness: Struggles over Livelihood and Nature Preservation in Africa*. University of California Press, Los Angeles and Berkeley, USA.

Oates, J. 2000. *Myth and Reality in the Rainforest: How Conservation Strategies Are Failing in West Africa*. University of California Press, Los Angeles, USA.

Odum, E. 1964. The new ecology. *Bioscience* **14(7)**: 14–16.

Roe, E. 1991. 'Development narratives' or making the best of blueprint development. *World Development* **19(4)**: 287–300.

Scott, J. 1998. *Seeing Like a State: How Certain Schemes to Improve the Human Condition Have Failed*. Yale University Press, New Haven, USA.

Sivraramakrishnan, K. 2000. State sciences and development histories: encoding local forest knowledge in Bengal. *Development and Change* **31**: 61–89.

Terborgh, J. 1999. *Requiem for Nature*. Island Press, Washington DC, USA.

Walker, A. 2001. The 'Karen consensus': Ethnic politics and resource-use legitimacy in northern Thailand. *Asian Ethnicity* **2(2)**: 145–162.

Walker, A. 2003. Agricultural transformation and the politics of hydrology in northern Thailand. *Development and Change* **24(5)**: 941–964.

Chapter 12

Berkes, F., Colding, J. and Folke, C. (Eds). 2003. *Navigating Social-Ecological Systems: Building resilience for complexity and change*. Cambridge University Press, Cambridge, UK.

Carley, M. and Christie, I. 1992. *Managing Sustainable Development*. Earthscan, London, UK.

Carnus, J-M., Parotta, J., Brockerhoff, E.G., Arbez, M., Jactel, H., Kremer, A., Lamb, D., O'Hara, K. and Walters, B. 2003. *Planted forests and biodiversity*. IUFRO Occasional paper 15.

Ellenberg, H. 2003. *"Ecosystem approach" versus "Sustainable Forest Management" – attempt at a comparison*. Federal Research Centre for Forestry and Forest Products and University of Hamburg, Hamburg, Germany.

Ferguson, I.S. 1996. *Sustainable Forest Management*. Oxford University Press, Oxford, UK.

Forsyth, T. 2003. *Critical Political Ecology: The politics of environmental science*. Routledge, London, UK and New York, USA.

Grundy, D. 2005. From plantation developer to steward of the nation's forests: the UK. In: Garforth, M. and Mayers, J. *Plantations, Privatization, Poverty and Power: Changing ownership and management of state forests*. Earthscan, London, UK.

Gunderson, L.H., Holling, C.S. and Light, S. (Eds). 1995. *Barriers and Bridges to the renewal of ecosystems and institutions*. Columbia University Press, New York, USA.

Hahn, K., Emborg, J., Larsen, J.B. and Madsen, P. 2004. Forest rehabilitation in Denmark using nature-based forestry. In: Stanturf, J.A. and Madsen, P. (Eds) *Restoration of boreal and temperate forests*. CRC Press.

Johnson, N.C., Malk, A.J., Szaro, R.C. and Sexton, W.T. 1999. *Ecological Stewardship*: A *common reference for ecosystem management*. Elsevier Science, Oxford, UK.

Kohm, K.A. and Franklin, J.F. 1997. *Creating a Forestry for the 21st Century*: *the Science of Ecosystem Management*.

Lee, K.L. 1993, *Compass and Gyroscope*: *Science and Policy for the Environment*. Island Press, Washington DC, USA.

Pollack, H.N. 2003. *Uncertain Science – Uncertain World*. Cambridge University Press, Cambridge, UK.

Rackham, O. 2001. *Trees and Woodlands in the British Landscape*. Phoenix Press, London, UK.

Ribot, J. 2002. *Democratic Decentralisation of Natural Resources – Institutionalising Popular Participation*. World Resources Institute, Washington DC, USA.

Ribot, J. 2003. Democratic Decentralisation of Natural Resources: Institutional Choice and Discretionary Power Transfers in Sub-Saharan Africa. *Public administration and Development* **23(1)**.

Sayer, J.A., Elliot, C., Barrow, E., Gretzinger, S., Maginnis, S., McShane, T. and Shepherd, G. 2004. *The Implications for Biodiversity conservation of Decentralised Forest Resources Management*. Proceedings of UNFF workshop on decentralised forest management, Interlaken, Switzerland. CIFOR, Bogor, Indonesia.

Schama, S. 1995. *Landscape and Memory*. Harper Collins, London, UK.

Schlaepfer, R. 1997. *Ecosystem-based management of natural resources: a step towards sustainable development*. IUFRO Occasional paper 6. IUFRO, Vienna, Austria.

Scott, J.C. 1998. *Seeing like a state*. The Yale ISPS series. Yale University Press, New Haven, USA.

Sedjo, R., Coetzl, A. and Moffat, S.O. 1998. *Sustainability of Temperate Forests*. Resources for the Future, Washington DC, USA.

Smith, R.D. and Maltby, E. 2003. *Using the Ecosystem Approach to Implement the Convention on Biological Diversity*: *Key issues and case studies*. IUCN, Gland, Switzerland.

Wilkie, M.L., Holmgren, P. and Cataneda, F. 2003. *Sustainable Forest Management and the Ecosystem Approach*: *Two concepts one goal*. FAO Working paper FM25, Rome, Italy.

World Bank, 2004. *Sustaining Forests: a development strategy*. The International Bank for Reconstruction and Development, Washington DC, USA.

ANNEXES

Annex 1

CBD Principles of the Ecosystem Approach

The 12 Principles of the Ecosystem Approach and their rationale (decision V/6 of the Conference of the Parties, www.biodiv.org/decisions/default.asp?lg=0&dec=V/6)

Principle 1: The objectives of management of land, water and living resources are a matter of societal choice.

Rationale:
Different sectors of society view ecosystems in terms of their own economic, cultural and societal needs. Indigenous peoples and other local communities living on the land are important stakeholders and their rights and interests should be recognized. Both cultural and biological diversity are central components of the ecosystem approach, and management should take this into account. Societal choices should be expressed as clearly as possible. Ecosystems should be managed for their intrinsic values and for the tangible or intangible benefits for humans, in a fair and equitable way.

Principle 2: Management should be decentralized to the lowest appropriate level.

Rationale:
Decentralized systems may lead to greater efficiency, effectiveness and equity. Management should involve all stakeholders and balance local interests with the wider public interest. The closer management is to the ecosystem, the greater the responsibility, ownership, accountability, participation, and use of local knowledge.

Principle 3: Ecosystem managers should consider the effects (actual or potential) of their activities on adjacent and other ecosystems.

Rationale:
Management interventions in ecosystems often have unknown or unpredictable effects on other ecosystems; therefore, possible impacts need careful consideration and analysis. This may require new arrangements or ways of organization for institutions involved in decision-making to make, if necessary, appropriate compromises.

Principle 4: Recognizing potential gains from management, there is usually a need to understand and manage the ecosystem in an economic context. Any such ecosystem-management programme should:

(a) Reduce those market distortions that adversely affect biological diversity;

(b) Align incentives to promote biodiversity conservation and sustainable use;

(c) internalize costs and benefits in the given ecosystem to the extent feasible.

Rationale:
The greatest threat to biological diversity lies in its replacement by alternative systems of land use. This often arises through market distortions, which undervalue natural systems and populations and provide perverse incentives and subsidies to favour the conversion of land to less diverse systems. Often those who benefit from conservation do not pay the costs associated with conservation and, similarly, those who generate environmental costs (e.g. pollution) escape responsibility. Alignment of incentives allows those who control the resource to benefit and ensures that those who generate environmental costs will pay.

Principle 5: Conservation of ecosystem structure and functioning, in order to maintain ecosystem services, should be a priority target of the Ecosystem Approach.

Rationale:

Ecosystem functioning and resilience depends on a dynamic relationship within species, among species and between species and their abiotic environment, as well as the physical and chemical interactions within the environment. The conservation and, where appropriate, restoration of these interactions and processes is of greater significance for the long-term maintenance of biological diversity than simply protection of species.

Principle 6: Ecosystems must be managed within the limits of their functioning.

Rationale:

In considering the likelihood or ease of attaining the management objectives, attention should be given to the environmental conditions that limit natural productivity, ecosystem structure, functioning and diversity. The limits to ecosystem functioning may be affected to different degrees by temporary, unpredictable or artificially maintained conditions and, accordingly, management should be appropriately cautious

Principle 7: The Ecosystem Approach should be undertaken at the appropriate spatial and temporal scales.

Rationale:

The approach should be bounded by spatial and temporal scales that are appropriate to the objectives. Boundaries for management will be defined operationally by users, managers, scientists and indigenous and local peoples. Connectivity between areas should be promoted where necessary. The ecosystem approach is based upon the hierarchical nature of biological diversity characterized by the interaction and integration of genes, species and ecosystems.

Principle 8: Recognizing the varying temporal scales and lag-effects that characterize ecosystem processes, objectives for ecosystem management should be set for the long term.

Rationale:

Ecosystem processes are characterized by varying temporal scales and lag-effects. This inherently conflicts with the tendency of humans to favour short-term gains and immediate benefits over future ones.

Principle 9: Management must recognise that change is inevitable.

Rationale:

Ecosystems change, including species composition and population abundance. Hence, management should adapt to the changes. Apart from their inherent dynamics of change, ecosystems are beset by a complex of uncertainties and potential "surprises" in the human, biological and environmental realms. Traditional disturbance regimes may be important for ecosystem structure and functioning, and may need to be maintained or restored. The ecosystem approach must utilize adaptive management in order to anticipate and cater for such changes and events and should be cautious in making any decision that may foreclose options, but, at the same time, consider mitigating actions to cope with long-term changes such as climate change.

Principle 10: The Ecosystem Approach should seek the appropriate balance between, and integration of, conservation and use of biological diversity.

Rationale:

Biological diversity is critical both for its intrinsic value and because of the key role it plays in providing the ecosystem and other services upon which we all ultimately depend. There has been a tendency in the past to manage components of biological diversity either as protected or non-protected. There is a need for a shift to more flexible situations, where conservation and use are seen in context and the full range of measures is applied in a continuum from strictly protected to human-made ecosystems.

Principle 11: The Ecosystem Approach should consider all forms of relevant information, including scientific and indigenous and local knowledge, innovations and practices.

Rationale:

Information from all sources is critical to arriving at effective ecosystem management strategies. A much better knowledge of ecosystem functions and the impact of human use is desirable. All relevant information from any concerned area should be shared with all stakeholders and actors, taking into account, *inter alia*, any decision to be taken under Article 8(j) of the Convention on Biological Diversity. Assumptions behind proposed management decisions should be made explicit and checked against available knowledge and views of stakeholders.

Principle 12: The Ecosystem Approach should involve all relevant sectors of society and scientific disciplines.

Rationale:

Most problems of biological-diversity management are complex, with many interactions, side-effects and implications, and therefore should involve the necessary expertise and stakeholders at the local, national, regional and international level, as appropriate.

Annex 1a

FSC Principles and Criteria

Document 1.2 Revised February 2000

Introduction

It is widely accepted that forest resources and associated lands should be managed to meet the social, economic, ecological, cultural and spiritual needs of present and future generations. Furthermore, growing public awareness of forest destruction and degradation has led consumers to demand that their purchases of wood and other forest products will not contribute to this destruction but rather help to secure forest resources for the future. In response to these demands, certification and self-certification programs of wood products have proliferated in the marketplace.

The Forest Stewardship Council (FSC) is an international body which accredits certification organizations in order to guarantee the authenticity of their claims. In all cases the process of certification will be initiated voluntarily by forest owners and managers who request the services of a certification organization. The goal of FSC is to promote environmentally responsible, socially beneficial and economically viable management of the world's forests, by establishing a worldwide standard of recognized and respected Principles of Forest Stewardship.

The FSC's Principles and Criteria (P&C) apply to all tropical, temperate and boreal forests, as addressed in Principle #9 and the accompanying glossary. Many of these P&C apply also to plantations and partially replanted forests. More detailed standards for these and other vegetation types may be prepared at national and local levels. The P&C are to be incorporated into the evaluation systems and standards of all certification organizations seeking accreditation by FSC. While the P&C are mainly designed for forests managed for the production of wood products, they are also relevant, to varying degrees, to forests managed for non-timber products and other services. The P&C are a complete package to be considered as a whole, and their sequence does not represent an ordering of priority. This document shall be used in conjunction with the FSC's Statutes, Procedures for Accreditation and Guidelines for Certifiers.

FSC and FSC-accredited certification organizations will not insist on perfection in satisfying the P&C. However, major failures in any individual Principles will normally disqualify a candidate from certification, or will lead to decertification. These decisions will be taken by individual certifiers, and guided by the extent to which each Criterion is satisfied, and by the importance and consequences of failures. Some flexibility will be allowed to cope with local circumstances.

The scale and intensity of forest management operations, the uniqueness of the affected resources, and the relative ecological fragility of the forest will be considered in all certification assessments. Differences and difficulties of interpretation of the P&C will be addressed in national and local forest stewardship standards. These standards are to be developed in each country or region involved, and will be evaluated for purposes of certification, by certifiers and other involved and affected parties on a case by case basis. If necessary, FSC dispute resolution mechanisms may also be called upon during the course of assessment. More information and guidance about the certification and accreditation process is included in the FSC Statutes, Accreditation Procedures, and Guidelines for Certifiers.

The FSC P&C should be used in conjunction with national and international laws and regulations. FSC intends to complement, not supplant, other initiatives that support responsible forest management worldwide.

The FSC will conduct educational activities to increase public awareness of the importance of the following:

- improving forest management;

- incorporating the full costs of management and production into the price of forest products;

- promoting the highest and best use of forest resources;

- reducing damage and waste; and

- avoiding over-consumption and over-harvesting.

FSC will also provide guidance to policy makers on these issues, including improving forest management legislation and policies.

PRINCIPLE #1: COMPLIANCE WITH LAWS AND FSC PRINCIPLES

Forest management shall respect all applicable laws of the country in which they occur, and international treaties and agreements to which the country is a signatory, and comply with all FSC Principles and Criteria.

1.1   Forest management shall respect all national and local laws and administrative requirements.

1.2   All applicable and legally prescribed fees, royalties, taxes and other charges shall be paid.

1.3   In signatory countries, the provisions of all binding international agreements such as CITES, ILO Conventions, ITTA, and Convention on Biological Diversity, shall be respected.

1.4   Conflicts between laws, regulations and the FSC Principles and Criteria shall be evaluated for the purposes of certification, on a case by case basis, by the certifiers and the involved or affected parties.

1.5   Forest management areas should be protected from illegal harvesting, settlement and other unauthorized activities.

1.6   Forest managers shall demonstrate a long-term commitment to adhere to the FSC Principles and Criteria.

PRINCIPLE #2: TENURE AND USE RIGHTS AND RESPONSIBILITIES

Long-term tenure and use rights to the land and forest resources shall be clearly defined, documented and legally established.

2.1   Clear evidence of long-term forest use rights to the land (e.g. land title, customary rights, or lease agreements) shall be demonstrated.

2.2   Local communities with legal or customary tenure or use rights shall maintain control, to the extent necessary to protect their rights or resources, over forest operations unless they delegate control with free and informed consent to other agencies.

2.3   Appropriate mechanisms shall be employed to resolve disputes over tenure claims and use rights. The circumstances and status of any outstanding disputes will be explicitly considered in the certification evaluation. Disputes of substantial magnitude involving a significant number of interests will normally disqualify an operation from being certified.

PRINCIPLE #3: INDIGENOUS PEOPLES' RIGHTS

The legal and customary rights of indigenous peoples to own, use and manage their lands, territories, and resources shall be recognized and respected.

3.1   Indigenous peoples shall control forest management on their lands and territories unless they delegate control with free and informed consent to other agencies.

3.2   Forest management shall not threaten or diminish, either directly or indirectly, the resources or tenure rights of indigenous peoples.

3.3   Sites of special cultural, ecological, economic or religious significance to indigenous peoples shall be clearly identified in cooperation with such peoples, and recognized and protected by forest managers.

3.4   Indigenous peoples shall be compensated for the application of their traditional knowledge regarding the use of forest species or management systems in forest operations. This compensation shall be formally agreed upon with their free and informed consent before forest operations commence.

PRINCIPLE #4: COMMUNITY RELATIONS AND WORKER'S RIGHTS

Forest management operations shall maintain or enhance the long-term social and economic well-being of forest workers and local communities.

4.1   The communities within, or adjacent to, the forest management area should be given opportunities for employment, training, and other services.

4.2   Forest management should meet or exceed all applicable laws and/or regulations covering health and safety of employees and their families.

4.3   The rights of workers to organize and voluntarily negotiate with their employers shall be guaranteed as outlined in Conventions 87 and 98 of the International Labour Organization (ILO).

4.4   Management planning and operations shall incorporate the results of evaluations of social impact. Consultations shall be maintained with people and groups directly affected by management operations.

4.5   Appropriate mechanisms shall be employed for resolving grievances and for providing fair compensation in the case of loss or damage affecting the legal or customary rights, property, resources, or livelihoods of local peoples. Measures shall be taken to avoid such loss or damage.

PRINCIPLE #5: BENEFITS FROM THE FOREST

Forest management operations shall encourage the efficient use of the forest's multiple products and services to ensure economic viability and a wide range of environmental and social benefits.

5.1   Forest management should strive toward economic viability, while taking into account the full environmental, social, and operational costs of production, and ensuring the investments necessary to maintain the ecological productivity of the forest.

5.2   Forest management and marketing operations should encourage the optimal use and local processing of the forest's diversity of products.

5.3   Forest management should minimize waste associated with harvesting and on-site processing operations and avoid damage to other forest resources.

5.4   Forest management should strive to strengthen and diversify the local economy, avoiding dependence on a single forest product.

5.5   Forest management operations shall recognise, maintain, and, where appropriate, enhance the value of forest services and resources such as watersheds and fisheries.

5.6   The rate of harvest of forest products shall not exceed levels which can be permanently sustained.

PRINCIPLE #6: ENVIRONMENTAL IMPACT

Forest management shall conserve biological diversity and its associated values, water resources, soils, and unique and fragile ecosystems and landscapes, and, by so doing, maintain the ecological functions and the integrity of the forest.

6.1   Assessment of environmental impacts shall be completed — appropriate to the scale, intensity of forest management and the uniqueness of the affected resources — and adequately integrated into management systems.   Assessments shall include landscape level considerations as well as the impacts of on-site processing facilities. Environmental impacts shall be assessed prior to commencement of site-disturbing operations.

6.2   Safeguards shall exist which protect rare, threatened and endangered species and their habitats (e.g., nesting and feeding areas). Conservation zones and protection areas shall be established, appropriate to the scale and intensity of forest management and the uniqueness of the affected resources. Inappropriate hunting, fishing, trapping and collecting shall be controlled.

6.3 Ecological functions and values shall be maintained intact, enhanced, or restored, including:

a) Forest regeneration and succession.

b) Genetic, species, and ecosystem diversity.

c) Natural cycles that affect the productivity of the forest ecosystem.

6.4 Representative samples of existing ecosystems within the landscape shall be protected in their natural state and recorded on maps, appropriate to the scale and intensity of operations and the uniqueness of the affected resources.

6.5 Written guidelines shall be prepared and implemented to: control erosion; minimize forest damage during harvesting, road construction, and all other mechanical disturbances; and protect water resources.

6.6 Management systems shall promote the development and adoption of environmentally friendly non-chemical methods of pest management and strive to avoid the use of chemical pesticides. World Health Organization Type 1A and 1B and chlorinated hydrocarbon pesticides; pesticides that are persistent, toxic or whose derivatives remain biologically active and accumulate in the food chain beyond their intended use; as well as any pesticides banned by international agreement, shall be prohibited. If chemicals are used, proper equipment and training shall be provided to minimize health and environmental risks.

6.7 Chemicals, containers, liquid and solid non-organic wastes including fuel and oil shall be disposed of in an environmentally appropriate manner at off-site locations.

6.8 Use of biological control agents shall be documented, minimized, monitored and strictly controlled in accordance with national laws and internationally accepted scientific protocols. Use of genetically modified organisms shall be prohibited.

6.9 The use of exotic species shall be carefully controlled and actively monitored to avoid adverse ecological impacts.

6.10 Forest conversion to plantations or non-forest land uses shall not occur, except in circumstances where conversion:
a) entails a very limited portion of the forest management unit; and
b) does not occur on high conservation value forest areas; and
c) will enable clear, substantial, additional, secure, long term conservation benefits across the forest management unit.

PRINCIPLE #7: MANAGEMENT PLAN

A management plan – appropriate to the scale and intensity of the operations – shall be written, implemented, and kept up to date. The long term objectives of management, and the means of achieving them, shall be clearly stated.

7.1 The management plan and supporting documents shall provide:

a) Management objectives.

b) Description of the forest resources to be managed, environmental limitations, land use and ownership status, socio-economic conditions, and a profile of adjacent lands.

c) Description of silvicultural and/or other management system, based on the ecology of the forest in question and information gathered through resource inventories.

d) Rationale for rate of annual harvest and species selection.

e) Provisions for monitoring of forest growth and dynamics.

f) Environmental safeguards based on environmental assessments.

g) Plans for the identification and protection of rare, threatened and endangered species.

h) Maps describing the forest resource base including protected areas, planned management activities and land ownership.

i) Description and justification of harvesting techniques and equipment to be used.

7.2 The management plan shall be periodically revised to incorporate the results of monitoring or new scientific and technical information, as well as to respond to changing environmental, social and economic circumstances.

7.3 Forest workers shall receive adequate training and supervision to ensure proper implementation of the management plan.

7.4 While respecting the confidentiality of information, forest managers shall make publicly available a summary of the primary elements of the management plan, including those listed in Criterion 7.1.

PRINCIPLE #8: MONITORING AND ASSESSMENT

Monitoring shall be conducted – appropriate to the scale and intensity of forest management – to assess the condition of the forest, yields of forest products, chain of custody, management activities and their social and environmental impacts.

8.1 The frequency and intensity of monitoring should be determined by the scale and intensity of forest management operations as well as the relative complexity and fragility of the affected environment. Monitoring procedures should be consistent and replicable over time to allow comparison of results and assessment of change.

8.2 Forest management should include the research and data collection needed to monitor, at a minimum, the following indicators:

a) Yield of all forest products harvested.

b) Growth rates, regeneration and condition of the forest.

c) Composition and observed changes in the flora and fauna.

d) Environmental and social impacts of harvesting and other operations.

e) Costs, productivity, and efficiency of forest management.

8.3 Documentation shall be provided by the forest manager to enable monitoring and certifying organizations to trace each forest product from its origin, a process known as the "chain of custody."

8.4 The results of monitoring shall be incorporated into the implementation and revision of the management plan.

8.5 While respecting the confidentiality of information, forest managers shall make publicly available a summary of the results of monitoring indicators, including those listed in Criterion 8.2.

PRINCIPLE #9: MAINTENANCE OF HIGH CONSERVATION VALUE FORESTS

Management activities in high conservation value forests shall maintain or enhance the attributes which define such forests. Decisions regarding high conservation value forests shall always be considered in the context of a precautionary approach.

9.1 Assessment to determine the presence of the attributes consistent with High Conservation Value Forests will be completed, appropriate to scale and intensity of forest management.

9.2 The consultative portion of the certification process must place emphasis on the identified conservation attributes, and options for the maintenance thereof.

9.3 The management plan shall include and implement specific measures that ensure the maintenance and/or enhancement of the applicable conservation attributes consistent with the precautionary approach. These measures shall be specifically included in the publicly available management plan summary.

9.4 Annual monitoring shall be conducted to assess the effectiveness of the measures employed to maintain or enhance the applicable conservation attributes.

PRINCIPLE #10: PLANTATIONS

Plantations shall be planned and managed in accordance with Principles and Criteria 1-9, and Principle 10 and its Criteria. While plantations can provide an array of social and economic benefits, and can contribute to satisfying the world's needs for forest products, they should complement the management of, reduce pressures on, and promote the restoration and conservation of natural forests.

10.1 The management objectives of the plantation, including natural forest conservation and restoration objectives, shall be explicitly stated in the management plan, and clearly demonstrated in the implementation of the plan.

10.2 The design and layout of plantations should promote the protection, restoration and conservation of natural forests, and not increase pressures on natural forests. Wildlife corridors, streamside zones and a mosaic of stands of different ages and rotation periods, shall be used in the layout of the plantation, consistent with the scale of the operation. The scale and layout of plantation blocks shall be consistent with the patterns of forest stands found within the natural landscape.

10.3 Diversity in the composition of plantations is preferred, so as to enhance economic, ecological and social stability. Such diversity may include the size and spatial distribution of management units within the landscape, number and genetic composition of species, age classes and structures.

10.4 The selection of species for planting shall be based on their overall suitability for the site and their appropriateness to the management objectives. In order to enhance the conservation of biological diversity, native species are preferred over exotic species in the establishment of plantations and the restoration of degraded ecosystems. Exotic species, which shall be used only when their performance is greater than that of native species, shall be carefully monitored to detect unusual mortality, disease, or insect outbreaks and adverse ecological impacts.

10.5   A proportion of the overall forest management area, appropriate to the scale of the plantation and to be determined in regional standards, shall be managed so as to restore the site to a natural forest cover.

10.6   Measures shall be taken to maintain or improve soil structure, fertility, and biological activity. The techniques and rate of harvesting, road and trail construction and maintenance, and the choice of species shall not result in long term soil degradation or adverse impacts on water quality, quantity or substantial deviation from stream course drainage patterns.

10.7   Measures shall be taken to prevent and minimize outbreaks of pests, diseases, fire and invasive plant introductions. Integrated pest management shall form an essential part of the management plan, with primary reliance on prevention and biological control methods rather than chemical pesticides and fertilizers. Plantation management should make every effort to move away from chemical pesticides and fertilizers, including their use in nurseries. The use of chemicals is also covered in Criteria 6.6 and 6.7.

10.8   Appropriate to the scale and diversity of the operation, monitoring of plantations shall include regular assessment of potential on-site and off-site ecological and social impacts, (e.g. natural regeneration, effects on water resources and soil fertility, and impacts on local welfare and social well-being), in addition to those elements addressed in principles 8, 6 and 4. No species should be planted on a large scale until local trials and/or experience have shown that they are ecologically well-adapted to the site, are not invasive, and do not have significant negative ecological impacts on other ecosystems. Special attention will be paid to social issues of land acquisition for plantations, especially the protection of local rights of ownership, use or access.

10.9   Plantations established in areas converted from natural forests after November 1994 normally shall not qualify for certification. Certification may be allowed in circumstances where sufficient evidence is submitted to the certification body that the manager/owner is not responsible directly or indirectly of such conversion.

The FSC Founding Members and Board of Directors ratified principles 1–9 in September 1994.

The FSC Members and Board of Directors ratified principle 10 in February 1996.

The revision of Principle 9 and the addition of Criteria 6.10 and 10.9 were ratified by the FSC Members and Board of Directors in January 1999.

The definition of Precautionary Approach was ratified during the 1999 FSC General Assembly in June 1999.

GLOSSARY

Words in this document are used as defined in most standard English language dictionaries. The precise meaning and local interpretation of certain phrases (such as local communities) should be decided in the local context by forest managers and certifiers. In this document, the words below are understood as follows:

Biological diversity: The variability among living organisms from all sources including, inter alia, terrestrial, marine and other aquatic ecosystems and the ecological complexes of which they are a part; this includes diversity within species, between species and of ecosystems. (see Convention on Biological Diversity, 1992)

Biological diversity values: The intrinsic, ecological, genetic, social, economic, scientific, educational, cultural, recreational and aesthetic values of biological diversity and its components. (see Convention on Biological Diversity, 1992)

Biological control agents: Living organisms used to eliminate or regulate the population of other living organisms.

Chain of custody: The channel through which products are distributed from their origin in the forest to their end-use.

Chemicals: The range of fertilizers, insecticides, fungicides, and hormones which are used in forest management.

Criterion (pl. Criteria): A means of judging whether or not a Principle (of forest stewardship) has been fulfilled.

Customary rights: Rights which result from a long series of habitual or customary actions, constantly repeated, which have, by such repetition and by uninterrupted acquiescence, acquired the force of a law within a geographical or sociological unit.

Ecosystem: A community of all plants and animals and their physical environment, functioning together as an interdependent unit.

Endangered species: Any species which is in danger of extinction throughout all or a significant portion of its range.

Exotic species: An introduced species not native or endemic to the area in question.

Forest integrity: The composition, dynamics, functions and structural attributes of a natural forest.

Forest management/manager: The people responsible for the operational management of the forest resource and of the enterprise, as well as the management system and structure, and the planning and field operations.

Genetically modified organisms: Biological organisms which have been induced by various means to consist of genetic structural changes.

High Conservation Value Forests: High Conservation Value Forests are those that possess one or more of the following attributes:

a) forest areas containing globally, regionally or nationally significant :
concentrations of biodiversity values (e.g. endemism, endangered species, refugia); and/or large landscape level forests, contained within, or containing the management unit, where viable populations of most if not all naturally occurring species exist in natural patterns of distribution and abundance

b) forest areas that are in or contain rare, threatened or endangered ecosystems

c) forest areas that provide basic services of nature in critical situations (e.g. watershed protection, erosion control)

d) forest areas fundamental to meeting basic needs of local communities (e.g. subsistence, health) and/or critical to local communities' traditional cultural identity (areas of cultural, ecological, economic or religious significance identified in cooperation with such local communities).

Indigenous lands and territories: The total environment of the lands, air, water, sea, sea-ice, flora and fauna, and other resources which indigenous peoples have traditionally owned or otherwise occupied or used. (Draft Declaration of the Rights of Indigenous Peoples: Part VI)

Indigenous peoples: "The existing descendants of the peoples who inhabited the present territory of a country wholly or partially at the time when persons of a different culture or ethnic origin arrived there from other parts of the world, overcame them and, by conquest, settlement, or other means reduced them to a non-dominant or colonial situation; who today live more in conformity with their particular social, economic and cultural customs and traditions than with the institutions of the country of which they now form a part, under State structure which incorporates mainly the national, social and cultural characteristics of other segments of the population which are predominant." (Working definition adopted by the UN Working Group on Indigenous Peoples).

Landscape: A geographical mosaic composed of interacting ecosystems resulting from the influence of geological, topographical, soil, climatic, biotic and human interactions in a given area.

Local laws: Includes all legal norms given by organisms of government whose jurisdiction is less than the national level, such as departmental, municipal and customary norms.

Long term: The time-scale of the forest owner or manager as manifested by the objectives of the management plan, the rate of harvesting, and the commitment to maintain permanent forest cover. The length of time involved will vary according to the context and ecological conditions, and will be a function of how long it takes a given ecosystem to recover its natural structure and composition following harvesting or disturbance, or to produce mature or primary conditions.

Native species: A species that occurs naturally in the region; endemic to the area.

Natural cycles: Nutrient and mineral cycling as a result of interactions between soils, water, plants, and animals in forest environments that affect the ecological productivity of a given site.

Natural Forest: Forest areas where many of the principal characteristics and key elements of native ecosystems such as complexity, structure and diversity are present, as defined by FSC approved national and regional standards of forest management.

Non-timber forest products: All forest products except timber, including other materials obtained from trees such as resins and leaves, as well as any other plant and animal products.

Other forest types: Forest areas that do not fit the criteria for plantation or natural forests and which are defined more specifically by FSC-approved national and regional standards of forest stewardship.

Plantation: Forest areas lacking most of the principal characteristics and key elements of native ecosystems as defined by FSC-approved national and regional standards of forest stewardship, which result from the human activities of either planting, sowing or intensive silvicultural treatments.

Precautionary approach: Tool for the implementation of the precautionary principle.

Principle: An essential rule or element; in FSC's case, of forest stewardship.

Silviculture: The art of producing and tending a forest by manipulating its establishment, composition and growth to best fulfil the objectives of the owner. This may, or may not, include timber production.

Succession: Progressive changes in species composition and forest community structure caused by natural processes (nonhuman) over time.

Tenure: Socially defined agreements held by individuals or groups, recognized by legal statutes or customary practice, regarding the "bundle of rights and duties" of ownership, holding, access and/or usage of a particular land unit or the associated resources there within (such as individual trees, plant species, water, minerals, etc).

Threatened species: Any species which is likely to become endangered within the foreseeable future throughout all or a significant portion of its range.

Use rights: Rights for the use of forest resources that can be defined by local custom, mutual agreements, or prescribed by other entities holding access rights. These rights may restrict the use of particular resources to specific levels of consumption or particular harvesting techniques.

Annex 2

Improved Pan-European Indicators for Sustainable Forest Management as adopted by the MCPFE Expert Level Meeting 7–8 October 2002, Vienna, Austria

Introduction

Since the first set of Pan-European Indicators for Sustainable Forest Management (SFM) had been developed in the early 90s, experience has shown that criteria and indicators are a very important tool for European forest policy. In the meantime knowledge and data collection systems as well as information needs have gradually developed further. Thus, initiated through the Lisbon Conference in 1998, the Ministerial Conference on the Protection of Forests in Europe (MCPFE) decided to improve the existing set of Pan-European Indicators for SFM.

This document contains the improved set of quantitative and qualitative Pan-European Indicators for Sustainable Forest Management.

An Advisory Group[1], representing relevant organizations in Europe, was formed to ensure that best use is made of the existing knowledge on indicators and data collection aspects in Europe and to assist the MCPFE during the improvement process. The Advisory Group consulted with a wide range of experts through a series of four workshops. These workshops ensured that the diversity of national situations and experiences as well as the work undertaken by various bodies in Europe were adequately reflected. The first MCPFE Workshop on the Improvement of Pan-European Indicators for SFM was held in March 2001 in Triesenberg, Liechtenstein. The second workshop took place in September 2001 in Copenhagen, Denmark, the third one in January 2002 in Budapest, Hungary. The fourth and final workshop was convened in May 2002 in Camigliatello Silano, Italy.

The indicators under all criteria, as presented in this document, are results of these four workshops and the work of the Advisory Group. The improved Pan-European Indicators for Sustainable Forest Management have been adopted at expert level at the MCPFE Expert Level Meeting, 7-8 October 2002 in Vienna, Austria.

More detailed information on rationales, international data providers, measurement units, current periodicity of data availability as well as underlying definitions is given in the supplementary documents "Background Information for Improved Pan-European Indicators for Sustainable Forest Management" and "Relevant Definitions Used for the Improved Pan-European Indicators for Sustainable Forest Management".

---

1 Members of the Advisory Group were: Mr. Michael Köhl (IUFRO/UNECE Team of Specialists TBFRA 2000), Mr. Thomas Haußmann (ICP Forests), Mr. Tor-Björn Larsson (European Environment Agency), Mr. Risto Päivinen (European Forest Institute), Mr. Derek Peare (IWGFS/Eurostat) and Mr. Christopher Prins (UNECE/FAO).

Table 1. Quantitative indicators

Criteria	No.	Indicator	Full text
C 1: Maintenance and Appropriate Enhancement of Forest Resources and their Contribution to Global Carbon Cycles	1.1	Forest area	Area of forest and other wooded land, classified by forest type and by availability for wood supply, and share of forest and other wooded land in total land area
	1.2	Growing stock	Growing stock on forest and other wooded land, classified by forest type and by availability for wood supply
	1.3	Age structure and/or diameter distribution	Age structure and/or diameter distribution of forest and other wooded land, classified by forest type and by availability for wood supply
	1.4	Carbon stock	Carbon stock of woody biomass and of soils on forest and other wooded land
C 2: Maintenance of Forest Ecosystem Health and Vitality	2.1	Deposition of air pollutants	Deposition of air pollutants on forest and other wooded land, classified by N, S and base cations
	2.2	Soil condition	Chemical soil properties (pH, CEC, C/N, organic C, base saturation) on forest and other wooded land related to soil acidity and eutrophication, classified by main soil types
	2.3	Defoliation	Defoliation of one or more main tree species on forest and other wooded land in each of the defoliation classes "moderate", "severe" and "dead"
	2.4	Forest damage	Forest and other wooded land with damage, classified by primary damaging agent (abiotic, biotic and human induced) and by forest type
C 3: Maintenance and Encouragement of Productive Functions of Forests (Wood and Non-Wood)	3.1	Increment and fellings	Balance between net annual increment and annual fellings of wood on forest available for wood supply
	3.2	Roundwood	Value and quantity of marketed roundwood
	3.3	Non-wood goods	Value and quantity of marketed non-wood goods from forest and other wooded land
	3.4	Services	Value of marketed services on forest and other wooded land
	3.5	Forests under management plans	Proportion of forest and other wooded land under a management plan or equivalent

Criteria	No.	Indicator	Full text
C 4: Maintenance, Conservation and Appropriate Enhancement of Biological Diversity in Forest Ecosystems	4.1	Tree species composition	Area of forest and other wooded land, classified by number of tree species occurring and by forest type
	4.2	Regeneration	Area of regeneration within even-aged stands and uneven-aged stands, classified by regeneration type
	4.3	Naturalness	Area of forest and other wooded land, classified by "undisturbed by man", by "semi-natural" or by "plantations", each by forest type
	4.4	Introduced tree species	Area of forest and other wooded land dominated by introduced tree species
	4.5	Deadwood	Volume of standing deadwood and of lying deadwood on forest and other wooded land classified by forest type
	4.6	Genetic resources	Area managed for conservation and utilization of forest tree genetic resources (in situ and ex situ gene conservation) and area managed for seed production
	4.7	Landscape pattern	Landscape-level spatial pattern of forest cover
	4.8	Threatened forest species	Number of threatened forest species, classified according to IUCN Red List categories in relation to total number of forest species
	4.9	Protected forests	Area of forest and other wooded land protected to conserve biodiversity, landscapes and specific natural elements, according to MCPFE Assessment Guidelines
C 5: Maintenance and Appropriate Enhancement of Protective Functions in Forest Management (notably soil and water)	5.1	Protective forests – soil, water and other ecosystem functions	Area of forest and other wooded land designated to prevent soil erosion, to preserve water resources, or to maintain other forest ecosystem functions, part of MCPFE Class "Protective Functions"
	5.2	Protective forests – infrastructure and managed natural resources	Area of forest and other wooded land designated to protect infrastructure and managed natural resources against natural hazards, part of MCPFE Class "Protective Functions"
C 6: Maintenance of other socio-economic functions and conditions	6.1	Forest holdings	Number of forest holdings, classified by ownership categories and size classes

Criteria	No.	Indicator	Full text
	6.2	Contribution of forest sector to GDP	Contribution of forestry and manufacturing of wood and paper products to gross domestic product
	6.3	Net revenue	Net revenue of forest enterprises
	6.4	Expenditures for services	Total expenditures for long-term sustainable services from forests
	6.5	Forest sector workforce	Number of persons employed and labour input in the forest sector, classified by gender and age group, education and job characteristics
	6.6	Occupational safety and health	Frequency of occupational accidents and occupational diseases in forestry
	6.7	Wood consumption	Consumption per head of wood and products derived from wood
	6.8	Trade in wood	Imports and exports of wood and products derived from wood
	6.9	Energy from wood resources	Share of wood energy in total energy consumption, classified by origin of wood
	6.10	Accessibility for recreation	Area of forest and other wooded land where public has a right of access for recreational purposes and indication of intensity of use
	6.11	Cultural and spiritual values	Number of sites within forest and other wooded land designated as having cultural or spiritual values

Σ = 35 quantitative indicators

Table 2. Qualitative indicators

A. Overall policies, institutions and instruments for sustainable forest management

A.1 National forest programmes or similar

A.2 Institutional frameworks

A.3 Legal/regulatory frameworks and international commitments

A.4 Financial instruments/economic policy

A.5 Informational means

B. Policies, institutions and instruments by policy area

Ind. No.	Crit.	Policy area	Main objectives	Relevant institutions	Main policy instruments used			Signific. changes since last Ministerial Conference
					Legal/ regulatory	Financial/ economic	Informational	
B.1	C1	Land use and forest area and OWL[2]						
B.2	C1	Carbon balance						
B.3	C2	Health and vitality						
B.4	C3	Production and use of wood						
B.5	C3	Production and use of non-wood goods and services, provision of especially recreation						
B.6	C4	Biodiversity						
B7	C5	Protective forests and OWL						
B.8	C6	Economic viability						
B.9	C6	Employment (incl. safety and health)						
B.10	C6	Public awareness and participation						
B.11	C6	Research, training and education						
B.12	C6	Cultural and spiritual values						

[2]OWL = other wooded land

Annex 3

List of Contributors

Per Angelstam
Associate Professor, School for Forest Engineers, Faculty of Forest Sciences, Swedish University of Agricultural Sciences, SE-739 21 Skinnskatteberg, Sweden
per.angelstam@smsk.slu.s

Josh Bishop
Senior Adviser Economics and the Environment, IUCN – The World Conservation Union, Rue Mauverney 28, CH-1196, Gland, Switzerland
josh.bishop@iucn.org

Bruce Campbell
Charles Darwin University and the Center for International forestry Research, Darwin, Australia
B_campbell@site.ntu.edu.au

José Joaquín Campos Arce
Deputy Director General and Director of the Department of Natural Resources and Environment, Tropical Agricultural Research and Higher Education Center (CATIE). Apartado 93-7170, Turrialba, Costa Rica, South America
jcampos@catie.ac.cr

Dennis P. Dykstra, Research Scientist
PNW Research Station, USDA Forest Service, 620 SW Main Street, Suite 400
P.O. Box 3890, Portland, OR 97208-3890 USA
ddykstra@fs.fed.us

Ian Ferguson
Professor Emeritus, School of Forest and Ecosystem Science
University of Melbourne, Parkville, Victoria, 3052, Australia
iansf@unimelb.edu.au

Bryan Finegan
Coordinator, Latin American Chair of Ecology in the Management of Tropical Forests
Tropical Agricultural Research and Higher Education Center (CATIE)
Apartado 93-7170, Turrialba, Costa Rica, South America
bfinegan@catie.ac.cr

Tim Forsyth
Development Studies Institute, London School of Economics
London WC2A 2AE, England
t.j.forsyth@lse.ac.uk

Richard W. Haynes
Program Manager, Human and Natural Resource Interactions Program, PNW Research Station, USDA Forest Service, Box 3890, Portland, Oregon 97208, USA
rhaynes@fs.fed.us

Elena Kopylova
Project Officer, Forest Programme, IUCN Office for the Commonwealth of Independent States ,
Stolyarny pereulok 3, Building 3, Moscow, 123022, Russia
elena-kopylova@iucn.ru

Horst Korn
Federal Agency of Nature Conservation, Insel Vilm, D-18581 Putbus, Germany
horst.korn@bfn-vilm.de

Pankaj Lal
Program Officer, Winrock International India, 1 Navjeevan Vihar, New Delhi, 110017, India

Michelle Laurie
Knowledge Management and Communications Officer, Forest Conservation Programme
IUCN - The World Conservation Union, Rue Mauverney 28, CH-1196, Gland, Switzerland
michelle.laurie@iucn.org

Marius Lazdinis
Faculty of Public Management, Law University of Lithuania, Ateities 20, Vilnius, LT-08303, Lithuania
marius@ltu.lt

Bastiaan Louman
Technical Director, CEDEFOR project, World Wide Fund for Nature – Peru Program Office, Calle
Trinidad Moran 853, Lince, Lima, Peru, South America
Bastiaan@wwfperu.org.pe

Stewart Maginnis
Head, Forest Conservation Programme, IUCN- The World Conservation Union, Rue Mauverney 28,
CH-1196, Gland, Switzerland
stewart.maginnis@iucn.org

Cléto Ndikumagenge
Coordonnateur, Projet d`Appui à la CEFDHAC, Union Mondiale pour la Nature / Conférence sur les
Écosystèmes de Forêts denses et humides d`Afrique Centrale UICN, B.P. 5506, Yaoundé,
Cameroon, Africa
cleto.ndikumagenge@iucn.org

Kinsuk Mitra
President, Winrock International India, 1 Navjeevan Vihar, New Delhi, 110017, India
kinsuk@winrockindia.org

Sushil Saigal
Program Manager, Natural Resource Management, Winrock International India, 1 Navjeevan Vihar,
New Delhi, 110017, India
sushil@winrockindia.org

Jeffery R. Sayer
Senior Associate, forests for Life Programme, WWF – International, Avenue du Mont Blanc, 1196
Gland, Switzerland
jsayer@wwfint.org

Roger Sedjo
Senior Fellow, Resources for the Future
1616 P Street, NW Washington, DC 20036, USA
Sedjo@rff.org

Douglas Sheil
Scientist, Center for International Forestry Research (CIFOR), P.O. Box 6596JKPWB
Jakarta 10065, Indonesia
d.sheil@cgiar.org

Robert C. Szaro
Chief Scientist for Biology, U.S. Geological Survey, 12201 Sunrise Valley Drive, Mailstop 300, Reston,
Virginia 20192, USA
rszaro@usgs.gov

Victor Teplyakov
IUCN Global Temperate and Boreal Forest Programme Co-ordinator, IUCN Office for the
Commonwealth of Independent States, Stolyarny pereulok 3, Building 3, Moscow, 123022, Russia
victor.teplyakov@iucn.ru

Johan Törnblom
School for Forest Engineers, Faculty of Forest Sciences, Swedish University of Agricultural Sciences,
SE-739 21 Skinnskatteberg, Sweden johan.tornblom@smsk.slu.se

Leonard Usongo
Director of the Jengi Programme, WWF Central African Programme Office, Bastos B.P. 6776,
Yaoundé, Cameroon
LUsongo@wwfcarpo.org

Róger Villalobos
Natural Resources and Environment Specialist. Tropical Agricultural Research and Higher Education
Center (CATIE). Apartado 93-7170, Turrialba, Costa Rica, South America
rvillalobo@catie.ac.cr

Index

Abbott, I. A. 154
aesthetics 23
Africa
    stakeholder values 12
    tree crops 124
    see also Congo Basin
agriculture
    Africa 126
    Central America 131, 133,
        134, 136
    conversion of forest to 21–2
    Germany 70
    India 75, 78
    integration in forests 63
    subsidies 25
    subsistence farmers 21
    traditional 20
    tree crops 124, 125
Amazon forest 51
American Forest and Paper
    Association 112
Asia-Pacific Economic
    Community 19
Association for the Development
    of Information on the
    Environment (ADIE) 120
Australia 147
    Accounting Standard 163
    BushTender programme 25
    codes of practice 154–6
    criteria and indicators 154
    Dept of Conservation and
        Land Management 152–3
    environmental changes
        153–6
    Forestry Standard 159
    groundwater salinity credits
        26
    indigenous people 161
    management plans 156–8
    media debate on science
        163–4
    National Conservation
        Reserve System 159
    polarized debate 178–80
    policy development 147–50

public participation 150, 160
Regional Forest Agreement
    148, 152, 153, 155, 159–61
resource security 160
social and institutional
    change 159–63
sustainable yield 158–9
Tasmania 150–1, 162
Victoria 151–2, 162
Western Australia 152–3, 162
Austria 71

Baltic states 69, 71
Barbier, E. B. 19
Bawa, K. S. 49
Belize 138
Bhopal India Process on SFM 75,
    91–3
biodiversity 1
    in the Alps 71
    in the Baltic states 69
    Central America 139–41
    conservation biology 49
    FSC principles and 235–6
    Guinea and 173
    information 34
    local management of 183–5
    market issues and 8
    monitoring 53
    in Sweden 68–9
    valuing forests for 22, 23
    see also habitat; wildlife
Biological Diversity Act (India)
    80–1
Bourke, I. J. 19
Brazil 187
Brown, Chris 19
Brundtland Report 112
Bureau of Land Management
    (USA) 101

Cameroon
    forestry laws 122
    integrated forestry 116
    Korup National Park 118, 119
    successes 124

Tropical Forestry Action
    Plan 119
Yaoundé Summit 121
Campbell, B. M. 5
Canada 177
    evolving approaches 101–2
    forest management 106–7
    management regimes
        107–8
    Model Forest Programme 12
    Pacific NW forests 102–4,
        109–11, 113
carbon sequestration 1, 22, 24–5,
    28
Carley, M. 189
Carlsson 42
Carrera, F. 136
CATIE
    see Tropical Agricultural
        Research and Higher
        Education Centre
Center for International Forestry
    Research 12
Central African Republic 116,
    120, 124, 125, 182, 183
    initiatives and institutions
        121, 122
    successes in 124
    see also Congo Basin
Central America
    achievements and challenges
        142–5
    certification 130
    changes and trends 134–8
    concepts and context 129–31
    cultural perceptions 138
    ecosystem approaches
        131–7
    forest management trends
        181–2
    people and resources 139–41
    special interest groups
        141–2
    stakeholders 131–4

Central American Commission on Environment and Development (CCAD) 136, 142, 145
Central American Indigenous and Smallholder Association for Community Agroforestry 133
Centre for Science and Environment (India) 78
Le Centre Technique Forestier Tropical (CTFT) 117
certification 50
  CBD principles 9–11
  Central America 130
  eco-labelling 25, 26
  monitoring programmes 56
Chile 19
China 187
Christie, I. 189
Clark, R. N. 42
Clark, T. W. 42
Clean Water Act (USA, 1972) 27
climate change 15, 50, 189
  Alps forestry 71
  effect on forest management 7
Committee of Ministers of Forests of Central Africa (COMIFAC) 121, 122
Conference on Dense Humid Forest Ecosystems of Central Africa (CEFDHAC) 122
Congo, Democratic Republic of 115, 118, 120, 122, 182, 183
  Ituri Forest 124, 183
Congo Basin
  approaches to SFM 119–20
  conservation and development 118–9
  domestic use of forests 117
  historical view of forests 115–8
  initiatives and institutions 121–3
  modelling 125
  successes 123–5
Congo Basin Forest Partnership (CBFP) 116, 123, 125
Congolaise Industrielle des Bois (CIB) 120, 123
Congolese Institute for Nature Conservation 115

Constitution Amendment Act (India) 80, 81
Consultative Groups on International Agricultural Research (CGIAR) 169
Convention on Biological Diversity (CBD) 1, 48, 102, 165
  compared to SFM 9–11, 177
  local institutions and politics 173
  principles 3–5, 8, 9, 15, 129, 177, 229–31
  see also Ecosystem Approach
Corcovado National Park 131
Costa Rica 130, 131, 182
  ecosystem approaches 131, 133, 135, 136, 143–5
  FONAFIFO system 25, 26, 28
  integrated rural development plan 140
  Maquenque National Park 141
  market instruments 129
  payment for environmental services 130, 134, 139
Costa Rican National Biodiversity Institute (INBio) 138
crime and corruption 15, 137
Criteria & Indicators (C & I) 37, 47, 154, 191
  establishment of process 2
  multiple stakeholders 11–12
  pluralist approaches 177

deforestation
  Central America 129, 136, 140–1
  Guinea, West Africa 172–3
  neotropical regrowth 51
  roundwood production 18
Denmark 187
developing countries 1, 18–20
development assistance agencies 78, 94
Dovers, S. 148, 156

Ecologically Sustainable Working Group 147
ecology
  assessing systems 39–42
  gap analysis 40–1
  information 34–7

monitoring and evaluation 35
restoration 36
social and biological components 43
economics
  of corruption 137
  ecosystem services 24–30
  externalities 23–4
  FSC principles and 235
  importance of 17–18
  integration 13–14
  issues and trends 29–30
  macro-economic impacts 18–19
  market value and forests 23–8
  multi-functional forests 13
  non-timber products 21, 22
  payment for environmental services 26, 130, 131, 139, 143
  public goods 23
  resource rich developing countries 20
  structural adjustment 18–19, 29
  subsidies 73
  valuing forests 20–3
  see also market dynamics; sustainable forest management; trade
Ecosystem Approach 3, 59–64
  CBD principles of 1, 3–4, 7–9, 67–8, 229–31
  Central America 142–6
  close to nature ecosystems 186
  decentralized management 183–6
  economic benefits of 21–3
  European experience of 73–4
  good practice 190–1
  local institutions and politics 173–5
  market values and 20–1
  new types of institutions 188–90
  plantations 186–8
  precautionary principle 5
  and SFM 111–12
Ecosystèmes Forestiers en Afrique Centrale (ECOFAC) 118–9, 121

education 2, 137
Ellenberg, H. 9
Emborg, J. 60, 62
Endangered Species Act (USA) 27, 104, 109, 110
Environment Protection Act (India) 80
environmental groups 183
    Central America 133
    certification and 11
    see also non-governmental organizations
Equitorial Guinea 115
erosion 171
Estonia 69
Europe
    the Alps 71–2
    Baltic states 69
    ecosystem approaches 179
    Germany 70–1, 73
    MCPFE pan-European indicators 243–7
    Russia 67–8
    Sweden 68–9
    UK 64–6
    Ukraine 72–3
European Landscape Convention 39
European Union
    agricultural subsidies 13
    ECOFAC programme 118–9
    multi-functional forests 13
    resolution on forest strategy 64

Fairhead, J. 172, 173
Federal Forest Agency (Russia) 67
Ferguson, I. S. 156
Finegan, B. 52–5
Finland 68, 179
Food and Agriculture Organization (FAO) 188
Forest Act (Thailand) 170
Forest and Rangeland Renewable Resources Planning Act (USA) 104
Forest Landscape Restoration initiative 13
forest management
    close-to-nature 70–1
    nature-based integrative approach 62

nature conservation approach 62
    plantation approach 62
    stand-level intensities 108–9
    standards versus pluralism 177
    thinning 109
    see also sustainable forest management
Forest Resources Assessment 2000 187
Forest Service (USA) 3, 101, 104–5
Forest Stewardship Council (FSC) 53, 112
    Central America 130, 136
    principles and standards 47–9, 232–42
Forestry and Logging Sector Cooperation Project 132
Forestry Commission (UK) 65–6
Forestry Communities Association of El Petén 133
forests
    functions of 166–7, 169
    global picture 178
    high conservation value 238
    natural and artificial systems 186
    set-aside conservation 183
    statistics and information 188, 189
    World Heritage sites 184
Foundation for the Development of the Central Volcanic Range 133
France 60, 115, 123
Franklin, J. F. 3
fuel wood 1
    Central America 139
    India 88
    subsidies 19

Gabon 116, 124
    bushmeat trade 118
    forest institutions 122
    see also Congo Basin
Galloway, G. 141
Gamborg, C. 61
Gandhi, Indira 95
gap regimes 50–1
Geographic Information Systems 41

Germany
    Central America and 132
    colonial Africa and 115
    concession in Congo Basin 120, 123
    forest management in 70–1, 73
globalization 7, 13
governance
    accountability 168
    Australian state system 147–8
    decentralization 6–7, 8, 183–6
    economic benefits and 21–2
    forestry departments 174–5
    Indian states 77
    issues and problems of 7
    new institutions 188–90
    politics of forest departments 168–9
    promoting forest benefits 25
grassroots organizations
    see environmental groups; local communities
Guatemala 146
    community concessions 129, 130, 131, 132, 133, 134, 142
    Maya Biosphere Reserve 130, 132
    non-timber forest products 138
    technical assistance 136
Guinea
    politics and forestry 172–4

habitat 1, 25
    Australia 155
    in Britain 65–6
    monitoring 52, 53–4
    Pacific Northwest 109
    retained forest system 106
    see also biodiversity; wildlife
harvesting rights 24
Hayes, John P. 52
High Conservation Values (HCVs) 48
Honduran Forest Management Fund 134
Honduras 129
    achievements 143

ecosystem approaches
134–5, 141
government institutions 130
policy changes 134
hunting 66

India
Bhopal India Process 91–3
conflict and resistance 94
corporate sector 79
development assistance 96
Ecodevelopment programme
86–8
forest resources of 75–6,
international commitments
97–8
Joint Forest Management 75,
82–6, 98, 99, 181
key players 77–9
Landscape Level Initiatives
88–91
local communities 100
National Biodiversity Strategy
91, 93, 181
National Forest Policy 95
Peoples' Protected Areas 88
plantations 187
policy and law 79–81
politics 98–100
regeneration 85
Terai Arc Restoration
Initiative 90, 96, 98
tiger reserves 86, 87–8, 89–90
Indian Forest Act 80
indigenous peoples 161, 234
Indonesia 187
information
adaptive management 43
assessing systems 39–42
decision-making 42, 44
developing and using 38–9
expertise 38
forest research 45
for modelling 36
Integrated Conservation and
Development Projects (ICDP)
4, 5, 131–2
Intergovernmental Panel on
Forests (IPF) 97
international law 97–8
International Monetary Fund
(IMF) 18

International Tropical Timber
Organization (ITTO) 14, 47,
121, 122, 181
on Central America 130
Iran 187
IUCN 159
Africa 117–8
principles of Ecosystem
Approach 4

Japan 187
Johnson, N. C. 3
Joint Forest Management (JFM)
75, 82–6, 98, 99

Kanha Tiger Reserve 87
Keith, D. A. 56
Keystone Center 3
Kohm, K. A. 3
Korup National Park 118, 119
Kyoto Protocol 163

land
government actions 25–6
ownership 139
Pacific Northwest use 107–8
residential values 24
Larsen, J. B. 61
Latvia 69
laws and legal rights
Cameroon 119–20
in Congo Basin 122
Ecosystem Approaches 9
FSC principles and 233–4
India 79–81, 97–8
Tasmanian inquiry 150
US debate on regulation 110
see also ownership
Leach, M. 172, 173
Lee, K. M. 154
Lee, Kai N. 33
Leitch, Jeanette 19
Lindenmayer, D. 156
Lithuania 69
local communities
accountable government and
168
Australia 160
Cameroon 119
Central America 129, 130
civil society 73, 74

decentralized governance
183–6
FSC principles and 234–5
India 77–8, 94–5
social choice and power
183–5
success of 178
Thailand 170–1

McKinnell, F. H. 148
McShane, T. 119
Madagascar 21
Malawi Principles 3
Maltby, E. 4
market dynamics
biodiversity issues and 8
competition 161–2
developing markets 28
forest values and 20–3
local marketplaces 137
valuing forests 23–8
Meggs, J. 155
Mesoamerican Protected Areas
System and Biological
Corridor 141, 144
Mexico 138
Millennium Assessment 188
Mills, T. J. 42
Ministerial Conference on the
Protection of Forests in
Europe (MCPFE) 59, 64, 68,
243
pan-European indicators
243–7
Mobutu, Sese Seko 118
monitoring and assessment 35,
53
Central America 146
development of mechanism
16
early warning capacity 190
flexibility 52
FSC principles 47–9, 237
hypothetical examples 54
inconsistency 52
information for 188
local circumstances 55–7
management tool 52–5
Montane Alternative Silvicultural
Systems (MASS) Project 106
Montreal Process 112, 154, 163
Morozov 67

Multiple Use-Sustained Yield Act (USA) 104

National Biodiversity Strategy and Action Programme (India) 75, 78, 91, 93, 98, 99
National Conservation Strategy (India) 97
National Council on Protected Areas (Guatemala) 132
National Environmental Policy Act (USA) 104, 110
National Forest Policy and Forest Conservation Act (India) 79–81
National Forestry Action Programme (India) 79
natural disturbances 49–51
    forest fires (Australia) 162
    Central America 138–140, 182
Naturaleza para la Vida 136
Nazarov, N. 73
Nepal 91
The Netherlands 20
Nicaragua 129, 130,
    ecosystem approach 135, 141
    government institutions 130
non-governmental organizations (NGOs) 47, 136, 162
    Central America 133
    development assistance agencies 78
    India 78
    local management and 184
non-timber forest products (NTFPs) 28, 139
    Africa 117
    economic value of 21–23
    India 78, 84, 88
    Yucatan Peninsula 138
Northwest Forest Plan (NWFP) 110
Nouabélé-N'Doki areas 124

Odum, Eugene 167
ownership
    Central America 139
    clarifying arrangements 15
    European 60
    FSC principles and 234
    India's corporate sector 79
    multiple stakeholders 11–12

Pacific Northwest 107–9, 110–11
    private non-industrial 74
    subsidiarity 12–13
    19th century values and 183
    see also laws and legal rights

Panama 134
Panchayat Raya Institutions 81
Pandey, Kiran D. 18
Peoples' Protected Areas 88
Periyar Tiger Reserve 86, 87–8
Pinchot, Gifford 104
plantations 186–8
    Australia 161
    FSC principles 238–9
pluralist approaches 6
precautionary principle 5, 15
Precious Woods in Costa Rica and Nicaragua 134
Project for Ecological Recovery 170
Project Tiger/Elephant 89–90
public participation
    see local communities; stakeholders
pulp and paper industry 1

recreation and tourism 1
    Australia 152
    in Britain 65–6
    Central America 138
    economics of 21
    Pacific NW forests 102
    value of forests 23
Resource Assessment Commission
    'Forest and Timber Inquiry' 147, 150
Rio de Janeiro Earth Summit 2, 31, 112, 163, 177
    conservation and development 116
risk assessment 36
rivers and river basins
    Ecosystem Approach 4
    information 38
    watershed protection 22–3
rural development
    market-based conservation 27–8
Russia 179
    plantations 187

western forests 67–8

savannah 172
Sayer, Jeffrey A. 5, 118
Scandinavia 60
Scherr, S. 19
science
    conservation biology 49
    information and 31, 33
    information for decision-making 44
    media debates 163–4
    narratives of explanation 174
    political discourse and 167, 169
    social values and 31, 33, 35
    see also biodiversity; ecology
Scotland 66
Sedjo, Roger 3, 15, 19
Sheil, D. 49
Shepherd, G. 4
Simpson 19
Smith, R. D. 4
Social Forestry System 141
Society for Promotion of Wastelands Development 78
socio-cultural contexts
    assessing ecological systems 39–42
    developing appropriate approaches 15
    for forest management 6
    policy implementation 41–2
    see also local communities; stakeholders
Spain 115
spatial analysis 4–5, 44
stakeholders
    adaptive management processes 43
    Australia 148, 179–80
    benefits of Ecosystem Approaches 21–2
    Central America 131–4
    diverse in Congo Basin 126, 127
    diversity of 11–13
    German timber industry 70–1
    India 88
    see also local communities; ownership
stand-level intensities 108–9
subsidiarity 12–13

sustainable forest management
(SFM)
adaptive management 37, 43,
45
alternative regeneration
systems 156
Central American lessons 137
certification 9–11
changing paradigms 7–9
compared to CBD Principles
9–12
debate over 5
definitions 2
determining yields 158–9
Ecosystem Management and
111–2
Europe 179
FSC standards 47–9
general versus specific
principles 49–52
good practice 6
information needs 31–9, 45–6
integrated strategies 40–1
locally appropriate 55–7
management plans 236–7
market forces and 23–8
natural disturbances 41,
49–50
Pan-European Indicators
243–7
quantifying 112
spatial scales 4–5
structural goals 157
Szaro's keys to 32
tenets of good practice
190–1
trends and issues 1, 6–7,
14–16
Sweden 68–9, 71, 73
Switzerland 71–2
Szaro, R. C. 32, 38–9
keys to sustainable
management 32

technology transfer 46
Terai Arc Restoration Initiative
90, 96, 98
Thailand
plantations 187
politics of community forestry
170–1
timber industry

Africa and economic
development 117–20
Australian Accounting
Standard 163
in Britain 65–6
Central America 134, 135,
136, 137
changing nature of 1
Congo Basin 119–20
cutting and retention systems
106
economic issues 29
Finland 68
German 70
illegal logging 18, 29, 72–3,
119, 170
market values 20–1
monitoring programmes 52–5
Pacific NW softwood 101–2,
107, 109–10
plantations 186–8, 238–9
polycyclic silvicultural
systems 48, 51
pulp and paper 1
roundwood production 18
rural poverty and 27
Russia 68
small and large scale 19
see also non-timber forest
products
tourism
see recreation and tourism
trade
liberalization 13–14, 19, 29
tropical timber agreement
13–14
tragedy of the commons 7
training programmes 46
transport 28
Tropical Agricultural Research
and Higher Education Centre
(CATIE) 131, 132, 135, 137,
181, 183–4
Tropical Forestry Action Plan
(TFAP) 119, 178, 182
tropical forests
neotropical rainforests 51
timber trade agreement
13–14
Turner 160

Ukraine 72–3, 187
United Kingdom 64–6, 187

United National Conference
on Human Environment
(UNCHE) 95
United Nations Conference on
Environment and
Development (UNCED) 2
Rio principles 31, 112, 177
United Nations Educational
Scientific and Cultural
Organization (UNESCO) 4
Man and Biosphere
Programme 4
United Nations Forum on Forests
98
United States
changing regulations 110
evolving approaches 101–2
management regimes 107–10
Pacific NW forests 102–4,
109–11, 113
plantations 187
United States Forest Service
ecosystem management 3

Van Zon, H. 73
Vanclay 158

Wales 63
Wang, S. 112
Washington Forest Practices Act
(USA) 110
water and watershed
forest functions 166–7
groundwater salinity credits
26
hydrological modelling 157
protection 22–3, 25, 28
rivers 4, 22–3, 38
valuing forests for 22
Wawashan - La Selva Biological
Corridor 141
Wells, M. 119
Wheeler, David 18
Wilderness Act 110
wildlife
in Africa 120, 121
African 117
bushmeat 118, 120, 125–6
FSC principles and 235–6
spotted owls 180
tiger reserves 86, 87–8, 89–90
Wildlife Conservation Society
(WCS) 120, 123–4, 182–3

Wildlife (Protection) Amendment
    Act (India) 80–1
Wildlife Trust of India 78
Wilkie, M. L. 9
Wilson, B. 114
World Bank
    Forest Policy 178
    macro-economic impacts 18
    support in Africa 125
World Conservation Monitoring
    Centre 173
World Heritage Convention 184
World Parks Congress 183–4
World Trade Organization (WTO)
    13
World Wide Fund for Nature
    (WWF) 124, 125–6, 183
    Central America 136
    in India 78, 90
Wunder, S. 20

Yaoundé Summit 121
Yonchaiyudh, Chavalit 170

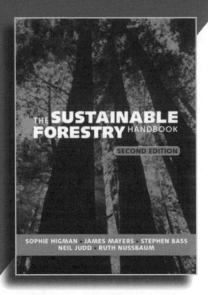

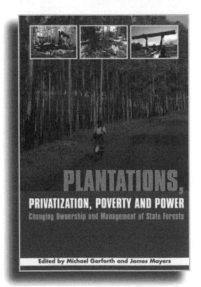

Also published by

EARTHSCAN

The UN Millennium Development Library

Project Directed by Jeffrey D. Sachs and The UN Millennium Project

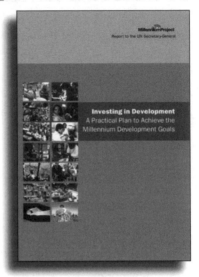

The UN Millennium Development Library presents a bold new strategy for overcoming poverty and achieving human development objectives embodied in the Millennium Development Goals, adopted in 2000 by world leaders.

VOLUMES IN THE LIBRARY

- **Investing in Development**: A Practical Plan to Achieve the Millennium Development Goals
- **Halving Hunger**: It Can Be Done
- **Toward Universal Primary Education**: Investments, Incentives, and Institutions
- **Taking Action**: Achieving Gender Equality and Empowering Women
- **Who's Got the Power**? Transforming Health Systems for Women and Children
- **Combating AIDS in the Developing World**
- **Coming to Grips with Malaria in the New Millennium**
- **Investing in Strategies to Reverse the Global Incidence of TB**
- **Prescription for Healthy Development**: Increasing Access to Medicines
- **Environment and Human Well-Being**: A Practical Strategy
- **Health, Dignity, and Development**: What Will it Take?
- **A Home in the City**
- **Trade for Development**
- **Innovation**: Applying Knowledge in Development
- **Overview**

The Atlas Series from
EARTHSCAN

Each book in the Atlas series includes:

- 50 full-colour global and regional maps
- essential facts and figures
- extensive graphics
- historical backgrounds
- expert accounts of key regions, issues and political relations
- world table of statistical reference

'The State of the World Atlas is something else – an occasion of wit and an act of subversion. These are the bad dreams of the modern world, given colour and shape and submitted to a grid that can be grasped instantaneously'
NEW YORK TIMES on *The State of the World Atlas*

Order online at
www.earthscan.co.uk